Grenfell of Labrador

Ronald Rompkey

Grenfell of Labrador

A Biography

UNIVERSITY OF TORONTO PRESS
Toronto Buffalo London

© University of Toronto Press 1991
Toronto Buffalo London
Printed in Canada
ISBN 0 8020-5919-8

Printed on acid-free paper

Canadian Cataloguing in Publication Data

Rompkey, Ronald
Grenfell of Labrador

Includes bibliographical references and index.
ISBN 0-8020-5919-8

1. Grenfell, Wilfred Thomason, Sir, 1865–1940.
2. Newfoundland – Social conditions.
3. Missionaries, Medical – Newfoundland – Labrador –
Biography.   4. Social reformers – Newfoundland –
Biography.   I. Title.

FC2193.3.G7R6 1991   610.69'5'092   C91-093540-8
F1137.G7R6 1991

All photographs are courtesy of Manuscript and Archives, Yale University
Library, Wilfred T. Grenfell Papers, except for the following: the *Albert* (Moses
Harvey Papers, Centre for Newfoundland Studies, Memorial University of
Newfoundland); WTG gives fresh air treatment (National Archives of Canada,
PA 178343); departure of volunteers for the coast of Labrador (Pascoe Grenfell
Papers, Richmond, Virginia). The maps were drawn at the Cartographic
Laboratory, Memorial University of Newfoundland.

This book has been published with the help of a grant from the Canadian
Federation for the Humanities, using funds provided by the Social Sciences and
Humanities Research Council of Canada.

For Noreen

Take up the White Man's Burden –
The savage wars of peace –
Fill full the mouth of Famine
And bid the sickness cease.

Rudyard Kipling

Contents

Contents

Photographs appear following pages 74 and 235.

Preface

For people growing up in Newfoundland and Labrador in the latter half of this century, the life of Wilfred Grenfell presents ambiguities. Some have regarded the man as a benevolent if not a saintly figure, an instrument of improvement in the northern districts of the province, others as an outsider, one who deliberately ignored the colonial governments of the day and imposed his own ideas about the direction the population should take. There is substance in each of these notions. In the broadest terms, however, Grenfell was a politician, for although he began his career as the agent of a missionary society, his true field of endeavour lay in the politics of culture. From the time he set foot in Labrador, he was seized with the desire to reform it, and that desire governed his actions for the rest of his life. This book is primarily a study of Grenfell the man, not a history of a missionary institution. Its purpose is to reveal how an individual possessed of certain powers intervened to change patterns of living.

In pursuing Grenfell's complex life, I have been fortunate to receive generous support. I first received travel funds while teaching at the University of Lethbridge, then a year's appointment as research associate at the Canadian-American Center, University of Maine at Orono. Subsequently, at Memorial University, I was granted study leaves and travel funds through the generosity of Averil Gardner, head of the Department of English, and Michael Staveley, dean of arts. Through the good offices of the dean of medicine, David Hawkins, I received a research fellowship that allowed me to complete the book on schedule. In the same faculty, I have also enjoyed the judicious and highly specialized advice of two successive John Clinch Professors of the History of Medicine, Kenneth Roberts and John Crellin. At the Queen Elizabeth II Library I have had the ready assistance of a highly professional staff and what I would consider privileged attention from Inter-library Loans and the Centre for Newfoundland Studies. From Administrative Services (Science Building office), under the supervision of Marilyn Hicks, I have received expert guidance in the delicate handling of paper and software. I am most grateful for all of this.

A study of this magnitude could not possibly succeed without the co-operation of those willing to grant access to privileged information. I therefore wish to thank the members of Sir Wilfred Grenfell's immediate family, Wilfred, Pascoe, and Rosamond, who have given me their time, their hospitality, and their willingness to discuss their father. I have also had the unique perspective of Eleanor (Cushman) Wescott (known in Grenfell circles as the 'Sphinx'), former secretary of the Grenfell Association of America. In the United Kingdom, I have had the unreserved support of Julian Grenfell, headmaster of Mostyn House School, and of Bevyl (Grenfell) Cowan, daughter of Sir Wilfred's brother, A.G. Grenfell. I also acknowledge the generosity and enthusiasm of Geoffrey Place, historian and school archivist, whose hospitality, guidance, insight, and editorial rigour, all bestowed over a period of years, cannot be adequately repaid. As well, I acknowledge the co-operation of the Royal National Mission to Deep Sea Fishermen, who have given me free access to their records.

I could not possibly mention here all those who have contributed to this book in one way or another. But I could not fail to mention in particular Peter Roberts, executive director, Grenfell Regional Health Services, St Anthony, for encouraging the book over the years. I also record here my enormous debt to Peter Neary for his unfailing encouragement and advice and his insights into the history of Newfoundland and to Diane Mew for her expert editorial direction. At the risk of giving offence to those neglected, I also mention the following who have assisted with the research, lent papers and photographs or granted me the benefit of their experience: Edward Andrews, David Ashdown, Alice Badger, Saul Bellow, Brigitte Berman, Pierre Berton, Julia Bishop, Rachel and Linwood Brown, Anne Budgell, Jessie Chisholm, Peter Churchill, Ivan Curson, the Reverend Norman W. Drummond, James M. Dunning, Sir John Ellis, Michael Feher, Elizabeth (Sears) Ferris, Stephen Friend, Andrew Golbert, F.G. Greenhouse, Vladimir Grenfell, Patrick Hare, Paula Hayden, David Haythornthwaite, James Herlan, Robert J. Higgs, James K. Hiller, Francis S. Hutchins, Sir George Kenyon, John W. Klopp, Victor Konrad, Barbara Leigh, Colleen Lynch, Janet Kahler, J.A. Mangan, Terence McCartney-Filgate, Elliott Merrick, Mary Mill-Blood, Geoff Monk, John Newell, Peter C. Newman, Anthony Paddon, William and Carolyn Rompkey, Francis

Rutter, Doris Sadler, William Savage, Betty Seabrook, Graham Skanes, Shirley Smith, Lord Southborough, Alice B. Thomsen, Edward Tompkins, Stephen Trombley, Norman Vance, Countess Mary Waldegrave, David Whisnant, George Whiteley, Jr, and Robin Winks.

I acknowledge the gracious permission of Her Majesty the Queen for the use of material from the Royal Archives. I am also pleased to acknowledge the generosity of the following for permission to quote from unpublished manuscripts: Bevyl Cowan, from the A.G. Grenfell papers; Julian Grenfell, the Mostyn House School papers; the secretary, the papers of the Royal National Mission to Deep Sea Fishermen; the Tower Hamlets Health Authority, the papers of the London Hospital and the London Hospital Medical College; the Bodleian Library, the Southborough papers; the Honourable Mrs Angela Eggar, the Amulree papers; Leslie Harris, the J.L. Paton papers; Marty Gendron, the Jessie Luther papers; Thomas Mayhew Smith, the papers of Dr John M. Little, Jr; Dorothea Moore, the Edward C. Moore Papers; the children of Eric S. Thomsen, the unpublished autobiography 'An American Odyssey'; Ruth Gimlette, the journal of Dr Eliot Curwen; Robert W. Wakefield, the papers of Dr Arthur and Marjorie Wakefield; Leslie T. Webster, Jr, the diary of Dr Leslie T. Webster; Mary Whiteley, the papers of Captain George Whiteley; David Ashdown, the Cecil Ashdown Papers; the Bentley Historical Library, the John Harvey Kellogg Collection; the Houghton Library, the Endicott Peabody Papers and the Houghton Mifflin Papers; the Rockefeller Archive Center, the Commonwealth Fund Archives and the Rockefeller Family Archives; and Manuscripts and Archives, Yale University Library, for the Wilfred Thomason Grenfell Papers, the Harvey Williams Cushing Papers, the Theodore L. Badger Papers, the Elizabeth (Page) Harris Papers, and the Hugh Payne Greeley Papers.

There remains the matter of money. Samuel Johnson once bitterly defined a patron as 'one who looks with unconcern on a Man struggling for Life in the water and when he has reached the ground encumbers him with help.' This insight is no less true today. No research project continues long without a patron of some sort, and I have been lucky to benefit from the generosity of granting agencies that encumbered me with help when I most needed it. I therefore record my thanks to the Canada Council for the granting of two non-fiction writing awards, the Hannah Institute for the History of Medicine for grants-in-aid, and the Social Sciences and Humanities Research Council of Canada for research grants.

Finally, I thank my wife, Noreen Golfman, for her tolerance and unwavering encouragement. It was not enough that one man should wrestle with the significances of another man's life. For the past few years, contrary to her own academic interests, she has occasionally had to wrestle with both men and perhaps learned more about each of them than she ever wished.

R.G.R.
Department of English
Memorial University

Prologue

In 1947, as the Physicians' Window in the north transept of Washington National Cathedral was about to be finished, a staff member of the New England Grenfell Association telephoned a Boston newspaper to announce the unveiling ceremony. 'The right lancet commemorates Sir Wilfred Grenfell,' the caller declared with some satisfaction. 'Never heard of him,' was the reply. 'Louis Pasteur is in the left lancet,' she persisted. 'Never heard of him either,' was the reply. 'Well, Jesus Christ is in the middle,' the exasperated caller shot back. 'Have you ever heard of him?' Each retelling of this exchange is usually aimed at calling into question the general knowledge of Boston reporters. But more important, it has also served as a reminder of the impermanence of reputation. Less than seven years before, Wilfred Grenfell's death had occasioned the most laudatory tributes from around the world; yet in this short space of time, his name had grown cold in the very city where he had lived and worked.

His name is still remembered in Boston, of course, and it is especially well commemorated in Newfoundland, where a coastguard vessel and a university college bear his name. Beside the legislature in St John's, a statute of him in winter dress overlooks the city where he first landed, and in front of the hospital in St Anthony a similar statue faces out to sea. But if you seek his true memorial, you must climb the hill behind the hospital and take a path into the woods to your left. There you will eventually confront a rock face marked with six brass tablets, one of them disclosing the location of his ashes. On that hill the simple tablet records his existence without any conventional Christian symbol or any of the maudlin and often sentimental language of the graveyard – only with a name, a date, and a short inscription, 'Life is a Field of Honour.'

The inscription catches one of the nuances of nineteenth-century

romanticism and offers the only clue to the kind of individual commemorated. For Grenfell was one of the last of that peculiarly nineteenth-century
breed, the spiritual adventurer, the manly Christian who carried the code
of service to the remote places of the earth at a time when such a chivalric
sense of life was still possible. Through his own efforts he built and
maintained in northern Newfoundland and Labrador an admirable medical and social enterprise that has left a distinctive philanthropic mark
for a century. What kind of individual was he, and what circumstances
produced such accomplishments?

This book sets out to answer those questions but not in the manner of
the heroic biographies by which Grenfell has customarily been treated.
Neither does it pretend to be 'definitive': many more details of his life
remain to be revealed. Rather, it endeavours to show how Grenfell's life
was shaped by certain social and religious movements in Britain during
the later Victorian period and by progressive trends in the United States
throughout the early twentieth century. I contend here that Grenfell is
most fruitfully understood not as a doctor or even as a missionary or as a
hero, but as a social reformer whose instruments were political and cultural. Once established in Newfoundland, he saw himself not simply as a
classical missionary bent on saving souls and healing bodies but as an
agent of change seeking broader improvements in cultural institutions.

Intervention of this magnitude raises numerous political questions.
Such questions have already been raised in a different context by writers
like Henry D. Shapiro and David Whisnant, who have made striking
observations about the response to perceived need in the Appalachians,
another region where the predominantly Anglo-Saxon culture was viewed
by benevolent workers as being somehow deficient. There, the pattern of
action depended upon regarding the region as somehow culturally disso-
nant – inhabited by people who were seen as different or at least less
developed – and then systematically changing it. At the outset, benevolent
workers in the South, mainly white, middle-class Protestants from the
northeast, ignored the diversity of local culture by directing their work at
meeting perceived needs at a human rather than a cultural level: the need
for health services, for education, and especially for institutions that would
foster community and the possibility of co-operation. But as time went on,
the role of the benevolent worker changed from missionary to community
worker, one who demonstrated by example certain alternatives to the
indigenous culture.

While the circumstances encountered by Grenfell in Newfoundland and
Labrador are not exactly parallel, the elaborate efforts brought into being
present a similar pattern of responses. It would be difficult to dispute the
value of the medical and social benefits that followed, but not everyone

tolerated Grenfell's attitude of social guardianship, as we may observe especially from the expostulations of church leaders, merchants, and governmental officials.

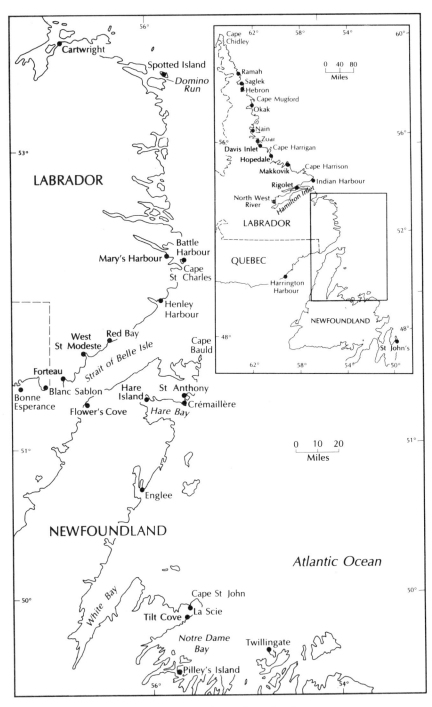

Labrador and Newfoundland

— PART ONE —

Deep Sea Missionary

—1—

Mostyn House School
1865 – 1882

The outline of Cheshire, as it protrudes from the west coast of England, suggests a shallow cup with two handles, one continuing east into the mountains of Derbyshire, the other, the Wirral peninsula, jutting out between two parallel rivers. The Wirral, a rectangular formation about eighteen miles long and six miles wide, is bounded to the east by the busy Mersey River, to the north by the Irish Sea. To the west, it is divided from Wales by the lower reaches of the Dee. Despite its proximity to the port of Liverpool, the Wirral remained relatively unpopulated during the last century and in the 1870s still featured large tracts of open countryside.

Overlooking the Dee estuary stands the windy hamlet of Parkgate, until recent decades hardly more than a single line of fishermen's shanties, houses, and inns overlooking a sea wall, giving rise to the Cheshire expression 'All o' one side, like Parkgate.' Apart from its shrimps, Parkgate had traditionally offered excellent sea bathing and a landing place for ships bound from Dublin. But the development of reliable roads through North Wales to Holyhead during the nineteenth century reduced its usefulness as a port, and the gradual erosions of the river virtually closed it as a packet

3

station by 1815, even though its lingering coastguard and custom house created a different impression.[1] In 1860, Parkgate still retained its air of importance, even possessing a hotel, built for the benefit of passengers delayed by contrary winds and bathers seeking the waters, breezes, and spectacular sunsets.

By 1865, the year of Wilfred Grenfell's birth, Parkgate had declined to the status of a quiet fishing village, its customary shipping diverted to more navigable havens and its sea-bathing visitors lured away by more attractive resorts. Twice a day the tide lapped at the sea wall, but by now the main channel of the Dee estuary had forsaken the English side for the Welsh coast. Even though, at the end of the nineteenth century, one could still stand on the wall and shoot duck and geese with the tide at one's feet, by the time Grenfell died in 1940 the tide had ceased to reach Parkgate with any regularity.

Overlooking the sea wall stands Mostyn House, a boys' school that has stood on the coast for more than a century. The school rests on the foundations of what was once the George Inn, transformed after the decline of the packet service to Dublin to suit a new age of travel and a different kind of customer. Enlarged and refurbished, it reopened in 1819 as the Mostyn Arms Hotel and continued to accommodate the remaining sea-bathing visitors under the proprietorship of Mrs Esther Briscoe. By the time Mrs Briscoe died in 1855, Parkgate's days as a bathing resort had expired, and the hotel closed. The building was let to the Reverend E.H. Price, a schoolmaster forced for financial reasons to move his school, now renamed Mostyn House School, from nearby Tarvin. Price had been a boy at Rugby with Thomas Hughes, whose *Tom Brown's Schooldays* promoted the myth of Thomas Arnold as a reforming headmaster,[2] and as a devotee of Dr Arnold's educational principles he himself was considered something of a pioneer of middle-class education. He had previously run a school for boys between the ages of seven and twelve, but now he took in boys between eight and eighteen and continued until 1862, when he moved to Maidenhead to found a preparatory school, the Philberds.[3]

The old hotel consisted of two buildings constructed in the Georgian style, with space for about sixty boys, some of them old enough to cultivate moustaches and wear waistcoats. One early school photograph shows that some of them stood taller than the headmaster himself, who was over six feet.[4] They attended for the 'half-year' rather than the term, living in what would now be considered rudimentary conditions. The school lacked adequate drainage or electricity: the boys passed their evenings by the light of candles or paraffin lamps constructed of tin, and slept four or five to a room on palliasses. By day they were taught in two large rooms and played what passed for indoor sports in two dismantled cowsheds, each open to the weather on one side and equipped with two or three swings, a horizontal bar, and a ledge to climb along. Lacking sufficient organized games at first, they devised their own.

From time to time the school transformed itself into a rifle corps, and the boys turned out in red serge coats and black trousers with a rib of scarlet running down the seam. Their 'weapons,' constructed of pitch-pine, offered a way of enforcing order. Once accused of being slack or disorderly, a boy could be ordered to march up and down a roofed passage with a rifle carried at the shoulder, and from a distance one could hear the tramp of feet as the condemned marched in silence. But youthful high spirits could not be contained completely. The boys found a vent in a two-storey cottage called the 'Devil's Hole,' where daily combats occurred. While one side garrisoned the upper rooms, the other would charge up the staircase until they were dislodged, on the way receiving a handful of lime and soot gathered from the base of the chimney breast. Despite these and other messy pursuits, they seldom changed their flannels, even after a game of football, but kept them in their play-boxes, where they absorbed the distinctive aroma of sardines, forgotten fruit, cake crumbs, spirit lamps, and other odorous contents. In January 1863 the Reverend Algernon Sidney Grenfell, eldest son of a Rugby housemaster, joined E.H. Price, his uncle, as assistant master and within a year succeeded him. Slowly, under his direction, the character of the school began to change.

By family tradition, the Grenfells claimed kinship with the Granville/ Grenville family and enjoyed the notion of tracing their ancestry to Sir Richard Grenville, who engaged the Spanish in the *Revenge*. Unfortunately there is no documentary evidence to support such a claim. More probably the Grenfells (who sometimes spelled their name Grenfield) represented a younger branch of this family sprung from Pascoe Grenfell, born in St Just, Cornwall, in 1689 and ultimately a merchant in Penzance.[5] His eldest son, John Maughan Grenfell, later moved to London, adopted the surname Granville, and married a daughter of the sheriff. He also adopted the Granville arms, which consisted of three gold devices on a field of red and the motto 'Loyal Devoir.' These devices present a highly stylized version of the clarion or pan-pipe (an instrument closely associated with the mouth organ). In the Middle Ages the Grenvilles owed feudal service to the *Clares*, the lords of Glam*organ*, and thus the clarion yields a double heraldic pun. At the turn of the last century, when the Grenfells were granted their own arms, these devices were blazoned on it on the presumption of kinship and styled 'organ rests.'[6]

John's second son, Algernon, was born in 1806. When he later became an assistant master at Rugby, he started a family tradition in schoolmaster-ing. His own son, Wilfred Grenfell's father, the Reverend Algernon Sidney

Grenfell, was born in 1836, a highly intelligent but neurotic individual, proud of what he perceived to be his family origins. His own life, however, did not begin auspiciously. His father died in 1845, soon after the birth of his sixth child, leaving practically nothing except a reputation as a good scholar, a Christian, and a gentleman.[7] His mother (*née* Maria Price, a Guernsey woman) took the family to Avranches, in Normandy, where they could live more cheaply. But she sent Algernon back to England to be taught Latin and Greek by an aged clergyman, who is said to have deprived the boy by keeping him from games and neglecting his diet. He did, nevertheless, prepare the boy to enter his father's old school in 1848.[8] There he excelled in both classics and mathematics and won an exhibition to Balliol College, Oxford, then a centre of educational reform.[9] Though gifted in languages, he soon exhausted himself with study and, as the family thought afterwards, ruined his health for life. At length he suffered a breakdown and took a pass degree in 1859. After recovering sufficiently at an asylum, he was engaged as a master at Bromsgrove School and then at Repton. Secure now at a reputable school, he met the woman he would marry.

Jane Hutchison, Wilfred Grenfell's mother, was born at Cossipore, near Calcutta, in 1832. Her father, Colonel John Hutchinson, was an Indian Army engineer and her mother a Thomason, daughter of the chaplain to the British residency. At the age of three she was sent to England in the charge of an aunt until her parents followed a few years later, Colonel Hutchinson having been appointed head of a new college for civil engineers in Kentish Town and later at Cooper's Hill. But the colonel seems to have tired of running a college full of young men, for he abruptly quit his job and moved to Boulogne, where the cost of living was considerably lower. The family stayed in France for about five years until the Revolution of 1848, when they decamped once more and settled in Cheltenham, among a small community of retired Anglo-Indians. Here the colonel died of what Jane described as a 'kidney disease.'

Jane Hutchinson met Algernon Grenfell in Boulogne, where both were holidaying in the summer of 1861. Grenfell, who liked to dance, would come round to her family's house in the evenings to do the polka, the waltz, and the quadrille, and sometimes the two families would go on long walks or picnics. Once he returned to Repton, however, he suffered bouts of loneliness, which he relieved by taking the night train to Cheltenham and throwing stones at the young lady's window until she came down to make him tea before anyone else had awakened. By now she was approaching thirty and had made up her mind to accept a proposal of marriage if the ardent younger man offered. They married in 1862, and Grenfell brought his bride back to Repton. Six months later he agreed to join Edward Price at Parkgate for one term as assistant master, arriving in August.[10]

Jane Grenfell regretted her decision to come to Parkgate as soon as she arrived in January 1863. Uncle Edward had sired a huge family whom she regarded as a 'loathsome' crowd, and the school was inhabited by an assortment of sixty boys, all with the unwashed look accumulating from their indulgence in school recreations. In those days they did not take regular baths, except small foot-tubs once a week, and an occasional dip in the sea in the summer. That first night at high tea, in they came and ranged themselves against the wall to stare at the bride. 'I remember so well how those boys looked at me that first night of my life at Parkgate,' she recalled. 'Evidently they thought that my advent ought to be celebrated in some very marked way. They were bursting with some request and I thought they would ask for a holiday or a picnic. Not at all; they begged for "a long lie-abed in the morning".'[11] Nevertheless, despite the uncomfortable impressions of the first six months, after which Uncle Edward left for Maidenhead to establish the Philberds, Algernon Grenfell took over the school and ran it for twenty years while Jane bore four sons of her own.

The first of these, Algernon George Grenfell, who eventually succeeded his father as headmaster, was born in the school on 4 November 1863, followed by Wilfred Thomason on 28 February 1865, Maurice Hutchinson (Mossy) two years later, and Cecil Martin Fearon in 1870. According to family tradition, Maurice, a brilliant child, died of meningitis before he reached adolescence, and Cecil suffered a blow to the forehead accidentally administered by Wilf with a croquet mallet held at arm's length while he swung around on one heel. The blow, as Wilf delicately put it, left him 'unable to share our play' for many years. The two older boys, left much to themselves, ought to have provided companionship for each other, but each was constituted of a different temperament, and their fraternal rivalry led to more serious consequences as time went on.

In those early years their father struggled to keep the school afloat. The school register shows that during his twenty years as headmaster he carried only 326 boys on the books, providing them with the two years of preparation expected for entry into a public school. But over half of these stayed for shorter times. Most entered at ten, eleven or twelve, but about thirty entered at fifteen or more, some remaining until twenty. Of these, ten went directly to university, 110 to a variety of public schools or equivalents, including Marlborough, Repton, Clifton, Rossall, Rugby, and Shrewsbury.[12] The numbers fell sharply from sixty at Edward Price's departure in 1862 to about thirty in July 1863, remaining low throughout the 1860s and climbing to fifty-four in 1879. By 1882 they had fallen again to thirty-seven and seem to have gone even lower, for when Wilf wrote Algie at Oxford at about this time he reported, 'The school is most *awfully* small now, only 33, no new fellows and five are leaving at the End of term. Papa is awfully despondent about it and thinks it will never recover, and of course it makes a great deal of difference as far as money goes.'[13] When their father resigned at the end of 1882 there were only twenty-nine left.

Mostyn House was both home and school for the Grenfell boys, and it provided them with considerable latitude, particularly during the holidays. Their father would take their mother abroad at the end of term, leaving them in the custody of the matron. They had the full run of the gymnasium and the field, but the vast sands were their chief playground, and they learned every new bank and gutter. The sweeping tide, as Wilf remembered it, created swirling currents around the Great Cop, the remnant of an attempt by the River Dee Company to reclaim the exposed acres before the sea broke through it. From here he would dive in and allow himself to be carried to the bank beyond or sleep out at night in an abandoned hut to be ready at dawn for unsuspecting ducks. As soon as he was old enough to shoot, he followed the flocks of sandpipers, plovers, dunlins, turnstones, oyster-catchers, and curlews that ranged back and forth across the estuary, following the ebb and flood. Sometimes these expeditions would take all day, during which time the channels freshly cut by the incoming tide would alter the landmarks, and he would have to swim part of the way home.[14]

Both brothers delighted in the feel and power of guns. At the ages of ten and twelve respectively, while their parents were abroad, they constructed in the night nursery a coffin-shaped, flat-bottomed 'canoe' named the *Reptile*. Unable to get it through the door, they dismantled the window frame and launched it out the window. With an ancient doubled-barrelled, twelve-bore muzzle-loader their father had acquired to keep birds from his pigsty and chicken-yard, they conducted clandestine warfare on the flocks offshore. To increase its range, they fed it double charges of powder preserved from old cartridges they stole from the coastguard station and carried loose in their pockets. Though the *Reptile* was wrecked twice, it remained in service until 1881, when Algie claims they sold it for twice the cost of manufacture.[15] Once the government abandoned the coastguard station and choked off their supply of ammunition, they could no longer waste a grain from a day's shoot. Instead, they simply removed the percussion caps and returned the weapon to its proper place on the mantle in their father's study.

As the two elder boys grew into adolescence and Cecil experienced what Wilf was to call 'behavioural problems,' they developed quite differently.

'He was my father over again,' Wilf thought later on, 'while I was a second edition of my mother.'[16] Algie was turning into a scholar with a grasp of languages, Wilf an athlete who had grown muscular from constant activity. He liked shooting snipe and working the fretsaw in the carpenter's shop, playing rugby and making jam, fishing and stuffing birds, preserving butterflies and mounting moths. Later he took up pipe-smoking, learned to waltz and polka, engaged in amateur theatricals, and played cricket. Never did he play a musical instrument, and he resisted his parents' endeavours to make him take up the study of music.[17] Quite simply, he possessed no ear or taste for it; he was to spend the rest of his life suffering through concerts and recitals he was obliged to attend or miming the hymns sung at innumerable services.

Once they had reached thirteen, each brother in turn ventured beyond Parkgate to school. In 1877 Algie won an open exhibition to Repton and entered the house of the Reverend Joseph Gould, who was married to his mother's sister Fanny. But his pranks did not endear himself to his uncle, and in January 1879 he was sent off to Marlborough. Wilf joined him there as a foundation scholar in September 1879. Wilf was miserable at Marlborough, for he missed his home and was forced to struggle with mathematics. But he loved natural history, enjoyed the cadet corps, and revelled in games. Algie remained at Marlborough only until the spring of 1881, when he won an exhibition to Clifton. Having reached seventeen, he appeared to have found his métier under the eye of the headmaster, J.M. Wilson. The next year he won a scholarship to Queen's College, Oxford, to read classics.

Wilf stuck out his comparatively brief public school career, with the exception of the winter of his sixteenth year, when he suffered a mysterious 'congestion of the lungs' and went to the south of France to live with a maiden aunt.[18] But his stay at Marlborough brought out a whole side of his identity – his love of games and athletics. By now, the school had been revolutionized under the headmastership of G.E.L. Cotton, who had introduced a program of compulsory games as a hedge against idleness and ill-directed boyish energy. According to a master who arrived there in 1875, the school produced a hardiness compounded of material discomfort, compulsory athletics, and regular study.[19] The days began at seven with a cold bath and chapel, and the boys were already at work in their classrooms before breakfast. There were two hours of school in the morning, three afternoons of two hours each, and two hours on Sundays, leaving three half-holidays. Evening prep took an hour, followed by chapel and bed. The characteristic dirty flannels hung on pegs and remained unwashed for weeks. Outside water closets still prevailed, and drainage remained an engineering conundrum.

During Wilf's years at Marlborough, classics formed the basis of the curriculum, leaving science as a marginal subject requiring extra time. Games, rapidly finding a central place in public school ideology, were compulsory. They were accepted as an important part of a boy's training, capable of inculcating not only physical and moral courage but loyalty, co-operation, and the will to command and obey. Indeed, letters in the *Marlburian* from old boys endorsed the arduous but satisfying life to be encountered overseas, and they drew a connection between the stamina and physical courage developed on English playing fields and the qualities required for pioneering success in Canada, soldiering in Burma, and baptizing in Melanesia.[20]

The school exemplified the Victorian cult of manliness – that collection of social and religious values of which Carlyle, Kingsley, and Thomas Hughes were the main proponents. First of all, manliness was associated with notions of good health: not only with the efficacy of sport and games but with the benefits of personal hygiene, a healthy diet, and the avoidance of tobacco and alcohol. It valued the simple life and, with its taste for camping and other outdoor pursuits, held the challenges of the frontier above the debilitating tendencies of the cities. It also associated itself with a code of fair conduct that valued honesty, decency, and honour. But manliness, as a social ethic, has been revealed as a morally ambiguous myth for the Victorians. J.A. Mangan writes, ' "Manliness," a substantive widely favoured by prelates on speech days and headmasters on Sundays, embraced antithetical values – success, aggression and ruthlessness, yet victory within the rules, courtesy in triumph, compassion for the defeated. The concept contained the substance not only of Spencerian functionalism but also the chivalric romanticism of an English Bayard: egotism coexisted uneasily with altruism.'[21] With its aura of physical and moral courage and decency, manliness has been viewed as a positive ethic, a vigorous counter to the perceived degeneracy of childishness, 'beastliness,' sensuousness, and effeminacy. But as one analyst has reminded us, the traditions of manliness, like those of chivalry and gentlemanliness, are social and literary phenomena, not religious ones:

> They have obvious relevance to those aspects of manly Christianity which reflect and operate in terms of the general social and literary atmosphere of the day. But they belong to the village green and the market-place, the houses of the great and the humble, rather than to the pulpit. Moral and religious considerations frequently arise ... but in the context of the world rather than the church. Since Kingsley in particular felt uneasy about hard-and-fast distinctions between church and world this may hardly seem to matter, but the preaching of Christian manliness in his novels and in those of Thomas

Hughes related to a tradition of preaching moral manliness as well as to more secular traditions.[22]

The language of the cult of manliness abounded with athletic and military images of running the straight race and fighting the good fight. Reflected in the religious writings of Coleridge, Thomas Arnold, and F.D. Maurice, it provided a strenuous model for a certain kind of spiritual life recognized among those of a certain social class on both sides of the Atlantic. The ideas of these thinkers, worked out in the fiction of Kingsley and Hughes as well as in the popular preaching and religious apologetic of certain evangelicals, created a context for one kind of educational philosophy in which 'playing the game' presented a substitute for religious idealism.[23] Wilf continued to admire the ideology of amateur sport after he left school and immersed himself in games of all kinds. He especially admired the athletic innovations introduced in Scotland at Loretto School by the hygienic optimist H.H. Almond, who went about reforming the health of his boys with the enthusiasm of a missionary.[24]

In retrospect, Wilf found the compulsory games policy at Marlborough an important influence. A shaggy, tough individual at this point, he was nicknamed the 'Beast' for his belligerent nature and his unruly hair. Besides revelling in compulsory games, he would go to extraordinary lengths to get an extra swim, joining the ragged few who chose to take an early morning dip in the open-air pool constructed out of a branch of the River Kennet, even though it did not officially count as a 'bathe.' He looked back upon these activities approvingly later in life when he reflected, 'The great desire of every boy who could hope to do so was to excel in athletics. This fact has much to commend it in such an educational system, for it undoubtedly kept its devotees from innumerable worse troubles and dangers.'[25]

But while he remained at Marlborough his father grew dissatisfied with the pace of his studies. At his present level, he clearly would not make it to a university. In December 1881, Algernon Grenfell took his son away to read for the London matriculation with a tutor, and during this period of independent study Wilf became acutely consumed with what he was to do with his life. The army beckoned, then the priesthood. The profession of arms, which towards the end of the nineteenth century had acquired increasingly religious overtones, fed his desire for action. Moreover, he admired such evangelical Christian soldiers as General Gordon. Then he changed his mind and announced to Algie, then at Oxford, 'I think I have given up finally all hope of [the Royal Military Academy] Woolwich and am I think determined to be a clergyman as I should like that next best.'[26] His father, who had grown depressed by the burden of the school, suggested he go to nearby Neston and speak to the local doctor, David Russell. During the course of this interview, the doctor took down from a shelf a pickled human brain and talked about the functions of the human body. 'I was thrilled with entirely new emotions.' Grenfell wrote later in life. 'I had never thought of man's body as a machine.'[27] The sheer pleasure of the body's physical functions fascinated him, and when his father offered him the choice of joining his brother at Oxford or going to London, he placed Oxford in the back of his mind until he had investigated medicine for himself. He entered the London Hospital Medical College in February 1883.

The Reverend Algernon Grenfell, an unstable and unpredictable individual, was at this time planning to move out of the school he had occupied for twenty years, ostensibly to confine himself to pastoral duties in London. But that was not the whole picture. He had grown more neurotic as time went on. As Algie remembered him, his behaviour sometimes suggested the manic depressive:

> He was an odd man: a marvellous teacher, but liable at any moment to fly into a devastating passion about nothing at all. His early religious training had been evangelical to the verge of Calvinism. My brother Wilfred and I were brought up on these lines. Unfortunately, about once a week my father's intellect rebelled against the dogma that had been thrashed into him as a child, and he launched out, after the daily family prayers were ended, into a riot of free thinking. The result was that by the time that I reached my tenth birthday, I was a finished atheist, convinced that one minus one equalled nothing at all. My brother began life as an enthusiastic evangelical.[28]

Algie preferred to think his father suffered from a form of insanity he had received through his mother from the Prices, a Guernsey family he claimed had intermarried far too closely. For this reason, he thought, several members of his family had suffered at times from periods of instability. For example, he regarded as unstable his Uncle Herbert, an inventor of gunsights for the Royal Navy who was dismissed for wrecking his ship. He knew that his Uncle John, a schoolmaster, suffered from a period of mental illness and that John's son Bernard, the Oxford Egyptologist who discovered the Gnostic gospels, died in an asylum. But a more dramatic event hastened their father's departure from the school and altered Wilf's view of organized religion.

William Ward, a twelve-year-old boy at Mostyn House and the son of a Neston evangelical who owned the local nonconformist Mission Hall, had died at the end of May 1882, and his father wished him buried in the churchyard. The Reverend Algernon Grenfell was called upon to conduct the funeral service. With a gesture of intolerance worthy of one of Hardy's vilest characters, the vicar would not permit the churchyard gates to be opened to allow the funeral procession in, and this act left an impression on the whole Grenfell family. Wilf remembered, 'My chum had only a legal right to be buried in the yard. The coffin had therefore to be lifted over the wall and as the church was locked, father conducted the service in the open air. His words at the grave-side gave a touch of reality to religion, and still more so did his walking down the aisle out of church the following Sunday when the vicar referred to the destructive influence of anything that lent colour to dissent.'[29] In fact, the sermon was preached by the curate, who as he prepared to leave the parish wanted to draw attention to the rise of dissent in Neston. Wilf's father, having now exhibited his disapproval of what one observer called 'ignorant bigotry,' had separated himself from the parish clergy.[30] He set out at once to find another job, and by November became chaplain of the London Hospital after competing against over twenty other candidates.

After leasing the school to William Barrett, his head boy when he took over in 1863, Algernon Grenfell brought his wife to Victoria Park, in the East End of London, where Wilf was immersing himself in the basic sciences at the medical college. Within a year the strain of the job overwhelmed him. Unlike the chaplains of other large hospitals, he lacked an assistant and found it impossible to take a day off. During the summer of 1885 he requested a leave of absence after his doctor ordered him to take three months' rest,[31] and Wilf attempted to prop him up by taking him on a fishing and sightseeing tour of Norway. Once they returned from their summer holiday in the open air, however, his father got progressively worse. The same pattern of behaviour returned to haunt him: periods of absolute clarity clouded by bouts of melancholy and recklessness. By October he was complaining to the house committee that he could not continue without an assistant, and at length they suggested he submit his resignation. Shortly afterwards he was committed to an asylum at Chiswick, and Jane Grenfell moved in with her mother in Hampstead.

The plight of Algernon Grenfell distracted the family for the rest of the year. He remained at Chiswick during 1886, where he could be visited conveniently. After one such visit, Algie wrote in his diary, 'See him in a Mr. Cook's private room – friend of his – nice bright fire & comfortable. Guv talks to me in a natural tone for 20 min – only begins to whine at end – Cook shut him up at once – then he attempts it in Latin – but getting no encouragement dries up.'[32] At lucid moments he wrote the most pitiful letters to his wife, beseeching her to liberate him. These letters include an undated *cri de coeur* written during a holiday with a male nurse at Aberaeron, a fishing village on the Welsh coast, with its forebodings of disaster:

My darling wife,

I send you my tenderest love. I humbly entreat you to remove me from Dr Tuke's – where I never can get well. Please ask George to come & see me to insist on it before too late. I cannot tell you more. Truly I told Algie the truth, or part of it. You cannot conceive it. Do, my Darling. I pray & beseech you remove me ere it is too late. Suppose only the need of *keeping patients* to pay for a private asylum, i.e. to make the doctor's profits. Suppose only how easy with a little neglect, a few drugs, a paid set of attendants & the company for hours of lunatics. Or of an attendant who does nothing to cheer you, ~~or the pretended company of the doctor's son who is half an idiot~~, and the misery of being watched & kept in prison – I am let out today on 'parole', i.e. promise to return, & I cannot break it, but if I stay at Chiswick you will soon hear that I am a helpless, hopeless lunatic. Oh I entreat you save me from *the Tukes*. Save me my darling, do try some other doctor, or I perish. God bless you.

Your own
Algernon.[33]

But no one did save him. Possibly no one could. Algie believed no amount of watchfulness could have prevented the disaster that followed. Letters from the asylum suggested that his health and spirits had improved during the summer of 1887. On the day in question, 18 August, he had been playing chess for three hours and after a walk with his attendant had cheerfully asked him to take a stroll by himself before dinner. After an absence of only half an hour, the attendant returned to find Grenfell's sitting-room empty and his bedroom door locked. And after breaking down the door, he found him hanging from the bedpost, dead. Wilf, who had been cruising off the Welsh coast, found a telegram waiting at Milford Haven and returned in time to receive his mother. Having suffered through her husband's anxieties, she looked upon his troubled face and found it calmer and happier than she had seen it since he had been taken to Chiswick. They buried him in a small hillside churchyard facing out to sea. Then, comforted by their friends, they prepared to inspect the will, not knowing that the provisions would generate contention and ill-feeling among them for the rest of their lives.

— 2 —

The London Hospital Medical College
1883 – 1889

A large number of these [lectures] are compulsory. This is unfortunate, for two reasons: the first is that many lectures are most uninstructive; the second is that it is often very inconvenient and injurious to have to attend lectures which clash with practical work, or which interfere with preparations for an Examination.

Charles Bell Keetley, *The Student's Guide
to the Medical Profession*, 1878

When Wilf entered the London Hospital Medical College in 1883, British medical education was passing through a period of reform that would change fundamentally the kind of practitioner sent out among the public. Such reform attempted to deal with a dilemma that has bothered the profession ever since: whether to give priority to educating the mind of the student or to preparing him for the practical job at hand. In its previous attempt to reform medical training in the Medical Act of 1858, the General Medical Council had developed a sound academic base for doctors in order to establish a professional culture free of the odour of commercialism. Academic education had aimed at developing a well-educated Christian gentleman with some professional competence, and the curriculum reflected that bias. But as the nineteenth century wore on, the Medical Council continued to find students deficient.

Required to specialize more and more in scientific subjects, they were left less time for other accomplishments, especially the use of the English language. As a result, between 1858 and the end of the nineteenth century the education of the average doctor changed in a manner familiar to our own time: the educative component was crowded out of the program by the weight of technical knowledge. As one historian has shown, 'The aim of the older education had been to give the student a good grounding in wisdom rather than knowledge, to form his character, and to let him learn the technical aspects of his profession in the course of a lifetime devoted to it. The aim of the new education was to prevent his being "an ignorant pretender." As so often happens in history, the mistakes of one generation have to be paid for by more than one of its successors.'[1] Thus, the examining board aimed at giving the candidate useful knowledge so as to produce a safe medical practitioner rather than a cultured gentleman. To encourage talent and avoid favouritism, it relied heavily on a sequence of rigorous examinations designed to develop the sound clinical skills that would satisfy one or more of the licensing bodies.

It must be remembered that attempts to regulate and improve medical training had not long existed in 1883.[2] The Medical Act of 1858 had established a licensing procedure, but entrenched interests in the various medical schools slowed the adoption of a common course of study for physicians. An amending bill in 1878 did, however, outline a program of study to be completed in two stages. The first included chemistry and chemical physics, anatomy, physiology, materia medica, and pharmacology, to be completed before the end of the second year. The second included pathology, medicine, surgery, midwifery, and forensic medicine. But these and other provisions were not finally made law until the Medical Act of 1886, well after Wilf had begun his training. What was once a two-year course stretched to four and then five years with the added requirement of a term of internship, whereby the student became a 'dresser' or apprentice to a surgeon.

Although Osler's classic textbook *The Principles and Practice of Medicine*, which set forth a scheme for the division of teaching hospitals, was not published until 1892, bedside teaching had already become an accepted practice in Britain. Separate clinics served separate wards, each under the supervision of a separate professor. More responsibility was offered the student and more opportunities for exercising new techniques in the laboratory.[3] These innovations were just beginning to take effect at the London Hospital. As the largest hospital in Britain, with its eight hundred beds and 75,000 patients a year, it offered enormous scope for observing and treating illness.

Soundly educated for his time but lacking scientific training (except for elementary chemistry), Wilf recognized that he had started at a disadvantage. As he later wrote, 'Men in my position suffered quite unconsciously a terrible handicap, and it was only the influences for which I had nothing whatever to thank the hospital that saved me from the catastrophes which overtook so many who started with me.'[4] When Wilf entered the hospital, there was no regular supervision of studies, no compulsory lectures, and no alternative to the many formal examinations – regular ordeals that carried a high rate of failure. Wilf's attendance record was high in his first year, when he became fascinated by the diagnosing techniques of Sir Andrew Clark. But in his second he attended only four of sixty lectures in medicine, two of thirty-two in midwifery, and six of thirty-four in forensic medicine. In the third year, his attendance fell in medicine, surgery, and pathology.[5] As clinical clerk during the summer of 1884, he attended only part of the time and received a mark of 'very poor.' He did not pass the examinations that October. But Frederick Treves, the London Hospital's senior surgeon, marked him 'very good' that spring as dresser, a role that required him to enter the wards after lectures to dress wounds, take out stitches, and renew bandages. On days prescribed for operations, he would stand in the well of the operating theatre, ready to hand Treves his instruments or sponge away blood. On others, as dresser on duty, he would take a turn in the casualty ward, ready day or night to respond to the bell installed over his head and treat the poor of the East End.

In Treves, Wilf found a sympathetic teacher and role model, not the brow-beating terror sometimes encountered in the medical schools of the time. Without Treves's influence he probably would not have finished his studies. As he claimed later, only when Treves became his lecturer in anatomy and surgery was it 'worth while doing more than pay the necessary sum to get signed up.'[6] An ambitious surgeon of yeoman stock who had qualified at the extraordinarily early age of twenty-two, Treves chased the twin bubbles of distinction and influence, then retired at the age of fifty after he had captured them both and left his mark on the practice of surgery.[7] A skilful publicist, he also seemed to possess extraordinary powers for teaching medical students, and he attempted to reform their training as he reformed surgical technique and social medicine. Wilf's fellow student, Dennis Halsted, tells us Treves could easily take a liking to a student or a strong dislike, but he remained on friendly terms with Grenfell and Halsted through a shared love of athletics and a common religious interest.[8] Aside from his innovative surgical ideas and his skill as a teacher, he also impressed them with his warm Dorset country style, his love of the outdoors, and his ideas on public health. In an encomium published years later, Wilf summed up his admiration for him in athletic terms: 'We used to say, when I was a school boy, that if a fellow was really good in one branch of athletics, you could pretty well count on his being good all round; when the cricket season was over a good man would find his place at football, and could generally be looked to for help when the Easter term brought the track team out. And so it seems to me of Sir Frederick Treves. To me he has always been the ideal all-round man; and I would just as soon to-day take his advice on how much of the mainsheet to get to claw a vessel best to windward, as I would on how far to venture in a delicate surgical operation.'[9]

Wilf had not yet reached twenty when he met Treves; Treves himself had just passed thirty and liked to give his free time to camping, sailing, and team sports. As a surgeon, he specialized in the treatment of intestinal obstructions, and Wilf watched him operate for his specialty, acute appendicitis. In 1898 Treves retired from the London to a more lucrative practice in Wimpole Street,[10] but he continued their friendship as his reputation widened through his subsequent service in the Boer War and his successful operation for appendicitis on Edward VII, who had been taken ill two days before his coronation. For this celebrated operation, the king rewarded Treves with a baronetcy and made him royal sergeant surgeon. Treves is best remembered, perhaps, for the exceptional attention he exhibited in the care of Joseph Merrick, the so-called Elephant Man, a victim of severe neurofibromatosis whose ghastly folds of cauliflower-like skin had turned him into a curiosity. With characteristic flair, Treves organized an appeal for the man and gave him a room in the attic of the London Hospital. Merrick was visited there daily by Wilf and the other students during their rounds and lived out his time with a degree of contentment he would not have otherwise expected.[11]

Wilf was also living through a period of fundamental change in surgical technique that gradually transformed the surgeon from an agent of pain and gross butchery, with limited expectations of success, to a saver of lives who could operate with considerably less risk.[12] Treves himself could recall a time when the surgeon, a gruesome figure clad in a black velvet coat, swiftly carried out his duties without any knowledge of anaesthetics or asepsis. In those days the operating theatre retained something of the air of the slaughterhouse, and the surgeon himself wore a frock coat, stiffened with blood and pus, that conveyed a sign of his experience and prowess. But the practice of surgery had since been transformed from a trade to a clinical science. With the discovery that putrefaction was caused by air-borne germs, Lister developed an antiseptic from carbolic acid. When he operated at the London Hospital he employed a special carbolic spray designed to kill germs in the atmosphere, requiring the surgeon to work in a cloud of carbolic steam that, Wilf recalled, 'spouted from large brass boilers over everything.' At the same time, Treves instituted the practice of scrupulous hygiene.[13] Through this practice in particular, the risk of operations was drastically reduced.

Having now grown into a muscular young man, Wilf revelled in the athletic opportunities presented in London. If he did not present himself regularly at lectures, he occupied almost all of his spare time with athletics.

He was successively secretary of cricket, rugby, and rowing, the last of which he broke into despite the condescension of the Oxford and Cambridge men who ran the sport. As he wrote to Algie at Oxford, 'I have a great reputation for rowing here as they see I occasionally coach the 'varsity VIII from horse back.'[14] In their first regatta, Halsted won the sculls and Wilf the double sculls. Wilf was also accustomed to carrying a sixteen-pound hammer around with him, and he won the hammer throw for the hospital as well. He played rugby and football for the hospital and for Richmond both at the same time. In 1885 he played with the outstanding hospital rugby team that won the cup and set the style of rugby football to come by playing four three-quarters. He also drew attention as an association footballer: 'A better all round man I never want to see,' declared a fellow player, 'his forward play was characteristic of his whole life, thoroughness was his watchword, and where the ball was, there you might with confidence look for Grenfell.'[15]

But though Wilf was gifted in some sports, he did not excel at them all. He possessed strength and stamina and the sheer joy of strenuous activity, but he lacked finesse, especially in gymnastics. Halsted described him as 'clumsy' in the gymnasium: 'When I saw him flinging himself about on the parallel bars, I was always afraid that he was going to break his neck,' he wrote. 'But it was, I suppose, typical of him that he always wanted to have a go at everything, whether he was any good at it or not.'[16]

Halsted knew Wilf's habits intimately since the two rented an unfurnished house in Palestine Place, Hackney. He soon learned that Grenfell, who needed only six hours' sleep at the most, liked to get up at 6:30 to study and then lecture the recumbent Halsted about wasting his time. Into their lodgings they put only the bare essentials: chair frames which they stuffed themselves and coconut matting for mattresses. Hardened to sleeping in unorthodox ways, Wilf had used a hammock at home, and now he slung one in his bedroom between the wall and the window-frame. After a few weeks his weight tore away the whole framework, and he was found one morning on the floor, surrounded by debris and glass. Both students shared an ascetic serious-mindedness despite the blandishments of London, and in their spare time they turned the ground floor and garden of their house into a boys' club in a section of the city already served by the 'settlement houses' of Arnold Toynbee and other middle-class intellectuals. 'We were both firm believers in the good effects of the physical discipline provided by athletics,' recalled Halsted, 'and so we set out really to put those boys through it, and I don't think any of them ever regretted the treatment we gave them.'[17]

Each Saturday night what passed for a dining-room would be transformed into a sweaty, noisy gymnasium with a boxing ring in the centre.

On Sunday afternoon it became a Sunday school. There were about a hundred boys eventually, ranging in age from eight to fourteen, most of them gone from school and out into the world to seek work. Wilf took particular satisfaction in organizing these events himself, even if he failed to carry through to the last detail, and Halsted thought this trait character-istic of him. 'He was always a man for the big things. That was his character. There was nothing equivocal in Grenfell's personality. He always aimed at the big things in life. The details, as I say, he left to others less competent. If the boys failed in anything, he would give them another chance with a kindly word, "Try again." '[18] Ample contributions of money came in from individuals and local firms eager to improve the state of the East End. Nevertheless, the two medical students insisted the boys themselves contribute a token penny a week so that they would not expect something for nothing. Having observed at the hospital the tragic lives about them in Whitechapel, the two insisted on putting their religious beliefs to some use despite the resistance they encountered. Cecil Tyndale-Biscoe, then curate of St Mary's, Whitechapel, respected what Grenfell tried to accomplish at this early age. 'A more gallant man never lived,' he remembered. 'He left his mark in Whitechapel as in every place he ever went. His tackling of drunken men and women, and scoffers at Christian-ity, and his great efforts in turning young hooligans into gentlemen, was an inspiration for all Christian workers.'[19]

If Wilf worked hard during the term, he made sure he got out of London during the long vacations, when he and Algie would charter a fishing smack with a few friends, sail out of Anglesey and cruise the Welsh coast, haunting the holiday resorts in their outlandish gear. This kind of holiday encompassed everything Wilf enjoyed, 'responsibility, yet rest, mutual dependence, and a charming, unconventional way of getting acquainted with one's own country.'[20] But even though they did not ordinarily need a chronometer or sextant in the Irish Sea, the crew did not share Wilf's confidence in his own navigating precision. On one of these free-wheeling voyages, with Wilf as chief navigator on the strength of his master's certificate, they attempted to reach the Isle of Man but found as it grew dark that the island remained seven miles to starboard. After convincing the navigator of his error, they worked their way to Douglas Harbour, avoiding a storm that probably would have swallowed them. Wilf used to terrify more careful sailors with the chances he took. He once shot a puffin in the Irish Sea and dived over the side to pick it up, even though a heavy tidal stream was running and they had already lost their dinghy in a squall. With the wind calm, the sails were useless. But once again, his athletic power saved him, and after a half hour he was able to swim close enough to reach the end of a rope.[21]

It occurred to Wilf that this was just the sort of experience needed to liberate his boys from their circumscribed East End lives, and during subsequent vacations he organized summer camps for them in Wales. The first year he took thirteen, and in ensuing years the numbers grew to a hundred. He made them wear a uniform of blue knickers and grey flannel shirts. They had to bathe in the sea before breakfast, although sometimes they managed to postpone the ordeal until noon, and they were forced to learn to swim before they could enter a boat. Towards the end of his residency at the London Hospital, when he could no longer find the time for these excursions, Treves found a way for them to camp in the grounds of Lulworth Castle in Dorset so that they would be near the sea still. By now the group had begun to look something like a cadet corps, with rifles and drill, and Wilf was demonstrating a gift for organizing people ill-equipped to help themselves. He also demonstrated a gift for advertising his achievements, as he later showed in his first piece of journalism in the *Review of Reviews.*

The boys themselves, who ranged in age from fourteen to twenty, were not the homeless 'lay-outs' discovered by his predecessor at the London, Dr Thomas Barnardo. They came from the ranks of what Wilf called the 'artizan class' and were already employed as apprentices, messengers, and factory hands in jobs that might pay from five to twenty shillings a week. Thus, by making weekly deposits, the group could build up enough capital to finance its own camp a year in advance. During their two or three weeks in the open air, they would look after themselves and when not rambling around the countryside engage in sports or country dancing. 'I may say we do not include alcohol in any form among our stores,' Wilf pointed out, 'being almost, if not all of us, teetotallers.'[22] Each Sunday the campers attended a church service, and each night they worshipped in the open. Having developed certain habits and values, Wilf expected them to return to their jobs and exert an influence for 'good.'

The most dramatic influence on Wilf's life at this time came not from medicine or athletics but from a new-found religious idealism. Growing up in Parkgate, he had been raised in an evangelical family, and he was impatient with the ritualistic and the sacerdotal. By the time he entered his second year of study he was looking for something more practical through which he could exercise his faith. Halsted viewed him at that point as 'an ordinary lad from the country' whose eyes had been opened by the London Hospital and the distress surrounding it. 'During our life at the house, too, with all those boys and the distress, I think he found he was gradually drifting into a way of persuading others to become Christians on definite lines,' he recalled, 'but of course, together with all that, there were the examinations and the medical education, so he could not give his time to his religion so much as to the practical side – getting qualified, etc.'[23]

Returning one night from a case in Shadwell, he entered a tent meeting conducted by the American evangelists Moody and Sankey and was so impressed by what appeared to be Moody's unvarnished, practical approach to living a Christian life that he made a private pact with himself to devote his energies to, as he put it, what Christ would do in his place if he had been a doctor. Moody possessed the ability to move large audiences, and undoubtedly Wilf responded directly to the unorthodox preaching style of the American: his quaintness, his vivid phrasing, his sense of humour – a directness that appeared fresh in comparison with formal British preaching. Moreover, unlike other evangelists, Moody did not weary his hearers with declarations about the wrath of God but insisted on the efficacy of God's love as a saving power over men. Wilf considered what followed to be one of the central events of his life.

At a subsequent meeting he went to hear J.R. and C.T. Studd, two cricketers who were helping Moody with his campaign. 'They were natural athletes,' Wilf recalled, 'and I felt that I could listen to them. I could not have listened to a sensuous-looking man, a man who was not master of his own body, any more than I could to a precentor, who coming to sing the prayers at college chapel dedication, I saw get drunk on sherry which he abstracted from the banquet table just before the service.'[24] When the call came to 'stand up' for Christ, he did so. 'I believed in free will: it seemed common sense,' he later told a Harvard audience. 'I knew that materialists did not, and that most of my comrades believed in Darwin and Huxley, and in the teaching that we are all slaves of unbreakable laws. I believed that I was at the fork of two roads, and could go down the one which I liked.'[25] Having spurned Darwin, he spurned his disciple, Herbert Spencer. Now he could articulate his religious inclinations better, and he felt secure in his mind about where his efforts should go – into some form of practical service.

Wilf kept missing lectures during his third year of training but learned enough on the practical side as a dresser to pass the examinations the first time round while Halsted failed twice. By January 1888 he had attained the conjoint diploma, LRCP, MRCS. What kind of physician was he? Halsted claimed he was not as tolerant as he might have been, not interested in individuals: 'He lacked sentiment, I would say. If he found anyone there wasn't much wrong with, he would not stand any nonsense. He would say, "Get some work to do, my friend, and you'll be better." Wilfred was perhaps right, but he put it in a very blunt, practical way – very practical. Sentiment did not appeal to him so much as the practical side of life. In private practice, you must have the sympathetic touch. Wilfred was never in private practice.'[26] Halsted also recalled Grenfell's personal crusade against drinking, for which he wore a badge around the hospital, proclaiming the benefits of abstinence. Such benefits had been impressed upon him by his clinical instructor, Sir Andrew Clark, who taught his students that alcohol was poison and reminded them that seven out of ten patients at the London Hospital owed their illness to it. But if Halsted thought Wilf lacked sensitivity as a physician, he ranked him very highly as a surgeon. Surgery seemed to suit his practical sense better.

With his basic training as a physician and surgeon finished, Wilf looked for a change of pace. He wanted to go up to Oxford, a necessary route if he were going to open a practice and find acceptance in Harley Street. Before he finished his medical examinations he wrote Algie's tutor at Queen's, T.H. Grose, to explore the possibility. It is reasonable to suppose that Grose procured a place for him in college since there was no regular system of admissions at the time and fellows often admitted students, provided they made satisfactory guarantees for fees. Grose accepted him for October 1888. There now remained the matter of finding something to do with his qualification before he proceeded further. He was twenty-two.

Treves suggested he could put his training to good use as a physician with the Mission to Deep Sea Fishermen, a newly formed charitable society to which he himself had become the medical adviser. The Mission was interested in seeing whether a physician could live and work at sea for an extended period, just as the fishermen did, and Treves must have realized that the job would not have appealed to most young physicians, for it obliged the successful applicant to go to sea with the North Sea fishing fleet for months on end, living under the same unsavoury conditions as the fishermen and treating crushed fingers and rotten teeth. It needed a strong young man with the agility to scramble up ladders and leap from one rolling deck to another. More important, the Mission was waging war on the grog ships that enticed fishermen on board with cheap liquor and pornography they could ill afford, and it needed someone indifferent to liquor. The challenge seemed to suit Wilf perfectly. Even though he informed Grose in February that he intended to come up to Oxford, the same week he was interviewed at the Mission headquarters by Ebenezer Mather, the founder, and Treves, chairman of the hospital committee. The Mission, he found, was looking for more than a doctor. It asked for more than expertise and goodwill from its applicants. It wanted a commitment to preach the gospel along strict evangelical lines and evidence of 'that distinct gift which is the prime credential of the true fisher of men.' Once it was satisfied about these contingencies, Wilf was taken on for a two-month voyage in the *Thomas Gray* at three guineas a week.[27]

Absorbed now in his first job, Wilf revelled in the responsibility and the rough life at sea, even if his patients did not stimulate him. These fishermen, attracted to the rough conditions aboard the fishing smacks by the relatively high wages, had acquired a 'superficial deadening apathetic gloss' difficult to penetrate. He reported to his mother, 'I am reading Charles Kingsley and enjoy it very much,' but he found it difficult to interest the crews in more than simple yarns and idle humour. He had brought some Twain, Artemus Ward, and Bret Harte to entertain them but complained 'they don't see the jokes.' The *Thomas Gray*, smallest of the Mission smacks, lacked adequate washing facilities, and thus the crew did not wash at all. Moreover, Wilf's cabin was not adequately heated. He revealed, 'It has no grate and I have to put up with a paraffin stove, which is rather nauseous and by no means over hot.'[28] By spring, he was still wrestling with common ailments and bewailing the lack of remedies. A patient suffered from pleurisy and congestion of the lungs. He wrote, 'It is the first time I have ever felt the responsibility so great, as my cabin is damp & I have continually to change & air his bed clothes – I do everything myself – my greatest difficulty is food.' Minor surgery presented special difficulties. He learned to stitch up a lip with the vessel in motion and the patient wedged in between crates of tobacco beneath the main hatch.[29] As he went about practising medicine under these conditions, both he and the Mission began to attract the interest of the press.

The *Thomas Gray* now embarked the correspondent for the *Leeds Mercury*, who was preparing a series of articles dramatizing the new venture in medicine of which Wilf had become the embodiment. In Wilf he discovered the kind of colourful character on which he could focus his story. He wrote:

> The doctor is a lithe, muscular Christian, with a pair of honest brown eyes and a breezy manner which is likely to be quite as powerful for good as one or two drugs in the British Pharmacopoeia. His experience, professionally considered, until the Thomas Gray fell in with the Great Northern Fleet was not encouraging – gales, snow, ice, rain, fog, and every variety of meteorological phenomena to be encountered in these latitudes in February and March. The Thomas Gray was beating about the North Sea for a whole week looking for the Hull fleets; and for nine days she was hove-to with a close-reefed mainsail while the stormy winds wreaked their will upon her. But on Saturday morning, when the doctor visited the home-going steamer Onward, there went thither men from every division of the then combined fleets to have their ailments attended to. And when he returned aboard the vessel, importunate patients followed. I saw him just outside the cabin door as the light was fading, steadying himself against the after-ladder, forceps in hand, extracting

a huge molar from the jaw of a fisherman who had not known sleep for a week. And a host of minor cases demanded his attention.[30]

He reported later that Wilf had run short of alkalis and was obliged to make a tour of the fleet in search of some bicarbonate of potash. Then he damaged his watch and took to measuring pulses by the ship's clock, an instrument of eight pounds he detached from a hook in the skipper's berth and bore aft whenever he needed it.

Despite the rough conditions, as he approached the end of his April voyage he wrote his mother to report that he was becoming hardened to the life and entering into the spirit of things as a mariner, adopting the affectation of a clay pipe and shag tobacco. The men, however, were required to suffer the rough conditions the year round. The fishermen, he told her, slept on the deck. Those fortunate enough to be assigned bunks tolerated bugs of various kinds, and occasionally holes had to be corked to keep the rats from racing across their sleeping forms. Yet, he assured her, 'I sleep here as heavily as I do on a bed or in my hammock, without a care – only I get my dip in the morning, though sometimes that is taken during a snow storm of which we've had more than I care for lately.'[31] He not only tolerated the discomfort, he enjoyed talking about it, and by the time he returned to Billingsgate he had earned the respect and goodwill of the fishermen.

When he arrived home in May 1888 and bunked in with Algie, now a master at Westminster School, his brother found him fit and enthusiastic after his ordeal, and the Mission work seemed to have entered into his blood. Now he faced a summer preparing for the MB examinations and getting himself ready to go up to Oxford. Two days later, when he dragged Algie to Exeter Hall for the Mission's annual meeting, Algie was surprised to find him getting to his feet and speaking, for Wilf was no orator. Yet he spoke out boldly, if confusedly, and his testimonial carried a ring of truth that went down well.[32] He had tapped something in himself he was not aware of – the ability to hold an audience with simplicity and directness. But when it came time to take his place at Queen's College, Wilf, whom Algie found to be 'quite a Radical' that summer, must have proceeded with some misgivings. He had found useful employment at sea and had enjoyed the respect of the fishermen. Now he was entering an utterly different world for an indefinite time and an unspecified purpose.

The term did not get off to an auspicious start. Late in October he went to London to sit the MB examination, and in November he learned that he had failed. The MB set at the University of London was conducted under a rigorous schedule that required the candidate to pass all examinations in pathology, therapeutics, hygiene, surgery, medicine, obstetrics, and forensic medicine. Wilf did not pass them all, and the result did not surprise Algie, who suggests in his diary that he was not properly prepared. 'He was ploughed for the MB,' he wrote, 'as was only natural: all the same, he very nearly got through.' Wilf returned to Oxford and engaged heavily in sports, never fully expecting to return after Christmas. There he proceeded to win Blues for rowing and rugby and a half Blue for athletics.

This appears to be a considerable achievement for one term until one realizes how much time he devoted to sports. In a letter written at the time, he describes a typical week's activities thus: 'We play Midland counties tomorrow, the London Hospital on Thursday. I row in trial torpids on Friday & we play Harlequins on Saty. & suitably a good programme. I am now rising at 7.20 & getting up Flemming & Wilson & we go for a run and a hammer throw before breakfast.'[33] But it was rugby that took most of his time. 'Quite took the place of doctor to the team,' Algie recorded, '& also experimented on numerous Queen's dons.'[34] By this time Wilf had developed into a determined if inelegant rugby player. A *Times* reporter covering one of his subsequent Labrador lectures could recall, 'nobody who remembers the Oxford Fifteen of that year, one of the somewhat lean years that followed the disbanding of Vassall's historic team of Internationals, will forget that "Grenfell, of Queen's," was a silent, indefatigable worker, always hard as nails, who made up for his lack of brilliancy by never relaxing his efforts for a moment until the call of "no-side" was heard.'[35] All the same, Wilf did not take readily to the Oxford style of life, and at the end of term he quietly left when Treves offered to take him back as house surgeon.

Algie and Treves agreed that Wilf was not ready for an excursion into academic life, although Treves thought he might still have benefited after filling the hospital post for six months. By June, however, he assessed Wilf's performance as 'indifferent.' In a part-time course in anaesthetics he was assessed as 'very poor.' The term at Oxford had confused him. Accustomed to a rough and practical way of life, he had not adapted easily to genteel pursuits and abstract learning. Many years later, he revealed his difficulty in a letter to Dr Harvey Cushing of the Harvard Medical School: 'I love Oxford – naturally – I loved the suavity, the polish, the real gentlemaness of its dons. I love them better than I did because I felt their apparent classical encasement. I had come from working in Whitechapel, and cruising in the North Sea. I loved them, but resented their self sufficiency – they were there to *educate* us – but for my problems they seemed so heavily handicapped as to be insufficient.'[36] Algie had revelled in Oxford and taken a second in Classical Greats two years before, having missed a first only because of his disappointing performance in the *viva*. Wilf, on the contrary, could not adjust to what he termed Oxford's 'sweetness.'

While Wilf struggled to find direction, Algie experienced difficulties of his own. He had learned in the spring that William Barrett had retained only twenty-one boys at Mostyn House and was giving notice to leave the following year to become the senior curate of the parish of Neston, with the expectation of succeeding as vicar. In the summer of 1889 Algie talked the matter over with Wilf and his mother as he contemplated what to do next.[37] The understanding arrived at during these talks would lead to important consequences stemming from the conditions of his father's will. When the Reverend Algernon Grenfell left Mostyn House in 1883, he leased it to Barrett, selling him only the furniture and goodwill of the school. Thus, when in 1889 Barrett gave notice, after allowing the build-ings to deteriorate and enrolment to fall, he placed the Grenfells in a serious dilemma. Should they sell off the property at a minimal price or try to build the school up again? Their younger brother Cecil had enlisted in the Royal Marines that year, and Wilf had not finished his medical training. It remained for Algie to take over the school, even though he had already found satisfying employment in what he termed the 'slums' of Westminster.

To understand fully the quandary into which their father's death placed the brothers, one must look at the conditions of the will.[38] Predictably, it provided charitable legacies of £100 for the Church Missionary Society, the British and Foreign Bible Society, and the London City Mission. All of his personal effects were left to his widow, together with £1,000. The rest of the real and personal property was left in trust to Algie, from which he was to pay his mother an income. However, since the full extent of the capital consisted of the school, which produced no dividends, Algie, in effect, was called upon to provide for his mother's support. Upon her death he was to pay Wilf £4,000 and invest funds that would produce an annuity of £160 for Cecil, who was not expected to outlive the other two. If Cecil died, this annuity was to be divided between the two surviving. If he predeceased his mother, another £1,500 was to be paid out of the estate to Wilf in lieu of his half of the expected annuity. But with the school in a run-down condition, the will did not accurately reflect the condition of the estate. As Algie's son Daryl speculated many years later, the will had not been brought up to date: 'Possibly, at one time or another when he may have made the will, he did have the money: but his latter days & some ill-health & other circumstances substantially reduced his substance. Dad declares A.S.G. knew & realized this before his death ... while in a nursing home, but too late to do anything about it in consequence of the nature of his complaint. A.S.G., Dad declared, talked to him on several of his visits to see him there.'[39] No one investigated the real value of the property, and when Algie attempted to sell Mostyn House in 1889 he could not find a buyer.

He was only twenty-six when he returned to Mostyn House in January

1890, after three years as a master at Westminster School. His explanation of the circumstances under which he assumed control, though it retains the air of a later difference of opinion between the two brothers, is important for understanding how that difference occurred. His father had purchased the property in 1875 from the estate of Thomas Brassey, the railway contractor, for £2,750; but Brassey had paid only £1,000 for it in 1852, and Algie thought he might at least attract a bid for that much.[40] When he failed to do so, he took over the school himself, for he 'loathed' London and thought he would be happier in Parkgate. He explained, 'I want you to understand clearly what it was I valued at £1,000 maximum in 1889: a bare, leaky, very ancient building infested with dry rot ... standing in a rough playground not even levelled, an odoriferous farm-yard with obsolete stable and shippons, lighting by paraffin lamps. Not a stick of furniture, no business or good will of any kind: father had sold these items to Barrett and I had to pay Barrett some hundreds of pounds for them out of income for three years.[41] In addition, he had raised a credit of £2,000 on the guarantees of his uncles, Hubert and John Grenfell, and with this in hand he shored up the main house, installed plumbing, and began to expand. By using what remained of the estate, he set about enlarging the premises, and during the first two years built a dining hall, a covered playground, and a swimming pool. In 1895, having raised the enrolment from eighteen to a hundred in five years, he felt confident enough to design a chapel, which he opened in 1897. Over the next decade he added a classroom block, changing rooms and a water tower, and doubled the size of the cottage, remodelling other interiors in the contemporary style. By then, he had built Mostyn House into a creditable school.

By 1895 he had also taken on as senior master 'Tommy' Price, a Queen's man who had accompanied him to Parkgate in 1890. Price, reputed to be a superb organizer, came at what Algie considered very high terms, including an option to rent the school should he himself give it up or die. So at this point he invited both his brothers to join him in setting aside their father's controversial will. This way, he could take over sole ownership of the school and develop it on his own terms, for he alone possessed the desire to save it. Accordingly, he proposed that Wilf take the rest of the estate and from it pay Cecil his £160 a year. 'I want nothing at all but Mostyn House,' he insisted, 'and that I want to have *outright – now*.'[42] Once this was done, he proposed making a new will that would make Wilf the owner of the school if he died and stipulating that Wilf should let it to Price at £1,000 a year. That spring Wilf wrote a sentimental letter reasserting his affinity with Mostyn House and granting Algie sole ownership. 'I believe as we grow older we feel like clinging together more than ever,' he told him. 'Blood is a good deal thicker than water.'[43] Accordingly, he agreed to set aside the will, giving Algie ownership of the school and dividing the remainder between Cecil and himself so as to preserve Cecil's £160 a year. He also agreed to the arrangements with Tommy Price. The solicitors, however, refused to take responsibility for carrying through the agreement since they considered it a breach of trust. There the matter remained suspended until Cecil retired from the Royal Marines in 1912.

The self-sufficiency of the two older brothers stood out more clearly as they advanced into maturity. As Algie shaped the school, he viewed himself as something of a cultural guardian, encouraging spelling and handwriting competitions and ensuring that the winners were acknowledged as much as any athlete. An uncompromising sceptic, he constantly ran up against his brother's wholehearted, unintellectual belief. Usually the two pulled each other's legs on matters metaphysical, preferring to score playfully off each other without disturbing the superficial unity of family relations. But at other times the discussion grew more serious. In 1926, during one of their rows over the distribution of the estate, Wilf expressed his disappointment and attacked what he perceived as his brother's materialism. He urged that as an educator, A.G. ought to have possessed a will to believe and cited the example of the missionary Cecil Tyndale-Biscoe, whom he had visited in Kashmir the year before. 'Personally,' he wrote sanctimoniously, 'I had far rather "be wrong with Socrates than right with Plato," especially if I had to make my calling the evolution of character. Tyndal Biscoe [sic] is changing the character of even Brahmin boys, as he says, by not emphasizing information but inspiration.' A.G. remained unmoved by the attack. 'Theories of permanised individuality after death rest on no evidence that I am aware of,' he replied. 'Nor do I see what such theories have got to do with religion, which (as you know) I hold to be the only possible driving force for this life. Socrates: Plato: Biscoe: all the Archbishops that ever lived knew exactly the same amount about the subject – viz. – nil.'[44] As the scholar of the family, he had discarded the family's studied puritanism and lived comfortably with himself while he threw his imagination and energies into his educational enterprise.

His mother, Jane Grenfell, returned to the school in 1895 as the lady of the house and remained there after Algie's marriage. Until her death in 1921 she provided an anchor for Wilf, who remained devoted to her and kept up a regular correspondence during his long absences in North America. As Wilf acknowledged, his mother exerted an unusually strong influence over him during this early stage of his life, and in later years he sentimentalized her shamelessly. He wrote, 'To the mind of every boy the mother he loves possesses naturally sources of wisdom which are not open to him. He does not query or analyse this fact. With our mother we somehow knew that she had a knowledge of truth which we did not have, and unquestionably she had. It was the inner light that Christ says comes from following in His footsteps. Even later in life, when our imperious personalities demanded a why and wherefore from everyone else ... we still found in her assurance something which satisfied us.'[45] Wilf was so deeply attached to his mother that no young women, except for religious or medical colleagues, seemed to enter his life. Even after he located his own family in the United States, he continued to regard Mostyn House as his spiritual and sentimental home.

—3—

The Mission to Deep Sea Fishermen
1889 – 1892

We have fed our sea for a thousand years
And she calls us, still unfed,
Though there's never a wave of all her waves
*   But marks our English dead:*
We have strawed our best to the weed's unrest,
*   To the shark and the sheering gull.*
If blood be the price of admiralty,
*   Lord God, we ha' paid in full!*

Rudyard Kipling, 'A Song of the English'

While Algie reflected upon the future of the school, Wilf decided to return to his work with the Mission to Deep Sea Fishermen. In December 1889 he received a temporary appointment to work in the North Sea fleet. In doing so, he joined a young organization on the verge of expansion. The Mission had begun, in effect, in August 1881, when Ebenezer Joseph Mather, secretary of the Thames Church Mission Society, made a voyage in a fish-carrier of Hewett and Company to the Short Blue Fleet situated along the Dogger Bank. He was distressed by the deplorable spiritual and medical state of the crews. Recent innovations in fishing technique had made it possible for fishermen to stay at sea for weeks on end. Packing the fish in ice slowed its deterioration; steam cutters rushed the fish to market; the system of fishing in fleets of fifty or more smacks ensured a steady supply. But the rapid growth of the industry demanded a ready labour force, and many recruits were boys apprenticed from workhouses in large cities.[1] Once they had finished the first voyage, however, they often failed to return to the oppressive conditions at sea. The risky business of fishing

31

and transferring boxes to the cutters created untreated injuries. The food was seldom adequate. The long passages produced sadistic bullying.

Mather was struck by the debilitating consequences of cheap spirits sold by what were known in the industry as 'copers,' vessels from Dutch ports that had originally sold clothing and fishing gear and now bartered tobacco and spirits for fish.[2] To buy the cheap tobacco, the fishermen were required to visit the coper, where the captain, free of the duty imposed in England, could sell it at less than half the price. Once on board, a man tired of the rigours of the North Sea could easily be tempted to drink, and too often he ruined his livelihood when he bartered away his gear, injured himself, or fell overboard drunk.

Mather's efforts to change this state of affairs exemplify the increasing importance of benevolence in late nineteenth-century missionary strategy.[3] Mather attempted to interest the Thames Mission in working in the North Sea but could not coax it beyond the Thames estuary. The next summer, with a generous donation from a sympathetic friend, he purchased the fifty-six-ton smack *Ensign*, registered it in his own name, and lent it to the Mission, under whose flag it sailed from Gorleston in July with a small dispensary and medicine chest. The following summer the Mission saw fit to establish a special fund for the work to supplement what the *Ensign* earned through fishing.[4] The same year, through further donations, the Mission purchased the smacks *Salem, Cholmondeley*, and *Edward Auriol*. With a scheme designed to undercut the coper, it consigned several tons of tobacco to Ostend, put it aboard a Mission smack, and sold it in the fleet duty free. Soon the firm of W.D. and H.O. Wills offered to supply tobacco at approximately cost price.[5] Once this occurred and the pretence of selling tobacco was revealed, the copers lost their market. At an international conference at the Hague in 1886 they were declared illegal.

So far, the Thames Mission had triumphed, but it could not sustain its rapidly developing fleet. Taking the matter into his own hands once again, Mather purchased the vessels by means of mortgages and advances from fishing companies; by November 1884 he had founded his own mission, the Mission to Deep Sea Fishermen, with a separate executive committee that paid his salary as secretary and manager. In this capacity he appealed to the general public for donations and in the first half of 1887 brought in over £14,000. Faced with a heavy financial administration, he expanded his committee to include such men as R.M. Ballantyne (author), G.A. Hutchison (editor of the *Boys' Own Paper*), Thomas Blair (merchant), Dr A.T. Scholfield (London Hospital) and Frederick Treves. In January 1886 Hutchison began publication of the monthly magazine *Toilers of the Deep*, sold for twopence, which soon reached a circulation of ten thousand. Within a year the circulation had doubled.

The Mission to Deep Sea Fishermen

The Mission to Deep Sea Fishermen saw itself primarily as an evangelical organization in search of souls, and only secondarily as a philanthropic agency. Although its first clergy and missioners appear to have been members of the Church of England, it strenuously maintained an 'undenominational' character. 'We cannot allow the bugbear of Church or Dissent to interfere with the progress of the work,' wrote Mather. 'It is not a question of the Establishment or of Nonconformity, but rather "Are you a fisheater?" [6] A later secretary would explain the Mission's theological stance this way: 'The sympathizers with the Society have always been able to claim that, while never degenerating into a soulless latitudinarianism, the Mission has been broad and common-sense in its outlook. It has not arrogated to itself the right of keeping the consciences of the fishermen, or any man's conscience; it has no cut-and-dried formula of doctrine or metaphysical confession of faith; it goes into the field with a wise, prudent, evangelical teaching, as I have already declared more than once, that teaching which has been the life-blood of the Church in all ages.' [7] And so the Mission drew its support from committed church people without entering into particular questions of belief. To high churchmen, it thus seemed to adopt a dangerously ambiguous theological position.

By the end of 1887 there were eight smacks at sea and a growing corps of evangelists. Mather himself acted as a kind of managing director, handling the day-to-day administration and speaking at meetings throughout the country to raise funds. When in January 1889 he requested that he be allowed to do this work in an honorary capacity, however, what was now the council began to look into his personal affairs. Some members expressed concern about his perceived extravagance, and there were unspecified charges of financial irregularity. Ten council meetings were held between March and August, during which time he failed to give satisfactory answers to inquiries. As the annual meeting approached, the council issued a statement explaining that he was no longer connected with the Mission. The council now took tighter control. From time to time, it met in Yarmouth to confer with skippers of the Mission vessels. The finance committee met weekly. The spiritual work committee and the hospital committee, the latter chaired by Treves, met whenever required. In order to administer the work more closely, the council next decided to divide the administrative duties between a superintendent, who would regulate the sea-going staff and do deputation (fund-raising) work, and a secretary, who would retain control of the London office. Mather's departure left a space that would be partially filled by Wilfred Grenfell.

Alexander Gordon became the first secretary and remained in the position until 1892, when he was dismissed for embezzlement and replaced by the senior clerk, Francis Wood. Grenfell, at the age of twenty-four was appointed tentatively as superintendent and given responsibility for the control and maintenance of the fleet, subject to three months' notice on both sides.[8] Considering the magnitude of the job, the appointment seems premature, for he had not held a full-time job before, and his Mission experience had consisted of only a few trips to the North Sea. Nevertheless, Treves testified to his impressive mix of zeal and physical stamina, and over the next three years he never spared himself. The Mission smacks, on the strength of their work with the Dogger Bank fleet, turned their attention to those of Brixham, Ramsgate, and Milford Haven and sought out the lobstermen of Dorset. The *Sophia Wheatley* worked among the Scottish fleets, and the *Euston*, with Wilf embarked, took station off the south coast of Ireland. During those expansive days, the Mission might have gone anywhere. 'In the same way,' wrote Alexander Gordon, 'if it were found practicable to open up work amongst the Greenland whalers or the Newfoundland codfishers, the Mission has a distinct call to engage in it, as, indeed, it has to preach the gospel to toilers on the deep to the uttermost end of the seas.'[9] Already it employed a hundred people, and a growing body of popular fiction celebrated its achievements.[10]

After establishing himself at Yarmouth and winning over the people of Gorleston with his vitality, Grenfell gave the Mission its first inkling of his independent reforming tendencies. He soon recognized that the fishermen ashore needed appropriate activities if they were to keep out of the public houses, and after holding a public meeting not officially sanctioned by the council he made himself honorary secretary of a committee to start a fishermen's institute. In this additional capacity he raised funds from a list of subscribers, including the fishing companies, and purchased the freehold of temporary premises while he raised more money for a permanent building to house a coffee bar, reading room, library, class-rooms, and space for reading and recreation. He also planned classes to teach fishermen first aid and elementary navigation, and an adult school to teach reading and writing.[11] At the same time, his 'lady visitor,' Miss Wilkes, had opened up a soup kitchen and supplied a hundred people a day. Her group of fishermen's wives began raising money for the Mission at its first bazaar in Great Yarmouth in August 1891. These and other innovations, such as a circulating library for the Mission smacks and a brass band, were introduced as a direct result of Grenfell's enthusiasm and energy. As the former manager of the Mission store in Gorleston recalled, he conveyed in those early days an infectious vitality. 'He had a very charming way with people,' he observed, 'and could get anyone to do almost anything. He hated speaking in public, though he would do it if necessary, but he was not a platform man, and his voice rather tended to go high pitched when he spoke to audiences.'[12] Oblivious to personal appearance or speaking style, Grenfell was more interested in the practical business of improving the lives of fishermen.

He also exhibited a talent for publicity. A former worker at the Fellows yard in Yarmouth recalled how he once displayed a Yarmouth smack at a London fisheries exhibition, leaving it just as it would have arrived in harbour after a voyage so as to demonstrate the difficult living and working conditions at sea. First, he had the smack towed to London and beached near Battersea. Then he set two crews to work: while one crew built a cradle around it, mounted it on rollers and hauled it through the streets to the exhibition, the other dug a pit in which it could be buried to the waterline. With the ground covered by artificial waves, visitors could then cross the plank and see for themselves.[13]

His talent was not confined to such elaborate schemes as this, however. He could also write. His regular contributions to *Toilers of the Deep* dramatized the spiritual and medical work of the Mission vessels and maintained a brief on the state of the fishing industry. He described the severity of wind and sea in romantic and often sentimental terms. He portrayed fishermen as innocent creatures menaced by nature and market conditions. In one of these early contributions he wrote:

> It is inky dark outside, and the only break to the blackness is the disappearing flash of the *Nicolas* lightship, which every now and again, rising over a sea, flings its vivid red glare at one in sudden bursts, as if to enforce its warning of the treacherous sands and terrible surf on the Scrobey beyond. The words of the old hymn keep running through my mind: 'For those in peril on the sea;' and, indeed, the very gas lamp below must sympathise with those battling with the gale to-night, for it seems maintaining a despairing struggle to keep its flickering flame alight. There will be many an anxious heart to-night in fishermen's homes all along the East Coast, longing for news of fathers, husbands, and brothers, and in none more than in those where the bread-winner is away on the West Coast fishery.[14]

Grenfell related from first-hand experience 'tales of sorrow,' details of collisions and drownings that often left families bereft of their wage-earners. He told stories of heroism, and he noted the general poverty of fishermen, such as those of the Loefoden Islands, so poor that in winter they overturned their boats and lived beneath them. He also carried on scientific work. He described in detail the specimens brought up by the Mission smack, preserved them in picro-sulphuric acid and alcohol, and dropped them off at the Marine Biological Association in Plymouth for analysis. Later the association asked him to deliver a series of lectures on the species associated with certain ports. He commented on fish prices and kept a chart of catch sizes to assist the International Fishery Commission with the conservation of stocks.

In the spring of 1891 he rejoined the *Euston* at Milford Haven. Except for a brief trip to London to speak at the Mission's annual meeting in the Exeter Hall, he laboured throughout the summer as the vessel fished along the coast of Ireland, visiting English fishing boats and holding mission services ashore. There was a notable meeting at the soldiers' institute in Queenstown for marines, engineers, and artillerymen at which temperance pledges were taken. The next day the missioners visited the artillery batteries and sent boats ashore to fetch anyone who wanted to attend a service on board. 'Several of the soldiers gave their testimony as to how they had been induced to take their stand as Christian men,' wrote Wilf with satisfaction, 'and as to the great joy they now had in life, in spite of the persecution, which the absolute impossibility there is of getting any privacy exposed them to.'[15] At Crookhaven he treated poor Irish patients and Manx fishermen and chatted in French as he treated those from Boulogne. In Valentia the boat was filled with men from the Isle of Man, Scotland, and Belfast who could find no place to visit ashore.

The *Euston* moved on to the Arran Islands and beat up-wind to the thinly populated Blaskets. 'Even on these desolate islands people dwell,' wrote Grenfell, 'and on the previous day, as we had approached Vickillane in our small boat, all the inhabitants, to the number of some dozen, had appeared on the cliffs above, hoping, I could only suppose, that we had come to visit them, but, alas, no opportunity offered.'[16] In the harbour of Killeany, fishermen accustomed to outdated methods of fishing asked to come aboard for a lesson in trawling. In Clew Bay the deck was crowded with islanders, but as Roman Catholics they would not come below decks to worship. Grenfell developed a fellow feeling for these Irish people and started work on a report to improve the Irish fisheries after holding a public meeting at the Catholic Temperance Hall, Greencastle. But he despaired of the widespread drinking he encountered.

An effective evangelist by now, Grenfell was also accumulating considerable personal knowledge about medical treatment at sea, fishing techniques, and market values and had become acquainted with numerous fishermen. Clearly, he enjoyed the life and the company of fishermen, but he neglected his office duties in Yarmouth. In February 1891 the council appointed a 'deputation secretary' to raise funds and informed Wilf that he was no longer responsible for the advocacy of the Mission. Instead, it defined his job of superintendent as a practical one requiring him to remain in Yarmouth and keep fixed office hours for handling routine communications.[17] To control his wandering further, the council expected him to report his intentions before going to sea even for a tour of inspection, so that it could keep track of him.

The sun rose over the North Sea on New Year's Day, 1892, to reveal Grenfell standing on the deck of the Mission smack *Alice Fisher*, accompanied by Treves, a Mission skipper, and six hands. As the vessel skimmed along, the blue Mission banner streaming in the wind, the rising sun caught the sails and wet decks, and a ruddy light danced upon the waves. 'It seemed,' wrote Treves, 'an omen of good promise!'[18] Returning from the *Alice Fisher*'s sea trials in Holland, the group felt pleased with the vessel's performance, for it was the first of the Mission's vessels built to specifications, incorporating a decade of experience. The *Alice Fisher*, a vessel of only fifty-five tons, had been designed exclusively as a hospital ship. The upper deck had been freed of the usual skylights and fittings. The lower deck, after careful consideration of the use of space, had been rigged out by the Mission's shipwrights under Grenfell's supervision. The crew's quarters and the galley were now situated aft, and the companionway was put abaft the mizzen, close to the wheel, allowing the crew immediate access to the deck. The three-berth hospital and the doctor's cabin, lit by a common skylight, were placed forward of this, and farther forward still was the main hold, incorporating the main lockers and bunkers and space for a bath. Here the huge load of tobacco was stowed. The vessel was also designed to accommodate large groups crowding aboard for services or medical assistance. Returning now to Yarmouth, where they had departed Christmas Eve, the crew savoured their new-found comfort, and the skipper delighted in the relative ease with which he could keep the ship's head up. Wilf and Treves stood to be photographed separately at the wheel, which bore the inscription, 'Jesus saith, Follow me, and I will make you fishers of men.' Their expectations that day extended far beyond what the *Alice Fisher* might accomplish, for they anticipated the further expansion of the Mission's activities across the Atlantic to assist the fishermen of Newfoundland.

As a colony of Great Britain with responsible government, Newfoundland based its economy almost exclusively on its cod stocks, yet it had virtually neglected the development and protection of the fishery. In the 1880s, faced with frequent failures in the fisheries, Newfoundlanders were experiencing despressed conditions, particularly on the Labrador coast. As early as 1886 the Mission had received an appeal from the Reverend Henry How, a St John's clergyman, proposing a scheme to make his communicants 'honorary agents' to improve the conditions of fishermen on the Grand Banks. At the time the council refused, explaining that it carried out its work 'upon undenominational lines,' but it offered to do anything it could 'without committing the Mission to any distinct Church of England principles.'[19] Now, five years later, after a decade of work improving the lives of British fishermen, it received another appeal.

This time, one of the council members, Francis Hopwood, an assistant solicitor at the Board of Trade, reported to the finance committee the substance of his interview with Sir William Whiteway, who as premier of Newfoundland had led a delegation to London in the spring of 1891 to protest the imposition of terms for fishing on Newfoundland's west coast, the so-called French Shore. Whiteway, who had chaired a joint committee of the Newfoundland House of Assembly to consider the construction of a railway, had identified the source of Newfoundland's chronic economic difficulties in his committee's report. He wrote: 'The question of the future of our growing population has, for some time, engaged the earnest attention of all thoughtful men in this country, and has been the subject of serious solicitude. The fisheries being our main source, and to a large extent the only dependence of the people, those periodic partial failures which are incident to such pursuits continue to be attended with recurring visitations of pauperism, and there seems no remedy to be found for this condition of things but that which may lie in varied and extensive pursuits.'[20] While the government considered alternative industries, poverty and unemployment rose amongst the fishing population. Hopwood was moved by Whiteway's appeal. He was about to undertake a trip to Canada to sit on a commission reviewing Canadian fishing legislation. To take advantage of the opportunity, the council authorized him to investigate the need for extending the Mission's operations overseas.

Hopwood arrived in St John's on 16 September 1891, bearing a letter of introduction to the governor from the colonial secretary, Lord Knutsford.[21] The letter declared that Hopwood was investigating the possibility of stationing a 'floating hospital' there and asked the governor to give him any facilities he needed for his inquiries. Hopwood then proceeded to interview prominent citizens of the city and visited Trinity Bay and Random Sound aboard HMS *Emerald*. His brief visit gave him a strong impression of the state of the colony. But his findings changed the orientation of the Mission for the next three decades.[22]

Newfoundland, an outstation of the British migratory fishery since the sixteenth century, was well known in Britain for its apparently inexhaustible cod stocks and its bracing climate. A Scottish physician who served there for five years reported that 'there are unfortunately no means of getting an accurate death-rate for the island, but I feel certain that, were it compiled, it would compare favourably with that from any part of the world.'[23] By the end of the nineteenth century the West Country merchants who dominated the fishery had transformed Newfoundland into a profitable colonial enterprise, and there was a growing self-awareness among Newfoundlanders themselves.[24] As a colony, Newfoundland had continued to depend upon the inshore salt cod industry (a notoriously unstable one on which to base its external earnings) as its single most important source of employment and market income even though, in response to fluctuations in the market, politicians had continued their efforts to widen the colony's means of production. From 1855 to the mid-1880s the industry flourished and prices rose. In 1884 there were sixty thousand men engaged in fishing.

During the late 1880s and early 1890s, however, the Newfoundland economy collapsed when export prices for salt codfish sank dramatically and production declined. France had instituted a system of duties and bounties that virtually shut off the lucrative French market, even though French fishermen still purchased large quantities of bait. When the Newfoundland government voted in a bait act excluding French and American fishermen, a further means of livelihood disappeared.[25] The employment levels reached in 1884 could not possibly be maintained, especially with the absorption of further population. Clearly, the fishery simply could not expand for ever, and the labour force fell from the 1884 level to under thirty-seven thousand in 1891. Whiteway, in his report, had shown clearly the choice open to government: 'Our fisheries have no doubt increased, but not in a measure corresponding to our increase in population. And even though they were capable of being further expanded, that object would be largely neutralized by the decline in price which follows from a large catch, as no increase in markets can be found to give remunerative returns for an augmented supply.'[26] He therefore recommended the development of other resource industries, especially mining and agriculture, in pursuit of the economic balance that eluded the Newfoundland government then and has eluded successive governments for decades since.

Hopwood, already acquainted with Newfoundland's economic status, now listened to complaints about political corruption and looked into matters ranging from the inadequacy of education to the abuse of the lobster fishery. As the representative of a benevolent agency, however, he was more immediately interested in the direct effect upon living conditions. On his first day in St John's, with Whiteway and the governor out of town, he called on the editor of the *Daily Colonist*, who gave him a list of influential people he should interview: merchants, judges, and government officials, especially Judge D.W. Prowse, Adolf Nielson (superintendent of fisheries), and the Reverend Dr Moses Harvey, a historian and Presbyterian clergyman of Irish descent. After only two days, he concluded that a North Sea hospital ship would not adequately serve the Newfoundland fishery.

Unlike the British fleet system, he found, Newfoundlanders practised 'single boating,' fishing in two-man dories launched from schooners. The thick fog and the greater distances between ships would make it too difficult for a banking schooner to find a hospital ship. Instead, he favoured giving medical instruction ashore, as the Mission did in the North Sea. He considered other related matters as well. Moses Harvey, his principal informant, told him that the law did not adequately cover the seaworthiness of vessels. The dories, he said, frequently drifted away and disappeared into the fog, and he recommended an act compelling bankers to carry life-saving gear for dorymen and provisions for limited periods. He also wanted to reduce the penalty for desertion. If fishermen deserted, he told Hopwood, the act was considered a criminal offence punishable by thirty to sixty days in jail, whereas in the United Kingdom an engagement was looked upon as merely a civil contract.

Finally, there was the broader matter of the truck system, a system of exchange open to widespread abuse. At the beginning of each fishing season a merchant would advance supplies to a fisherman and at the end deduct his share of the catch from the amount owed. While there was nothing unusual about the system itself, especially in the agricultural world, in Newfoundland it always produced a loss for the fisherman and a continual state of indebtedness. On a larger scale, the colonial government participated in the financial risk inherent in such a system, assuming a portion of the cost of production by making miscellaneous grants to the fishing industry and giving able-bodied relief to fishermen during the off-season. Thus the government contributed substantially to the value of the product, but in years of low fish prices it could not avoid heavy deficits. If a fisherman withstood all these conditions, he might be eligible for as much as $100 a year, but through the truck system he would receive payment in clothes and provisions instead of cash.

So far, these reports did not disturb Hopwood. He was confident the conditions could be changed through regulation. His demeanour changed, however, when he heard about the deplorable conditions existing on the Labrador coast. In Labrador, Harvey told him, about twenty-five thousand men, women, and children sailed every year in July, mostly from Conception Bay, and lived in temporary huts on the shore. These annual migrants, as distinct from the permanent Labrador settlers ('livyers'), survived there until October with no administration, no means of preserving law and order, no relief, and no medical care. They too were paid in provisions. For two or three years, he added, a coastal steamer had been sent up with the mail, carrying on board *one* person, sometimes a student, with medical knowledge. 'He is, however, besieged by the wretched people & on one or two occasions when one of H.M. ships has visited the scene the people have begged the crews for the ordinary necessaries of life,' Hopwood added.[27]

The governor's secretary, for his part, told Hopwood that an acute shortage of clothing existed and that consequently women and children working ashore were being left 'practically naked.'

Harvey did not exaggerate these conditions. They had been observed before by other visitors to Labrador, such as Commander William Chimmo, RN, who had been sent to the northeast coast aboard HMS *Gannet* in 1867 to seek out new fishing grounds and devise sailing directions. Chimmo was shocked by what he saw of the way people survived. 'Their wretchedness for five or six months in the year quite baffles description,' he reported, 'apart from the cruel and dangerous manner in which they are brought to and from the Coast, as I have attempted before to describe! surely something should be done to lessen their hardships.'[28] At the time, Chimmo had made recommendations for improving the most fundamental conditions: a safe form of transportation to and from the fishing grounds, clean housing free of rent, and a means of chartering a vessel so that fishermen could acquire their own provisions instead of purchasing them from their employers, the fish merchants. Lastly, he recommended that the fishing agents allow the fishermen the chance to pay for the goods received instead of carrying credit year by year and remaining perpetually in debt. But none of these recommendations had been adopted.

As Hopwood admitted in his report, these conditions had taken him completely by surprise. From the information disclosed by Harvey and others, he had found the state of affairs 'scandalous' and refrained from describing the circumstances in detail for fear of being thought guilty of 'exaggeration.'[29] While still in St John's he had suggested the Mission might send out the *Queen Victoria*, one of its three hospital ships, for a short period the following summer to conduct medical work and distribute clothing along the Labrador coast, and the idea had met with great enthusiasm from both government members and the merchant community. But in his London report, he chose his words carefully: he suggested sending out the *Queen Victoria* not as an 'institution' but as an 'experiment,' contingent upon the report of the doctor on board before the Mission committed itself to more permanent work. He also warned against the danger of pauperizing the population by giving them handouts. Even though he knew people lacked money, he insisted the Mission should attempt to foster a sense of independence.

Hopwood might have expected his report to be received with universal applause in London. Instead, it provoked an exchange of anonymous letters to the *Canadian Gazette*, a London trade paper, raising a difference of opinion that would cling to the Mission's actions for years to come. One comfortably placed correspondent offered an exaggerated view of Newfoundland's pastoral prosperity and insisted that the government already provided 'all the medical assistance they can.' Another took issue with that opinion. 'Many a snug villa in Devonshire or on the Clyde is the product of the "truck system" in Newfoundland,' she wrote, 'the younger members of the Old Country firms going out to make their "pile," and no more than the necessary capital left in the business.'[30] Despite this exchange, the report moved the council at its December meeting and caught the imagination of Grenfell, who hoped the council would let him as superintendent take charge of the venture. By February he was looking for a qualified skipper acquainted with the Labrador coast. The council had decided that the *Albert*, not the *Queen Victoria*, should undertake the voyage and that Grenfell should be embarked as doctor. 'The Doctor is not only an expert medical man,' Hopwood wrote in a letter to the *Canadian Gazette*, 'he is a scientist, and on his return we shall receive both a practical account of work done for the benefit of the fishermen, with recommendations for future guidance, but also much useful information as to the fish life, temperature of water, sea bottoms, &c., which Commodore Sir Baldwin Walker told me would be of great use to the public as well as the fishermen.'[31] Just as it had examined species and gauged temperatures in British waters, the Mission hoped it could add to the understanding of fishing conditions.

Hopwood's remarks also stirred up the popular press, which circulated the 'lamentable' and 'deplorable' details of starvation and want, particularly the effects on women and children. Perhaps the most severe commentary appeared in a *Daily Chronicle* editorial, casting doubt on the authenticity of his claims. The editorial argued, 'Hunger and want cause, at certain times, not a migration, but an exodus of Newfoundland fishing families to Labrador, where they live in a state of squalid promiscuity – if Mr. Hopwood is to be believed – which it is sickening to hear about. Women and children share the awful life in this land which the Puritans, if they saw what was going on there just now, would describe as "the abomination of desolation." Yet all this goes on because people who make money by it can control the Government of Newfoundland by help of its manhood suffrage and freedom from Imperial restraint.'[32] From the relative anonymity of his place at the Board of Trade, Hopwood now found himself the centre of controversy. The wide circulation of his findings, including a separate edition issued by the Mission in pamphlet form, raised one other difficulty that would impede the work later: the acute embarrassment of Newfoundlanders, particularly those living in London.

Some sense of that embarrassment is reflected in a letter to the *Canadian Gazette* from 'Newfoundlander,' suggesting political bias and exaggeration. Hopwood protested. The hospital ship could never change the economic plight of the colony, he argued. The long-range solution rested with the Newfoundland government. But he had put the case strongly, painting the mercantile class uniformly as disinterested predators, and Moses Harvey found it necessary to write himself to soften the language in case anyone thought the fishermen were living in a state of serfdom. The relationship between employer and employee was much the same as in any other country, Harvey insisted. Otherwise, he supported Hopwood's findings in case anyone doubted their authenticity. 'I am in a position to state that he sought information on these matters in a most careful and impartial manner, among people of all ranks and denominations, and of all shades of opinion, and that he spared no pains to arrive at an exact knowledge of the facts,' he wrote.[33] However, he carefully avoided blaming individuals for the malignant truck system, especially since the merchants took a risk in carrying fishermen over hard times, and suggested that it ought to be abolished gradually, not through legislation.

The *Albert*, a hospital vessel of 155 gross tons, had been designed for capacity rather than manoeuvrability. Just over a hundred feet long, she had been strengthened during construction to provide for her unusual twenty-five-foot beam and her twelve-foot holds. While she was limited to working in larger harbours, she could carry considerable cargo. For this voyage she required extensive modification, and while the press played up the deplorable state of Newfoundland fishermen, Grenfell supervised her refit at the yard of Henry Fellows and Son in Great Yarmouth, neglecting his duties at the Yarmouth office. After Alexander Gordon received a complaint from a local solicitor, the council discovered that he also practised medicine privately, and Treves, as a member of the council, wrote him unofficially in February to advise him of his error. 'If it grows sufficiently large to become remunerative it will take you away from the Mission work,' he argued. By April the finance committee had also agreed to write him on the subject.[34]

Fellows modified the *Albert* for ice conditions just as he had refitted the Moravian Mission vessel *Harmony* for work in northern Labrador. First, he covered the vessel from the stem to the rigging with 'ice chocks.' Then, three feet of 3 1/2-inch oak was laid over the planking down to the waterline and seven feet of elm of the same thickness below, all of which was tapered off neatly and painted like the rest of the ship. Two large beams forward provided further reinforcement. As a precaution, a yard of forty feet was rigged in front of the mainmast to accommodate a square sail in case the vessel had to go astern suddenly or stop dead. In all, the refit cost the Mission £1,400, which increased to nearly £2,000 by the time the trip ended.[35]

In addition to these structural modifications, the *Albert* took on navigation and safety equipment she would not ordinarily require in the North

Sea. An outfit of charts and sailing directions came aboard that revealed the inadequacy of marine surveys, for some charts still featured information dating from Captain Cook's brief visit in 1765. Two boats appeared, a regulation lifeboat and a naval whaler to be used as a gig. There were added a sheet anchor, fittings for launching flares, and arrangements for not-under-command signals: three red globe lanterns to be hung vertically at night and three large collapsible balls by day. The letters MPNV were assigned as an international call sign, to be displayed by flags from the International Code of Signals. The *Albert* was also victualled for five months and supplied with suitable 'literature,' including religious tracts, bibles, and testaments that poured in from enthusiastic donors. As bale after bale of books and used clothing piled up, the living space for the nine crew members shrank. Later, as these were distributed on the Labrador coast, the vessel rose eight inches.

The *Albert*'s crew was recruited especially for the voyage. Although Grenfell could claim to be a master mariner, his qualification applied exclusively to yachts. To find a certificated, foreign-going master mariner to serve as captain the council had to look outside the membership, and their choice fell upon Joseph F. Trezise of Penzance, a man with twenty-five years' experience, mostly in steamers. Accustomed to the relaxed cruising style of the North Sea, Grenfell regarded him as a martinet who expected everything to be 'just so.' Besides, by his own admission, Trezise was 'always off colour' in sailing vessels.[36] As mate they engaged a former Mission skipper, Joseph White, Jr, now caretaker of the Gorleston Fisher Institute, and as boatswain Robert Hewer, once skipper of the Mission ship *Ashton*. One member of the crew did double duty as carpenter, another as sailmaker.

The ship stood ready for the first leg of the voyage on 15 June, having been detained since the 11th by an anchor that failed to meet the Board of Trade specifications. But now the lines were let go, the tug *Reaper* took the strain, and the *Albert* crept out of her Yarmouth berth into the stream, to the accompaniment of a flurry of hats and handkerchiefs from the spectators on the quay.[37] Three Mission vessels alongside dipped their colours, and a salute of nine guns was fired by the Royal Navy. Grenfell thought the send-off was 'right royal' and stood on deck taking photographs. Pausing only to have the compasses adjusted, the vessel remained under tow as far as Corton, where the tug took off the visitors, then headed into a North Sea gale alone.

Grenfell could not stay still. As the crew settled into their seagoing routine, he immediately found himself in a conflict fundamental to leadership at sea. Though nominally in control of the vessel, he did not command it. Trezise commanded it and took responsibility for its safety but did not control it. Grenfell chafed under the arrangement. As the *Albert* thrashed down the Channel against a headwind, he started a bible class, and everyone attended but the man on duty at the helm. He also started a pictorial log and developed his own pictures in the dispensary. But the conflict with Trezise, who was not a Mission worker, continued to irritate him. At first he found the captain, with whom he shared a cabin, a 'good fellow' but 'a trifle slow.'[38] As the voyage progressed, however, he grew more intolerant and thought Trezise overly cautious. He zealously wrote his mother, 'With all respect to him he is the most awful duffer I ever met at sea things, and constantly afraid of something happening to him. I am determined to capsize him out of the dingey [*sic*] one day. He can swim, but is afraid of his life to do anything but smoke. Well I hope I haven't been guilty of speaking evil. Perhaps it's his "Eddication" as Mr Gladstone would say, which is to be blamed. Well he is having a new one now, for the men persuade him that life isn't worth a moment's purchase & a little trouble would send him to bed in a life belt.'[39] Trezise, a nervous sailor, rarely left the upper deck. Unknown to Grenfell, some years before he had been wrecked in a barque on the Grand Banks. After three days and three nights adrift, only he and two others survived. The memory still haunted him.[40]

After picking up the gig at Lulworth, the *Albert* punched into head winds and thick fog for several days. Beating around Land's End, Trezise discovered he was making thirty inches of water a day in his well, and on the 27th he decided to put the vessel on the mud in Crookhaven to inspect the hull in case a trunnion had been left out during the refit.[41] After a careful survey, no obvious leak could be found. Having suddenly manifested itself, it mysteriously disappeared, and the *Albert* departed again on 4 July. Trevise shaped a course along the well-travelled great circle route to Newfoundland, making to the north so as to cross the meridian of 18°W in latitude 50°N, then to the south to strike the Grand Banks at 45° to 46°N. The head winds blew for the next fortnight, but the *Albert* continued to ride comfortably and by the 16th had covered half the distance. Then the wind came round. For the first time, the square sail could be set, and the vessel could lie along its course. Grenfell kept himself busy harpooning porpoises, shooting petrels, and second-guessing the captain.

He now felt the benefit of his yachtsman's certificate. 'The Master Mariner work has been most useful and interesting,' he reported to his mother. 'I feel now as if I could easily navigate the ship myself, and anyhow my observations are often a check on arithmetical errors by the Skipper and also occy are the only ones taken, when perhaps he has been up 48 hours on end.' He read a book she had given him and, following his habit, entered the important ideas in his bible. He was also reading *The Revelation of the Risen Lord*, a collection of sermons by Brooke Foss

Westcott, the reforming bishop of Durham, given him by a young woman named Harriet Walker. He helped out painting ship to smarten up the *Albert* for their arrival. 'The microscope and camera, with observations on temperature etc. have helped to fill my time up,' he revealed, '& I seldom seem to have a moment.'[42]

On the 21st, still two days out, a barque bound for England brought jarring news. St John's, a city of mostly wooden construction and a population of twenty-five thousand, had caught fire on 8 July and was almost totally destroyed. These events threatened Grenfell's careful plans. As the low line of coast came up on the horizon, the smoke reached his nostrils. With the glasses he could pick out forest fires blazing on the surrounding hills, making it easy to find the narrow entrance to the harbour. Keeping the revolving white light of Cape Spear lighthouse to port, Trezise would ordinarily have entered the harbour by lining up two red lights exhibited on the foreshore, but both had been destroyed. Instead, he passed a tow rope to the steam tug *Favorite* and went to an anchorage in the harbour, shifting later to a berth at a merchant's wharf.

As the ship came alongside, Grenfell could feel the oppressive heat. Luckily, the wooden wharves still stood, but an inferno encompassed the bowl of hills surrounding the harbour. The city itself, already lying in ruins, reminded him of Pompeii after extensive excavations. He wrote, 'The sides of the hills were densely black with charred remains, and on every hand rose hundreds of variegated pillars, in many places packed closely together like remains of Greek classic temples. These were the chimneys of the houses – all the rest had gone – but even in wooden houses square brick chimneys were built, and so on closer inspection one could see that these pillars had without exception some two or three fireplaces let into them one above the other: these dispelled effectually the illusion.'[43] Moses Harvey came aboard first and took them to his house. Along the way, they observed fugitives crammed into every structure still standing. Temporary wooden huts, fourteen by twelve feet, were going up in the public park, side by side with bell tents supplied from HMS *Blake*. Recognizing the acute shortage of clothing, Grenfell landed a portion of his Labrador stock, and with every doctor in the city burnt out, he set up a temporary clinic on board.

He now decided to stay a few days to lend further assistance and acquaint leading citizens such as Sir William Whiteway with his intentions. At the same time, he took the extra precaution of engaging Captain Nicholas Fitzgerald of Harbour Grace, a former Labrador planter (in Newfoundland parlance the owner of a fishing boat & fishing premises), to pilot him through the numerous uncharted rocks, islands, currents, runs, and tickles of the Labrador coast. He took a train to visit the cod hatchery in Trinity

Bay at the invitation of Adolf Nielsen, superintendent of fisheries, and with an eye to his scientific objectives he then invited Nielsen to join him in the *Albert* as soon as the hatchery had closed up for the season, so that together they could observe currents and estimate fish stocks. Never one to worry about enjoying himself when conditions worsened, he went trouting with a local merchant whom he found to be an Eton man and a 'splendid fellow.' After a delay brought on by fog and head winds, the *Albert* was towed out again on 2 August. Throughout the visit, no fees or duties were paid, and the government agreed to pay Captain Fitzgerald a fee of $200. Grenfell thought he could feel already the sympathy and encouragement of the St John's people.

— 4 —

The Voyages of the *Albert*
1892 – 1893

The fogs that occur in calms, especially after strong winds, are frequently so dense as to conceal a vessel within hailing distance.

The Newfoundland and Labrador Pilot, 1897

Along the Newfoundland coast, in the days before radar penetrated the void, the fog-horn was the seaman's precious ally. Newfoundland ships liked to carry the conch (pronounced *conk*), a large seashell with the narrow end removed. Standing somewhere in the bows, a man would cradle it with the sensitivity of a chamber player. By inserting one hand into its mouth, the thumb on the outside, he would apply his lips and produce a shrill, piercing laugh that warned invisible ships and cracked off unseen headlands. He could produce a more mellifluous sound with a different contrivance consisting of a bellows operated by a crank or lever. Whichever he employed, under foggy conditions the shrieking and baying punctuated the watch for days on end, and the crew unconsciously screened it out, just as they learned to ignore the constant play of the waves. After the *Albert* left St John's, the fog-horn rarely sat silent. Grenfell used the time to take readings from his reversing thermometers, tracing a freezing current three hundred fathoms below. On the third day out the weather cleared to reveal Cape Bauld, jutting out from the northernmost tip of the island. Captain Fitzgerald, left to his own devices in these latitudes without the benefit of chart, lighthouse, or channel buoy, took note of the procession of ice on all sides and prudently recommended that Trezise manoevre in amongst the islands. He also insisted on anchoring at night, and the first evening the *Albert* lay in Domino Run amid crowding icebergs, spouting whales, and flocking petrels.

During his first days working among the fishermen, Grenfell's illusions about Labrador were soon dispelled. Such was his ignorance, he admitted afterwards, that he thought he would be dealing with sealers working on ice floes.[1] But he soon discovered a fundamental difference between the fishing population here and the one in the North Sea. Instead of one constituency, there were several. First, there was the native population, consisting of the hunter Innu of the inland and the coastal Inuit, the latter served since 1752 by the United Brethren, a German sect popularly known as the Moravians.[2] On the northern part of the Labrador coast the Moravian missionaries had traded with the Inuit for fish and furs and had at the same time introduced medical care, agriculture, music, and other European amenities while encouraging them to maintain their native culture. Then there were the permanent settlers, the 'livyers,' descendants of British servants, sailors, and artisans who had come out with the fur trading companies and intermarried with the native population. Finally, there were the migratory fishermen, a cheap, abundant source of ready labour divided into two groups. The 'floaters,' who came north as permanent crews of fishing schooners, operated the vessels throughout the season; the 'stationers,' who arrived aboard schooners and coastal vessels together with their families, went ashore to their allotted harbours, where they put up temporary huts and erected stages for landing and drying the fish before it was taken to foreign markets. In the autumn, when the season drew to a close, these latter would crowd aboard the schooners again and return to Newfoundland. The schooners would proceed to St John's for winter supplies, then lie up in their home ports until the following spring.

As he acquainted himself with Newfoundland fishing techniques, Grenfell found a sharp contrast between these and the British practice of loading up for a quick sale at Billingsgate market. Unlike the North Sea trawlermen, the Newfoundlanders deployed a cod trap, a simple but expensive device consisting of a long net or 'leader' running out from the shore to direct the schools of cod into a large, square net, closed at the end, floated by corks and moored at the corners by four large buoys. The trap employed no bait. Instead, the cod were permitted to swim as they liked, for as soon as they encountered the leader, they would follow each other in. Three times a day a crew in a small working boat would haul the net up.

As they brought the catch alongside, the lead hand would examine the contents from the surface with a fish-glass in order to determine whether the haul was worthwhile. If it was, a complex process began. As Grenfell explained it, 'The boat then is fastened to the middle rope near the door, and the free edges of the line pulled up and passed over the boat, and out again; then the boat is pulled nearer the opposite wall to the door, and so on, gradually shaking all the fish down into the far end, till they are so confined they can be baled out with a large hand net, or driven into a large cod-bag.'[3] The fish, counted by the quintal, or hundredweight, were then taken on board. During a good season it was not unusual to take over forty quintals a day this way. Thus, to earn his share, a fisherman was required to possess not only strength but knowledge, timing, and endurance for the season. The slightest injury, soreness, or minor ailment might cost him his livelihood and that of his family. In October, when the trapping season finished, hand-lining began. Now the 'planter,' or owner, issued his men with 'bultows,' several thousand fathoms of line baited with herring, squid, or caplin, set out from the boats and secured to the bottom. He also employed a method called jigging by which a fisherman would let down a pair of large hooks secured back-to-back with a piece of lead shaped like a herring. Having sent it to the bottom, he would then jerk it up and down so that it caught the cod somewhere about the body when it approached.

Grenfell observed not only the species and the fishing techniques but the processing. He saw the fish landed on stages built of pine poles and then piked up to be headed, gutted, and washed, each part of the operation conducted by a specialist of some skill. He wrote, 'A woman or boy generally "heads" and "throats" the fish – that is, cuts off the head and slices the throat open. The splitter, who is a skilled hand, splits the fish and takes out the backbone with a knife like a razor, and at an amazing pace, yet I have only seen one cut himself in this operation. The fish is then washed, stacked in salt, and on suitable days dried.'[4] When the fish were running, the whole operation might keep the flares burning far into the night, and after two or three days the catch was ready for loading aboard British or European cargo vessels, to be sold in the traditional markets in the Mediterranean, the West Indies, or South America. At the end of the season the merchants met to agree on a price. In 1892 it was $2.80 (twelve shillings) a quintal.[5]

Only the most rudimentary medical service was provided for these people by the colonial government. According to Dr R.J. Freebairn, the medical officer on the coast in 1894, he himself left St John's in July aboard an old sealing vessel with no hospital facilities or nurse on board and did not return until November.[6] Since he could not provide any continuing care, the sick had to be transferred to the coastal boat at Red Bay or Battle Harbour. Each day the vessel moved from one harbour to the next, and under these conditions a single medical officer soon exhausted himself, managing only four or five hours of sleep a night.

The *Albert*, flying the distinctive blue banner of the Mission to Deep Sea Fishermen, made a spectacular arrival in these remote harbours, and within an hour a collection of small boats would tie up around her. Before the end of August the vessel had visited five ports, and Grenfell had gone in the whaler with his portable medicine chest and box of books to seven more outharbours. By then, he had treated over three hundred patients and a wide range of illnesses. Apart from the usual run of accident cases brought on by a vigorous outdoor life, he saw untreated cases of lung disease, the consequences of an influenza epidemic, pneumonia, and pleurisy. Evidence of other epidemics, including diphtheria, was also common. He observed the effects of poor diet and hurried eating, manifested in multiple cases of prolonged constipation, indigestion, haemorrhoids, xerophthalmia, peritonitis, scurvy, pellagra, beri-beri, edema, and rickets.[7] And there were other unpreventable ailments of fisherman such as water boils, night-blindness, strained back, sore muscles, broken fingers, rotten teeth, inflamed nerves, mouth ulcers, rheumatism, conjunctivitis, urine retention, strangulated hernia, and arthritis. Emergency dentistry also took up considerable time and required treatments not exactly prescribed by the textbook.

Then there was the non-medical Mission work. Grenfell handed out clothing and religious tracts and held prayer meetings in the North Sea tradition, both on board and in sheds and wharf houses ashore. The Reverend John Sidey, a resident Methodist missionary, could hardly contain his excitement as he reported the unexpected arrival of the *Albert* in Red Bay. Apart from the medical facilities that suddenly appeared, he was impressed by the relative comfort on board. He wrote:

> The little saloon aft was a picture, as cosy as could be wished, a small library at one end gave it an air of refinement also. Through a door leading out of the saloon was the Doctor's private apartment. This, too, was fitted up with every requisite. Another door led out into the ambulance room; here were swinging beds, tables, &c., for the performance of operations, while all around were hospital beds and other appurtenances absolutely necessary to a vessel whose office was a refuge for the injured or sick seamen. Folding doors were now thrown open, revealing quite a large-sized room, used as a mess-room for the crew in ordinary, and another set of folding doors at the other end opened into a large spare space, which the steward seemed to appropriate to himself; when thrown in one this hold would accommodate over 100 people.

Before long, Sidey observed for himself how this space was used and how Grenfell performed at prayer meetings:

> In one corner stood a very fine American organ, at which the writer was seated by invitation. Just behind him knelt the Doctor, a very unclerical looking figure in a tight-fitting tweed hunting suit, but whose countenance spoke of

the life within which makes all outward appearance a thing of nought. By his side, the Rev. George Stoney, the mate and ship's carpenter, while the crew gathered around the organ. We were soon making the vessel ring with the strains of a well-known Sankey's hymn. What voices those seamen had! I had not revelled in such song for a long time, it was grand. Then came the prayer by the minister, another song, then the address by the Doctor, simple and impressive, but wonderfully practical, the tone, animation of the speaker spoke the power within – a hidden fire; one could hear a pin drop, it was more of a Bible reading, several references to Scripture, but the main points were kept well in hand, and none could go away without carrying something of that word with them. A solemn feeling pervaded the whole ship.[8]

Grenfell was now working his personal magnetism on these fishermen and revelling in the opportunity to do so much good. Even more, he took pleasure in reporting that a number of men and women had publicly 'stood up' for Christ and that for this reason alone they would be grateful for the *Albert*'s visit to the coast.

After beating up a narrow run, so hazardous that the lookouts on the yardarms spelled each other off continually, the *Albert* reached Hopedale, the most southerly station of the Moravian Mission. Here Grenfell stayed with the fishing fleet for ten days, attending to over two hundred vessels, then turned south again. After only a few weeks in Labrador, he had already begun to feel a rising excitement brought on by what he perceived as the great missionary opportunity presented to him. He could hardly contain his eagerness as he wrote to London, 'If ever the people of Newfoundland and Labrador get an opportunity of expressing to our friends at home the emotions that the very expectancy of the *Albert*'s arrival, to say nothing of the actuality, has undoubtedly created in their hearts, there can be no possible doubt that this voyage to the Labrador would become an annual feature – nay, a regular branch of the work of the Mission to Deep Sea Fishermen.' A month later, he reported he had treated 693 patients, including one operation under chloroform for a bone disease of the leg, and he speculated that he could have doubled the number with the use of a steamer or small steam launch such as the ones loaned him by the local planters. He now appealed sentimentally through *Toilers of the Deep* to his own supporters in Britain, citing cases of the most abject poverty and hunger. He asked, 'How could any human being, with a heart of flesh, after seeing such sights, enjoy a Christmas dinner in old England, as we hope to, with our minds haunted with these hungry, pale faces, of our own blood and race? Think of them feeding only on mussels they could pick up, and perhaps the dust of hard bread or biscuit, if even that was procurable, if at the same time we knew in our hearts that by any self-sacrifice we could have seized the opportunity so providentially afforded of giving this cup of cold water in the name of a Master who did so much for us.'[9] Already he looked to the future, preparing for the extended missionary venture he hoped would come. But, with the frost approaching, he needed to make his way back to St John's, and he arrived in the Narrows on 21 October. By that time he had treated over nine hundred patients.

In the city of St John's in the late nineteenth century, despite the oppressive provincialism and the periods of unmerciful weather, it was possible at a certain economic level to enjoy a pleasant social existence. As the wife of a Harvey and Company employee wrote, there existed a 'lively, interesting, and warm-hearted community life, a social atmosphere of friendly kindliness, pleasant to live with and especially heartening to the stranger within its gates.'[10] For the coterie at Government House, the merchant community, and the small body of professionals and clerics, life in St John's could indeed be lived comfortably as long as fish prices remained high and connections were maintained with the mother country. But as an outsider, Grenfell detected behind the façade of decent hospitality a desire not to upset the social and political status quo. For the first few days of his return he could barely contain his condescension as he went about the business of organizing a public meeting.

In general, he found St John's disappointingly small and its colonial government, with its devotion to parliamentary convention, pretentious. The government of Newfoundland had by this time fallen under the virtual control of a few St John's merchants: powerful, wealthy men of English and Protestant background on whose capital the fishery depended.[11] They, together with those they supported, composed the dominant social class and formed the core of the Conservative party, leaving the Liberal party as the party of reform and social agitation. What the colony lacked was a substantial middle class, and a huge gulf of wealth and power separated what another British observer called the 'fishocracy' from the ordinary fisherman, a virtual peasantry to whom the commercial wharves of Water Street symbolized exploitation. 'There is no colony belonging to the British Empire where influence and name tend so much to form caste in society, and where it is more regarded than in St. John's,' Philip Tocque had written twenty years before. 'This distinction of caste has a very pernicious influence. It prevents the amalgamation of fellow citizens, and destroys mutual confidence.'[12] The class division was further reinforced by a religious sectarianism sustained by the education system. Instead of state schools, the sectarian schools were all separately financed by government grants. Thus the public institutions emphasized the religious and ethnic differences and sustained them.

Such political conditions continued virtually unchanged until the 1930s, when the Amulree Commission inquiring into Newfoundland's political and financial affairs revealed a political tradition still tainted with corruption and paternalism. Elected members were still regarded as conduits for public money. Respectable citizens still refused to enter political life for fear of personal abuse and the taint of corrupt dealings – even though they were permitted to carry on their businesses. The civil service also bore the stigma of corruption. The commissioners observed, 'The educated class, from which the administrative grade of the Civil Service is recruited, is very small: the members of it are all known, if not related, to each other: everyone knows everyone else's business and it is a simple matter to ascertain which way any particular Civil Servant voted or, if he did not vote, what are the political leanings of his family and his relations.'[13]

Grenfell had observed these same manifestations forty years before: 'It is most odd to an Englishman to go and look for a Prime Minister behind a grocer's counter, or a colonial secretary selling boots,' he wrote. 'But such is the case almost & one learns to be surprised at nothing.' He also grew sensitive to the conflicts of interest in St John's society. Convinced that it was the merchants who must be fought, he wrote his mother, 'Everything is political here. People know where you buy everything, what you say & what you do & if you don't allow your constituents to break the law or get an unfair share of relief money or get them out of poaching affrays, why you haven't a chance of being prime minister again. This is literally true.'[14] Such an attitude presented a dilemma, for he needed to work hand-in-hand with such people if he wanted to improve conditions on the coast. A few days later, when Governor Terence O'Brien convened a public meeting of those same individuals at Government House, he expressed his pleasure, taking full advantage of what one close observer called his 'personal magnetism.'[15] Important Labrador merchants praised the medical work enthusiastically, and Grenfell responded with a detailed account of the deficiencies encountered. By now, some grander gesture was plainly required if he wanted to develop what the Mission had inaugurated in Labrador, without draining its supporters in Britain.

Adolf Nielsen had already raised the central issue in a letter to the governor the day before: the need for better medical care as a first step in sustaining productivity in the fishing industry. 'Besides all this loss, suffering, and miseries a sick fisherman has to bear himself, he often also causes a great loss to the planter or merchant who supply him, when deprived from prosecuting the fishery, perhaps in the best part of the season, especially in such cases which nature takes a long time to heal, but which by professional treatment and attention very likely would have been cured in a short time,' he said.[16] A medical service would not merely cure sick fishermen, he argued; it would benefit the merchants as well by ensuring a continuance of labour. Such an appeal to the profit motive was already recognized in other parts of the empire, where medical intervention clearly served the colonial interest as long as it did not threaten profitability and individual enterprise.[17] When two ship's captains urged the building of a hospital on the Labrador coast, Moses Monroe, a colleague of Whiteway who had been in the business of supplying fishermen on the Labrador coast, suggested forming a committee to co-operate with the Mission and encourage it to return the following summer: 'Every one of our commercial houses would gladly contribute towards the carrying out of so laudable an object, if the suffering of the sick fishermen would be in any way alleviated,' he said.[18] Sir William Whiteway seconded the motion, which was carried unanimously, and a merchants' committee had suddenly come into being. Grenfell now possessed the public endorsement he required. But he had also placed himself in the hands of the very commercial interests who had created the social problem in the first place. Sooner or later, the conflict would return to plague him.

With the *Albert* in the St John's dock for an overhaul, Grenfell spent the next few days ashore conferring with the governor. In return for the Mission services, he learned, the Newfoundland government was prepared to erect and furnish two small hospitals and make a direct grant for their upkeep. The commercial interests also pledged to hand over a house at Battle Harbour and one at Smoky Run, at the mouth of Hamilton Inlet. They also undertook to contribute fifty to one hundred dollars apiece and to assist with the local transport of patients by launch. In return, they expected the Mission to provide a steamer, a launch, a nurse for each of the hospitals, and the equipment. In a letter to Treves just prior to his departure, Grenfell seemed encouraged about the possibility of public support, even if the government decision had still not been officially made.[19]

More important, in the course of these negotiations he was learning about the extent of religious influence in the colony. At the public meeting he had carefully emphasized the Mission's medical objectives but not its religious ones. As he explained his aversion to church influence to his mother, 'If I had said a word of religious work, the whole pack would have been at one another's throats in a twinkling. The truth is that here exists a bitter struggle between the Church [of England] and Methodism. The Church is dead, appears to have no life, no soul & merely to be seeking the bread that perishes. Methodism is alive, earnest, spiritual – seeking the conversion of the souls of the people and putting up with any sacrifice for it. The result is that it is making great inroads both in Church & I am glad to say Catholicism.'[20] Furthermore, he had lost his respect for the Church of England bishop, Llewellyn Jones, who after the fire had destroyed the city had set about launching an appeal to rebuild his stone cathedral while the faithful went unclothed, unhoused, and unfed. 'The Bishop dare not say anything against us,' he wrote, 'but is not with us, and told a great friend of mine here, that our preaching the gospel and people being converted [is] directly pulling down the work of the church. However, his mouth is gagged, for we are popular here.'

Grenfell reserved his severest scorn for the questionable political practices of the colony, which he characterized as '*very*' corrupt. Lacking a professional middle class or a landed interest in the Westminster tradition, the legislature depended for its membership upon merchants, lawyers, and minor officials – men who dispensed patronage and often profited from their advantage at the same time. 'Even K.C.M.G.'s out here are by no means above peculation,' he told his mother, 'and small shopkeepers and almost bootblacks fill the house of assembly.' Though rooted in the facts, these opinions sound a trifle naive and quickly formed. Quite obviously, he could not have mastered the intricacies of Newfoundland politics in such a short time by himself. These details he must have learned from Governor O'Brien, a former army officer and Indian governor unused to the latitude accorded a self-governing colony. 'He told me he would suggest as the only cure, that Nfd should become a crown colony with a peppy old Anglo-Indian as Governor, who would liberally [*sic*] sit on the slightest deviation from the straight path,' he wrote.[21] By now he had formed an understanding of where Newfoundland was headed, and as he sailed for England he knew what the Mission ought to do next.

In January the council received the Government House resolution and decided to support the worthy but expensive venture overseas, provided they could find sufficient public support there. A month later the St John's committee reported that it had accepted a house in Battle Harbour donated by the merchant Walter Baine Grieve and intended to erect another. It had also opened a subscription list to raise £250.[22] Encouraged by these developments, Grenfell, who had returned to his duties as superintendent, got busy advertising the work ahead. In the February issue of *Toilers of the Deep* he published a lively account of the Newfoundland fishery, illustrated with his own photographs of rugged coasts, costumed natives, and settlers' hovels. These he made into slides and exhibited at meetings around the country, hoping to raise enough money for a steam launch, for the finance committee of the Mission did not feel disposed to provide it. Throughout the winter he had petitioned them for extra money for the *Albert*, for lantern slides and other equipment, but had been put off. Now he found he would have to raise it himself.

The council, once more, felt dissatisfied with his neglect of his duties as superintendent. Recognizing the plans already in motion, they changed his terms of reference again so as to bring him under tighter control.[23] The superintendent's office was moved to London, where he was directed to take sole responsibility for the work at sea, leaving the Yarmouth establishment in charge of a ship's husband. He was directed to report on the efficiency of the fleet but forbidden to make appointments without the authority of the council or interfere with the operation of the vessels. The council also made him answerable for equipping the vessels, especially with drugs and medical instruments, but would not allow him to pledge the credit of the council without specific instructions. Instead, he was required to keep a diary for the finance committee, to be handed in each week. Under these terms, he was offered £300 a year (with another £80 for his rooms) and given six weeks' holiday.

If the council found it difficult to restrain Grenfell in his sudden zeal to alter life in Labrador, the membership of the Mission roundly supported him. On 19 May a throng turned up on the quay in Gorleston for a farewell service at which he introduced the volunteer medical staff for the second voyage of the *Albert*: two physicians, Eliot Curwen and Alfred Bobardt, and two nurses, Sister Cecilia Williams and Sister Ada Carwardine of the London Hospital. With the experience of the first voyage, this time he planned a busier and a more complex undertaking. On the morning of 23 May a crowd mustered on Gorleston Pier to see the *Albert* away, and the Mission band stood on board, playing at intervals during the passage out the harbour while the customary salutes were exchanged. Grenfell himself returned to London. At the annual general meeting of the Mission two days later, his description of the forthcoming summer's work was loudly cheered.[24]

After joining the *Albert* at Exeter, he proceeded to Exmouth, Cleveland, and Bristol, where he spoke at large public meetings. To his great surprise, at these last ports of call, two donors came forward with enough money to procure a steam launch, and as the ship made its way west, he quickly diverted to Liverpool to make the purchase. There he found the *Clwyd*, a six-year-old vessel that appeared serviceable but was not ideally suited to the task of bumping about the rocks and ice of the Labrador coast. Though capable of making nine knots and clearly more manoeuvrable than the *Albert*, she was apt to roll heavily in a beam sea, and her small cabin, which needed to be raised to accommodate patients, caused her to dive when steaming into the wind. But the *Clwyd*, forty-five feet long and eight feet at the beam, was strongly built of oak and copper-fastened.[25] In Liverpool he saw her sheathed in copper and overhauled for hospital work; then he left to rejoin the *Albert* while the *Clywd* was hoisted aboard a steamer of the Allan Line for shipment to St John's.

From Dr Curwen's journal we have a detailed picture of the *Albert*'s second voyage to St John's. Apart from the practical business of standing watches and maintaining the ship, the medical team kept up their reading, and sometimes the crew of thirteen would form itself into a choir under the direction of Bobardt and rehearse for the services to come. There were daily sports on deck when the weather permitted. The first day out of Queenstown, during a game of cricket with broom handle and pail for bat and wicket, the ball went overboard, and Trezise was obliged to heave to while Grenfell tore off his clothes and plunged in after it. Thereafter, the ball was tethered by a line, and deck cricket established itself as a regular feature of seagoing life. As he reported entertainingly for the benefit of the boys at Mostyn House School, 'A break from the "off" or "leg" was equally easy when the boat rolled. Fielding was delightfully simple, there being no running after the ball – for we counted a slog into the sea 3, and on deck 1. It gave us no end of fun and exercise.'[26] For the rest of his spare moments, he occupied himself with his clubs and quoits and, he informed his mother, managed to get in three hours of medical reading a day.[27]

His arrival in St John's, still busy with reconstruction, differed dramatically this time. The *Albert* saluted by firing a rocket at the entrance to the Narrows, and after it reached its berth, friends, former patients, and the committee of government and opposition members crowded on board. Governor O'Brien, who was taking a personal hand in the arrangements, took the time to school Curwen in the art of Newfoundland politics, just as he had done with Grenfell the year before. The Labrador fishermen, Curwen discovered, formed a large part of the electorate, and with an election expected in November the committee were going about their business with great enthusiasm, encumbering Grenfell and the crew with hospitality and waiving customs and shipping charges. Curwen also made himself familiar with the peculiarities of Newfoundland sectarianism. He concluded:

> Sectarianism seems to be the root of the miserable want of honesty and all the quarrels & bitterness here; Catholics, Anglicans & Wesleyans (including Congl. & Presby.) are about equal in number throughout the Island but in St. John's the R.C.s preponderate greatly; there is a truce between the parties, the terms being that what one has the others have too; consequently, there are 3 Boards of Education, 3 School Inspectors, 3 Everything where possible, and where it is not possible to have three men in one post – e.g. head clerkship of Post Office – when a R.C. resigns he must be succeeded by a Wesleyan & he again by an Anglican; the result is that promotion by merit is unknown, e.g. since last year the R.C. head clerkship of P.O. died & was succeeded by a Wesleyan grocer who knew nothing of the work, the other clerks of the P.O. not having a chance as they were R.C.s or A. Separate Gov. grants are made

to the three different sets of schools; a village is either without a school altogether or has to have three – three bad ones with teachers who scarcely know more than ABC instead of one good one. This is only one example of the system.[28]

The committee seemed to have made progress during the past winter. The Battle Harbour structure had already been donated and required no further work to function as a small hospital. The Indian Harbour hospital was under construction in St John's, to be conveyed in sections for assembly before their arrival. A day after the *Albert* arrived, the *Corean* followed through the Narrows, bearing the *Clywd*, the nurses, and the supplies. On 5 July, in an elaborate ceremony at the waterfront, Lady O'Brien renamed the launch the *Princess May* in honour of Princess May of Teck (later Queen Mary). The following day Curwen departed in the *Albert* with the two nurses, glad to be relieved of the constant attention. 'We have had a very good time in St. John's,' he wrote, 'but have been oppressed by the kindness, generosity & extreme hospitality of the people; we have had *no* time to ourselves and are wanting a little quiet.'[29]

—5—

The Voyage of the
Princess May
1893 – 1894

If you want to know what the worst human poverty is like you should try not London, but Labrador. In the meanest courts and alleys of the world's metropolis there is still a picturesqueness mingled with the squalor, the great chance, the broader outlook, the variety of vicissitude. But in Labrador, amongst Englishmen, it is only dull cold and stupid hunger – large families, much English pluck and pride, a little hope and resolve to make the best of it – and a great deal of gratitude for any attempt to improve their condition.

Beckles Willson, *The Tenth Island* (1897)

Grenfell now undertook to steam the launch to Labrador himself. That way, without Trezise looking over his shoulder, he could command it as he wished. The next day he took Bobardt, an engineer, the steward of the Battle Harbour hospital, and two hands and departed without checking the launch's seaworthiness. The *Princess May* had not yet received a mechanical check. The funnel had been lost on the *Corean*, and the shaft was not fit for sea.[1] But he was too eager to bother with such details. He encountered mechanical failures twice during the first five miles and considered turning back. But he held on, and with a remarkable feat of seamanship that few might possess the daring or folly to undertake, he bounced up the northeast coast in a dense fog, hugging the land.

The first night, he groped his way into Catalina, Trinity Bay, where he took on coal. The next day, with thick fog and an onshore wind, he considered staying put but instead crept along to Greenspond amid numerous icebergs. On the third day he suddenly realized that his compass, secured by iron screws, had placed him far off course, but he managed a further eighty miles and dropped anchor in Twillingate, Notre Dame Bay. Next, by poking in and out, he made an anchorage in Pacquet, then crossed White Bay and anchored in St Anthony. With a fresh northeaster blowing, it took him two attempts to cross the Strait of Belle Isle before he joined the *Albert* in Battle Harbour on 13 July. He had made the four hundred miles in a week under these conditions without injury or breakdown.

By the time he arrived, Curwen and Sister Williams, busy with the Battle Harbour hospital, had already made their own inquiries into the state of the local inhabitants and found what they determined to be an 'extraordinary' state of affairs.[2] Landing at Fox Harbour, a community of ten houses, they collected information about living conditions. Then, while Curwen drew the men out of the house, the nurse asked about the condition of the women's clothing. Six of these houses consisted of only one room in which the entire family lived. In one, an Inuit widow with three sons and three daughters all lived together, clothed in rags. Clothes were so scarce that on washing days they all turned in under a wool quilt they had received from the Mission the year before. Poorer than these was a widower of sixty-two with eight children, six of whom his neighbours had taken off his hands. He was blind in one eye and had started a cataract in the other. Though he could not read, he displayed on one wall the front page of the Sunday school anthology *Great Thoughts of Israel* with a portrait of the compiler, Edward Augustus Horton. When asked when he last had any money, he replied, 'God knows when I had any money; afore I was married I had a scattered shilling.' Another man lived with his two sons and two stepdaughters in a log hut banked with three or four feet of earth. A hole let in light through the roof. He and the boys slept on a shelf, and the girls slept on two other shelves, one above the other. Others had barely enough food to keep alive and survived only through the kindness of neighbours or the local agent. As the summer's work progressed, scenes such as these became commonplace. Each day uncovered more extreme cases of want. Unprepared for the extent of the hopeless poverty they witnessed, the medical staff could not imagine where to begin.

An Englishman touring the coast of Labrador in the late nineteenth century would know that the most northerly tip of the Labrador peninsula lay in the same latitude as the north of Scotland and that Battle Harbour, to the south, lay almost due west of London. He would therefore realize that day and night would run to the same length in both places. He would also know that Labrador, despite these small resemblances, presented an inhospitable face to all but the most durable kinds of habitation. The Atlantic coast, where white settlers had visited regularly to hunt and fish from the middle of the eighteenth century, manifested most markedly the natural force that gave it its inhospitable character – ice. Long centuries of glaciation had fashioned the region into a huge sculpture of immense variety: gingerbread hills of the inland transformed themselves in winter into broad strokes of fluid white; primordial lakes pock-marked more than a quarter of its surface; rivers sliced their way through sharply outlined valleys to the sea. On the coastline itself, sheer cliffs and steep fjords presented an impenetrable barrier to migration.

During Wilfred Grenfell's introduction to the Labrador coast, the resident population dwelt in harbours formed by spectacular indentations.[3] Hamilton Inlet, the largest, extended inland for over 150 miles. Others commonly ran thirty to fifty miles deep, walled in by cliffs that could rise to four thousand feet and drop to one hundred fathoms. To reach these, it was necessary to negotiate a fringe of small, uncharted islands, the bane of the navigator who had not yet acquired the necessary local knowledge. And outside of them lay the inner banks, a shallower region extending out to about fifteen miles and enclosed by the frigid waters of the Labrador Current.[4] Sweeping down from the Arctic, the current in effect fed the fishes of the Labrador coast with its microscopic life forms, at the same time bringing thousands of icebergs and throwing one more hazard in the path of the northern navigator. Some icebergs could stretch to one-third of a mile, leaving only a proportion of their bulk visible from the surface, and could advance at a speed up to twenty miles a day until in the end they melted, fractured, or grounded off the coast of Newfoundland.

Inland, the climate ranged from cold temperate to arctic, discouraging all agriculture except for what was carried on under the most contrived conditions. For there were only two seasons. The transition from winter to summer occurred generally during the first two weeks of June, with the gradual disappearance of all but the most stubborn ice and snow. The snow started to fall and the ice reformed about the middle of September, and from early October it stayed, concluding a growing season of only three months at most. Temperatures as low as $-40°F$ or $-50°F$ had been recorded in Grenfell's time and others as high as 80°F. Nevertheless, at the end of the nineteenth century, one survey reported potatoes and other root vegetables grown in a latitude as far north as 54° and easily cultivated in the micro-climate at the head of Hamilton Inlet. During his voyage in the *Albert*, Dr Eliot Curwen found in the Hopedale gardens of the Moravian Mission a good supply of celery, cucumber, cauliflower, beet, lettuce, spinach, and parsley as well as beds of flowers in full bloom. In Nain, by building walls against the east wind and covering the crops at night, the Moravians had successfully grown garden vegetables despite summer frosts.[5] Such a cold climate made the raising of livestock impossible, however, for there was no grassy plain. Instead, a carpet of moss and lichens covered the ground.

Grenfell probed the coast for the rest of the unusually rough and windy summer and autumn of 1893 in the *Princess May* while the hospital at Battle Harbour was fitted up and painted. 'There can be not the slightest doubt as to the necessity of a doctor at Battle,' wrote Bobardt; 'the people here are unprovided for, their life is hard, and when ill, they must either work or die.'[6] While the work progressed, Grenfell proceeded south into the Strait of Belle Isle, seeing patients at the fishing stations along the way and putting the first dents in the copper sheathing of the launch when he went aground entering Blanc Sablon in a fog. He then turned north to meet the *Albert* in Indian Harbour, where the coastal steamer would deposit the components of the second hospital. On his return, Curwen and Sister Williams had already arrived, bringing the disappointing news that inordinately foul weather had prevented the steamer from landing the timber. The components would have to travel up the coast and back again before construction could begin.

This reversal left Grenfell with all his resources concentrated in one place, and he quickly needed to consider how to redeploy his staff before going any further. 'We are very disappointed not to be able to get into the Hospital this year,' wrote Curwen, 'and it is not easy to settle how we can best spread our influence: at present we are concentrated strongly in Indian Harbour; Dr. G. will go North in the launch & I am anxious the "Albert" should move on too as the Capt. can do good Mission if not medical work, but Sister & I cannot stay here if we have no house to stay in.'[7] Thus, while Curwen remained on board, Sister Williams returned to Battle Harbour in the mail steamer *Windsor Lake* with a sick patient. As for Sister Carwardine, she did not yet enjoy Grenfell's full confidence, even though he was satisfied with her medical work. He wrote priggishly, 'I fear greatly nurse Carwardine is not a Christian. Oh it will be a pity. We must make it a matter of earnest prayer that she may become one or she will be a terrible hindrance.'[8]

It was 15 August before the *Albert* was ready to start north. As it headed for Hopedale, Grenfell himself detached to Hamilton Inlet in the *Princess May* with one of the crew and visited the Hudson's Bay Company station at Rigolet before doing the rounds of the neighbouring islands. The farther north he went, the less he could depend on an elementary hydrographic survey. Heading into Double Island, an Inuit summer settlement, he reported, 'Our first difficulty was to find where it was, for though among countless islands of bare rocks, those we sought were not marked in the chart, and the way was unknown to us.'[9] With only the most elementary devices, he now attempted something quite unnecessary, a daring if not hazardous sprint to the most northerly stations to leave his presence on the full extent of the coast. Assisted by an Inuit pilot, he made Hopedale safely, finding the *Albert* already anchored there and in touch with the Moravian missionaries. It was now 25 August. If he were to continue as far north as Nain, he would need to leave immediately, before the winter weather closed in. The next morning he set off at 7:30 in company with a Moravian, the Reverend P.M. Hansen, and made for the mission station at Zoar, about sixty-five miles north.

At this latitude Grenfell's charts were useless, especially for identifying the numerous islands and shoals. In order to carry on, he needed to take other measures for the safety of the vessel. By borrowing a long wooden ladder from the mission station and lashing it upright against his mast to elevate a lookout, he felt his way along, locating the rocks by their wash before they presented any danger. At nine o'clock the same night Hansen brought him safely into Zoar, where his whistle roused the surprised missionary, the Reverend S. Schultze. Still not satisfied, he resolved to reach as far as Nain after lying over the following day, a Sunday. Far beyond his coal supply by now, he dumped five sacks to burn during the return journey, then smothered his upper deck with wood, leaving no room to move from one end of the *Princess May* to the other.

All that day he steamed north. Hansen had visited Nain only once before by komatik, and on that occasion the countryside had been buried deep in snow. Now he could not identify his usual landmarks. As it grew dark, he sighted cliffs resembling the entrance to Nain harbour, and Grenfell stood on, expecting at any moment to see the lights of the mission house. Suddenly, the lookout warned him of shallow water, and before he could stop the launch had hit the bottom. Fortunately, it had not been damaged. So going astern a short distance, Grenfell dropped anchor in two fathoms and waited for daylight. In the middle of the night, the odd angle of the *Princess May* awakened him, and he got up to find that Hansen had rolled out onto the deck. The launch by now was high and dry and would not refloat until morning. After getting under way again, he encountered a young Inuit with a boatload of salmon-trout bound for Nain and offered to tow the man in. But again, his eagerness got the better of him. Disregarding an elementary rule of seamanship, he steamed too fast and buried the bow of the man's flat-bottomed dory, delaying himself again while the man collected his cargo.

The Reverend C.A. Martin, superintendent of the Moravian mission, gave Grenfell an enthusiastic welcome in Nain. Indeed, the Moravians, the sole missionaries on the coast since the eighteenth century, were heartened by the arrival of an ally and considered the two new hospitals an 'unspeakable boon.'[10] They hoped Grenfell might add another hospital further north. After a day of fine weather, Grenfell could not resist the temptation to finish one final leg to Okak, where the Inuit would be assembled at their fishing stations. With no chart on board and an old Okak man as pilot, he made the extra ninety-five miles in another day. He could see Cape Mugford in the distance, rising a sheer three thousand feet out of the sea, and he had ventured as far north as he dared. It was 30 August. 'Being late now in the year, and the weather being already boisterous, while at night it froze and during the day we had some snow, I thought it advisable to go no further north this year in a vessel only 8 ft. wide, and not a good sea boat,' he wrote with unconscious irony.[11] After treating patients for two days, he turned south again, this time steaming at night through a field of ice brought in by an easterly wind. By sheer good fortune, steaming watch on and watch off with the sole crew member he employed as mate, boatswain, able seaman, and steward, he luckily encountered calm seas all the way back and reached Nain by breakfast.

It was 4 September before they had cleaned up the *Princess May*, loaded up with wood, and got under way again. The first thirty miles passed without difficulty, thanks to a rough sketch provided by the captain of the *Harmony*, together with one he himself had made on his way north. But as he emerged into open water, heavy seas and fog forced him into an uncharted bay for the night. At daylight, he steamed through the fog and arrived in Zoar for breakfast, leaving again at midday for Davis Inlet. At approximately 6 p.m., he ran the launch upon a narrow reef with a falling tide and could not muscle it off. For a short time his dash to Hopedale had come to a halt. To prevent the hull from chafing, Grenfell and his crew of one rolled the *Princess May* over onto the port side, then ran their borrowed ladder under the starboard. Between this and the bilge they lashed a large block of wood and rolled the vessel back on top of it, putting the weight on the starboard side. Then they slept two hours by turns until the tide floated the vessel free at 2:15 a.m. An hour later they anchored in Davis Inlet.

Grenfell reached Hopedale at about 5:30 on the evening of 6 September, having passed part of the fishing fleet going south. By this time he did not expect to find the *Albert* in the harbour, for he had given orders for Trezise to start south. Yet there was the *Albert*, with flags up and guns firing as if a royal visit were in progress. The *Albert*, he found, had been detained when Trezise and Curwen were called to inquire into the deaths of four women poisoned by hemlock. During his twelve days' absence, a jury had been sworn in, an investigation made, and the evidence sent to St John's. Meanwhile the ship had received no word of his whereabouts from any of the schooners making the passage home. The next evening, after one day in, he preached at a meeting attended by 350 people. His subject: sleep as the urging of the devil.[12]

Grenfell now put the *Princess May* ashore to look at the hull and the engine. As he expected, three gouges lay exposed in the keel and an assortment of dents in the hull, despite the copper sheathing. While none of these appeared serious, the shaft that he had ordered made up in St John's displayed an obvious bend and a good deal of rust that demanded attention. While the maintenance was being done, the crew continued the taxing medical and missionary work as the harbour began to fill up with home-bound schooners. At one point there were seventy-six vessels, all requiring medical attention of some kind. On Sunday, 10 September, four services were conducted. At one there were 250 people present, at another 350, and Grenfell reported with satisfaction:

> To all these the message of God's love was proclaimed. A token of Christian affection was given to all, as they came for it, in the form of a pair of woollen cuffs or mittens, and a good solid bundle of excellent literature, well assorted, to each ship. Those that did not come to us we visited, while after evening service Dr. Curwen had patients till eleven o'clock, and we visited two schooners, whose sick men were too bad to come off board. There was hard work for all hands, and had work not been systematically distributed, we could not have got through it.[13]

The next day Grenfell departed in the launch to visit more southerly coastal communities such as Chensovik, Ailik, and Makkovik, leaving orders for the *Albert* to follow a few days later, after tending to the oncoming schooners, then to call at Turnavik Island, some distance offshore. This plan of action nearly cost Grenfell the ship.

Trezise took the *Albert* out of Hopedale on 18 September, unconvinced of the need or the wisdom of visiting West Turnavik, for the harbour entrance, approached through dangerous runs, presented only a narrow opening. Besides, Grenfell had already called there in the launch going both north and south, and Curwen had spent two days there himself. Moreover, Hopedale was proving to be a most advantageous position. In the course of their long stay there, the crew had become attached to the inhabitants, white and Inuit alike, especially the Moravians, who had brought fresh flowers as a gesture of farewell. Curwen remarked, 'Capt. is in a very uncomfortable position as Dr. G., who is Superintendent of the Mission and has Capt. Trezise's appointment in his hands, gives orders as to where the "Albert" shall call but takes no share in any of the responsibility should a mishap occur in the attempt to carry out an injudicious or unsafe order.'[14]

It was nearly dark when Trezise arrived off the mouth of the harbour and fired a flare, bringing Captain William Bartlett, the resident planter, on board to pilot them in. Relieved to see the vessel placed in experienced hands, Curwen went below to finish a letter, but ten minutes later the sound of running feet brought him springing up again, and by the time he had reached the upper deck he found the *Albert* lying beam on across the mouth of a cove, the bowsprit nearly touching the steep rocks on one side and the stern grinding upon a low ridge on the other. (Later, in St John's, Lloyd's surveyor found the after-length of keel fractured and estimated repairs at £150.)[15] Bartlett had mistaken the opening for the harbour; as soon as he realized the error Trezise let go both anchors to stop his bows from jamming between the rocks. With a strong wind blowing onshore, it would not have taken long to break up.

Over fifty men scrambled aboard. Extra anchors were taken out in boats and dropped to seaward. Then the men heaved in, and the *Albert* was warped off in three hours. Even so, the whole effort would have been useless had the wind not suddenly died. Later that night, with the *Albert* tucked into the harbour, it freshened again and blew so hard that no vessel could leave the next day. There Trezise remained until 25 September, when it took him five hours to set the anchors and haul the *Albert* out again. When he reached Holton two days later, Grenfell came out in the launch to tow him in. But Trezise, who was probably still furious at the wasted effort, refused. By now he saw more clearly than ever the need to put the safety of his ship first. Indeed, he was convinced that a sailing vessel of the *Albert*'s dimensions did not suit the running about demanded in these tricky harbours. The next day he took a full morning to moor fore and aft to avoid swinging into the numerous craft anchored there.

From Holton the *Albert* made an easy run to Indian Harbour, where Grenfell found that the hospital, with the exception of the chimneys, had been erected in six weeks. Wishing to mark the occasion with a ceremony, he announced that he would give a lecture with lantern slides featuring scenes from the Holy Land and events from the life of Christ, just as he had done up and down the coast. The building was already packed an hour before the lecture, and with the hymns projected onto a sheet fixed to the wall, a hearty meeting took place. Now that the hospital had been constructed, he could leave with the knowledge that it would be ready the next year. And after entrusting the keys and equipment to the agent of Job Brothers, the next day he crossed Hamilton Inlet to Cartwright and joined the *Albert* again at Indian Tickle. It was now 4 October.

While the *Albert* rode at anchor, Curwen took the opportunity to see for himself the misery endured by the families taking passage home. Called aboard a schooner to examine a fisherman's wife, he was surprised to find he had to lower himself into the hold and then crawl along some distance to see his patient, who was lying so close to the deckhead that she could not sit up. He himself had to lie on his side to examine her. The vessel, he observed, had been loaded with no regard for the comfort or safety of the passengers: 'The schooner had been down the shore fishing and had 400 quintals of fish in this hold; planks & bark were laid over the fish and a tarpaulin and then the space above this was divided among the crews that were taking passage home in her; into this space they had to put all their belongings – traps, crockery, window frames, barrels of clothing, molasses, food &c. &c. and on the top spread their bed; it was a curious sight as I lay talking to my patient & looking about; all sorts of things were lying about and the rain was coming in & wetting much.'[16]

These people, however, considered themselves fortunate to have only two and a half fishing crews of five to ten people on board. As many as twelve or fourteen had been crammed into the hold side by side, in some schooners, and not everyone had the privilege of standing on deck. The women were required to remain below for the entire voyage, so that at night not all the men had a place to lie down. If a vessel loaded like this encountered a storm, forcing the captain to batten down the hatches, some of these people would suffocate. 'I am not surprised the owners & skippers try to keep us from visiting these places where the people are stowed,' Curwen wrote; 'the skippers take as many crews as they can get into their schooners because of the freightage money; the people have to provide their own food and wait their turn to cook at the galley, which is on deck, in even the worst of weathers.'[17]

As the voyage of 1893 drew to a close, it became apparent to Grenfell and his staff that Labrador fishermen did not suffer simply from poverty, for they worked willingly and hard. Rather, they suffered from a subtle form of economic exploitation they were helpless to change. By its very presence, the Mission to Deep Sea Fishermen had already exposed the repressive practices of the vested interests as well as the entrenched power of the political system. Grenfell knew a fisherman newly elected to the House of Assembly who was appointed revenue officer and who cruised the coast with his own duty-free liquor. Others kept unlicensed gin shops. The agent of Job Brothers at Indian Harbour thwarted the work considerably, even though Job himself served as a member of Grenfell's committee in St John's. Not everyone on the coast opened their arms to the Mission.

Curwen quickly took in the obvious source of difficulty: nothing would change while the merchants controlled the only supply of cash. Such stringency, he noted, led to numerous absurdities:

The merchants seem determined not to allow the people to make money, in fact to get as much out of the people as they can; they take their salmon, cod, herring & fur at a price they name & give in return what provision they like, always arranging the prices so that there is nothing on the credit side; it makes little or no difference to the settler if he makes a good fishery during a season: for example, Mangrove does not expect any more provisions for the winter this year than he got last (viz., two barrels flour, 1/2 cwt. bread, 7 gallons molasses & 3 lbs. tea) although he has taken more salmon ... Geo: Holley has not had an ac[coun]t since 1884, so that he does not know if he is in debt or not; he has a cod trap & with his 3 brothers has no doubt he has made $700 this year, but he does not for a moment believe he has anything on the credit side and fears to ask.[18]

Other abuses became apparent as well. It was not uncommon to see a schooner go on the rocks after a bad voyage, the hulk and the catch to be sold without notice to recoup enough for the owner's winter supply. Grenfell himself thought the churches did not help matters. He continually drew attention to the poverty among the settlers and had stated publicly, 'They live and die without the knowledge of God.' The implications of this exaggeration enraged the Church of England missionary, who took it as an affront to the established church. 'What we are bound to say about the condition in which we find the people is sure to lead us into trouble with those who have interest in keeping matters much as they stand,' predicted Curwen, 'and already much exception is taken to a remark or two in one of the letters published in Sept. "Toilers." '[19] Grenfell's statements in subsequent numbers of *Toilers of the Deep* incited further protests, especially from those defending the work of the religious denominations. 'Probably this is because they have found that, though they be half-starved, they are not so outrageously wicked or indifferent to religion as the English North Sea fishermen,' wrote an observer in Harbour Grace. 'Morally and religiously our people, though perhaps nothing to boast about, may safely be claimed as being far ahead of the English working classes. They have had some to look after their welfare long before the M.D.S.F. ventured in the field.'[20]

In the mean time, as the weather worsened, Grenfell would not stay put but steamed off to the adjoining island to visit Red Point, Domino, and Batteau, even though the deck of the *Princess May* had sprung so many leaks he could not keep her rugs dry. The crew of the *Albert* found his behaviour unnecessarily reckless and hoped that as time went on his good fortune would desert him long enough to show him the risks he took. Curwen observed, 'He is a great anxiety to us.'[21] As he worked his way down the coast towards the Strait of Belle Isle, he got into Tub Harbour 'somehow' with a gale blowing up. Two days later, attempting to round a headland in the heavy sea that followed, he lost his buckets and loose gear over the side and put into Snug Harbour. 'And here we are still, Sir,' he wrote the editor of *Toilers of the Deep*, 'learning to be patient.'[22] Finally, on 16 October, he reached Battle Harbour, where he found the *Albert* and a relieved hospital staff waiting for him. The next day it snowed.

Sensing he was staying a bit too late in the season for the safety of the vessel, he now made plans to return to St John's. He himself would navigate the *Princess May* with two of his own crew members, as usual. Sister Williams would join the *Albert*. Bobardt and Sister Carwardine would follow a week later in the *Windsor Lake*, the coastal steamer Curwen believed was working against their interests. ('Many lying reports has she spread along the coast about us; every man on board save one is a Roman Catholic & all hate us,' he wrote.)[23] On 20 October Grenfell left some of his coal and equipment aboard the *Albert* so as not to be too heavy crossing the Strait of Belle Isle and departed in the general direction of Newfoundland, leaving obscure instructions for a rendezvous on the other side. Said Curwen, 'Dr. G. left in "Princess May" at 6:30 but whether he was going down Strait of Belle Isle or across to the "French Shore" I do not think he knew himself. He left instructions that we are to proceed to St. Anthony, if we don't find him there to some other place, & if not there we shall find him at a third harbour. Sufficiently vague.'[24]

Later that day the *Albert* followed in tricky sea conditions: the wind blew from the west, but the tide ran north, up the strait. Under the lee of the island, Trezise took in two reefs of his main. In the evening the wind dropped, and the *Albert* rolled within sight of Cape Bauld when the main boom, fourteen inches in diameter, snapped in two places, leaving him without any mainsail at all. At the same time, the sail itself split from the peak to the foot and had to be lowered. Two days later the ship's boat was lifted up by a rising sea and dropped onto a bucket, staving in one of its planks. Resolved to preserve the safety of his vessel, Trezise decided to run for St John's, knowing he could not possibly beat up into a harbour to meet Grenfell even if he wanted to. Under these conditions, he made St John's by 23 October, still not knowing whether Grenfell had crossed the Strait of Belle Isle or not.

By early November no one had seen Grenfell. Acting upon the great concern about his safety in St John's, Governor O'Brien wired every tele-graph station around the island to make inquiries, and the mail boat *Virginia Lake* was instructed to look in every harbour and cove – even to cross the strait. The sealing vessel *Leopard*, employed in electioneering for the general election of 6 November, was also ordered to take part in the search. In response to the governor's wire, several schooners reported seeing Grenfell detained on the Labrador coast. Others had seen him later at St Anthony. But when Bobardt and Sister Carwardine arrived on 2 November in heavy weather, he had still not been heard from, and a wire reporting him missing had been carelessly sent to London. Two days later he reported from Twillingate.

After leaving Battle Harbour on 20 October, Grenfell had been driven by strong winds into Henley Harbour. Four days later he had crossed the Strait of Belle Isle, a distance of twenty-eight miles, in four and a quarter hours, expecting to find the *Albert* waiting with his coal and supplies. Pressing on along the French Shore, harbour by harbour, in order to pass around Cape Bauld, he had kept up steam by procuring fragments of abandoned flakes and pieces of fence. Before he reached Fortune, the *Princess May*, with only three feet of freeboard, had rolled heavily and tossed the only spirit compass over the side. Then, after crossing White Bay and reaching Cape St John blind, he had made a run of forty miles across Notre Dame Bay to Twillingate, where he had picked up coal and carried on again by stages. Finally, by accepting a tow from the sealing steamer *Nimrod*, he had kept the line as far as Cape St Francis, where his competitive instinct surfaced again. 'Here we let go our line, and racing the *Nimrod* into the Narrows, beat her by about a quarter of a mile,' he related with some satisfaction.[25]

In the space of four months, Grenfell had travelled approximately twenty-five hundred miles in a small launch under some of the most difficult seafaring conditions and arrived without injury. His recklessness vexed a good many people, but he had returned better informed than anyone about conditions in Labrador, and the volume of work he was able to perform showed the magnitude of the task at hand. In the course of 109 days he had visited eighty-seven ports, some twice, and treated 794 patients.[26] He had also held sixty services, attended by an estimated five thousand people, and given twenty lectures with the aid of lantern slides. Curwen had treated 1,052 patients in the *Albert*, but with the frequent movements of the vessel, only three in-patients. The others he had sent to the Battle Harbour hospital, where Bobardt had treated thirty-three in-patients and 647 out-patients. The *Albert* had visited ten harbours for extended periods, some twice, and had held prayer meetings attended by approximately six thousand people.

Back in St John's, Grenfell stepped from the convulsive decks of the *Princess May* to the ornate formality of Government House, where Governor O'Brien insisted on housing the medical staff for the next three weeks, while they caught up with their correspondence and made plans to return home. Grenfell's first letter was sent to mollify his mother, still terrified that he might have drowned. Although she and others who knew him had been sent into what Treves later called 'a fine panic,' Grenfell chose to put a brave face on and lecture her pompously about the need for optimism. He wrote, 'Is it not extraordinary how our humanity would nullify all our professions of faith & confidence in the absolute "bestness," if there is such a word, of Our Father's will. Drowned – well best drowned. Spared – well spared to work – best so. Now you will be amused to know I was never in danger. Tho' I put out in the gale I simply put into the next harbour & had a great time among the people.'[27] He also acknowledged the opposition his recent accomplishments had aroused. As a pioneer in Labrador, he had uncovered irregularities few outsiders were in a position to notice, but he explained the antagonism by suggesting that people were jealous of his success. 'The Church of England is our most bitter antagonist,' he wrote. 'Alas. Alas.'

During the next three weeks, while he met the St John's committee and waited for the *Albert* to be repaired, Grenfell was pleased with the public response. At a crowded public lecture chaired by the governor, he showed lantern slides depicting elements of Labrador life which, as the *Evening Telegram* reporter put it, 'Newfoundlanders, with few exceptions, knew little or nothing about.'[28] Yet despite events such as this and the work of his committee, he could not possibly raise enough money himself to make the improvements required. Moreover, he felt thwarted by the Church of England diocese, which he found to be 'high ritualistic' and indifferent to his evangelical bent. Without consulting the Mission, he now decided he would take part of his annual holiday and tour Canada with Bobardt at his own expense, endeavouring to find support and raise money in the larger cities.[29] Suddenly, on the strength of his recent work, he was taking the initiative for the Labrador venture and the busy days in St John's were coming to a close. 'The dear old govr. will miss our noise & smoke & our always being late for meals,' he wrote his mother. As he left St John's, he grew excited about his prospects. 'I have heaps of introductions & am going to try & push the Mission,' he added.[30] As for the Mission, it was left without a superintendent to look after the busy North Sea activities. For several months there would be no one to provide the leadership there.

Calling first at Halifax, Grenfell balked at turning himself into a kind of commercial traveller. But, at Bobardt's insistence, he met the premier, the general of the garrison, and other public officials and spoke at a public meeting chaired by the bishop of Nova Scotia. There followed meetings sponsored by the Halifax churches and a large gathering at Dalhousie University, so that by the time he left by rail for Montreal he had established a new branch of the Mission to Deep Sea Fishermen without the Mission's knowledge. In Montreal, where the Canadian Foreign Mission Society had supported a Labrador mission under the Reverend Charles C. Carpenter and Miss Jane Brodie until 1878, he met with even greater enthusiasm.[31] Here he emphasized the Mission's potential benefit for the Canadian portion of the Labrador coast. The Anglican bishop of Montreal as well as Sir William Dawson, the principal of McGill University and a leading anti-Darwinist, agreed to promote another public meeting, and Grenfell sought out Sir Donald Smith, who was intimate with the Labrador coast after years of service with the Hudson's Bay Company. Smith was now president of the company as well as president of the Canadian Pacific Railway and the Bank of Montreal and a worthwhile ally.

Grenfell liked the way Bobardt's Australian 'cheek' brought results so readily, realizing the same style would not be greeted so warmly in England. 'You have to be advertised in American ways here,' he wrote his mother half apologetically. 'One of the newspapers, the largest here, "the Gazette," & the government organ insisted on specially photographing me & putting it above an article on our work to draw attention. These things surprise no one here, hateful as they are.' The lack of ceremony and cumbersome social convention also appealed to him. 'One thing I like about these people is their solid matter-o-fact business ways – you walk in – say "I'm Dr. Grenfell – I want you to work up a meeting for me – so & so said you would if I asked you." He says "I will" or "I won't" & off you go again –.'[32]

By now his lectures had acquired a heavily anecdotal style, encompassing romantic tales of 'brave deeds' performed by lonely Labrador 'Vikings' amid storms, perils, and hardships. The 'trials' of daily life and the manners and customs of the north were illustrated by his own slides. A reporter noted: 'Dr. Grenfell tells earnestly of their great needs, their spiritual and bodily wants – a strange and thrilling story throughout. The listener marvels that he knew so little of these men.'[33] By the time he left Montreal he had formed another committee under the chairmanship of Sir Donald Smith, pledged to raising $1,000 annually, and a ladies' committee that would supply sheets and household effects for the Indian Harbour Hospital. Already he had collected $1,300 in donations.[34]

On the strength of Grenfell's appeal, the Board of Trade had passed a resolution encouraging the government of Canada to co-operate with Newfoundland for the benefit of Canadian fishermen. As he moved on to Ottawa, he was rapidly learning what it took to promote the cause, even though he still found public speaking decidedly uncomfortable. 'Well you will say, I shall get proud – not so I think – I like Labrador work better than this,' he wrote defensively to his mother. 'I am now again little better than the professional mendicant.' After the events of the past summer and his own personal success, he was beginning to see the Labrador work as his personal creation. 'There is great scope for work out there,' he announced, '& I feel I should like to inaugurate it myself, if the Mission agree.'[35] In Ottawa he and Bobardt petitioned the minister of marine and fisheries for a grant of $5,000 to erect a hospital on the Canadian coast west of Blanc Sablon. However, the scheme was blocked by Commander William Wakeham of the Fisheries Protection Service, who advised the government against involvement in missionary activity. 'Do our people on the Labrador require any such assistance and unless they are in extremities is it wise to make paupers of them, as the gratuitous distribution of unnecessary relief of this kind is sure to do?' he asked.[36] In view of this report, the cabinet turned down the request.

Even so, Grenfell had established a foothold in Canada on his own terms. Before he returned to his duties as superintendent, he and Bobardt accepted a CPR pass from Smith and took the railway as far as they could go, ending up in Victoria, British Columbia, without actually applying for leave from the Mission.[37] Early in the new year, Treves chose his words carefully in conveying to the wandering superintendent the council's growing impatience. 'Everybody is pleased with the trip to Labrador this time and think you have done first rate,' he told him. 'In fact it has been an entire success and has done a great deal of good for the Mission. I quite sympathise with your desire to have a trip with the whalers and did what I could with the Committee. They were however all dead on your coming home and had I pressed matters there would have been a row and a split in the camp.'[38] Indeed, in Grenfell's absence the council had delayed some business decisions. It had considered getting rid of its two oldest smacks; it had looked at new premises, thought about starting a coal shed, and proposed a move to Lowestoft. But no one was taking charge of these ventures. Treves therefore advised Grenfell to return as soon as possible. 'The next time you go out make arrangements beforehand,' he added. 'It is impossible to do everything at once.'

By March 1894 the two had returned to England, Bobardt to enter the navy, Grenfell to return to the fishing fleets. When Bobardt applied to the Mission for reimbursement, however, the finance committee rejected his claim, and their response left no doubts about their attitude to the Canadian initiative. Since they had not authorized the Canadian tour, they considered the two doctors' formal connection with the Mission had at that time 'closed.'[39] Technically, they were correct, for Grenfell had written to announce they would proceed from St John's at their own expense (since they intended to take a holiday). But the Mission had also come to realize uncomfortably that they were beginning to lose control of developments overseas. Grenfell, as a result of a few vigorous months abroad, was more deeply committed to this new phase of the work than they. When he applied for ten days' leave before returning to Labrador the next spring, they denied it. 'You will recollect that you were asked to return from Canada for the specific purpose of looking up the North Sea work,' they replied, 'and the Committee therefore feel that they would be stultifying their own resolution on the subject if they do not ask you to carry out the wishes they then expressed.'[40]

The Rev. Algernon Sydney Grenfell, WTG's father

WTG at Queen's College, Oxford, 1888, front row left

WTG at the helm of the *Alice Fisher*, North Sea, January 1892

The Grenfell brothers: Cecil, Algie, and Wilf, *c.* 1905

The *Albert,* at Stewart's wharf, St John's harbour, hoists sail for Labrador, July 1892

Mostyn House School, 1908

WTG with Jack, April 1908. Grenfell wears the rugby outfit and dog skins in which he survived the ice-pan adventure

Wedding party, Chicago, November 1909

WTG with Labrador livyers, 1908

Dr John Mason Little and WTG with crew of *Strathcona I, c.* 1910

WTG and his mother at Mostyn House School, May 1912

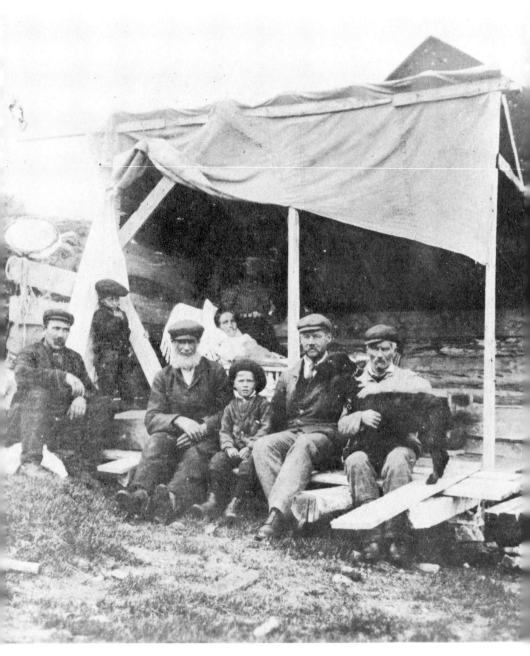

WTG gives fresh air treatment to patient at Harrington Harbour, *c.* 1912

PART TWO

Social Reformer

—6—

Hard Times in Newfoundland
1894 – 1897

Come all you good people, I'll sing you a song
About the poor people, how they get along;
They start in the spring, finish up in the fall,
And when it's all over, they've nothing at all,
And it's hard, hard times.

'Hard, Hard Times,' Newfoundland folksong

The literature and folklore of Newfoundland abound with instances of the powerlessness and poverty imposed by the truck system. Year after year, fishermen sank deeper into debt, and each generation handed the legacy of financial impotence to the next, secure in the knowledge that the merchants in St John's would be the only ones to reap the benefits. However, the merchants themselves, though far more secure than the fishermen, were not immune from the malignancies of the system. They would surely have preferred a more conventional cash economy, for as it stood they could recover their investment only after the fish had been sold in the foreign markets. While they waited, they in turn existed on large advances from local banks. From the late 1880s poor fishing and low prices inflicted heavy losses on the merchant faction in St John's, and in these circumstances the banks should have prudently let the weaker firms sink in order to avoid a general disaster.[1] But the same merchants, some of whom sat on Grenfell's committee, also served as directors of the Newfoundland banks. As they exhausted their own resources, they borrowed all the more heavily until they cut deep into the depositors' funds, so that in December 1894 both the Commercial Bank and the Union Bank of Newfoundland closed their doors for ever, leaving the colony to drift for two weeks in an economic void. Only after the Bank of Nova Scotia and the Bank of Montreal opened branches in St John's could Newfoundland advance on a surer footing. As Grenfell prepared to return to Labrador in the spring of 1894 he could not have known that the colony he wanted to reform was headed for an economic collapse that would absorb the Mission's resources even further.

Grenfell's visit to Montreal in the winter of 1894 had brought unimagined benefit when two small vessels were suddenly offered for his use. Sir Donald Smith had agreed to purchase and refit the steam yacht *Dahinda*, a vessel capable of manoeuvring better in close quarters than the cumbersome *Albert*. Measuring seventy-eight feet long and fourteen feet at the beam, the *Dahinda* was registered at just over thirty-three tons and carried two thirty-five-horsepower engines as well as a foresail, main, and mizzen. She was built of oak with iron beams and brass fittings; her deck housings had been reinforced with teak for Labrador work, and she carried two small boats launched from davits.[2] Thomas Roddick, the Newfoundland-born Montreal doctor, had also presented £50 for the purchase of a hospital launch, to be named the *Eurilia McKinnon*, after his first wife. These two vessels, in addition to the gift of hospital appliances from the ladies' committee in Montreal, gave Grenfell the leverage he needed for dealing with his superiors. By the annual general meeting of the Mission in May, he had completed a set of plans for the summer with all the thoroughness of a naval operation.

This time the *Albert* left Yarmouth in June with Trezise in command and sailed directly to Labrador, carrying on board Dr J.H. Bennett, destined ultimately for the China mission field, and Dr Frederick Willway, assigned to Battle Harbour and scheduled to remain there throughout the winter before proceeding to another foreign mission himself. The *Albert* would land Bennett and Sister Carwardine at Battle Harbour, then proceed to Indian Harbour to assist Willway and Sister Williams with opening the new hospital before Grenfell brought the *Dahinda* downriver from Montreal. Meanwhile Grenfell himself had gone to Birkenhead and purchased from Rutherford's a small, transportable sailboat equipped with a centre board and dipping lug and easily operated single-handed. To be later named *Eurilia McKinnon*, it was intended for harbour work. In company with W.B. Wakefield, a volunteer travelling at his own expense, he then sailed to St John's by steamship, arriving on 24 June. After meeting his committee at Government House, he decided to gather a crew and transport them to Montreal to fetch the *Dahinda* so that the vessel could be laid up the following winter in St John's and the crew paid off. The *Princess May*, still undergoing extensive repairs from the abuse of the previous year, was to be despatched to Indian Harbour, where Willway could work with her along the coast and up Hamilton Inlet.

Trezise, detained by a solid wall of drifting ice, took twenty-eight days to reach Battle Harbour and after leaving Bennett there failed to reach Indian Harbour with Willway until 20 July. The new hospital, Willway found, had survived the winter intact but still consisted of nothing more than four walls and a roof. He would require the *Albert's* carpenter and crew to finish the interior and install stovepipes while the chimneys were built. The lack of adequate heating, however, almost brought catastrophe. Without adequate protection from the pipes, one wall caught fire, and the hospital would have burned to the ground except for the prompt action of the local people. But each of the two new hospitals operated as planned, and the staff awaited Grenfell's arrival in the *Dahinda* to bring the medical work to its anticipated peak.

Meanwhile, in Montreal, an enthusiastic group of Protestant supporters stood in the stern of the *Dahinda* on 13 July, the vessel dressed over-all with signal flags for a christening ceremony. From one mast flew a small white pennant with 'Sir Donald' in red, from another the large blue flag of the Mission. All the fittings had been cleaned and polished, and the saloon had been decorated with large vases of flowers. After a few words from Grenfell about the vessel's intended employment, Dr Roddick's sister, one of the mainstays of the Montreal women's group, renamed it the *Sir Donald*. There was a benediction by the bishop of Montreal and three cheers for Sir Donald Smith, the former Labrador agent who was backing Grenfell generously. Two days later Grenfell left for Labrador with the goodwill and satisfaction of his Montreal supporters, who saw the presentation of the *Sir Donald* as a reproach to Commander Wakeham and his brief to the government of Canada the year before. When Wakeham's remarks appeared in London in the *Canadian Gazette*, the *Montreal Gazette* responded with a strong editorial praising the Mission's undertaking on the other side of the Labrador boundary. 'These people, it is presumed, know what the Newfoundland Labrador requires as well as Dr. Wakeham can know what the Canadian Labrador does not require,' it insisted, 'and their attitude may be taken as indicative that charity extended to the work in question will not be misapplied.'[3]

The voyage down the St Lawrence and through the gulf took longer than expected. At Rimouski further carpentering needed to be done, and iron clamps had to be forged to fix the new deck pieces. After leaving on 26 July, Grenfell worked his way downriver and through the gulf, and in a few days he could observe the familiar features of the Labrador coast. In Harrington, where he held a clinic and a service, he received a warm welcome. During three days in Bonne Esperance, where he was looked after by the merchant William Whiteley, another warm supporter of the Mission's work, he began to think of his arrival in Battle Harbour. The crucial rendezvous with the rest of his staff approached as he made his way up the coast, stopping along the way at such places as Pigeon Island, Bradne, Isle de Bois, and Barachoix and then running into familiar harbours such as Blanc Sablon, l'Anse au Claire, Forteau, West St Modeste, and Red Bay, where former patients came aboard to welcome him back.

It was blowing hard when the *Sir Donald* left Red Bay, carrying one or two surgical patients for the hospital and pressing to make Battle Harbour in a day. Was the *Albert* still there? Was the hospital in operation? There had been no news for six weeks. The vessel floundered from headland to headland against the gale before anchoring in Henley Harbour. But the next morning, with the weather calm, Grenfell knew he would see Battle Harbour that day. 'Everyone was soon busy,' he wrote, 'patients and all, as far as possible, cleaning and polishing and tidying up, so that we might make a good impression for the new vessel.'[4] Now Cape St Charles appeared, and the steward hurried the midday meal to save time for securing everything below. With the captain standing attentively on deck and Grenfell acting as pilot, only one more cautious manoeuvre among the shoals remained before they were in. All they required was a little careful ship-handling. But once again, Grenfell was in a hurry. The worst reefs had fallen astern, and they had just rung on full speed again when they felt a subtle grating sensation, followed by a jerk to one side. The *Sir Donald* was left rolling helplessly in the swell, stuck amidships. With twelve feet of water beneath the bows, they had caught at low, low tide the edge of a reef running off Indian Cove. An hour either way would have been seen them safely through; and, in fact, the vessel soon floated free, but they could not get under way again. A quick survey revealed a shaft broken, a propeller lost, the sternpost twisted, and the rudder knocked to one side.

Grenfell decided to walk overland with Wakefield and a guide to find a steam tug in Battle Harbour, luckily the only place on the coast he could have found one. Humiliated by his own eagerness, he virtually ran across the barrens while the embarrassment of his predicament ran through his mind. A few hours before, the vessel had been decked out with bunting for a triumphal entry. Now he and Wakefield, caked with mud, shocked the crew of the *Albert* with the discouraging news. 'Glad I was to have no one to blame,' he wrote. 'I was pilot myself. The passage was well known to me, as I had passed and repassed through it, both in the *Princess May* and the steam-launch *Bandit*. A few yards to one side would have saved us.'[5] By late afternoon the launch had towed the *Sir Donald* in and moored her alongside the *Albert*, the larger vessel still incongruously hung with flags in her honour.

His careful plans had fallen apart. The *Albert* would have to divert from her planned passage to tow the *Sir Donald* to St John's, where the dockyard would find the hull unsound and thus unfit for further work that year. Disappointed by the survey of the hull, Grenfell later told the Mission he thought the Montreal committee had been 'quite unaware' of her structural condition at the time of purchase and had probably been 'taken in.'[6] For the present, only the *Princess May* remained for coastal work; but after making two attempts to leave she, too, remained in St John's. With the season already well advanced, only a fraction of the patients could now be seen, and the two hospitals would not receive the expected supply of more serious cases.

Quickly formulating a new plan of action, Grenfell sailed to Indian Harbour in the mail boat *Windsor Lake*, taking with him the twenty-foot *Eurilia McKinnon* to reach some of the coastal communities. Only then did Willway, who had met Grenfell once before, fully understand the extent of his intensity and endurance. Later he recalled,

> How glad we were to see him, how much there was to talk about and, dare I add it, how glad we were to have him go again! Nothing tired him, no day was long enough, nights were wasted unless you spent them in strenuous tasks that could wait until the fading daylight put an end to other equally tiring efforts. I thought I had been busy, but when he came I found it was only my ignorance and inexperience that had made me think so. At last he left us and actually sailed that crazy boat all the way back to Battle Harbour. It is true he shipped a man as deckhand, but he so terrified him that the man broke his contract before the journey was half done, preferring as he naively said, living a little longer to leaving a little money to his relatives.[7]

With this simple work boat and the co-operation of the coastal service, Grenfell was able to seek out patients until mid-October. After launching it in Indian Harbour, he cruised down Hamilton Inlet to Rigolet, then returned to assist Willway through much of September until he found a schooner to take him and the boat south again. On 26 September he left Seal Island in the *McKinnon* with a livyer he had engaged and was attempting to reach the communities around Venison Tickle when a sudden head wind cracked the bamboo mast in the middle, so that sail and gaff fell on top of them both, and they were required to continue the journey with a jury rig until a replacement could be found.[8]

Through a succession of short sails and tows from passing schooners, Grenfell continued to visit patients along the coast for three weeks until he got himself dropped off at Battle Harbour again, the season now nearly over. Bennett had already departed, and there was no doctor in the hospital. Even though he had just spent a month at sea in a twenty-foot craft, he turned again to surgery without a pause. He wrote, 'I had several visits to make that afternoon, and the next day three operations to perform – one being a tumour from the neck of a fisherman brought to the hospital by the mail doctor, another a cleft palate in a girl of ten years, and a third a tumour of the face, that had come all the way from Black Tickle, 130 miles to the northward of Battle. All these have been completely successful.'[9] By 14 October Willway had abandoned Indian Harbour and joined him in the Battle Harbour hospital. Two weeks later Sister Williams arrived from Rigolet in time to accompany him to St John's on the last mail boat of the year. Only Willway remained, looking ahead to a winter in which he would be required to act not only as doctor but as parson, schoolmaster, choir leader, district visitor, and relieving officer. In the new year he would be absent three and a half months, travelling approximately twelve hundred miles by dogsled as far north as Davis Inlet,[10] then for three weeks into the Strait of Belle Isle. By the opening of the next fishing season, he was an experienced Labrador missionary with more local knowledge than Grenfell himself.

When Grenfell returned to St John's that fall, he began to feel the quickening of public interest in the Labrador mission, and it placed him in an awkward position. How was it possible to publicize the conditions existing on the Labrador coast and appeal for aid without embarrassing the very people he intended to help? It was not possible. Once aroused in defence of their own dignity, Newfoundlanders did not readily accept criticism from outsiders, no matter how well intentioned. Grenfell gave a tactful interview to the St John's *Evening Herald*, deftly answering specific questions about the misfortunes of the past summer.[11] But later in London he made more serious statements in an interview with the *Illustrated London News*. These, coinciding with the Bank crash of 10 December 1894, added to the ignominy already surrounding the colony. Generally, Grenfell made balanced observations. He not only described the misery but provided his own photographs. He even tempered his attack on the merchants by suggesting that they would gladly abandon the inherited truck system if they could find a way to replace it. But the article exaggerated Grenfell's observations by portraying Labrador fishermen as 'British outcasts' working at the beck and call of absentee merchants, 'many of them as much their property as the slaves of the South were the property of the cotton lords before the Civil War!'[12] As soon as it appeared, Grenfell back-pedalled, and the next number carried his corrections as well as a list of the improvements already under way.

At the same time he wrote apologetically to the Anglican bishop of Newfoundland, Llewellyn Jones, perhaps to offset what he had said about the 'deplorable' spiritual neglect in the Labrador settlements. The bishop had not seen the article, but he took the opportunity to object to the Mission on doctrinal grounds and point out why he thought it might have been rejected by his clergy and people. Above all, Jones challenged the concept of 'undenominationalism' and charged that the Mission to Deep Sea Fishermen proceeded without fixed beliefs other than their anti-Catholicism. The Mission workers, said Jones, did not attach sufficient importance to distinctive truths of any kind and made it difficult for committed churchmen to support their work. He asked:

> Is it any wonder if our clergy feel sure that this grievous wrong is being done under the guise I will not say of 'undenominationalism' – for that means nothing, I suppose an infidel might claim to be included under that term – but of *Christmanship?*
>
> What Churchmen feel is that it would be more honest if the M.D.S.F. would come out in its true colours as a Dissenting institution.
>
> Our people would then know where they are.
>
> 'Undenominationalism' is the worst enemy the Church of England has to contend with – because it is an enemy posing as a half friend.[13]

While Grenfell defended himself, he sought the sympathy of Governor O'Brien, now trapped in a financial crisis that threatened the colony's constitutional position.[14] Faced with a minority government he could not manage and a financial tangle he could not resolve, he applied to London for aid and asked for a royal commission of inquiry. But the Colonial Office decided that a grant-in-aid would serve no useful purpose. It hoped that if the colony went bankrupt, it could then perhaps be nudged more easily into confederation with Canada. Subsequently, O'Brien associated himself with a movement that collected several thousand signatures calling for a royal commission, but still the Colonial Office refused to alter its policy. Grenfell himself complained to Francis Hopwood, who as a government official and a member of the Mission council worked confidentially to 'pull the wires' behind the scenes; but there was nothing he could do.[15] By February 1895, as a result of a bill passed in the Newfoundland House of Assembly, a cabinet took office formed almost entirely of men previously disqualified on a finding of bribery and corruption. O'Brien felt his office degraded, and handed in his resignation. By mid-March, Herbert Murray, a British treasury official, arrived in St John's as relief commissioner. 'Things are very bad but the Colony must drift into Confederation even on bad terms & that is the very best thing for your work,'

Hopwood assured Grenfell.[16] This was cold comfort indeed, and as Grenfell made plans for the next summer the prospects for the Labrador mission seemed more uncertain than ever. The crisis in Newfoundland had given him back the burden of the Indian Harbour hospital and the renovations in Battle Harbour.[17] He would have to look elsewhere for the money he expected from government.

During the winter of 1895 he turned to writing again and finished the draft of his first book, *Vikings of To-day*, brought out in the spring with a strong introduction by Treves. In commending the book, Treves endorsed Grenfell's Labrador initiatives in dramatic language – language so romantic that it clung to all subsequent accounts of his work and placed it on a heroic plane. 'It is claimed that the splendid physique and the heroic courage of the British race are both deteriorating, and that those who seek for the time of noble deeds and sturdy hearts must turn back to the days of Elizabeth – to the stirring times of Drake and Raleigh,' declared Treves.[18] But clearly, he thought, the British could still perform such deeds, and his rationalization drew on the assumptions of moral manliness. He wrote that the book at hand would transport the reader from the heated, unnatural, and debilitating atmosphere of the city, from the enervated, the pampered, and the self-indulgent people who inhabited it, and bring him to a place where conventionalities were replaced by the simplest elements and rudimentary problems of life. A skilled travel writer and lecturer, Treves also made a crucial connection with Grenfell himself. Grenfell was not only hardy and skilled. He had responded to the same magical attraction of the sea that had emptied the coves of Cornwall and Devon centuries ago, and the book demonstrated how the same spirit of enterprise and daring had survived to the present time.

In *Vikings of To-day*, Grenfell set a pattern for a sequence of Labrador natural history books to follow. In placing the Mission's work in context, he described the country and its natural features, the people, the history, the birds, the fishes, and the fur-bearing animals. He explained how to handle dogs and hunt seals, how the cod fishery and the truck system worked. At the same time he interspersed these details with a full account of the Mission voyages to date, complete with medical statistics, reports from his medical officers, testimonials from local people, and offers of help. Treading a cautious path between travel and promotion, he aimed at something unexpected: bringing the Labrador work out of the missionary domain and placing it before the public at large. To preserve his disinterest, he resolved to take no profit from the book's sale and turned over the royalties to the Mission.[19]

Having bullied the council once again, Grenfell returned to Newfoundland in the summer of 1895 and sailed from St John's as master of the *Sir*

Donald, for the Board of Trade had advised him to surrender his yachts-man's certificate to the Canadian board and apply for a fresh one.[20] At the same time the thoroughly refitted *Princess May* headed for Indian Harbour under the command of a Newfoundlander, George Newell. As Grenfell made his way north, he found that, instead of setting his work back, the recent financial catastrophe in the colony had provided him with even greater opportunities. Herbert Murray, the relief commissioner, had authorized him to distribute salt and other relief supplies, and with all his vessels operating at once, he could cover more territory than ever before. The *Sir Donald*, reinforced with oak sheathing, carried a full supply of drugs forwarded by the ladies' committee in Montreal as well as a new diptheria antitoxin presented by the British Institute of Preventive Medicine and 130 packages of clothing. 'Never was there so great need of this mission as at the present time,' the *Evening Herald* judged. 'It appears that the necessities of retrenchment have led the government to dispense with the services of a medical man on board the mail steamer on Labrador, in order to save his salary. But for the mission, therefore, there would not be a single medical man whose services would be available.'[21]

For the next few months, as the medical staff and crews worked to lift the poverty and starvation, Grenfell's personal stature on the coast continued to grow. The small hospitals now treated a full range of medical and surgical cases, and their influence extended far beyond purely medical care. Moreover, Grenfell himself did not simply make medical decisions; he touched the way people conducted their lives. A St Anthony man whose wife had died at Battle Harbour begged him to take him and her body to his home in Newfoundland so that he could proceed to earn a living through the summer. Reluctant at first to make the unnecessary expenditure, Grenfell relented. He then ordered the *Sir Donald's* carpenter to fashion a rudimentary coffin and sent the *Princess May* across the gulf, the flag at half mast. 'These trips will cost us £3 in coal,' he estimated. 'It is very dear here just now, but we had practically no alternative. The poor fellow offered to sell anything he had to be able to pay part of the expenses, but I would not allow him to do anything till we see how the fishery turns out.'[22] In Bateau in November he was called upon to help fourteen people he found sleeping together in a small house of mud and boards. 'As for clothing,' he noted, 'all are badly enough off. Bed clothes appeared to be entirely wanting, and naked feet and cotton dresses with wretched underclothing was the condition of the children.'[23] Having set himself up as relieving officer, he then went a step further. In West St Modeste, with no merchant at hand to advance supplies, he made his first venture into establishing a co-operative. 'The scheme seems feasible,' he wrote, 'and as under the present circumstances it is almost impossible for the people to keep out of debt, while many are on the verge of starvation, no one will be injured by these people supplying themselves.'[24] Thus Grenfell acknowledged early on the inevitable. In circumstances like this, it was impossible to run a purely medical mission and ignore broader social problems.

Early in August he penetrated Hamilton Inlet as far as North West River, then turned north to catch the schooners fishing at the more remote points and attend to the coastal Inuit. At Nain, lying at anchor next to the Moravian ship *Harmony*, he heard about the typhoid epidemic that had carried off ninety-two people the previous winter, unfortunate folk who had lacked the most elementary medical aid. Willway had managed to reach only as far north as Davis Inlet that winter and could not help them. Whole families had died together, he discovered, some burning their own houses for fuel. Further north, at Cutthroat, he again encountered typhoid, traced to two men who had visited Nain. At Okak the epidemic raised its head again: three more were suffering from the disease. The Moravians strongly welcomed his presence. 'We owe a debt of gratitude to him and the excellent Society which sends out such Christian helpers to the distant Labrador,' they recorded.[25] Stretching now to accommodate the remaining schooners, he hoped to reach Cape Chidley, the most northerly point, and round off his investigation of the Labrador coast. But by the end of the month, having steamed to within forty miles of it, he turned south again, any day expecting to hear the grating of ice against his hull. He did not wish to risk further damage to the *Sir Donald*.

By early November Grenfell had returned to Battle Harbour, satisfied that he and his two doctors had visited virtually every coastal family from Blanc Sablon to the tip of the Labrador peninsula as well as the end of Hamilton Inlet and Sandwich Bay: a considerable achievement under any circumstances. Running along an uncharted, unmarked coast, he had touched ground (officially) only six times. During these voyages the three doctors had kept case notes, giving the first picture of the level of health in the region. But the winter ahead already looked bleak. The government of Newfoundland had cut its meagre winter supplies almost entirely, so that on his departure Grenfell was obliged to leave twenty-five barrels of flour in two of the harbours, together with molasses, tea, gunpowder, and hard bread to help prevent starvation. Warned against turning people into paupers by giving them handouts, he left these in the custody of the securest men and instructed the others to saw wood at £5 a thousand feet, intending to return and pay for it the following summer.

Once again the summer staff dissolved. Dr Augustine Robinson stayed behind to travel the coast during the winter, then depart for missionary work in South Africa after being relieved by Dr Graham Aspland. Sister

Carwardine would spend her first winter in Battle Harbour and Sister Williams part of the time in Canada visiting the committees of volunteers. She would then return to replace Sister Carwardine the next winter. Willway, by now an accomplished northern hand, had been recalled by the London Missionary Society to work in Mongolia. But Grenfell valued his work too highly to allow this to happen. 'He loves the work,' he protested to his council, 'we work together as brothers.'[26] After the council's intervention, Willway was released by the LMS in November 1895 and continued as one of Grenfell's strongest allies.

Feeling a heavy drag on its resources that summer, the Mission asked Grenfell to visit Canada and raise funds. So far, the British government had not delivered the expected assistance to the colony, for, as Hopwood wrote, 'At home the prevailing opinion is that everything connected with Nfld is corrupt & rotten & that wholesale condemnation is the best thing for the place.'[27] Grenfell sprang at the chance, since he wanted to form a fourth committee in Toronto and raise enough money for a steam launch to serve Battle Harbour. But although the council had encouraged the visit, it worried about losing control of its budget and neglecting its work in Britain during his absence. When it asked him to return to his duties in the North Sea, he replied at Christmas with a strongly worded letter from Montreal, arguing that he could not do much good in England in the time remaining before he returned to Labrador again. He also asked whether he could remain on the coast the next winter.

This letter constituted the most passionate declaration of his devotion to social reform so far. He wrote: 'Here they have no representative, and I want very much to have a complete year at least with the Newfoundlanders and Labrador fishermen, that I may better know and understand their ways. I assure you I feel very anxious to carry out this programme. This really is getting a more important work each year as our facilities of reaching the people increase. I feel certain I could make a good record in work if I remained in Labrador next year. I believe I could do better afterwards in organizing, arranging and [doing?] the work I most dislike of deputation work. I have worked hard at this branch – my whole soul is in it.' This outburst failed to move the council. Having granted him leave to observe the seal fishery, it ordered him back as soon as he had returned from the ice so that they could arrange what they tactfully called the 'future conduct' of his work in England.[28]

The delicacy of language did not conceal the council's impatience. The developments in Labrador had shown them they needed to exercise greater control over Grenfell's initiatives to prevent him from weakening the Mission's primary task at home, for after more than a decade of work it saw itself as a considerable force for good in the maritime world. In

February 1896, as Grenfell was finding new support in Toronto, it added the word 'National' to its name; by the end of the year, Queen Victoria recognized its growing importance by granting it the use of the prefix 'Royal' during the Diamond Jubilee. Treves, who had protected Grenfell's interests in council, had endorsed his request to go to the seal hunt, but now he urged him to come home. Tactfully, he congratulated him on his pioneer work but pointed out that the Mission had no replacement for him in the North Sea. 'Things are not going well at Gorleston,' he wrote. 'In fact they are going very ill. We want someone there badly. There are all sorts of difficulties in one way and many enemies to be met. As a matter of duty I think you ought to return.'[29] Thus, as soon as he arrived in England at the end of April, Grenfell was summoned by the council for a confrontation.

Instead of backing down, he insisted on returning to Labrador, arguing as he always would that the work had become too closely identified with his name. His withdrawal might jeopardize the efforts of his supporters in North America and blemish the Mission's reputation. Still the council would not move. If Grenfell wished to remain general superintendent, they insisted, he would have to spend more of his time in England. The question was referred for the moment to a committee composed of the four committee chairmen, and as a result Willway was appointed assistant superintendent. Nevertheless, Willway supported the Labrador effort fully in *Toilers of the Deep*, in case anyone still thought the Mission was departing from its original purpose. Like Grenfell, he maintained that the Mission existed to assist 'wherever our fisher brethren are found in circumstances of need.'[30] That spring both superintendents returned to Labrador, to be faced with the worst conditions they had seen so far.

Leaving St John's in the *Sir Donald* in June 1896, Grenfell called at Tilt Cove to pick up Aspland, then stopped at Englee, on the northern peninsula. Here he witnessed the demoralizing spectacle of hunger and depression even before he reached Labrador. Within minutes of his arrival the decks were crowded with hungry people who had not tasted flour or tea for weeks. Grenfell wrote, 'All our baked bread, with butter and also hard biscuit, was given out at once, and many hungry persons ate ravenously on deck all they could get. Herrings had been in the harbour the last fortnight, and that had helped to eke out their existence; for some pathetically told us 'the beach had been picked clean of mussels and winkles.' But boiled herrings without any bread, or anything but cold water, became nauseating. Several could hardly keep herrings down any longer.'[31] Even with cash in hand, these people would have still gone hungry and ill-clothed, for there was no food to buy and no boots, stockings, coats, and shirts to be had. To make matters worse, the codfish had started to run, but there was no salt in the harbour and not enough hooks and lines for a satisfactory fishery. Grenfell went ashore to distribute flour for general baking and meditated on the evils of the truck system.

On Sunday Aspland preached at a bleak service in the Wesleyan church, taking his text from Luke's narrative of the events on the road to Emmaus. Sorrow may sometimes blind the believer, he assured the crowd, but never hide him from the eyes of Christ. There followed a community meal with the results of the day's baking, and Grenfell, who could not have missed the scriptural parallels, estimated that 150 people gathered and soon finished off 'all the loaves, buns, ten cans of meats, four tins of marmalade, one tin of butter, and half a dozen buckets of lime juice.' Then the children who could not attend (simply because they owned no clothes) remained to be fed, and for the rest of the day the crew sought them out. Faced with extreme cases like this, Grenfell was moved to some of his most articulate appeals for continuing the Mission's work. 'For surely even in this age, when scientist, but not science, teaches us the "fittest only should survive, and the sooner the weak go to the wall the better for all the race",' he wrote with an eye to the social Darwinists, 'we may be allowed to consider a desire to help ... as still an attribute of humanity as distinct from the lower creation, and not one implanted by God in the hearts of Christian people only.'[32]

The spectacle at Englee convinced Grenfell more than ever that the surest answer to Newfoundland's difficulties lay in reforming the credit system, even though it would alienate his merchant supporters in St John's. That summer he experimented with a small-scale co-operative in an endeavour to introduce cash, choosing Red Bay as an appropriate community for pioneering it. In Red Bay the men had enjoyed a good fishery the year before, and they were mostly independent. Moreover, a windfall provided by two nearby wrecks had yielded enough flour and other goods to see them through the summer; and they could sell their fish to anyone they liked after they had paid for their salt. The heads of the families entered into a bond to purchase goods, appoint a storekeeper, and keep the store intact. The profit left over after the payment of simple charges and the cost price applied to goods was to be divided equally among them.

With this arrangement, Grenfell sensed he was exposing himself to criticism, for he had supplied most of the goods himself and freighted them to Red Bay aboard the *Sir Donald*. The Mission could thus be perceived as entering into trade, jeopardizing its precious detachment from affairs. 'Already,' he wrote in June, 'unkind whispers float about that we seek to make a profit.'[33] A.A. Chesterfield, the Hudson's Bay Company agent at Rigolet, recalled, 'As is the case in all crusades, the change brought hostility on the part of the established traders, whose profits were cut by the change and some of them initiated a smear campaign against the good work. They said it was all right to cure the sick. It was all right to preach the gospel. These were the recognized work of the missionary. To correct economic wrongs was the function of the government. Interference in the economic lives of the people smacked of some kind of religious graft.'[34] But Grenfell insisted on showing how such a system would benefit the trader as well and hoped other communities would adopt it, for clearly no one could sell shop goods in a place like Englee without customers. That year, he reported, the Red Bay Co-operative sold $1,488 worth of goods and declared a profit of $50. By the fall most of the community had paid for their salt and purchased their supplies for the winter, but Grenfell would continue to be haunted by charges of commercialism.

As the season progressed, Willway saw an even bleaker winter approaching, for to make matters worse the fishery had failed. Preparing for his second winter in Labrador, he expected he would have to feed some of the livyers himself or else they would die. 'God help us to face this problem soberly and honestly,' he wrote. 'We dare not let these poor creatures go hungry whilst we prate about the expensiveness of missions.'[35] By early September he reported that over two hundred people had been sent home from his Indian Harbour station by planters eager to avoid the unnecessary expense of feeding them. Day by day, vessels arrived prematurely en route for Newfoundland, and with the exodus under way he feared he himself would need to send away the *Princess May* and pay off the crew. As Grenfell prepared to leave the coast, he sounded discouraged. Acquainted with practically every settler on the Labrador coast, he realized that nothing would change unless the whole system of living and dealing were altered. He wrote, 'As I pass up and down, and repass this fall, visiting some places for the fourth time, I can only say I see no other hope for them, unless the Newfoundland Government grants them free passage to Canada or the States to try elsewhere to do better.'[36] By November Willway had been empowered by Robert Bond, Newfoundland's colonial secretary, to co-operate with the Hudson's Bay Company agent in relieving starvation along the stretch of coast between Battle Harbour and Sandwich Bay and in devising public works for recipients of pauper relief.

Grenfell arrived in St John's with the council's endorsement of his plan to raise further funds in Canada. After Christmas he lectured in Halifax, Montreal, Toronto, Hamilton, London, and Ottawa, establishing a pattern for many such tours to come. At the outset, he asked the Toronto branch for money to renew the *Sir Donald's* tired boilers, but the request provoked a sharp reply from the council on a matter of principle. Ordinarily, money raised by public subscription had been placed in the general fund for the

Mission's use. If donations were diverted to serve special projects, the council argued, it would lose control, and a letter written to Grenfell by the secretary made this position clear.[37] When Grenfell requested a holiday in Canada, he was told to be home by 1 March 1897 and to 'incur no further responsibilities.'[38] However, during his visit to Montreal the committee who had provided the *Sir Donald* in the first place offered to sell her and purchase a new one. When Grenfell conveyed their intentions, the finance committee, unaccustomed to such independent action, could barely contain its rage beneath its characteristic understatement. 'In view of the communication which had been addressed to Dr. Grenfell on the subject of the Society's finances, and its ability to run a steamer, or provide a third Doctor for Labrador this season, some surprise was expressed at Dr. Grenfell's communication,' it recorded.[39] That spring Grenfell's activities agitated the council further when the Mission's auditors could find no vouchers to support the Labrador expenditures. With no vouchers at hand to verify the expansion, it required him to sign a statement validating the costs.[40] For while he had developed the ability to organize others and move audiences to generosity, he had not mastered the accounting sense required to use money to the greatest advantage. Together with his venture into the commercial market, this awkwardness with figures would haunt him later.

The council's summons cut short another new initiative, a tour of New England churches and schools paid for by the new Toronto committee with the aim of placing a crucial foothold in the United States. As he set off, Grenfell was met in Massachusetts by the Reverend Charles Carpenter, the former Labrador missionary with support in Montreal and a columnist for the *Congregationalist*. The eight days of lecturing in the Boston area captured the attention of the daily newspapers and the church weeklies. He had started a similar round of meetings in New York when he received word from London and sailed home directly. Nevertheless, he had advertised the Labrador venture and expanded his network of acquaintances in the Protestant community there. He now possessed a sense of a greater constituency eager to help this kind of missionary work. Whether the council desired it or not, the American interest in Labrador had already acquired a momentum of its own.

91

— 7 —

Exile in England
1897 – 1899

God speed thee on thy mission; a loving woman's gift,
Sent forth in holy hope, and trust, our sailors to uplift.
Our generous hardy fishermen, who toil from dawn till dark,
In wet, and weariness and cold. Be thou to them God's Ark,
Laden with comfort for them, a boon and blessing both.
In sickness or in accident, science and love go forth.

Isabella Murray,'On the Christening
of the "Julia Sheridan" '

When Grenfell returned to England in the spring of 1897 he soon realized that his role as superintendent had expanded with the Mission's expanded view of itself but altered with the alterations in the technology of fishing. First, at the request of the long-liner and trawler interests in Hull, the Mission sent him in the *Sophia Wheatly* to Iceland and the Faeroes to investigate how to serve British fishermen working in that region. As a result of this voyage the *Temple Tate* was converted to a floating seamen's institute at Aberdeen and the *Thomas Gray* berthed for the same purpose at Ostend. Then, the following year the Mission consolidated its work among the spring herring and mackerel fishermen around Crookhaven. Secondly, with the fishing companies converting quickly to steam propulsion, the Mission required new hospital ships to continue serving the men adequately at sea. Thirdly, the changes in technology were bringing fishermen higher earnings and more time ashore, and thus the Mission needed to expand its shore services to provide alternatives to the public houses. All of these new ventures preoccupied Grenfell as superintendent for the next two years and forced him to put Labrador to the back of his mind.

In mid-June he weighed anchor from Thorshavn in the Faeroe Islands to begin searching for the Shetland trawlers fishing around the Great Faeroe Bank. But finding that most of these vessels fished farther to the north, he spent much of the time off the Vestmann Islands and the mouth of Brede Bugt and eventually sailed into Reykjavik to arrange for the translation of religious tracts into Icelandic and Danish. There he was permitted to hold a public outdoor service in English, side by side with a Salvation Army officer speaking in Icelandic. He was impressed by what the Army had done. 'Much travelling among fishermen in many parts convinces me they do really good work,' he noted condescendingly, 'even if we do not agree with all their ways.'[1] For two weeks he cruised off the north coast of Iceland and boarded vessels to distribute tracts, hold prayer services, and advertise the presence of the Mission. Returning at the end of July, he brought back an unavoidable truth from the fishing grounds: only a steam trawler equipped as a hospital vessel could serve such an extended fleet.

He had come to the same conclusion earlier, after a short voyage aboard a steam trawler in the North Sea. Everywhere the fishing industry was changing rapidly. Even within the brief span of Grenfell's experience, inshore boats had given way to large cutters for running the fish to market. These, in turn, had given way to fleets of sailing yawls serviced daily by steamers. Now the yawls themselves were surrendering to fleets of fishing steamers out of Grimsby, Hull, Boston, Yarmouth, Sunderland, and Aberdeen as well as those from Holland and Belgium. No longer did the skipper pace the deck, calculating the strength of a breeze, deciding when to shorten canvass or shake out a reef. He positioned himself in the deck-house and responded to the machinery, hollering orders down the voice-pipe and ringing on revolutions with the engine telegraph. 'Speaking as a landsman,' Willway would write the Mission members, 'it seems that the fisherman's calling has lost all its romance.'[2] The smart new vessels fished night and day at greater speed. They no longer drifted along conveniently together, and a Mission smack under sail could not possibly continue to work among them. If the Mission wished to continue as a positive force at sea, Grenfell concluded, it would soon have to find a way to reach the fishermen and for the fishermen to find the Mission ships. Without a doubt, the North Sea work required a steam trawler.

The Mission also needed to face the changing conditions ashore. More efficient fishing equipment produced greater earnings. Fishermen spent longer periods ashore and faced new 'temptations.' Suddenly, Grenfell observed, fishing was becoming a more lucrative vocation with hidden dangers for Christians unprepared for them, especially new opportunities to drink. At Yarmouth the Mission's 'temperance refreshment rooms' provided cheap meals on the quay as a successful competitor for the public houses. ('It isn't everyone can give a hot dinner with a cut off the joint for $3\frac{1}{2}$d., and not be ruined over it,' he wrote with some satisfaction.)[3] There were also new institutes opening at North Shields, Milford, and Grimsby. Nevertheless, Grenfell found it difficult to find volunteers to act as local secretaries and organize in the other fishing towns. In January and February 1898 he himself undertook an organizational tour with almost daily meetings. Following his own advice to volunteers, he employed the business techniques favoured by Moody: strong publicity, ministerial endorsement, the encouragement of lay workers, and a relentless appeal for money. In each region he organized a series of small gatherings that would lead to a large, well-publicized event. Lecturing with a set of coloured slides illustrating the fishing practices of the British fleets, he felt justified in charging admission and did not hesitate to ask for donations for the Mission's work. This method, which he would employ in the United States in later years on behalf of Labrador, took him through Clifton, Portishead, Weston-super-Mare, Bath, Liverpool, Birkenhead, Chester, and Dublin.

The most important public meeting of the year was held in London in March. During the past year the Mission's income had amounted to £25,000, only a small proportion of it collected from Londoners. The meeting at the Mansion House, presided over by the Lord Mayor, was aimed at publicizing the Mission's accomplishments and commending it to businessmen in the City. On the platform sat Donald Smith, now elevated to the peerage as Lord Strathcona and Mount Royal and appointed high commissioner for Canada. With him sat Sir Terence O'Brien, Hopwood, Grenfell, and others. During the past year, announced the Lord Mayor, the Mission doctors had treated sixty thousand fishermen. For their efforts on behalf of a lucrative industry, they deserved greater public support. Grenfell, in his turn, sketched the expansion of the British fishery and the scope of the Mission's work, and Strathcona, together with Willway and O'Brien, testified to the value of the Mission's efforts on the Labrador coast. The meeting brought to a climax an unrelenting winter of fund-raising. It was the kind of successful publicity venture at which Grenfell was becoming expert.

He had developed a distinctive platform presence with a breezy, robust delivery and the style of a seasoned mariner. To present the fishery as justifiably important and worthy of public donations, he liked to cast it romantically within the myth of Britain's heroic heritage, portraying fishermen as hardy Anglo-Saxons whose God-given destiny it was to feed the world from the oceans around their shores. Fishing, like fighting, was a national inheritance that had to be properly safeguarded, he maintained, and in an essay published in *Toilers of the Deep* he pressed the point with a strongly patriotic tone borrowed from a new book by the Reverend W.H. Fitchett, *Deeds that Won the Empire*. In this compilation of British military and naval victories, Fitchett had appealed to the British as an 'Imperial race' with a great tradition of manly struggle that stood as a legacy 'bequeathed' to the present generation in order to maintain a 'robust citizenship.' 'They represent some, at least, of the qualities by which the Empire, in a sterner time than ours, was won, and by which, in even these ease-loving days, it must be maintained,' he wrote.[4]

Similarly, Grenfell argued, the mastery of the seas was a God-given inheritance of the British people, whom he liked to portray as a race of latter-day Vikings. 'Some will no doubt smile at this insular and possibly quite erroneous prejudice,' he carefully added, 'but history seems to tell me that God has given to the Anglo-Saxon race this invaluable and peculiar power to help safeguard our invaluable inheritance also – an open Bible.'[5] What were the racial qualities exhibited by British fishermen on the high seas? A natural genius, resource and daring, and an innate ingenuity and stubbornness. Grenfell also enjoyed the romantic idea that constant contact with the ocean had produced another important effect: a refinement of human nature that had inculcated manly virtues and sheer virility. Thus, in Darwinian terms, fishermen constituted a special breed. 'Patient and persevering, hardy and resourceful, generous and open-hearted, they represent all that is best in the Viking spirit of their ancestors,' he concluded.

Grenfell was eager to show that Christian fishermen possessed the best qualities of manliness – virtuousness mixed with toughness – contrary to the misconception that they somehow lacked virility. He once took satisfaction in showing this side of their nature to a group of public school boys on board one of the Mission vessels. Fishermen, insisted Grenfell, showed that they were truly 'Godly.' 'Their utter absence of conventionality and selfishness afforded a lesson that struck home also, while their downright earnestness, without either suspicion of cant or stilted unreality, with their high ideal they expect of a professing Christian, were a strong call to increased personal loyalty in ourselves, and a noble refutation of the slur of "unmanliness" so commonly cast on those making any open and therefore useful confession of faith on land,' he wrote.[6] It was a proposition he would employ again and again. Conceived of in this way, fishermen were somehow admirable, and they deserved the public's attention.

Grenfell liked what he perceived as their lack of cant and conventionality, and he felt comfortable with their uninhibited habits of worship. At the Mission's annual meeting of 1898, presided over by Lord Strathcona, he returned to these notions again. He took pains to offer a way of offsetting the inducements of drinking saloons and ensuring that fishermen continued to use their God-given talents. His address borrowed the social Darwinist rhetoric influential among health reformers of the time. By placing Britain within the framework of inter-racial and international competition, he suggested that British fishermen had already demonstrated their superiority by taking upon themselves the task of feeding the Latin countries. 'Why the Latin speaking races do not catch their own fish I do not know, or why they do not handle a boat like the Anglo-Saxon race I do not know,' he said. 'But they do not – at least, that is our opinion of them.'[7] The notion of Anglo-Saxon superiority at sea had now become a permanent part of his presentations.

Meanwhile, as Grenfell preoccupied himself with the Mission's broader objectives and assumed more responsibility for its leadership, Willway continued to look after its winter operations in Labrador. After two seasons of dogsledding and snowshoeing, he was by now more experienced in winter work than Grenfell himself and indeed reported he had never felt better. Throughout the winter of 1897 he had kept the readers of *Toilers of the Deep* entertained with exciting communications about his travels through the sub-arctic wastelands and disclosures about working conditions experienced at low temperatures. He had related the perils of travel by dogsled:

I have been shot off head first, thrown off sideways, disappeared into snowbanks, been partially submerged in brooks, barked all possible portions of my anatomy, and in various other ways suffered all the indignities common to the comatic [*sic*] traveller. My belongings likewise have at various times been equally unlucky. We have started with a full cargo at the top of a hill and have arrived at the bottom with everything scattered far and near – with decks clean swept, in fact.

He had described the difficulties of taking pictures in fifty to sixty degrees of frost:

By the time you have erected your camera you begin to doubt the existence of fingers, and possibly have to thaw out your hands by putting them in your pocket or other method; then you attempt to focus, and your fur cap falls over your eyes; that being adjusted, your ground glass is coated with ice, whilst your ears protest loudly against the whole procedure; finally, the plate is exposed, packed up, carried a few hundred miles with the baggage, and eventually being developed, the finished picture becomes a conundrum for one's friends.

But he had also conveyed the wretched living conditions, such as the nakedness of a family of nine:

> There being no evidence of beds or bedding of any kind, I asked the man where they all slept. 'Oh, down there anywhere,' was his answer, pointing to the floor. If you can picture these nine people lying down when night came on in a heap upon the floor, probably crouching together for additional warmth, without a rag to cover them, without any attempt at privacy, like the very dogs that did their bidding, keeping themselves from freezing by the abundance of firewood which, thank God, cost them nothing, then you will have some conception of what I saw that Saturday evening the end of last February.

And he had told of a man whose family was about to starve:

> He was badly clothed; his children were in bed, partly for warmth, partly to quiet them. The only food in the house was a cupful of peas. The man had not broken his fast since some time the day before, when he had some of the peas boiled with water. Got him something to eat, and carried him with me back to Cartwright, first sending a little tea and flour for the children, to be replaced on the man's return. Very cold fresh wind all day. The man and I ran for a considerable distance to keep warm. Arrived at Cartwright in the afternoon; gave the man a shirt and some vamps [heavy socks] to put on his feet.[8]

As he prepared to leave the coast that spring, Willway again raised the question of encouraging settlers to emigrate but dismissed the idea as impracticable. 'They know nothing of the world at large,' he said, 'and did they leave it would be but to become pauper immigrants in some other land.'[9] Instead, he joined with Grenfell in recommending a sinking fund to continue paying people in return for wood and work.

When the new season opened in the autumn of 1897, the Labrador staff changed again. Aspland returned to Battle Harbour, this time bringing back Ada Carwardine as his wife, and the two would remain there the following winter to relieve Willway. Sister Williams returned to Indian Harbour with Dr Grierson, a Halifax physician. Willway himself cruised the coast in the *Julia Sheridan*, a harbour tug of nineteen tons donated anonymously by Miss Julia Greenshields, a member of the Toronto committee, in memory of her mother. The *Sir Donald* still lay in St John's awaiting new boilers. The *Julia Sheridan*, formerly Job Brothers' *Lance*, had been christened there at a ceremony attended by the new governor, Sir Herbert Murray.[10] This latest addition, clearly inadequate for transporting equipment and patients together with the inevitable sacks of used clothing, provided Willway with his transportation. Only forty-six feet long and sixteen feet abeam, she soon acquired a reputation as a 'dancer.' As he prepared to leave that fall, Willway complained, 'When you have to gather your plates and dishes in your arms and keep strict watch over the vagaries of the coffee-pot; when you find the steward sitting on the floor in his galley, using his legs as fiddles for his improvised table, then you can conceive the possibility of a stranger considering the *Julia Sheridan* to be of a somewhat flighty, not to say frivolous, disposition.'[11] Already Grenfell had approached the Mission council with a proposal for a new steamer to replace the growing flotilla of dinghies, tugs, and sailboats that could barely keep up with this branch of the Mission's work. But the council, ever cautious, deferred a decision until it could weigh the additional costs against its widening responsibilities in Britain. The Labrador branch had begun to threaten its operating capital. It could neither go forward nor go back.

Early in 1898 Willway pressed for a special council meeting to discuss the Labrador finances.[12] The total cost of running the Labrador venture had now risen to £1,600, and contributions from all sources accounted for just over half that amount. While the council remained committed to the northern work, encouraged in large measure by Treves, it could not devote more than £1,500 a year to it without encroaching on its capital or running into debt. So it refused to authorize £2,500 for a new steamer and would not sanction such an undertaking, knowing it would require another £700 a year for maintenance, unless more subscriptions could be raised. But Grenfell *could* raise them. Starting with a donation from Lord Strathcona, he managed to draw in £1,500 by May, and at the annual general meeting of the Mission Willway backed Grenfell while warning the assembly, 'Unless we keep a grip on Dr. Grenfell he is likely to run away with us, and now we have to give him scope and then haul him in, and so I have to tell you that we cannot have that new steamer until we have got the money to run her.'[13]

Throughout the winter, while Willway returned to replace Aspland in Labrador, Grenfell again confined himself to the United Kingdom, keeping up his rigorous schedule and looking for a way to build a new ship for his purposes. On his own initiative he sought out F.W. Barry, a naval architect he knew, and persuaded him to draw up plans free of charge. At first these provided for a wooden-hulled, steam-driven vessel of eighty-three feet, capable of carrying only thirty tons of coal and also ketch-rigged. But by November 1898, as Grenfell oversaw the opening of the Mission's new seamen's institute at Gorleston, he also reported that construction had already started at the Dartmouth shipyard of Philip and Sons on what was by now a steel-hulled vessel, to be launched in the spring.[14] (By contrast, the Mission's first North Sea steamer, the *Alpha*, was not launched until December.) Early in the new year, with the Mission clearly beginning a new decade of development, he offered to write a book about the work in the North Sea and the council welcomed such a publication. But Grenfell was so distracted by his construction plans that he failed to get it out for another five years. By that time he had widened the book's scope to embrace the work on both sides of the Atlantic.[15]

As Grenfell looked ahead to several months of deputation work, lecturing in parish churches and schools, he allowed himself a rare moment of despair. A special meeting of the council received his long report on the disposition of the fleet and the changes taking place in the fishing industry. The report also showed that he had grown tired of lecturing, fund raising, and fussing with day-to-day administrative detail. He wrote: 'I have a month's deputation work now, and I confess I don't look forward to it, knowing as I do so many places where our work really needs more personal supervision and more intelligent forethought.'[16] He had lost patience with the relentless routine of shore life and desired to be back at sea, where his energies and imagination could bring more immediate results. Soon the opportunity arrived. Early in February Willway wrote him a private letter ostensibly devoted to the business of the Red Bay co-operative. In this letter he also revealed two major difficulties that settled the matter of Grenfell's future employment and the direction of the Labrador work.

The previous spring Willway had married and brought his wife with him to Labrador. After a few months, however, she had developed a strange, undiagnosed illness that had left her weak. Willway confessed he was 'very anxious' about it but asked Grenfell not to mention her condition to anyone so as not to worry her mother. Willway also showed signs of fatigue. The grim task of dispensing relief supplies, together with the attitude of the people and the iniquities of the truck system, had worn him down. In the pages of *Toilers of the Deep* he reported cheerfully on the way the Mission helped people survive, but privately he presented Grenfell with a much bleaker picture:

I am simply sick of constantly doling out flour & tea & molasses & finding *at the end* that the people are no whit better than at the beginning. I believe the poverty down the shore this winter is appalling and now I have to go down and feed the poor creatures who really in their hearts *blame me* because they get no more. I am looked on as a sort of ogre by not a few from Square Islands down. I honestly try not to be ruffled & pray for help too, but it is horrid work. Do have a long & serious talk with 'those in power' when you come out. Urge on [Dr] Robinson [at Battle Harbour] the utter inadequacy of sending

[Cousens?] to dole out flour &c for labours that *never can* be commensurate with the help given.[17]

Willway's attitude ran counter to the Mission's policy. Both Willway and Grenfell had publicly advocated encouraging destitute settlers to remain where they were rather than adopt the Canadian practice of relocating them further south. In Grenfell's view, it was better to improve people's lives than place them arbitrarily somewhere else. But Willway had asked public officials the previous fall to take people away. The Hudson's Bay Company, which had allowed their stores to be used for keeping provisions and honoured orders signed by Willway, was growing impatient. By 1901 it would refuse to honour relief orders it did not benefit from directly.[18] These difficulties were compounded by the high price of provisions. Willway continued:

I see that one of HM Gunboats visited Sop's Arm last fall and made an official report to Governor Murray about the shameful prices charged for inferior flour &c and the low starvation point prices given for labour. The old fox published it. Good for him, say I. Couldn't we have a warship that would for a few days leave lobsters & larceny alone and come and look at how we live? Let them visit Cartwright & Rigolet & Red Bay &c & instead of Exchanging Compliments with 'the powers that be' let them collect the evidence of the people themselves and then let the light of public opinion shine in on Molasses darkly sold for 70 & 80¢ a gallon, tea (such tea!) at 75¢ a pound, pork at Klondike prices. Where is the fault? What is the remedy, God knows. I can't see my way through it.

Unable to point the finger of blame directly, he attributed the state of affairs to general economic conditions, the general urgency to make money. What stirred him most was the well-known cycle of corruption in the colony itself. He went on:

Dishonesty eats like a canker into every class out here. The fisherman cheats, the planter cheats, the trader cheats, the merchant cheats until one's head is in a whirl & one wonders can good ever come out of such a mass of corruption. I am getting into such a state that there are some men whom I hate to hear pray because I know that their lives don't square with their talk. I know it isn't only in Labrador that this phenomenon is to be observed, and I dare say that in three months (when you get this) this letter will read as a rather incoherent utterance but never mind. I know your sympathies are more than with me in this endeavour to find an end by which to unravel the present tangle. One thing is certain. Government relief must be suppressed as far as possible and we want to shake ourselves clear as much as we can of the flour & molasses trade.

Willway did not suggest abandoning the starving. Rather, he was interested in finding ways of encouraging their independence, especially through co-operatives. At this low point in his life he knew he lacked the vigour to throw himself wholeheartedly into the gargantuan task of changing how business was done. He also knew that Grenfell possessed an abundance of such energy.

For the rest of the winter, in addition to his duties as superintendent, Grenfell followed closely the special requirements of the new Mission vessel, to be named *Strathcona,* which was an unusually large construction project for the yard of Philip & Sons. The *Strathcona* had grown to ninety-seven feet over all and eighteen feet abeam with a displacement of 130 tons. Her up-to-date machinery could produce 150 horsepower and a speed of nine knots. The upper deck was fitted with a wheelhouse, a charthouse, and a steam winch convenient for hauling off wrecks and groundings. Below, besides the usual crew accommodation and a saloon that could be transformed into a mission hall, there were spaces for a dispensary and a hospital equipped with specially contrived swinging cots and x-ray appara-tus – perhaps the first of this kind to be so mounted for use at sea.[19] She would be launched on 27 June and christened by the wife of Captain A.G. Curzon-Howe, RN, formerly commodore of the Newfoundland station.

Grenfell decided he wanted the honour of taking the *Strathcona* to Labrador under his own command, and when he submitted his Labrador report to the hospital committee for 1898 he pressed for it. On the grounds of experience, his proposal conveyed considerable weight, even though he lacked the requisite papers. He argued:

I am anxious to go master of her, it will save in money and I feel myself perfectly competent. I have worked the [astral] sights three years in the 'Albert' on the way to America and I have tested my work on the North Sea since. When you realize we send a vessel to Iceland under a man like White, and when you realize many much larger steamers go every day all over the North Sea, all over the Bay of Biscay, all round Shetland, Rockall and Iceland, I can see absolutely no danger whatever to the Society in making over the boat to me for the voyage, if that formality is required.[20]

The committee, chaired by Treves, remained unmoved by his certainty and deferred their decision until they had confirmed their insurance position as well as their status under the regulations of the Board of Trade. They then conveyed their objection to the council.[21] Since Grenfell's Board of Trade certificate as master mariner authorized him to sail only a yacht he owned himself, they would have been obliged to register the *Strathcona* under his name. And, in fact, Grenfell liked the idea. He especially liked the flexibility of such an arrangement, and later that year he pursued the matter with the Finance Committee, arguing that registering *Strathcona* as a yacht would reduce costs and lower the registered tonnage. Moreover, the 'incidental difficulties which crop up with the Board of Trade regulations' could frequently be avoided.[22] To the council, however, any such advantages appeared slight, and they instructed the secretary to register the vessel under the Merchant Shipping Act. Before it sailed the following summer, they brought over a qualified captain and crew from Newfoundland.

While the Mission remained preoccupied with these arrangements, its expanding overseas interests required firmer leadership and stronger public representation than ever before. In June 1899, when Aspland arrived in St John's on his way north, he became aware of serious public criticism aimed at the Mission by the Roman Catholic bishop of St John's, M.F. Howley. Howley, an ardent Newfoundland nationalist with a taste for stepping into political issues, had involved himself in the controversy over a railway contract the government had signed with the Canadian contractor R.G. Reid for the construction of a Newfoundland railway that would open up new territories for exploration and development.[23] During a lecture tour of Canada and the United States, Howley had castigated the government for the generous terms accorded Reid and described the contract as an unconscionable sell-out to a monopolist. He also took the opportunity to criticize the work of the Mission to Deep Sea Fishermen in Labrador and reveal for the first time the dissonance created by the Mission's portrayal of Newfoundland life. Asked by the *Ottawa Free Press* to comment on whether the conflict between ritualism and evangelism in the English church had spread to Newfoundland, he dismissed the work being done. 'The Grenfell mission to Labrador and Newfoundland is regarded with tolerant amusement by well-informed Newfoundlanders,' he said. 'The idea is good, but the mission is uncalled for and the enterprise is looked upon as an innocent fetish upon which to squander misdirected religious enthusiasm.'[24]

By the time Aspland arrived in St John's, Grenfell's supporters had already taken issue with Howley's remarks. Moses Harvey, eager to play down the missionary dimension of the work, had written in his fortnightly submission to the *Montreal Gazette*, 'Dr. Grenfell is accustomed on Sundays and occasionally on week days to hold simple religious services at which short addresses are delivered, hymns sung, and prayers offered; but he has never been charged with any proselytizing efforts or any sectarian utterances, or any interference with the creeds of others. Only those who choose attend such meetings. Surely there should be nothing offensive to any one in such services, which do not at all form the main object of the mission, and are only incidental thereto.'[25] Aspland, though he recognized the tense sectarian rivalry in St John's, was himself amazed that the annual treatment of twenty-five hundred patients over the last seven years should be reduced to these terms. In a reply published in the *Evening Herald*, he played down the Mission's evangelism. 'Medical assistance is our primary object,' he wrote defensively, 'and added to it under suitable circumstances – christian work for body and soul.'[26] This statement of priorities suggested a significant change of attitude. In the early years on the coast, Grenfell had ranked evangelism as high as his medical work, sometimes higher. Even with the increased medical and social demands imposed, he himself had never suggested that the priorities had been reversed.

For several weeks, while the controversy continued in the sensationalist and abusive Newfoundland newspapers, there was strong support for Grenfell personally. 'No doubt to the Clerical mind the Doctor's fad about religion and his work as a lay preacher are very objectionable,' wrote 'Catholic,' taking into account the dissatisfaction of the Church of England clergy. 'Cannot they overlook his little peculiarities and eccentricities in this respect in view of his noble philanthropy and his increasing and most successful efforts in the cause of humanity[?]' 'True Catholic' disagreed. 'The Mission is entirely sectarian and is deeply interested in the voluntary distribution of religious literature along the coast,' he replied.[27] Such acrimony and misinformation, displayed in the subsequent correspondence, prompted a further reply from Aspland later that summer, when he attempted to answer some of the charges by citing the surgical treatment accorded Roman Catholic patients and the access provided to priests. 'I have been very earnestly trying to discover why our Roman Catholic friends have suddenly taken such a dislike to us; yet cannot believe it possible,' he wrote.[28] But such ingenuousness convinced no one, and when the exchange concluded, public perceptions about the nature of the Mission's work did not disappear with it. The increase in the Mission's activities in Labrador, each year growing more independent of the St John's interests, had aroused suspicion. A strong voice was needed to speak on the Mission's behalf.

In Labrador, while the controversy continued, events had not progressed as Willway had planned. To begin with, he had lost the use of the *Sir Donald* after taking the hull to Battle Harbour the previous summer to serve as a dispensary. At the end of the season he had moored her in Assizes Harbour, a land-locked inlet that should have served as a safe haven for the winter. But when the ice went out in the spring, it tore the vessel from her moorings, dragged her through the entrance, and bore her into the Strait of Belle Isle, where the Newfoundland sealing fleet encountered her moving slowly south, covered with snow and surrounded by whitecoat seals.[29] Towed to St John's, the derelict was sold at auction, and part of the proceeds were lost to salvage. Then, early in July 1899, the Mission received an urgent telegram from Willway, announcing that he would have to bring his wife home immediately. Mrs Willway, despite her husband's ministrations, had continued sick throughout the winter even though she had exhibited no signs of disease. Willway was convinced she had suffered a nervous breakdown and hoped that a shift to familiar surroundings would restore her health. After placing Aspland in charge of the Battle Harbour hospital with the *Princess May* and leaving his other assistant, Dr Sharples, in charge of Indian Harbour with the *Julia Sheridan*, he departed with his wife for England, where she underwent surgery but did not regain her previous health (she died in 1902). Willway now asked the Mission to send out Grenfell to replace him. So now, unexpectedly, Grenfell had a reason for going back to sea and saving himself from another year of fund-raising and routine administration.

By 9 September he was sailing to Tilt Cove aboard a steamer of the Cape Copper Company, leaving Willway in charge of the increasing demands of the work in England.[30] But he planned to return to England in the spring to make the first overseas voyage of the *Strathcona* after Willway had spent the winter with the vessel on deputation work. To salvage what he could of the remaining time, he planned to make a final trip around the coast in the *Julia Sheridan* and then walk to Quebec, visiting settlements along the way and continuing on with a lecture tour of the major centres. Once he had reckoned the distance involved, however, he abandoned this plan in favour of walking across the ice in the Strait of Belle Isle in February and linking up with the closest point on the new railway.

But he soon saw the folly of this plan too. Instead, he resolved to spend the time putting up a new building in St Anthony as a permanent winter hospital to answer the needs of people on the French Shore, the western Newfoundland coast on which the French had been granted fishing rights by the Treaty of Utrecht (1713). Arriving there in November, just before freeze-up, he left the *Julia Sheridan* frozen fast and spent his first and only winter in Newfoundland travelling by snowshoe, ski, and dogsled. All of this was accomplished without visiting St John's. Yet Grenfell did not neglect to convey these developments to the capital, and in a letter to Moses Harvey he outlined his plans. Even so, he realized he could not depend on others to display his achievements in the right light. He would have to take charge of his own public relations.

Without any formal decision having been taken on the subject by the council, the Mission now in effect opened up a new branch on the Great

Northern Peninsula, an area more densely populated than the Labrador coast. During the winter of 1899–1900 Grenfell set up his medical head-quarters in St Anthony at the house of Frederick Moore, financed to some extent by the Newfoundland government, while A.J. Beattie, a Scot he had known at Oxford, started teaching twenty children in the empty schoolhouse. Grenfell also exercised his office as a lay reader with a licence from Bishop Jones (though so far it allowed him to preach only in Labra-dor).[31] He fitted up a room in the unused courthouse where he could give St John Ambulance lectures and started people playing simple board games that many of them had never played before.

With the winter before him, he began his most serious program of cultural intervention yet. On a patch of level ground he had a space cleared and at the new year scheduled outdoor sports, including komatik and snowshoe races, shooting contests, an obstacle course, and a greasy pole contrived from a ship's spar that had been frozen in the ice and mopped over with cod liver oil. The prizes? Half a barrel of flour, twenty pounds of pork, twenty pounds of beef, a coat and trousers, and other precious commodities.[32] And, inevitably, there was football. Grenfell does not say where he procured the football, but he may have been inspired by the winter football played at Loretto. One day he kicked off on his frozen playing field, and a new sporting era began. (The following summer, he distributed six footballs along the Labrador coast, all donated by Mostyn House School.) Amused by the winter conditions imposed upon the game in St Anthony, he wrote, 'It has proved the greatest attraction, and, among other things, both Mr. Beattie at his school to the boys [sic], and in the evening, have been instilling the orthodox rules of Association football into the settlers. The fun is fast and all the more furious when the forwards suddenly disappear out of sight through the crust of the snow, and, perhaps, even funnier when two or three others fall into the hole on the top, and what the people call a "tangle" occurs.'[33] Christmas came and went. At the Mission's Christmas party, ninety-three children crowded into a room with the adults to witness a slide show and the lighting of the tree. A sheet dropped to reveal Santa Claus perched at the top of a ladder, but after Grenfell had discoursed on who exactly he was, only a few children found the courage to come forward and give the costumed figure a kiss. Each child received a present, a doll or a furry cap, and many experienced the fun of Christmas for the first time.

In the course of the winter, living in only one Newfoundland commu-nity, Grenfell made notes about how life could be improved. He was becoming expert at handling dogs and komatiks but regretted the absence of reindeer, the versatile northern animals capable of pulling the sledge but also feeding themselves and providing milk. Presented with the opportunity to make extensive observations, he regretted there was no hospital on the coast and no sources of income for the inhabitants. There were women producing mats and other craft items at home, but no one to market them. There was plenty of fish, but no co-operative store such as the one in Red Bay. Barratry was commonplace on the coast, but no one could lay charges. Not until the advent of the *Strathcona* did Grenfell begin salvaging wrecks and laying charges on behalf of Lloyd's of London.[34] During his trips to the adjoining communities he discovered an incidence of tuberculosis 'out of all proportion' and considered how he could deal with it. In keeping with current thinking on the transmission of the disease, he thought it might be promoted by 'carbonic acid air' given off in crowded rooms and resolved to issue a tract on the subject. His most spectacular achievement that winter, however, was to harness the voluntary labour of the community to begin a new hospital.

Grenfell spent his thirty-fifth birthday hauling the first pieces of the frame, to be constructed near the harbour of St Anthony. 'I have been given an excellent site,' he wrote, 'shaded, near the wood, flat, with room to graze if necessary, and a good stream running through it all the year round.' He and Beattie had already drawn the plans for the modest structure and reckoned the necessary posts, beams, sills, sleepers, wall pieces, and couples required. Now they organized a gang of about forty volunteers, divided them into five parties and, with two men to cook and a dozen teams of dogs to carry supplies, led a procession into the woods for a week's work. Living in temporary tilts erected that same week, each man was allotted a share of hard bread, pork, butter, and molasses as well as flour for 'dough boys' and peas for soup on 'pork days.' In all, they hauled out by dog team over three hundred pieces, ready for construction at the first thaw.[35]

With his first winter in Newfoundland behind him and his plans taking shape, Grenfell wrote enthusiastically to his brother about the great possibilities for social reform in northern Newfoundland. He wrote in July 1900, 'I expect to go out again & settle possibly in north Nfd for a year or two. I think I can be the means of emancipating the people & the life has great attractions also. I'm going to improve the breed of dogs & introduce new & improved methods – old at home but new here. And I can do this all along the coast.'[36] Already his imagination was reaching far beyond what the Mission had envisaged. That summer the *Strathcona* treated over a thousand patients, and the Mission spent £2,084 to maintain the Labrador branch, barely one-third of which had been paid out of public contributions.[37] With expenses mounting, the council became increasingly cautious and urged more assistance from North America to support the North American branch. The days of the Grenfell Mission were about to begin.

—8—

The Hero Ascendant
1900 – 1905

To the members of the Brown-Harvard expedition to Labrador last summer, this mission was a revelation as to the possibilities of a wisely-conducted, practical philanthropy. It is undoubtedly the most important and promising feature connected with life on the Atlantic side of Newfoundland and Labrador, being an economic and moral force of the greatest significance.

E.B. Delabarre, Report of the
Brown-Harvard Expedition, 1900

On his first tentative visits to New England and New York, Grenfell experienced the concerted power of American philanthropy. He discovered Americans entering the twentieth century with a sense of self-assurance and progressiveness reinforced by the knowledge that the United States remained in the broadest sense a 'Christian' nation with an orderly style of life. These optimistic assumptions of Theodore Roosevelt's generation were rooted in the stability of a white middle class whose religious, government, business, cultural, and intellectual leaders sprang in large measure from Anglo-Saxon and Protestant origins. Many Americans believed that Christian civilization was destined to dominate the world, not militarily but peacefully, and such expectations gave greater force to missionary endeavours at home and overseas.[1] Thus, as Protestant missions pushed abroad through the activities of denominational missionary societies and a variety of non-denominational agencies, their emphasis changed. Missionary work no longer dedicated itself primarily to saving souls but to reforming and improving life as it was found.

In the United States itself the nature of the reforms and the imagination operating behind them are epitomized in the life of Joseph Lee, the so-called father of the American playground. Lee, a Boston brahmin who eschewed personal luxury and extravagance, successfully promoted measures that strengthened community life and individual development rather than social assistance and dependency. In his first book, *Constructive and Preventive Philanthropy* (1902), he drew an analogy between the benefits of constructive social institutions and those of public health, and argued that philanthropy should not consist of the efforts of one class for the benefit of another but of the efforts of all for the benefit of the community. Lee's efforts were directed towards specific social goals, such as strengthening local government, improving education, and cultivating recreation. He encouraged, among other things, systematic saving, building and health laws, model tenements and lodging houses, street cleaning and sanitation, home industries, summer vacation schools of four to eight weeks, kindergartens, playgrounds, public baths, youth clubs, industrial training, gardening, and prohibition. These were the improvements already under way when Grenfell visited the United States.

One other notable progressive, Helen R. Albee, fostered home industries. Mrs Albee argued that American philanthropy, in concentrating upon the needs of the sick and the poor, had neglected the needs of healthy, able-bodied youth in rural districts.[2] She thought the answer lay in 'profitable philanthropy': encouraging hand-made furniture, weaving, and rug-making – the last her special achievement. In rural New Hampshire the hooked rug had been elevated to something of an art form, with fresh materials and original designs that departed radically from conventional American practices. The reputation of the Abnakee rug spread rapidly from the New Hampshire mountains and found outlets in Boston and Philadelphia. But Mrs Albee was quite clear about how the industry should be developed by philanthropy. While home industries served as useful occupational therapy, she thought, to pay their way they required gifted people with a marked aptitude and means of continuing while the industry developed.

Perhaps the most dramatic instrument of social reform, however, was the settlement movement, an optimistic scheme to establish houses in slums and immigrant neighbourhoods, staffed by middle-class volunteers, to attack problems arising from insufficient housing, unemployment, and ignorance. The settlement houses, principally in Boston, New York, and Chicago, grew into imaginative combinations of the neighbourhood centre, homemaking class, school, housing office, and employment bureau. They had their origins in the religious settlements begun in the East End of London by Charles Kingsley and F.D. Maurice at the very time Grenfell was a medical student.[3] Thus, the early American settlement houses were founded by individuals with strong religious and social convictions –

people like Jane Addams, the founder of Hull House in Chicago – who believed that social reform should be entrusted to the 'better element' in American society, the educated and enlightened upper middle class whose duty it was to mediate between the upper and lower classes and thus secure stability and progress.[4]

The overwhelming proportion of workers drawn to the settlement idea were church members – active Congregationalists, Presbyterians, Baptists, Episcopalians, and Methodists with a sense of mission arising out of their Calvinist upbringing. Of these, a substantial number possessed theological training. Others were writers attracted to the settlements as a source for muckraking and realistic fiction. Still others served for short periods to advance their own careers or hung on while they decided upon which course to take in life. And there were those who simply found the life interesting and stimulating, young men and women of comfortable family backgrounds in no hurry to earn a living but happy to operate at the leading edge of social reform. The early success of such institutions attracted the interest of churches, training schools, and missions, and in time the term 'settlement' lost something of its significance.[5] The idea had lent itself to wide adaptation, and its central value had entered into the activities of many different institutions. Though settlements existed in Europe and Asia, the largest number existed in the United States, where they had been adapted for rural communities.

The American reformer who influenced Grenfell most directly at the turn of the century was Lyman Abbott (1835–1922), a Congregational clergyman whose social conscience had been aroused during the Civil War by the anti-slavery position of Henry Ward Beecher. A self-styled progressive, he once described himself as 'an evolutionist, but not a Darwinian; a Liberal, but not an Agnostic; an Antislavery man, but not an Abolitionist; a temperance man, but not a Prohibitionist.'[6] Though not a socialist either, he believed that social reform involved a new recognition of the partnership between labour and capital. When Grenfell's cause attracted his attention, it was Abbott who promoted it in the United States. Abbott succeeded Beecher as pastor of Plymouth Congregational Church, Brooklyn, and assisted him with the editorship of the *Christian Union* (later the *Outlook*), a weekly magazine he took over in 1881 and edited until 1922. Under Abbott's direction, the *Outlook* became the great popularizing vehicle of liberal Christianity. It subsequently acquired a following as an influential forum for reformist ideas, advancing the platform of the Progressive party and the candidacy of Theodore Roosevelt. By 1902 it had reached a circulation of one hundred thousand, and it exceeded that figure for the next twenty years.[7]

The *Outlook* also advocated a broad concept of Christianity. Theologically, Abbott himself represented the Progressive Orthodoxy movement, a liberal entity pioneered by Horace Bushnell to challenge the traditional Calvinist doctrines of salvation and judgment within the Congregational church.[8] He also took a broad view of the authority of Scripture, and as a 'theistic evolutionist' he propagated an interpretation of Darwinism acceptable to orthodox Protestants. Politically, he espoused American expansionism. He once wrote: 'Without these three elements, law, commerce, and education, no community is civilized or prosperous, no community has liberty or justice. It is the function of the Anglo-Saxon race to confer these gifts of civilization, through law, commerce, and education, on the uncivilized people of the world.'[9] At home he supported Roosevelt's progressive Republicanism in the presidential elections of 1904, 1907, and 1912, and when Roosevelt left office after his second term Abbott invited him to join the *Outlook* as a contributing editor. Grenfell once wrote Abbott, 'I do not think, as far as theology goes, there can be a pin of difference between your views and my own.'[10]

Throughout 1901 and 1902 the council of the RNMDSF authorized Grenfell to make deputation tours of Canada and the United States during the winter. While these tours attracted some interest in parishes and schools, the cause did not attract the attention of the public at large until the winter of 1903. That year, beginning early in February, Grenfell worked his way through Nova Scotia, New Brunswick, Quebec, and southern Ontario, then Boston and Chicago. In Ottawa he met one of his most useful Canadian allies, William Lyon Mackenzie King, deputy minister of the new Department of Labour and editor of the *Labour Gazette*. As an idealistic young Christian and social reformer, King had worked with Jane Addams for two months at Hull House in 1896–7 and understood the possibilities for social change in an urban setting. He immediately recognized Grenfell as a kindred spirit and counted their meeting as 'one of the most fortunate happenings' that had come his way for many years.[11] Impressed with Grenfell's new co-operatives and his other imaginative reforming ventures, he described them in an anonymous article in the *Labour Gazette*.[12] He introduced Grenfell to handball, and the two became friends. He would open doors to the Canadian bureaucracy that Grenfell could never have opened himself. King also formed with two of his contemporaries from the University of Toronto, Reginald Daly and Norman Duncan, an influential trio. Daly, whom Grenfell met during a Harvard expedition to the Labrador coast in 1900,[13] assisted the cause while serving with the Geological Survey of Canada and joined the New England Grenfell Association when he later became professor of physical geology at the Massachusetts Institute of Technology. Duncan pursued a reputation in muckraking journalism and the literature of local colour in the United

States and 'discovered' both Newfoundland and Grenfell for American readers.

After delivering a succession of addresses in Boston, Grenfell next attracted the attention of Edwin D. Mead, the reformer, anti-monopolist, and social gospeller. As editor of the *New England Magazine*, Mead was known as a strong progressive. He was also president of the Twentieth Century Club, a collection of the leading liberal intellectuals in Boston, and after Grenfell addressed the club he wrote, 'Few people have ever spoken at the Twentieth Century Club who have taken warmer hold of our people. Here is missionaryism of the sort that we all believe in.'[14] Once Grenfell reached New York in mid-April, however, he found his true audience. This time, the scheduling of his meetings and lectures was handled by Abbott's son, Ernest Hamlin Abbott, who provided him with an office at 287 Fourth Avenue. Grenfell reported, 'I don't think I have ever been busier in my life than here in New York. For the necessity of trying to keep pace with my engagements made it necessary for a stenographer to come to my room at 5:30 that I might dictate till breakfast, while the lectures seldom let me home before midnight.'[15]

The lectures on Labrador also kindled the interest of the newspapers. After a short article appeared in the *Sun*, reporters started to arrive at the office from the *Herald*, the *Telegram*, the *Tribune*, and the *Times*, all of which printed illustrated articles. In the *Times* interview Grenfell demonstrated how well he understood his American audience, for he carefully distanced himself from the traditional missionary. Instead of converting people, he insisted, he was interested in 'hewing rough material' into attractive individuals, using the influence of sea life, his medicine chest, and a Bible to change the way people lived. Once again he returned to his romantic image of a noble aristocracy of the sea. Working in deep water, he explained, brings those like the Labrador fisherman an unconscious refinement composed of the balanced temperament, poise, and bearing of a man who has found himself and knows the environment in which life has placed him. He did not apologize for their station in life but admitted that developing these traits constituted the most attractive phase of his work. 'They have in the first place an utter indifference to danger that covers a multitude of sins,' he said, 'and the waves and the wind have toned them down and refined their character.'[16] Thus, the 'civilizing' influence of simplicity remained an important element of his promotion and later served as a counter to those who would recommend moving the population to more settled districts.[17]

There was more. Grenfell himself was suddenly recreated in the popular press as a saintly figure. The Reverend William Forbush's *Pomiuk: A Prince of Labrador* (1903), a children's book about an Inuit boy who had been exhibited at the Chicago World's Fair and who later died at Battle Harbour Hospital, portrayed Grenfell as his saviour. Other articles appeared in magazines such as the *Christian Herald*, the *Missionary Review of the World*, and *Youth's Companion*. But it was Lyman Abbott's word that counted most. With his endorsement in *Outlook*, the myth of the heroic, adventurous Labrador doctor was launched. 'This surgeon-mariner, unconventional missionary, rugged, enterprising, modest, so forgetful of self that he would be likely to resent being termed unselfish, adventurous, brave, indefatigable, is Dr. Wilfred T. Grenfell,' wrote Abbott in an editorial. Listing Grenfell's accomplishments over the previous decade, he concluded: 'If there is any better preaching of the Gospel of Christ in the world than this we do not know it.'[18] In the same number Abbott printed Grenfell's own account of his life to date, emphasizing the victory over the copers in the North Sea and the initiatives in Labrador.[19] This piece was later printed separately and distributed as a pamphlet entitled 'A Bit of Autobiography,' providing the model for numerous lectures and articles to come.

In other ways, however, Grenfell felt the burden of raising funds. The Mission had ended the previous year in debt, and its auditors urgently pointed to the dangers of over-extension. In five years it had opened premises in eight new locations in Britain, and the rapid expansion had drained its assets, which in property and investments amounted to approximately £55,000. If it were to keep control of its finances, it would need to keep a more careful and continuous watch over its diverse activities. In 1902, when Grenfell opened a New York account at Brown's Bank in his own name, the finance committee ordered him to add the words 'Superintendent of the R.N.M.D.S.F.' and to treat it as a strict Mission account. The following year they ordered the Labrador accounts audited locally twice a year and the statements sent back to London.[20]

The council encountered another difficulty. With the growth of the Labrador branch, Grenfell now spent most of the year in North America, leaving Willway to look after changing conditions in Britain without the full authority to do so. What they needed was a full-time superintendent, and that spring, they named Willway 'Co-superintendent' so as to maintain continuity. Grenfell was getting increasingly out of touch with the Mission's primary task, so that Willway in effect became superintendent.[21] (Willway would dedicate the rest of his life to the RNMDSF. He later became its secretary and did not retire until 1937.) By recognizing the distinction between the two branches of the work, the council undoubtedly wished to set its finances in order. But by so doing, it also hastened the formation of a separate organization in the United States.

In 1904, with a new hospital in operation in St Anthony, the funds dedicated to Labrador increased to $20,000 a year, and the council refused to send another doctor there for the summer. To further cut costs, they withdrew the *Julia Sheridan* from service. By now, the three hospitals and the *Strathcona* treated nearly three thousand patients annually, and the personal strain on Grenfell was increasing. When not raising money, he piloted the *Strathcona* up and down the Labrador coast, sometimes tending to patients, sometimes acting as magistrate and investigating wrecks for insurers. In St Anthony he rapidly developed a headquarters at the new hospital and started a sawmill and a fox farm. Willway added to the medical returns this summary of Grenfell's other activities:

> Dr. Grenfell is captain of his ship, Lloyd's surveyor, wreck commissioner, peripatetic magistrate, and poor law commissioner, as well as evangelist and missionary, from the Straits of Belle Isle to the Hudson Straits. In his leisure (!) he botanises, makes charts (not always wise to follow them implicitly), hunts and fishes for the sake of his larder, carries on a voluminous correspondence, much of which is written on odd fragments of paper, and engages in literary work. I think it would be well inside the mark to say he is often actively at work eighteen hours out of the twenty-four. Work, too, that is frequently of a very exhausting character.[22]

But regardless of how much energy he put into the work, Grenfell had reached an impasse. Without more money he would have to cut back his medical services. The Mission had now operated in Newfoundland for twelve years, yet so far it had not received the grant long promised by the Newfoundland government. Furthermore, his new St John's committee had failed to maintain public interest and stir up local politicians. After spending a disappointing week in St John's to begin the summer's work, he turned to his London connections for assistance. In a letter exhibiting an uncharacteristic tone of despair, he laid his troubles at the doorstep of Sir Francis Hopwood, now permanent secretary of the Board of Trade and well positioned to influence others. Having failed to move the Newfoundland prime minister, Sir Robert Bond, he asked Hopwood to speak to the new governor, Sir William MacGregor.

Grenfell pursued the government grant with greater confidence in 1904, perhaps because the colony had enjoyed a period of unaccustomed economic success. The expansion of the timber and mining industries, combined with increased catches and high prices in foreign markets, had swelled the government treasury, so that in fact Bond was operating from year to year with a surplus. The same year Bond negotiated an Anglo-French convention that gave Newfoundland undisputed possession of the French Shore. By influencing the governor, Grenfell hoped he could impress upon Bond the urgent need of government money. He wrote to Hopwood:

> Would you see the new Governor for us & put the matter to him. I don't come out here for pleasure. I do not *mind* the isolation, but I do very much mind the financial responsibility. We now raise a large sum in Canada, & a larger sum in the States. The interest there is *growing* rapidly: we have *never had one American visiting Labrador* who has not gone away intending to help us, but they come slowly, & I do not intend to spend every holiday I get in future going round everywhere with a hat, though I am as ever prepared to do a reasonable share because I love these fishermen. *They are [easily] the best material our Anglo-Saxon blood is capable of.* But the Mission now orders me to sell our second steamer as she costs us £100 a year!! & we are to shut down one of our hospitals!![23]

Convinced that indifference had prevented his St John's committee from pressing the government sooner, he prompted them to prepare a case for submission.

Hopwood, who had once seriously considered taking on the governorship of Newfoundland himself, failed to reach MacGregor but wrote him a strong letter urging payment of the grant and mentioned the matter to Bond, who had come to see him in London. In this manner he continued to use his office to promote Grenfell's schemes. But Grenfell could not have been prepared for Hopwood's attitude to the future of the Labrador branch. As an officer of the Mission, Hopwood had closely watched the work drain its resources, and now he expressed his doubts, as well as those of Treves. He wrote:

> As Treves said in a letter to me recently & I quite concur it is extremely doubtful whether you ought to continue this laborious work however interesting; I allude especially to the hard necessity of sending round the hat. I am disposed to think that we must seriously discuss matters in the spring if we have not got a grant by then & if necessary consult Sir Fredk. as to how we can best put pressure on the Colonial Government. If all is well I shall be delighted to go into the whole subject with you on your return.[24]

At this critical stage of his work Grenfell was not heartened by the reservations of his two chief patrons; nor was he cheered when MacGregor told him he doubted the government would act.[25] By the time he returned to St John's that summer, however, MacGregor did report progress and suggested he was pressing Bond to accompany him on a trip to Labrador the following year.[26] At the end of 1904 the Newfoundland government did indeed vote the annual grant of $1,500, and the St John's merchants once again undertook to raise the same amount. This news encouraged Grenfell, but it made the council less comfortable about the future of their activities overseas. At their first meeting in the new year they considered for the first time handing over the entire Labrador work to a joint Canadian-American committee. Meanwhile, they dispatched the secretary, Francis H. Wood, to St John's to appoint a finance committee and explain the Mission's accounting system.

Gratified to some extent by the American help, the council recognized that the rapid expansion in Boston and New York would eventually deny them control. Indeed, as time went on they realized that the Labrador work was being identified more and more with Grenfell himself rather than with the RNMDSF.[27] A Grenfell association had now sprung up in Boston, administered by Miss Emma White, and in Toronto the indefatigable Miss Julia Greenshields had started a quarterly magazine, *Among the Deep Sea Fishers*, that published Grenfell's high-minded preachments, articles reprinted from *Toilers of the Deep*, and lists of donors. That year Grenfell's second book, *The Harvest of the Sea*, a summary of the Mission's activities narrated from a fisherman's point of view, was published in New York by Fleming H. Revell. Now into his fortieth year, Grenfell was receiving continual attention from journalists as a strong moral presence advocating social change.

With the possible exception of Lyman Abbott, the writer who contributed the most to Grenfell's transformation into a figure worthy of American attention was Norman Duncan, the friend of Mackenzie King. When the yachtsman George Durgin ran into Duncan on the Labrador coast during the summer of 1903, Duncan was on his way north aboard the *Strathcona*, making notes for a proposed novel. 'He [Duncan] is the same dreamer I had pictured when I finished his first story,' Durgin wrote. 'His face is an open page to his sensitive, highly strung nature, and it was easy to understand his ability actually to feel the sad and futile strivings, the disappointments, the pathos of the Newfoundland life.'[28] After reading an article Duncan had prepared for *Harper's*, Edgar Briggs, managing director of Fleming H. Revell, assured Grenfell, 'I can safely promise you that when published it will do more good for your Mission than any one single literary effort that has thus far been made.'[29] And it did. The readers of *Harper's* suddenly learned from Duncan of a 'well-born, Oxford-bred young Englishmen' whom he admired unreservedly. In his idealization of Grenfell, whom he had grown to know during his summer voyages to northern Newfoundland, Duncan wrote: 'The doctor is very far from being a daredevil; though he is, to be sure, a man altogether unafraid; it seems to me that his heart can never have known the throb of fear. Perhaps that is in part because he has a blessed lack of imagination, in part, perhaps, because he has a body as sound as ever God gave to a man, and has used it as a man should; but it is chiefly because of his simple and splendid faith that he is an instrument in God's hands – God's to do with as He will, as he would say.'[30]

By the time he made his next tour of the United States in 1905, Grenfell admitted that Duncan's books were 'the most helpful agencies' he had acquired, bringing in large audiences. However, he thought Briggs and Duncan had taken advantage of him, for he had given them information as well as the use of his photographs with the understanding that the royalties would go to the Mission. None of them ever had.[31]

The same sense of admiration permeated Mary Bourchier's children's book *The Wandering Twins* (1904) and Duncan's personal tribute, *Dr. Grenfell's Parish: The Deep Sea Fishermen* (1905). In this latter volume, which leaned heavily on his series of Labrador articles, Duncan allowed himself to become an instrument of Grenfell's intense publicity. 'Dr. Grenfell is indefatigable, devoted, heroic,' he wrote; 'he is more and even better than that – he is a sane and efficient worker. Frankly, the author believes that the reader would do a good deed by contributing to the maintenance and development of the doctor's beneficent undertakings; and regrets that the man and his work are presented in this inadequate way and by so incapable a hand.'[32] That same year, during Grenfell's lecturing tour of New York and Boston, Abbott published a full-page portrait of him in *Outlook* and an admiring editorial.

Grenfell received greater attention than ever before in New York when he spoke at churches, clubs, and social settlements. A story carried on the front page of the *New York Times* revealed that about $60,000 [*sic*] had been contributed in the larger cities and that Andrew Carnegie had donated money for loan libraries on the Labrador coast. More significantly, it reported Grenfell's first experiment with the social settlement idea. Two young professional women of the type attracted to the settlement movement had volunteered to go to Labrador at their own expense to work with fishermen's wives and teach girls to weave. Miss Isabel Harris was said to be 'independently wealthy.' She had done settlement work for several years and was connected with the Episcopal church. Miss Clara Koonz had worked with the Tenement House Commission and was regarded as an 'expert' in the industrial system. Clearly, Grenfell had the settlement model in mind when he told the *New York Times*, 'Both Miss Harris and Miss Koonz propose to aid our work by helping the wives of the deep-sea fishermen to help themselves. They will establish at the various stations along the coast what you call here Settlements.'[33] For this purpose, he had purchased the necessary looms, and the two women added to the trickle of American students arriving on the coast as a consequence of Grenfell's appeal for volunteers.

At a dinner in his honour attended by New York ministers and educators and chaired by Dr Henry Van Dyke, Presbyterian and poet, a New York Grenfell Association was formed. Van Dyke was elected president, Ernest Hamlin Abbott secretary, and Eugene Delano of Brown Brothers Bank treasurer. Later the directors would attract such genteel, like-minded men as Stephen Baker, president of the Bank of Manhattan; William deWitt Hyde, president of Bowdoin College; Hamilton W. Maybie, associate editor of *Outlook*; William R. Moody, son of the evangelist; and Francis Lynde Stetson, a prominent lawyer identified with the Morgan interests. These men, some of whom were close friends,[34] assumed responsibility for the Battle Harbour hospital and in their first year of operation collected $12,596.[35] They also placed upon the enterprise the unmistakable stamp of Fifth Avenue liberalism.

The day following the dinner, the *Times* carried a story about Grenfell's address at the Majestic Theatre, showing why he was arousing what it called 'widespread interest and support.' Besides relating the history of the Mission to date, Grenfell, in his customary fashion, showed slides illustrating life on the Labrador coast. Said the *Times*, 'Various episodes of hospital life were shown on the stereopticon, with incidents in the everyday life of the natives at sea and ashore. The picture of a barefooted little girl, poorly clad, and standing in the snow, gave the audience an idea of the poverty which had to be combatted.'[36] Such scenes undoubtedly impressed the New York audience, but their constant exhibition represented Newfoundland and Labrador as a squalid part of the world that wanted only the sympathy of more fortunate Americans to bring it closer to the mainstream of North American culture. The persistent image began to haunt the businessmen and government officials of Newfoundland, and before long their protests would be heard.

Meanwhile, reports of Grenfell's activities on the coast came back from the summer visitors who observed him at first hand. Grenfell had found it necessary in the beginning to make a rule restricting summer visitors to the three hospitals, but the council could not help seeing that this rule had been observed by everyone but him. During the summer of 1905, they noted, there had been an unusual influx of distinguished doctors, teachers, and curious sightseers, people like William R. Moody, invited north to observe the work going on. Moody, for example, gave his American readers a selective view of Grenfell's varied roles highlighted by this picture of the *Strathcona*:

> The chart room of the *Strathcona* is in itself suggestive of Dr. Grenfell's varied ministries. One of the first objects one's eyes rest upon is a row of dentist's forceps that are in frequent use. In the corner are gun cases and boxes of shells, for the Doctor is a keen sportsman and it is due to his prowess that

his larder is well stored with game. Upon a shelf are his books most in use, among which I noticed, in strange association, 'The Justice's Manual,' Denney's 'Death of Christ,' 'The Other Side of the Lantern' by Sir Frederick Treves, 'St. Paul' by Frederick Myers, 'The Diseases of Children,' and 'The Castaway' by F.B. Meyer. Interspersed with these were scientific works and surgical treatises with unpronounceable names, while medical journals and religious publications filled a rack on one side.[37]

A more detached view was presented by the Reverend Edward Moore, a Harvard professor of theology and history who accompanied Grenfell that summer and observed his idiosyncrasies daily. Moore, who was assigned no specific duties himself, was highly sympathetic to the cause but constantly reminded, during the daily demands on Grenfell's time, of the inadequacy of the staff and funds. He soon concluded that Grenfell needed most of all someone to superintend the numerous projects going on ashore and keep things moving during his frequent absences.

First, there was the *Strathcona*. She was obviously too small. Despite Grenfell's ability to respond to many of the demands placed upon her, Moore observed that life aboard carried on in a state of confusion, partly because Grenfell refused to suffer details and partly because the crew could not cope with the inefficiency. His portrait of the crew, together with the assembled livestock, is reminiscent of Defoe. The crew, including Grenfell's 'secretary,' G.A.A. Jones, a Harvard student, consisted of the following:

> Jones whom Grenfell took for his [Jones's] sake rather than for the help which he himself so much needs. A funny old white-haired Englishman for cook who delights to say 'we seamen' though I doubt if he has ever been outside of the galley. A skipper much tried by Grenfell's unaccountable doings and the uncertainties which attend all his movements. Two engineers and two seamen beside a cabin boy. Two grown dogs, a collie and a retriever, three pups, two of which are the retriever's own and one an Esquimau komatik dog which she is willing to suckle with her own, and three little fox pups for the fox-farm, which Grenfell picked up a few days back from a schooner. They had been put in a blubber-cask and their coats are still very sticky. But they play with the pups and are very tame and very amusing. This menagerie is all over the deck, falls down the companionway, is always having its feet or its tail trodden upon and yelping for pain when not yelling for food.[38]

After a week of this, Moore could not tolerate the accumulated filth covering the decks, for in addition to the crew and animals the *Strathcona* carried a variety of cargo. He added, 'She carries everything, fire-wood, coal, lumber, all on her decks, beside freight of every description. And the crew is too small for what is expected of them. Grenfell does not care in the least for any thinkable form of discomfort. And I like that. I can stand that, too. But I never saw an Englishman who was so indifferent to dirt.'[39]

During the summer of 1905 Moore witnessed the visit of Governor MacGregor. Making good his promise to visit Labrador, MacGregor proceeded along the coast by naval vessel as far north as Nain, giving public speeches to the assembled Inuit and the Moravian missionaries with solemn assurances of the sovereign's continuing interest in their welfare.[40] In St Anthony he caught Grenfell by surprise and provoked a thorough but unceremonious tour of the station. Moore recalled:

Grenfell put about, landed at once – so did the governor – took him on a tour of inspection of every blessed thing, hospital, house, library, dispensary, laundry, school, not a living soul except the poor servants out of bed – imagine the feelings of the American ladies, governors arriving while they were in bed, four or five drawling young Englishmen at his heels – 'Well, I say, now, by Jove, rather fine, this, old boy,' etc., fifty Esquimau dogs at their heels, packing boxes everywhere, looms half set up, in the parlor, reed organ taken to pieces by one of the Penn boys and not yet got together again, coal all over our decks just as the men knocked off the night before, one of the little foxes washed through a hawse-hole in the two inch stream from the hose wherewith we were trying to trim the ship while the governor visited the ladies ...[41]

Not only did the governor surprise Grenfell, who was counting on him to influence the Newfoundland government, but also the two zealous New York ladies, who had revealed their ignorance about weaving. They quarrelled violently. After a short stay, they went north to collect furs, and the so-called weaving industry stood temporarily in disarray.[42] Moore continued his ministrations and observed what was delicately called Grenfell's 'impatience' as a navigator.

The Newfoundland fisheries vessel *Faiona* was steaming north with the minister of marine and fisheries embarked so as to pick up the governor on his way south, and Grenfell hoped to impress upon the minister the need for accurate charts and navigational aids along the Labrador coast. Off Cape Harrigan the pilot engaged by the *Faiona* abruptly declared that his contract had run out and that anyway his competence as a pilot did not extend beyond that point. Grenfell was obliged to go aboard and take responsibility on the strength of his local knowledge, not knowing that the *Strathcona's* accustomed route was not satisfactory for the larger *Faiona*, which generally steamed to seaward of the numerous islands and inlets. Once under way, he simply followed in the *Strathcona's* wake, proceeding along an inside passage, and as he attempted to pass he bantered with the crew about their sluggish pace. A humiliating experience followed. Moore noted, 'Just before the group of huts which constitute the Hudson's Bay Station were reached she ('The Faiona') veered from the course and went hard aground. She was going nine knots an hour and rammed the shoal in great shape, ran high up at the bow and then the bow settled off into deeper water, but she remained hanging about amid ships. Fortunately, it was only sand or mud, though there were rocks all round. And fortunately the tide was nearly half down.'[43] As the vessel settled into a list, the passengers and crew were required to stay on board overnight, sleeping at an angle, before the tide lifted them off. For the next ten days, as they proceeded north again, the minister of marine fretted about his vessel's safety and made Grenfell's enforced presence miserable.

Despite this demonstration of Grenfell's navigational powers, Moore marvelled at the almost universal respect he had earned among the population, a respect borne out by the ritual repeated time after time whenever he entered a harbour. As soon as Grenfell came in sight, dories and punts would emerge from every hand, and men would grasp the lines arranged every six or eight feet along the rail, sometimes securing their painters to a stanchion before the anchor hit the water. Once the sick and the poor had come on board, it was impossible to say when Grenfell could get under way again, and thus he seldom arrived anywhere at the expected time. This ritual had also been observed by George Durgin, who wrote, 'I have been witness to his infinite patience, for when his steamer drops anchor all the inhabitants for miles about flock to her deck. Everyone has an ailment or trouble; all are listened to; something is done for each. I wouldn't be surprised if sometimes a healthy but complaining man gets a bread pill, but he departs satisfied.'[44] But once Moore reached St John's, he also learned of the growing opposition to Grenfell's personal involvement with his co-operatives. Part of the St John's traders applauded the way in which he had given fishermen a degree of independence and respectability. Others insisted that a missionary ought to keep trade at arm's length. The uneasy alliance between philanthropy and commerce was bound to be troublesome sooner or later. That autumn their animosity found a vent in the St John's press.

Late in November 1905 the *Trade Review*, a weekly commercial paper, published a petty, mischievous editorial charging Grenfell with illicit trading. Since the Mission was permitted to import used clothing duty free, it had always left itself vulnerable to the misapprehension that it sold clothing at a reduced price, thereby undercutting traders who had operated on the coast for years. To make matters worse, Grenfell had recently been promised a government grant of $1,500, and the grant was now construed as a means of enhancing his profit at public expense. The *Review* charged:

> Last season the nominal value of the goods coming in this category was $2,714, tho what the actual value was no man knoweth. As far as can be learned, these values the Customs' authorities take the Doctor's word for, and the goods are passed thro without further examination. If the Doctor were a dishonest man (and we do not say that he is), the actual value of the goods might be $10,000, instead of two. If these goods were given away for charitable purposes, there would not be much to object to, but, when they come into competition with goods of the trader, who has to pay from 40 to 50 per cent. duty, it is a different matter.[45]

At the same time the efficacy of the Mission's work was called into question. Citing recent statistics, the editorial showed that the death rate had doubled in Labrador since the Mission's arrival. Adopting a nationalistic stance, it took up the cry of M.F. Howley (now archbishop) and objected to the need for 'itinerant, self-dubbed philanthropists' to exploit the poverty and misery of the colony and make a name for themselves.

But a week later the *Trade Review* was forced to print a retraction. Pressed by one set of St John's interests, it had not bothered to investigate the matter thoroughly. Its offices had been besieged with letters and telephone calls from another group, the outraged supporters of the Mission, some of them merchants. After a meeting with his committee, Grenfell sought a retraction and, threatening a libel suit, retained the services of Sir Edward Morris, the minister of justice.[46] The *Trade Review* now hastened to interview Grenfell, who speculated that the false reports probably arose because he had interfered with the long-standing practices of trading in illicit liquor and barratry. In the face of this opposition, the paper admitted it had been misinformed, made a full *amende honorable,* and promised to send a reporter to Labrador to investigate the matter at first hand.[47] Unfortunately, the whole matter of mixing trade with missionary work did not rest there.

On 4 December Grenfell addressed a large gathering of supporters to which Governor MacGregor lent his support as chairman and, departing from his usual extemporaneous style, took the trouble to defend what had been construed as trading practices over the past thirteen years. Instead of attacking his accusers directly, he laid down an axiom for interpreting what the Mission was trying to do and went to the heart of the matter. 'The axiom is simply this,' he said, 'that there are people living in this Twentieth Century whose conception of success in life does not involve the size of their money-bags.'[48] There were those who had volunteered to work in Labrador, he continued, some without any pay at all. As for his own involvement in financing trading ventures, he acknowledged, 'Most severe criticisms of late if not merely malicious have arisen simply from a wrong conception or interpretation of the real object of our ventures more especially in productive and distributive co-operation.' For these he took full responsibility and accepted any blame attached to them. But he also explained at length the other methods being applied to relieve poverty and hunger: the housing of orphans, the exacting of work for used clothing, the opening of five co-operatives, and the opening of a sawmill that had put him personally in debt. In defence of what had seemed to some a futile act, he said, 'Surely it can only be shallow and sordid minds that have contended that to invest money without any desire for pecuniary returns is the act of a fool. For the fact that such investments in their higher issues can never be really lost, alone stamps them as a gift.'

He also mentioned the most recent innovations in St Anthony: a bait freezer, an industrial building for woodwork, a circulating library. But since the criticisms had rested on the handling of money, he took pains to mention how these other ventures were financed. At that point, the annual cost of medical and social activities amounted to $20,000, only $1,000 of which was collected in St John's, for the government grant had still not been paid. 'Over $3,000 has been contributed in Canada during the year,' he said, 'and over $10,000 in the United States, exclusive of special gifts for the new hospital, library work, etc.' Finally there were the student volunteers. Each year more volunteers from American universities were appearing on the coast eager to help. These, he suggested, ought to have inspired young Newfoundlanders to do the same, but so far they had not.

If Grenfell had temporarily cleared up the matter of trade, the whisperings about outside interference continued. The next morning, in a letter to the anti-Bond and pro-confederate *Daily News*, Archbishop Howley again took up the nationalist complaint against cultural intervention, describing the Mission as a 'mistaken Charity' and a 'positive evil.'[49] Recalling the Wakeham report eleven years earlier, he repeated the charge that the Mission pauperized the people and demanded that Grenfell abandon his trading interests. And quoting from the annual report of the registrar general, he repeated the claim that over the past four years the death rate in Labrador had doubled. On the strength of this outburst, the next week there followed an exchange of petty accusations between the *News*, managed by H.A. Morine, and the *Evening Herald*, edited by P.T. McGrath, each attempting to discredit the other.

On 11 December Howley published a second letter, this time advancing the nationalist argument against the Mission. Now he took issue with the substance of Grenfell's lecture and challenged the idea that the Mission operated solely as a charity. But he reserved his third letter, two days later, for what appeared to trouble him most: the way in which Grenfell's publicity had degraded his countrymen. Without doubt, Grenfell's slides depicted life as it was lived in the north and in Labrador and ignored the more comfortable and respectable life lived in St John's. The slides were realistic, Howley, conceded, but heavily weighted to create an impression of need. 'These views are indeed taken from life, but that does not prevent them from being veritable and most offensive caricatures ... These pictures, taken from the very lowest and poorest of our people's homes, are highly colored by an exaggerated verbal description, and the impression left upon the mind of the hearers is that such is the general and normal state of our people.'[50]

To balance these impressions, he took great pains to assemble contemporary accounts of the wretchedness and misery experienced in the East End of London and the mining and industrial towns of the north of England, and he urged Grenfell to seek an outlet for his zeal there. 'I maintain then that this whole Grenfell business is a huge mistake and an indignity to us as a Country and a Government,' he concluded.

In his final letter, Howley answered the claims of Grenfell's lecture. He acknowledged Grenfell's open admission of personally investing in trading ventures even though he received no profit, but he urged him to cease. If Grenfell continued to trade, he urged, he should give up any privileges not accorded to other traders. As for his acknowledged role as a missionary, Howley objected strongly to the implied assertion that the religious denominations neglected their people in Labrador. As one who had served his time in the smaller communities, he wrote, 'I do not object to Dr. Grenfell's preaching (I don't know what he preaches), what I object to is making such a *fuss* about it.' Missionaries of all denominations worked quietly among the people, he observed, yet they had never thought of themselves as heroic. Speaking on behalf of them all, he repudiated the implication that they neglected their work.

Howley's attack constituted the fullest response to Grenfell so far, and it drew forth a flurry of letters and editorials defending him, for Howley had put the case strongly and broken through Grenfell's composure. (In a private letter to Mackenzie King, Grenfell referred to Howley as a 'mean, sordid, bigotted prelate' aided by the rum sellers and barrators.)[51] As a Newfoundlander, Howley had defended Newfoundland's dignity and pride well enough, but he had chosen his evidence a little too carefully, suppressing other important details without acknowledging that the Mission's work answered a need. Unfortunately, Grenfell had now reached a point where he was treading a fine line between the classical missionary and the social reformer, expecting to succeed in both roles at once. While he had done nothing wrong, he had perhaps expanded his influence beyond what he was competent to do and cast doubt upon the integrity of the Mission. In the new year, the Mission's hospital committee considered the matter in light of the unfavourable publicity and decided that trading operations were 'inexpedient' for the Mission's purposes. It then recommended they be discontinued.[52]

No matter how weighted Howley's remarks, the exchange revealed an uncomfortable truth. Regardless of the good the Mission accomplished in the northern parts of the colony, there existed in St John's a body of political opinion opposing its presence on cultural as well as economic grounds. The St John's establishment was highly resistant to change, and its economic growth was not matched by a sense of social responsibility, for when the Fishermen's Protective Union rose at the turn of the century under William F. Coaker, bent on political revolution, the merchant community and Howley opposed it.[53] Grenfell had lately been the subject of eulogy in the British, American, and Canadian press, and the international attention had brought the difficulties in Newfoundland into the open for international scrutiny. Clearly, Howley's remarks bore some merit. Unlike the Mission in the United Kingdom, still advancing the cause of deep sea fishermen, the North American branch had involved itself in a variety of schemes that looked like social reform. By now Grenfell's aspirations had departed substantially from those of the parent body. In the years to come, leading up to the First World War, his American organization prospered, but his relationship with the London offices, though cordial, would grow even more tenuous.

—9—

Grand Almoner
1905 – 1908

*Some people once asked me what were the essentials for life with the
Grenfell Mission. I told them: a sense of humor, a good digestion and
love of one's fellow men. After several years of pioneer work and
four summers wandering along the coast of Labrador, I would add:
patience, powers of adjustment, and resignation.*

Jessie Luther, 'Mission to Labrador'

In December 1906, as Grenfell brought the *Strathcona* alongside one of
the wooden wharves that used to fringe the harbour of St John's, he secured
it to one of the enormous bollards, then stood back and regarded its
condition as he reflected upon a year of extraordinary activity. A glance at
the superstructure revealed not the smart new acquisition of 1900 but
the tired remnant of five years grinding through uncharted waters. The
topmasts, sacrificed during a recent gale, lay below, the rigging stripped
and stowed. The mainmasts, normally weathered and salted, now bore
the additional grime deposited from the stack, and the varnished housing,
peeled by long exposure to sleet and spume, had assumed the colour of
skimmed milk. Two feet above the railing, the woodwork, exposed to
deckloads of raw pine recently hauled out of the woods and transported to
the hospitals for the winter, had been scraped bare. The sleek black sides,
assaulted daily by innumerable fishing boats, had acquired the mottled
look of frosted glass, and the harbour murk concealed a multitude of
scrapes, gouges, and dents exacted by the still unnamed and uncharted
hazards of the Labrador coast. What remained of the large blue Mission
flag drooped from a temporary gaff lashed into the large topgallant iron.

Grenfell did not observe these details regretfully. Rather, they reminded him of how far he had taken his scheme to reform the north since his last visit to St John's. The changes brought about in Labrador during the year had succeeded largely through the growing network of support created in Canada and the United States, gradually making him more independent of the council. This now presented the council with a dilemma: should it give up control of a valuable and highly visible organization for which it was still legally responsible, or should it hand over control to those in North America better placed to finance and staff it? From the time of Willway's appointment as superintendent, the council had tacitly though not formally accepted the inevitable: except for visits to the United Kingdom to lecture or attend meetings, Grenfell would occupy himself as master of the *Strathcona* during the summer and raise funds during the winter. But if the council thought the overseas branch would settle into an established pattern, they had underestimated Grenfell's desire to reform. He wanted to do more.

After laying up the *Strathcona* for the winter of 1906–7, he wrote the council, urging the secretary, Francis Wood, to attend a conference that would define the legal position of the New York branch and its capacity to handle the money it received. Pressed by these events, the finance committee entertained a question it had never before contemplated, namely the possible transfer of the Labrador work to one of the overseas auxiliaries.[1] Wood raised the matter during his visit, but the New York committee resisted. For the moment, it merely wished to be incorporated as an association so that it could legally receive legacies or property as gifts. Wood, however, recognized the growing influence of the New York committee. Soon the Boston auxiliary would incorporate itself as the New England Grenfell Association, to be followed by the Southern Grenfell Association (Baltimore), the Grenfell Association of Chicago, and the Grenfell Association of Buffalo. On his return to London he told the council that American support would surely increase and predicted that all the money required for the Labrador work would issue eventually from American hands.[2]

In the summer of 1905 the London office realized that Grenfell planned to expand when he again approached the Canadian government for a grant to build a hospital at Harrington Harbour, situated on the southern part of the coast and well into Quebec territory. By this time he was more experienced with governments and could count on the influence of Reginald Daly and Mackenzie King. Having secured the gift of $5,000 towards the construction of a small hospital from the philanthropists Mary and Jessie Dow, daughters of an eminent Montreal brewer,[3] he next pursued an annual maintenance grant of $2,000 from Ottawa and the same duty-free privileges the Mission enjoyed in Newfoundland. Meanwhile, he convinced Dr Mather Hare, a Halifax surgeon two years his senior with seven years' missionary experience at the Canadian Methodist Mission in West China, to start the new hospital and sent him to Harrington.[4]

Hare soon reported that the able-bodied men in the community were prepared to haul out the sills, construct the foundation, and guarantee a supply of firewood annually if Grenfell could wire 'Proceed with the hospital.'[5] But the finance committee, unsure of the level of American sympathy, refused to entertain this new initiative unless Grenfell could produce $2,000 of the $5,000 they estimated such a hospital would cost annually. King strenuously lobbied both sides of the House of Commons for the grant, and Grenfell wrote the Montreal committee, asking them to wire 'Go ahead' if they could arrange it. Without waiting for a reply, he then took a gamble. He ordered Hare to proceed with construction, promising to pay for the work himself if the maintenance money miscarried and assured him he could move his family up the following August.[6] (So eager was he to start the new hospital that he subsequently offered to pay some of Hare's expenses out of his own pocket.)[7] By the time Grenfell arrived in Battle Harbour, a telegram from Montreal awaited him. 'Proceed with hospital,' it said; 'money forthcoming.' This was indeed lucky, for the Laurier government had already rejected the idea, refusing to set a precedent by funding a charity from parliamentary estimates. That winter the wood was cut and sent to Harrington by schooner, ready for construction the following spring. By that time, as he put it, Grenfell was 'fagged out' and clearly indicated that he wanted Hare to look after himself. In the summer of 1906 Hare received his first hospital patients under makeshift conditions. The new hospital did not open until January 1908.

Despite Grenfell's success, the episode exposed the lingering animosity in the Department of Marine and Fisheries, where Commander Wakeham remained in charge of the coastal services. Wakeham supported the new hospital in practical ways, and he remained friendly with Dr Hare. But he was still troubled by the notion of paying for a charity, and he influenced the thinking of his deputy minister, Colonel Gourdeau.[8] Both men had been appointed under the previous Conservative regime. Liberal members had asked several times for Wakeham's dismissal without success, and this had made ministers such as Sir Frederick Borden, the minister of militia and defence, all the more determined to prevent him standing in Grenfell's way.[9] But King, who Grenfell thought stood by him 'like a brother,' also knew such matters could not be forced. Though he professed a high regard for Grenfell, he recognized his impulsiveness and advised caution. Despite the delay, King felt confident that the cabinet would give its approval in due time. Meanwhile, he advised Grenfell to have the proposal resubmitted through the people actually living in Harrington.

The following year, after the death of the minister of marine and fisheries, King began to agitate again by approaching the prime minister through the sympathetic leader of the opposition, R.L. Borden, and the equally sympathetic governor general, Earl Grey, for he thought the extra $2,000 could be turned to good advantage. 'If it does nothing other than enable you to do the work on a larger scale, and gives what prestige there may be in Government recognition, it is worth fighting for,' he wrote.[10]

Grenfell made a second attempt to set up a modified social centre on the settlement house model in 1906, when he acquired the services of Jessie Luther, a Rhode Island artist who was also a qualified crafts instructor. Miss Luther was a disciple of Jane Addams, having directed the Labour Museum at Hull House, which contained an elaborate display of weaving and other textile techniques from around the world. She had also taught the crafts Grenfell had in mind. As a pioneer in the field of occupational therapy, she had since moved to the Butler Hospital in Providence but now took time off to assist Grenfell. During the summer she set to work to begin a wood-carving class in St Anthony and ordered the materials for basketry and dyeing. Most important, through correspondence with Helen Albee and her rug-making manual, she set up the idle looms and began classes in weaving and mat-making.[11] Grenfell was delighted with the progress during one of his stopovers. Miss Luther observed, 'He is looking very well, rather heavier than when I saw him a year ago, and with a young beard which changes him somewhat. I was impressed, more than ever, by his strength and manliness.'[12] Grenfell, who was growing enthusiastic about home industries, showed her how he had fashioned the clay found beneath the topsoil into flower pots, dried them on the kitchen stove, and baked them so that they had come out looking like terracotta. He wanted her to come back and start a pottery class the next summer.

In her journal Jessie Luther gives the impression that she had maintained a close rapport with Grenfell that year and that Grenfell had confided in her the nature of his changing role. She summed up the dilemma this way: 'It evidently troubles the Doctor that he is obliged during several months of the year, to go about "with hat in hand" for Mission funds. Apparently the English Mission office wants him to give a year to evangelical work, but he wants to be *doing* instead of preaching, and seeing him, one can understand his point of view. I cannot imagine him an orthodox evangelist; his influence and appeal are through action, sincerity, and example rather than exhortation.'[13] On a visit to Providence the next winter, Grenfell discussed another option with her: the possibility of making jewellery from native copper and from Labradorite, a variety of feldspar that flashed blue when polished. He also wanted to make brick to replace the hazardous stovepipes in use. Thus, through Grenfell's lectures and her own overtures, she subsequently acquired a potter's wheel and material for a kiln. She also sought out a one-man brickyard in Cape Cod and learned the process of brick-making. Grenfell was so enthusiastic about developing 'fireside' industries like those already successful in the United States that he approached the superintendent of the Butler Hospital and arranged a year's leave of absence for Miss Luther so that she could work in St Anthony. With her arrival, Grenfell's latest vision, the 'industrial department,' set up shop.

Passing through Massachusetts, he paid a call upon another kindred spirit, the Reverend Endicott Peabody, headmaster of Groton School. Peabody, a few years older than Grenfell, shared the same manly assumptions, for he had been educated in England at Cheltenham and developed a love of athletics. At Trinity College, Cambridge, he had read the life of Charles Kingsley, whose vigour and enthusiasm had inspired him to devote his life to correcting social problems.[14] A committed anglophile, Peabody had created at Groton a happy admixture of the British and American boarding school systems. He had also been moved by the ideas of Benjamin Kidd (1858–1916), whose particular strain of social Darwinism appealed to certain Americans at the turn of the century. Kidd defended religion as a race-preserving force, and Peabody was especially interested in his theory that the Anglo-Saxon race should predominate 'for the good of the world.'[15] Grenfell and Peabody admired each other's accomplishments and remained friends. On this tour Grenfell sent the headmaster a copy of William DeWitt Hyde's book *The Art of Optimism as Taught by Robert Browning* (1900) because, as he put it, it suited his own temperament admirably.[16]

The recognition of Grenfell's accomplishments in the United States continued in other ways. That same year he published two books of reminiscences, *Off the Rocks* and *Northern Neighbours*, the former with an introduction by his New York president, Henry Van Dyke. And his organization acquired a more formal shape. With New York promoting Battle Harbour and the summer station at Indian Harbour (Dr E.R. Mumford), Toronto looked after St Anthony (Dr George Simpson), including its growing orphanage and industrial work. With the work of the major hospitals in hand, the Montreal committee was left free to concentrate on the new hospital situated in Harrington. But in Britain the recognition of Grenfell's fourteen years of toil was manifested in a different way. In the king's birthday honours list for 1906 Edward VII named Grenfell a companion of the Order of St Michael and St George, the honour conferred on the strength of a recommendation from Earl Grey, as Mackenzie King revealed.[17] King, who had made it his business to cultivate Grey and provide him with details of the Mission's accomplishments, had undoubtedly promoted the idea himself. Indeed, he was gratified to think that Grey and Grenfell shared a similar outlook.

During the winter of 1906–7, with all this falling into place, Grenfell set aside four months for touring the United States. He visited hospitals for briefings on up-to-date treatments and came away with his pockets bulging with new instruments. He received from the Dutch Reformed Church the money for a new launch to serve St Anthony. He was brought by Lyman Abbott to have lunch with President Roosevelt at the White House. He maintained a bewilderingly arduous speaking schedule, speaking over two hundred times under a variety of circumstances. As he reported wryly to the Mission, 'During these months I have had chances to speak alike in universities, public schools, and kindergartens – to men, women, and children; in churches and Sunday schools of many denominations; in social clubs and before scientific societies; in public halls and in private houses; at opera houses and in operating theatres; at breakfasts, luncheons, and dinners; at paid meetings, at free meetings, and by special invitations; with lanterns and without them. No form of opportunity seems to have been denied me. I have given formal talks and informal talks, and what some would call "talky" talks.'[18]

One important source he failed to win over for a large grant, however, was the Rockefeller Foundation. Beginning in 1907, Grenfell made representations to John D. Rockefeller, Jr, but although the Rockefeller Foundation admired Grenfell personally it shied away from an organization that depended for its existence on the personal appeal of one man. The Labrador mission, it noted, lacked the supervision and management of a missionary society whose history tended to create a feeling of confidence.[19] Nevertheless, Grenfell's personal charisma attracted other interests. Miss Greenshields marvelled in particular at the enthusiasm of audiences in Toronto. 'No place is large enough for those who want to hear him,' she told Mackenzie King, 'the Massey Hall being for once in its history – inadequate! I feel sure all this means increased financial help, and we must go to work to secure its continuance while the impression of Dr. Grenfell's personality is deep.'[20]

As he lectured that year, an even grander scheme was developing in his mind. For some time he had noted the success of his counterpart in Alaska, Dr Sheldon Jackson, a Presbyterian missionary who had successfully introduced reindeer as the 'camels' of the north.[21] These animals, Grenfell thought, would provide the perfect replacement for the vicious sled dog, often a threat to man and beast. A single reindeer could draw a load of three hundred pounds up to a hundred miles a day and thus accomplish the work of a whole team of dogs. At the same time a herd could supply meat and milk as well as skins. As Governor MacGregor confirmed the previous summer, the species could subsist on the Labrador lichens, which were strikingly similar to those found in northern Europe. 'Labrador seems to be so favourably suited for this animal that the introduction of the domestic reindeer there would hardly partake of the nature of an experiment,' MacGregor observed.[22] A group of Boston supporters, led by William Howell Reed, had already started a subscription list for a reindeer fund, and it had grown to $8,500.

Grenfell wrote to Earl Grey apprising him of a Canadian scheme modelled on the Alaskan initiative, thinking it would assist the native population and attract settlers. The Inuit and Innu population of Labrador and Hudson Bay, he pointed out, had decreased with the gradual reduction of their traditional food supplies. Knowing Grey's imperial sentiments and his eagerness to bring Newfoundland and Labrador into confederation with Canada, he also emphasized the political benefits. He suggested to the governor general that 'the introduction of these deer would seem to me to be an important step in imperial policy. For I can conceive of no reason why, with attention paid to this department of work, and possibly to some experimental farms destined not only for Northern Canada, but for Northern Labrador and the Northern Hudson Bay country, these now un-settled regions might not be settled, and the policing of Fullerton and Baffin's Land and North Chesterfield Inlet become at once more than matters of sentiment merely.'[23] He then requested an interview to discuss how to finance the transportation. King's efforts and Grey's intercessions began to show results that spring when the Canadian cabinet unanimously approved a grant of $5,000 and urged the minister of agriculture, Sidney Fisher, to do anything he could to help.[24]

In view of subsequent events, the precise terms of the agreement signed by Grenfell and the minister require some consideration.[25] The grant made provision for a herd of reindeer to be imported to the *Canadian* portion of Labrador. Grenfell was appointed as the herd's agent or trustee, charged with the responsibility of transporting the animals and distributing them among the residents. But since he had undertaken to do this voluntarily, he was not strictly liable for the grant or for the disposal of the animals, only for making a report of his activities. At the end of April 1907, as he boarded the *Oceanic* for England to visit his mother and receive his CMG, he intended to present his reindeer scheme to the Mission.

At the Mission's crowded annual meeting in May, Treves took the chair, accompanied by L.P. Brodeur, the new Canadian minister of marine and fisheries. Treves's strong speech on Grenfell's behalf, encouraged by the king's recognition, eclipsed any doubts about his sympathy and the Mission's support. Treves took full credit for introducing Grenfell to the Mission in the first place, praising the way Grenfell had looked after the medical needs of people overseas and given them self-respect through mercantile ventures and education. But he also wanted to encourage the Mission's interest for the future. He said: 'The schemes he has now are curious in their scope, extending from the introduction of reindeer, on the one hand, to making teapots out of native clay on the other.' And mindful of recent criticism about the Mission stepping outside its primary role, he argued that it ought to continue its work even though the business of social reform seemed to fall within the purview of the colonial government. Governments operate officially, he argued. They do not possess sympathy or sentiment. What comes from the Mission comes from the hearts of English people. As a recent example of this distinction, he cited the work of Florence Nightingale during the Crimean War. 'The whole essence of her work lay in the fact that it was voluntary, spontaneous, and actuated by no single thought but kindness, tenderness of heart, and sympathy,' he said. 'And the work Dr. Grenfell has done for Labrador is, in certain of its phases, very much like the work that Florence Nightingale did at Scutari.' He then asked for the work to continue in Labrador just as it continued in the North Sea.

When Grenfell rose himself, he spoke with the confidence of a man whose name was now recognized in the capitals of the North Atlantic, one with a private vision of improving a small corner of the empire. Labrador was not a dreary place in which to live, he maintained, but a better place to live than the Dogger Bank. Returning again to his cherished Darwinian theme, he reminded the gathering that the best things are bred out of hard circumstances, not on peaceful southern islands. 'You are going to get them out of the very same circumstances that produced a Drake, a Frobisher, and a Hawkins, and the great men who made the history of the sixteenth century, and who gave this great country of ours its open Bible and its maritime supremacy, and that which makes nations great,' he said. He recalled being asked in Boston why he had not used his money to move the Newfoundlanders and Labradorians to a more welcoming place rather than try to improve their present conditions (a question asked by economic reformers before and since). The present solution, he had responded, was no more futile than spending millions on a temple 'to worship a crazy woman [Mary Baker Eddy] – as the Christian Scientists are doing.' Instead, he had advocated encouraging positive racial qualities – the 'stable equilibrium' required of people who survived in the north. He told the meeting:

> We want to cultivate those hardy qualities which made the Vikings of old. If you walk down the Strand you have not much trouble in telling a deep sea fisherman if you see one; he does not walk as if he had anything to be ashamed of. I believe it was Herbert Spencer who said that the physical qualities of a nation go a very long way towards making that nation great. 'Mens sana in

corpore sano.' We say that and then we forget the splendid body of men we
have on the deep sea.

The speech was interrupted time after time by applause. Though not gifted
as an orator, Grenfell had seized upon an idea with broad appeal. For the
moment he did not need to fear whether or not the Mission would stand
behind him.[26]

Before the month was over he received more public recognition. Oxford
made him an honorary doctor of medicine, the first such degree the university had ever conferred. He acquired the convocation robes of scarlet box
cloth and carmine silk for this occasion and journeyed back to the university he had last left so precipitately. And now, accompanied by his cousin
Professor Bernard Grenfell as his sponsor, he proceeded solemnly to the
ceremony and heard himself praised by the orator as a truly Christian hero
walking in the footsteps of Christ himself. Three days later, on 31 May,
he was brought by Treves to an audience with Edward VII, who handed
him the insignia of the Order of St Michael and St George and talked
enthusiastically about Newfoundland and Labrador, the 'splendid seafaring genius' of the people, and the American assistance pouring in. The
next day he was hailed in the *Pall Mall Gazette* as one of those who leave
their mark on their generation.

With $13,500 in hand, he now convinced the council to support his
most daring reform to date, the introduction of a herd of three hundred
domesticated Norwegian reindeer, fifty of which Lord Northcliffe had
agreed to purchase for his Newfoundland lumber camps. But once again,
when the plans were ready he left the details to others. Returning to North
America, he placed total responsibility for engaging herders and chartering
a specially adapted vessel in the hands of the Mission secretary, Francis
Wood, who was prepared to take on the responsibility but not to carry
through with the details. Wood soon found, however, that the fund would
not allow him to employ an expert to superintend the shipment. He would
have to go himself to northern Norway and negotiate a contract to purchase
the deer and a quantity of moss for the voyage. He would also have to
engage four Lapland families to go out as herders (though he knew nothing
about herding) and purchase ten herding dogs.[27] Even before the project
began, it had acquired that distinctively Grenfellian air of amateurism.

After a summer in the *Strathcona*, Grenfell exhausted himself with a
lecturing tour of Canada and the United States to swell the reindeer fund
and encourage university volunteers. Reginald Daly, now a professor at
MIT, reported excitedly to King:

We had Grenfell here for two nights, he had large crowds at Harvard and Tech
and has secured much money. I attended my first meeting of the board of

directors for the New Eng. Grenfell association and was much interested in
the way men like Carroll D. Wright [labour commissioner and President of
Clark College], William Brewster [distinguished ornithologist], Prof. Moore
of Harvard, as well as a number of Commonwealth Ave. millionaires were
taking hold of the work. Grenfell is a power in this land. It is my ambition to
get a half million out of the 80 millions Mrs. [Margaret] Sage wants to give
away and I mean to try for it as an endowment for Grenfell. He needs it, for
this life is slowly wearing him out.[28]

At the time, the Sage millions were being incorporated into the Russell
Sage Foundation, inaugurated in 1907. In fact, the foundation did become
interested in social reforms of this kind, but Daly was not successful. Mrs.
Sage subsequently donated $5,000 towards the construction of Grenfell's
seamen's institute in St John's but not the substantial grant desired.[29]
Meanwhile, despite his anxiety about the reindeer, Grenfell could not get
back to St Anthony until January 1908, too late for the herd's arrival.

He had left the Mission's affairs at St Anthony in the hands of a dedicated
group. With a need for more room to accommodate his expanding staff,
he had bought a small house near the hospital, adding several rooms and
a glass-enclosed porch. This dwelling, known as the Guest House, he
intended as a residence for those not living in the hospital or the orphanage
as well as a home for himself.[30] Here he kept a study with his books,
writing table, chairs, and rugs and displayed his athletic trophies, silver
tea service and plate in the dining room. Another small room he and the
male staff had taken over as a gentlemanly 'gun room,' where they kept
their sporting equipment, cleaned their firearms, developed photographs,
and smoked after dinner with a touch of that eternal boyishness that did
not appear out of place in an outpost like St Anthony. Besides Grenfell,
there were five principal occupants, whose varying careers offered sufficient
dramatic interest for an Edwardian novel.

First, there was Jessie Luther, the mother of the group, the organizer,
interior designer, sometime cook, mender of clothes, supervisor of the two
maids, and teacher of crafts. A graduate of the Rhode Island School of
Design, she was accomplished in metal work and enamelling, wood carving and carpentry, basketry, leather tooling, book-binding, weaving, pottery
and associated arts, including tailoring. It was her task to introduce these
skills to the population and to some extent offset their dependency on the
fishery. Five years older than Grenfell, she respected him enormously but
took a detached, ironic view of his boyish, erratic behaviour.

Then there was Dr John M. Little, Jr, thirty-two years old, a Boston
surgeon who had accompanied Grenfell aboard the *Strathcona* the previous
summer. The son of a real estate tycoon from the Back Bay, Little had

served in Boston as something of a 'society' doctor and now sought some higher purpose in life. Attracted by the stimulation of useful work, he had volunteered to stay the winter at his own expense, and he wrote long letters to his parents, detailing his cases and his new-found utility. A keen outdoorsman, singer, and *bon viveur*, he amused himself by composing entertaining verse and proved to be archly companionable. With Dr Arthur Wakefield, he once came to a Hallowe'en party dressed as a nurse with a snowy kerchief folded neatly across a substantial 'bosom.' On that occasion, wrote Mrs Wakefield, the deportment of the two was fastidious, but 'Nurse Little showd a decided tendency to "toe-in" and Nurse Wakefield evinced a deplorable penchant for the society of the men-folk!'[31] Together with his pursuit of fun, however, Little did all the major surgery in the St Anthony hospital.

The compleat Boston gentleman, he possessed the forthright manner and confidence provided by an established merchant family.[32] His grandfather had died a millionaire in 1880, and his father, who had built Boston's first extensive office building, the Little Building, had married into a family of Boston bankers. But Little was not simply passing time. He was also a gifted surgeon who had graduated from the Harvard Medical School in 1901 and, after a year's study in Vienna, finished with a surgical residency at the Massachusetts General Hospital, where for five years he served as assistant to Dr Samuel Mixter. 'His exceeding skill and great experience as an operating surgeon up to date, has been invaluable, not only to your medical officers at the various hospitals, but also to many of the patients that have come into our hands,' Grenfell told the London office.[33] Intelligent and perceptive, Little identified what he thought was Grenfell's major weakness, his management of finances. 'Dr. G. is not careful about such things, having too many irons in the fire to enable him to give attention to details, tho' he makes the mistake often of trying to,' he observed.[34]

There were three other inhabitants, all genteel individuals importing their attitudes and skills into the north. Miss Ruth Keese, a young schoolteacher from Ashburnham, Massachusetts, who had come to introduce kindergarten methods, was descended from a family of clerics. Admired for her sparkling personality, she nevertheless suffered from deafness. She would marry Little in 1911. Then there was Cuthbert C. Lee, a husky young Philadelphian of seventeen with a keen sense of humour and a gift for mimicry. Lee planned to enter Harvard, but for the time being he had been sent by his father to mature. He now performed general maintenance duties and helped out at the school.[35]

The most complex personality of the group, however, was Lieutenant William G. Lindsay, formerly an officer of the Fifth (Irish) Volunteer Battalion and a veteran of the Transvaal campaign. Lindsay was heir to a family estate in Cork, but for the time being he lived off an allowance from his widowed mother and spent his time abroad seeking useful things to do. He had reportedly been engaged for fifteen years to a woman whose father forbade the marriage until Lindsay could become financially independent. After testing himself as an officer in the Boer War, he had lately entered into a business venture in the United States that had failed. At the suggestion of a friend, he then decided to offer his services to Grenfell without knowing exactly what Grenfell did or where he did it. The previous summer, when he climbed aboard the *Strathcona*, he surprised even Grenfell, who suspected he was a criminal at large. (There was nothing unusual in this, for volunteers, especially nurses, occasionally showed up in St Anthony on the strength of what they had read about the place.) Once Lindsay produced membership cards from several reputable British clubs, however, his services were accepted. He was later put in charge of the peat bog project and subsequently given overall supervision of the reindeer, even though Miss Luther did not think he was well prepared for the animals. 'When one considers the importance of the reindeer venture and its widespread publicity,' she wrote, 'it is really appalling; arrangements are so vague and so dependent on conditions, that nothing can be definitely planned.'[36]

As the winter set in, the group took measures against the anticipated monotony and kept matters on a formal but friendly level befitting genteel mixed company. They edited a chronicle of daily incidents and laughed heartily over the barbs embedded in the personal items, bits of advice, and corny doggerel. They held dinner parties, sketched, took photographs, wrote serious articles for the Mission magazine, cut each other's hair, played the phonograph, and occasionally took out a pack of cards, even though card-playing was frowned upon by the local Methodists. They were preoccupied with food simply because their isolation denied them their accustomed fare, and they revelled in the fish and game they could occasionally bring home themselves. But it was the work that sustained them best. 'Those at home, who picture this a long, monotonous winter of drudgery and self-sacrifice (with a halo attached), should know that it is more interesting than any winter life I have experienced, or even imagined,' wrote Jessie Luther.[37] And Grenfell's presence was felt daily. In his absence he had left a bisque figure of the three wise monkeys that sat at the centre of the table.

Christmas Day brought the coastal boat *Portia*, carrying the Harmsworth men who would take fifty reindeer to Lewisporte. Grenfell was not with them. At New Year's they held the annual children's Christmas party. Then, on Sunday, 5 January, the Norwegian steamer *Anita* appeared off the coast after a voyage of twenty-two days. Prevented by the ice from crossing the Strait of Belle Isle, it landed the three hundred reindeer at Crémaillière, two miles south of St Anthony. Despite the long voyage, the beasts had travelled well, and the Mission suddenly had on its hands 250 does, comparatively small creatures about the size of a yearling red deer, and twenty-five bucks the size of an average horse, broken to harness. Besides these, there were twenty-five oxen (unbroken bucks) for breeding.[38]

Equally interesting were the Lapps themselves, an exotic-looking group consisting of three couples and a fourth with two boys. Short in stature with small features, both men and women dressed in deerskin breeches and knee-length coats made from what looked like innumerable scraps. Only their headdress differed. The women wore a close-fitting hood and the men a cap with four stuffed cloth horns. A sheath knife and tobacco pouch hung from their belts, for the men chewed, and both men and women smoked. With them they had brought ten Lapland herding dogs, mostly black and similar in shape to the husky, though smaller.[39] Protective of their reindeer, they had signed a contract to work for two years, during which time they were to train local herders to replace themselves. Lindsay appeared unsure about how to proceed at first, but when Grenfell arrived on the next *Portia*, the pace of life suddenly increased. 'Dr. Grenfell is full of plans of all kinds,' wrote Jessie Luther, 'with sometimes little regard for details.'[40]

From the moment of his arrival Grenfell was preoccupied with adapting the reindeer to local conditions and impatient to demonstrate their usefulness to the population. With a deer harnessed to a sled-like *pulka*, he set out across the countryside with an interpreter and a Lapp familiar with the animals' behaviour. But instead of galloping along, as he expected, he was forced to sit in the *pulka* while the Lapp, on skis, led the deer forward until at length it tangled itself in one of the traces and sank to its neck in the spring snow. Leaving the Lapp behind, Grenfell and his interpreter set off to drive the deer instead of lead it but only succeeded in reaching Englee, where they spent the night. They had travelled nine miles, not sixty as planned. 'The Doctor came in disgusted with the conduct of both Lapps and deer,' Jessie Luther recorded, 'convinced that pulkas are only fit for firewood and that the Lapps know nothing about reindeer.' He later discovered that two of the 'herders' he had left Wood to hire were village Lapps with no herding experience at all.) The next time he harnessed two deer to a komatik and with his interpreter aboard coaxed the animals into a trot. 'We watched them with excitement until they vanished over the hill, a splash of colour on the snow for the Doctor wore a gorgeous costume of white deerskin jacket, blue sash and red cap, grey trousers, high yellow skin boots and black fur mittens,' wrote Jessie.[41]

The Lapps were not the primitives they first appeared, for they capably looked after their own material needs and exhibited a strong business sense. But they did not take to the northern Newfoundland climate, and after the first year one family returned home. A raise in salary kept the other three, and the following year they asked for a further raise. With the government grant withdrawn, Grenfell refused and let them go as well, relying instead on the knowledge of local men.[42] As for the deer, they continued to flourish and increase rapidly. Under the right conditions they could draw a komatik thirty miles a day. Their milk was preserved in rubber-capped bottles, and now there was cheese to add to the local diet. During the busy summer season at the hospital a deer was slaughtered every fortnight. But despite these advantages, at length Grenfell accepted the obvious: the reindeer would never fully replace the sled dog.

Once the Lapps had set up camp, a new difficulty presented itself. The local dogs, as if sensing the presence of rivals, began to attack the deer and in one or two cases devoured them. In his capacity as magistrate, Grenfell now drew up (with the owners' agreement) a set of regulations requiring all the dogs in the community to be tied up, muzzled or clogged, or to be shot. But these measures imposed other difficulties. While the deer were adapting to the countryside, the local people still required their dogs daily for hauling through deep snow, for the long-legged deer found the going difficult and often sank out of sight. Dogs remained indispensable, especially for bringing patients long distances to the hospital. For the first few weeks the experiment did not progress well.

Despite the demands of training deer and running a medical service, Grenfell revelled in the challenge and in spare moments enjoyed the mix of temperaments at the Guest House, adding what Jessie Luther ironically called his 'unusual' personality to the group. Indeed, her journal entries for this period manifest a strong affection for him, tinged with an awareness of his single-mindedness and boyishness. As soon as his trunks arrived, he asked her to help him unpack the assortment of practical and formal wear he had brought with him. 'He pranced around the room in his khaki overalls, flannel shirt and skin boots,' she noted, 'wearing his silk hat to show me how he looked in such an article.'[43] Then he made her dress up in his Oxford doctoral gown. She never failed to notice Grenfell's theatrical side, and Grenfell himself liked her unconventionality and forthrightness, qualities he admired in American women. He had once written his mother, 'I *like* the American girls – i.e. the Christian ones. They are so practical, so full of go & capacity.'[44] But so far, none of them had attracted him strongly enough for him to give up his precious independence. Life was exciting and full of activity. No individual woman was strong or capable enough to distract him from his absorbing task of reforming the north.

At first he forgot about regular meals, preferring to eat at the hospital on the fly. But as time went on he gradually joined in the rhythm of the household. Jessie Luther noted with some satisfaction:

> It is interesting to have him consult me about household matters and he seems to enjoy the whole atmosphere of the house. I see on his face what I call the 'purring' expression which means content. He comes in and takes off his boots by the fire, puts on his felt slippers which he keeps behind the stove, while he talks about patients he has been to see or about some plan he has in mind. He leaves things all over the house and I meekly go around or send the maids to pick up after him without a murmur. That was only at first, however; now that he has settled down I find he likes an orderly house and manner of living as well as the rest of us, and if things are disorderly he notices it. He even changes his coat for dinner at night.[45]

After the evening classes and hospital rounds, the group would gather for cocoa, and the men would sit around and smoke. Little would sometimes play the banjo, and Grenfell would tell stories or read from Kipling until late at night. But he was never completely one of them. He kept himself at a distance. At his birthday party in February, when they each impersonated an important figure he had met on tour, they thought the skylarking had gone too far and encroached on Grenfell's dignity. But he accepted the fun and often got away with some of his own, including his collection of nicknames. Lee, who reminded him of the young David, became 'David.' Lindsay, director of peat excavation, became 'Pete.' Ruth Keese, whose name seemed too serious for her personality, became 'L.M.K.' (Little Miss Keese). In this way he subtly imposed his status on the group. However, Jessie Luther was known behind her back as 'The Missus' and Little was 'Dr. Little.' Grenfell himself was known universally as 'The Doctor.'

For two weeks in February, dressed spectacularly in deerskin and furs, Grenfell and Little carried out a tour of the outlying communities. 'Miss Keese and I feel quite widowed,' wrote Miss Luther, 'and the house does not seem a house at all – only a shelter.'[46] Upon their return, plans began for the annual St Anthony sports and Grenfell contributed his accustomed element of disorder. He had casually mentioned that the participants who had travelled from a distance would be fed, and the response was so great that the visitors had to be accommodated in the sun porch of the Guest House. Otherwise, the sports were a great success. Grenfell had ordered the figure of a running deer cut out at the carpenter's shop and had painted on a head so that the whole apparatus could be drawn across the firing line for the shooting competition. In the afternoon there were races across the snow. Grenfell entertained the assembly by performing with his Indian clubs, then took on Little in a boxing demonstration during which he received a black eye and Little sprained his thumb. On the second day there was a sack fight in which six men tied in sacks butted each other with their shoulders until only one remained standing. When the doctors took on the clergy, Dr Stewart, the huge Scottish medical officer of the hospital, prevailed. Finally the sports ended in a tug-of-war, pitting the Mission staff against the local fishermen. This event ended quickly, for few could match the hauling ability of fishermen.

There were now subtle signs of spring. Preoccupied with getting his herd of reindeer across to the mainland and sustaining it, Grenfell again approached Earl Grey, asking him to intercede with the minister of agriculture for an annual grant of $2,500. He then wrote the minister himself, conveying his intention to transfer the herd when the ice broke up.[47] (The following spring Parliament voted an annual grant of $1,000.) The group in the Guest House got ready to disperse for the summer and make way for the visitors arriving to look after Grenfell's more conventional projects. A nurse was coming from Johns Hopkins Hospital to conduct public health visits, and someone was expected who would make drains and build roads. There were visitors coming from St John's, including Governor MacGregor. There would be others from Montreal and Toronto, all requiring accommodation. And there would be squads of young men from Harvard, Princeton, Yale, Columbia, and various boys' schools, all seeking meaningful work. The pace of life was picking up again. In the midst of these preparations came a horrifying sequence of events that in the space of one day altered Grenfell's life permanently.

— 10 —

The Hero Confirmed
1908 – 1910

Through the long, long years,
With their laughter and their tears,
*   We'll be true to the motto that has bound us to you –*
And in fine or dirty weather
We'll still be boys together –
*   For the dark, dark green and the light, light blue.*

Mostyn House School Song

Grenfell was uncharacteristically late for breakfast on Easter Sunday morning. He had been up rummaging through his steamer trunks and appeared at the table just as the others were finishing their oatmeal, looking stern and unusually well groomed, for he had taken the trouble to wax his moustache. As he reached his place, he swung a leg over the back of a chair, playfully revealing a pair of red, yellow, and black stockings of the Richmond Rugby Football Club and a pair of dark blue serge shorts, then looked around the table mischievously and broke into the grin he usually reserved for boyish pranks. That morning, still wearing his athletic gear underneath his outer clothing, he presided at the church service, the lessons focusing on death and resurrection: Psalm 23 ('Yea, though I walk through the valley of the shadow of death, I will fear no evil') and Psalm 90 ('The days of our age are threescore years and ten, or, if men be so strong, they may come to fourscore years'). As the Guest House circle returned, they observed a komatik drawn by nine dogs crossing the ice in front of the hospital, an unusual appearance for a Sunday, since the local people did not normally take their dogs out that day unnecessarily. The team had come up from Canada Bay, about fifty miles due south, to take

141

Grenfell to a young man he had operated on for acute osteomyelitis during his last call. In the interim, the patient's family had treated his leg improperly, and now he appeared to suffer from blood poisoning. Possibly Grenfell would have to amputate.

Pausing to put on his travelling gear and take the midday meal, Grenfell started off behind a komatik loaded with instruments, dressings, and drugs. For the long journey he took his seven best dogs, a team to which he was personally devoted: the clever Brin, the gentle Doc, the wiry Spy, the lop-eared Moody, the young Watch, the wolf-like Sue, and the agile Jerry. He also took his pet spaniel, Jack. With the ice on the bays breaking up and the brooks forcing their way through the snow, it would have been safer, perhaps, to travel with a companion, but the other team was exhausted, and he pressed ahead to save time. 'We watched him climb Fox Farm Hill and turn near the top for a final wave of the hand,' recalled Jessie Luther; 'Jack ran on ahead, wild with joy at being allowed to go.'[1] By going on ahead, Grenfell planned to make Lock's Cove that night and stay with friends, then carry on across the ice to his tilt at the bottom of Hare Bay, a way station prepared for just such an emergency. There he planned to rendezvous with the other team the next day. By crossing Hare Bay he would save himself considerable time and effort.

It rained that night. Water soaked the interior of the glass porch at the Guest House, and the next day no dog or deer stirred out as usual to haul logs out of the woods, for the soft snow had made the going difficult. The Guest House awoke to the unfamiliar roar of the open sea, which had gradually worked its way to the end of the wharf. Then a door was thrown open, and a reindeer apprentice rushed in calling for Mr Lindsay. Someone had seen Grenfell out in the middle of Hare Bay, marooned on a large, flat piece of ice. Within a few minutes, a small crowd gathered at the hospital and stood around murmuring. According to a messenger from Lock's Cove who had stopped at the reindeer camp, someone had seen Grenfell just at sundown, drifting out to sea with his dogs around him. Before anyone could launch a boat, it had grown too dark to see him.

The Mission staff now stood helpless. The breakfast hour passed unnoticed, then the time to begin work. Two men arrived from Goose Cove, situated at the mouth of Hare Bay, with the news that someone else was on the ice pan, someone coming in the other direction who appeared to have only five dogs with him. This news provided momentary hope, and the staff were prepared to believe an unknown traveller was drifting slowly out of Hare Bay, even though they knew it could have been no one else but Grenfell. Late that morning a messenger arrived from Lock's Cove with further news. George Reid, the 'elder' at Lock's Cove, had heard about the man on the ice. Taking his glass, he had scanned the expanse and recognized Grenfell from about three miles away, his dogs gathered around him, drifting towards the open sea. Reid did not expect the ice would hold together until morning, and he could see no possibility of mounting a rescue.

Out on the ice, Grenfell reflected on what had happened. During his stopover at Lock's Cove the wind had shifted to the northeast, bringing rain and sending in a heavy sea that carried enormous blocks of ice to the landwash. Half a mile out, he could see open water. He had set off at nine o'clock that morning, and with some difficulty crossed Northern Arm to Hare Island. The ice had seemed firm, and he felt sure he could cross to the other side. Indeed, he had made his way successfully enough until he was less than a quarter of a mile from shore. 'Then the wind suddenly fell,' he recalled, 'and I noticed that I was travelling over loose "sish," which was like porridge and probably many feet deep.'[2] Relieved of the pressure of the wind, the ice had parted around him, making retreat impossible, and to his surprise he realized he was trapped where he stood, unable to move dogs and sled.

He had been through the ice before but never alone. Once during the annual seal hunt he had been stranded on a huge pan with a sealing party when a similar shift of wind moved them a quarter of a mile from the next pan and separated them from their ship. Now he instinctively urged the dogs towards the shore, hoping to make the short distance before his whole outfit sank. But the dogs became confused and hesitated, and the komatik with his dry clothing and extra food sank slowly into the mass of icy fragments known locally as 'slob' ice.

He cut the traces from the sled and dragged himself through the frigid water by pulling on them until he reached a small piece of ice. Once on top, he heaved the dogs up beside him. By standing up, he could see another huge raft about twenty yards away, and he tried to get the dogs to move to it and carry the traces with them. But each time he threw them off, they acted as if they were all engaged in some hearty game and struggled back upon the pan where he stood. Only by throwing a piece of ice to fetch did he manage to get Jack to move to the pan, and when he threw them all off again they followed, taking with them the precious line. As soon as he reached the pan himself, however, he realized the collective weight of dogs and man was sinking it, and the whole process had to be repeated again. This time, when he scrambled out of the water, he was not standing on an ice pan at all but a body of frozen slob measuring about ten by twelve feet. Lacking sufficient open water to risk a swim, he could sense the wind taking the whole tableau out to sea as he stood there, and about fifty yards away he could still see the komatik with his food, thermos bottle, dry clothing, matches and wood. His outer clothing, which he had stripped off for freedom of movement, had also been left behind. Standing in his athletic gear, soaked with ice water, he cut off his knee-length skin boots, split the legs, and made a jacket that protected him to the waist. At least he wouldn't freeze to death.

By midday he had drifted past the island he had crossed that morning; within a few hours the movement of the ice had detached it from the mainland. The wind and tide were conveying him in the direction of the open ocean, well out from the north shore of Hare Bay, which rose in sheer cliffs up to 160 feet and made rescue difficult. Without his outer clothing, he needed more protection in order to survive the night. So even though he was emotionally attached to his dogs, he threw one on its back and stabbed it through the heart with his clasp knife, receiving a bite on the leg in the process. He sacrificed two more dogs this way and received another bite, all the while expecting that his exertions would cause the ice to break apart. 'A short shrift seemed to me better than a long one,' he remembered, 'and I envied the dead dogs whose troubles were over so quickly.'[3] As a result of the slaughter, he was better protected, but he had drifted another three miles, and as the afternoon wore on it began to get dark. He could see the lights of Lock's Cove, where he had spent the previous night, through an aperture in the walls of the cliff, an entrance so narrow it permitted a signal to be seen only briefly. Having crossed the inhabitants' range of vision, he had drifted over six miles.

As the temperature continued to drop, he took steps to preserve his body heat. His coat, hat, gloves, and oilskins remained on the other pan. All he retained were his knee-length football shorts, Richmond socks, a flannel shirt and a sweater vest. By continually taking off these and swinging them around one by one, he kept them partially dry, but by the afternoon everything had frozen stiff. He laid out the dogs' skins as a kind of rug and piled up the carcasses as a windbreak. But during these exertions, his fingers froze, and his wet feet began to bother him. He pulled apart the rope from the dogs' harnesses and stuffed them into his wet shoes to keep his feet warm. Then he put his wet football socks inside his knickerbockers, where they at least served to keep out the wind. He also ripped the layers of flannel from the harnesses and bound them on his legs like puttees.

Having protected his feet, he next sought protection from the wind. As the night wore on, he ordered Doc, who weighed ninety-two pounds, to lie down. Then, lying close against the dog, he wrapped the skins of the three carcasses around him and eventually fell asleep. Unfortunately, in this position one hand continued to freeze badly. 'One hand I had kept warm against the curled up dog,' he remembered, 'but the other, being gloveless, had frozen, and I suddenly awoke, shivering enough, I thought, to break my fragile pan.'[4] At this point the wind fell and the surface went calm. If the bay froze up again, he hoped his pan would hold together longer, and he would perhaps be visible at daylight to the people in Goose Cove, the last settlement to be passed before he left the bay and drifted on into the open sea. Again he slept, then awoke with the idea that he must put up a flag. By removing the frozen leg bones of the dead dogs, he intended to lash them together and hoist his shirt as soon as it was daylight.

As the sun rose, it revealed the icy mass reduced in circumference and littered with the carcasses and debris of the night's work. Soon the makeshift flagpole thawed and went limp. He could not raise it more than three or four feet above his head. A shift of wind brought him back in a northwesterly direction, so that instead of lying offshore, visible to anyone searching for him, he began to close upon a cliff face known as Ireland's Point and near it the fishing station of Ireland's Bight. This place, Grenfell knew, stayed deserted in winter, when the inhabitants shifted inland to their winter quarters. There would be no one there to see him float by. As the chances of a rescue narrowed, the lines of a hymn of resignation by Charlotte Elliott recurred unconsciously in his mind:

> My God, my Father, while I stray
> Far from my home on life's dark way,
> Oh, teach me from my heart to say,
>   Thy will be done!

But there was someone there. The day before, a group of young men had gone up on the hill above Ireland's Bight and reported to George Reid an object out on the ice with crows circling around it. They suspected it might be Grenfell.[5] Reid, who possessed one of the rare telescopes on the coast, easily confirmed the report but too late to launch a boat. He decided to wait until first light, at about five o'clock the next morning, before going to have a look. Meanwhile the men walked the cliffs to note any further changes in the direction of the wind, and a 'sealing' boat about eighteen feet long was loaded with snow shoes, guns, and food for a few days.

Fortunately, Tuesday morning was sunny, and a heavy sea was running. Out in the middle of Hare Bay, Grenfell began to imagine he could see rescuers. He saw men against the cliffs, but they turned out to be trees. Once or twice a glittering object appeared on the surface, but it turned out to be ice sparkling. The dogs moved about restlessly. How long would it take before they tipped over the coagulation of ice and snow or broke it into fragments? How long would it take before he ran onto the breakers at Spring Shoals, where he seemed to be heading? The idea that he would have to try to kill one of them to eat crossed his mind, for by now he had eaten nothing for twenty-four hours and suppressed his hunger and thirst by chewing on a rubber band he had worn instead of a garter. Now that the sun grew warmer, he got busy drying out his matches so that he could make smoke. Once or twice he imagined the rhythmic glint of an oar but dismissed the possibility until he could no longer deny he could see the shape of a hull. There was no doubt about it: he could see a boat making its way laboriously through the slob ice. By the time it reached him, he had drifted to a position south of Goose Cove, as much as fifteen nautical miles.

The boat contained George Reid with four young men at the oars: Reid's two sons together with George Davis (who had seen Grenfell from the cliff) and George Andrews.[6] Though we cannot know Grenfell's position exactly, to reach him they would have had to push and row their boat almost the same distance through slob ice and open water at great risk to themselves – an outstanding athletic performance. At that point, they still did not know whether he was even alive, and they were prepared to bring back his body. But he moved as they approached, and the emotion of the past twenty-four hours finally broke. They could hardly recognize him, for his face was drained, and the dehydration had given him the appearance of a much older man. They burst into tears. Then they hoisted him, together with the trophies of his survival, into the boat and gave him food and hot tea. Once he had eaten, they ploughed their way back through the shifting pans to Lock's Cove.

The news of the rescue spread quickly along the coast. Jessie Luther claims that by one o'clock the regulars at the Guest House were still delaying at lunch when they heard it was under way. When Grenfell arrived at St Anthony that evening, Jessie and Miss Keese went immediately to the hospital, where he was treated for frostbite and exposure. 'He was so changed one would scarcely know him,' wrote Jessie. 'His eyes were bloodshot, his face a curious dark red and his hands so swollen with frost he could barely use them. His voice was strange and weak as he told us of his terrible experience.' But Grenfell would not surrender. Released from the hospital to go to the Guest House, he decided to demonstrate how he had used the dog-skin cloak and flagstaff. He had by then put on his shirt but took it off again and hoisted it on the pole to show how it might have looked. Someone helped him put on the jacket made of boot-tops and adjusted the dog-skin cloak and puttees. 'As he stood outside the door, waving the flag, everyone tried to laugh at the queer object he made, and someone suggested photographing him,' Jessie Luther added. 'Then he hobbled home and collapsed.'[7]

Grenfell moved like someone twice his age. He sat near the stove half asleep, sometimes singing the hymn that had stayed with him during the night. He talked about the dogs and imagined he was still sinking through the slob ice. His feet and hands ached from frostbite, and the two bite wounds required attention. Later, Jessie put him to bed with a hot-water

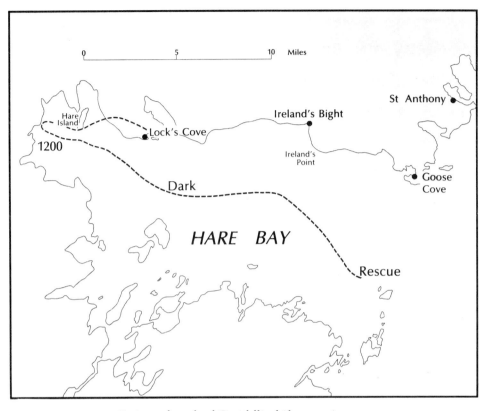

Estimated track of Grenfell's drift on an ice-pan

bottle and a protective 'cradle' she devised to raise the bedclothes above his feet. But he could not sleep until Dr Little administered a strong sedative consisting of thirty grains of bromide and a half-grain of morphine.[8]

For the rest of the week he endured the discomfort, moving about without the aid of a walking stick. The mental trauma of facing his own extinction had made him uncharacteristically moody, but he was moved by the universal show of concern. 'One of the hardest things (to a sentimentalist like myself) has been the expression of love and sympathy from all the shore,' he wrote. 'I've had a lump in my throat many times since I landed as the strangest of visitors have come and shaken hands, and I've seen the tears roll down their cheeks when they couldn't speak.'[9] Thus, he overreacted to trivial events and became periodically depressed, but he kept himself busy making a model dog team and worked on a projected book about Labrador. In the evenings, at cocoa time, he read aloud from the poetry he liked or sometimes from his own book or the religious fables of Laura E. Richards. The following Sunday he again led the service at the church. In this way he occupied himself until mid-May, when he stirred out to fish and shoot and began to think about the summer's work. By the end of the month he had left for St John's in the *Strathcona* to inspect a building he wanted to take over as a seamen's institute. As for the patient in Canada Bay, he was brought to St Anthony, where he recovered. In July Grenfell returned to Hare Bay aboard the *Strathcona* to present engraved watches to his rescuers. He put up a plaque at the hospital to commemorate the sacrifice of the three dogs and an identical one in the chapel of Mostyn House School.

As a result of the excursion on the ice, Grenfell's personal reputation stood higher than ever. The bare details of his survival now circulated through the wire services, and sensational accounts appeared in the British and American newspapers. The *New York Tribune*, for example, on 4 June ran on its front page the headline 'DOGS TRY TO EAT MAN' and recounted how he had battled for forty hours against a pack of 'hunger-maddened' dogs. His own account of the mishap, which he dictated to Jones the day after his rescue, intending to sell it to *McClure's*, appeared instead in the *New York Tribune* under the Arthurian headline 'A Voyage Perilous,' and the newspaper mailed out fourteen hundred copies to the supporters of the Grenfell Association of America as a fund-raising venture. *Wide World* published it in London.[10]

As a modern-day fable of endurance, the ice-pan story served to attract growing numbers to his lectures, especially after it appeared as a booklet the following summer, published with a biographical sketch, photos of dog-team travel (including one of Grenfell wearing his survival gear), and an account of the rescue given by George Andrews, rendered into an approximation of northern Newfoundland dialect by Jessie Luther. The booklet turned into an outstanding publishing success; in December Grenfell informed his mother that it had already gone through three editions.[11] By 1920 it had reached an eighteenth edition, and three years later the publishers were required to make a new set of plates. Equally important, Houghton Mifflin, through the expert handling of its distinguished literary editor, Ferris Greenslet, found a ready market for the book as part of their Riverside Literature Series, aimed at schools. This edition sold fifty-eight thousand copies by 1924, bringing a new generation of Americans into touch with the exploits of Wilfred Grenfell.[12]

When the excitement subsided, the staff returned to their accustomed duties at St Anthony. That spring, with the sudden influx of patients, adventurous young students, visitors, and onlookers, the group in the Guest House went their separate ways. Dr Little, who had spent the previous summer with Grenfell in the *Strathcona*, took charge of the St Anthony hospital and in the course of the following year turned himself into the surgical authority in the region. To his delight, he found almost limitless opportunities for surgery, opportunities curtailed, he thought, only by the Mission's other priorities. 'I have not a doubt whatsoever that should I want to stay here I could have the whole surgical practice of Newfoundland in a not very long time,' he wrote his mother.[13] Though he tended to exaggerate his own importance and clearly ignored the other capable surgeons resident in the colony,[14] Little was conscious of working long hours as a volunteer and considered the experience invaluable. Nearly ten years later, when he looked for a position in the more competitive Boston market, he would view his accomplishments more modestly. But for the time being, he wanted to make himself a first-class surgeon and knew he could never achieve the same breadth of experience elsewhere. In two articles published in the *Journal of the American Medical Association*, he described the attraction of northern practice with a view to convincing other American practitioners to join him. 'One is dependent entirely on oneself up here,' he wrote, 'and that is a stimulus which should be invaluable, and which, I think, is too often absent in the work at our large centers.'[15]

Little was now receiving referrals from other Newfoundland communities, including St John's, and thought that the St Anthony hospital was doing superior work. He performed a wide range of procedures, often under less than ideal conditions and without sufficient rest. Prone to regard his accomplishments with great self-satisfaction, he once suggested that no one else in Newfoundland should be allowed to do surgery except Grenfell, 'and he is self-confessedly not qualified for the class of work we are now doing,' he added.[16] By following the British and American medical journals and maintaining a good medical library, he found he could keep up with recent developments and occassionally publish a paper on northern medicine, such as his analysis of Inuit dermatitis. But the work he performed presented Grenfell with a dilemma. The St Anthony hospital, though limited by its size, was clearly capable of performing superior work. He needed to decide whether to direct more money towards advanced surgical care and expand the facility, or maintain his programs for social reform. In the end, he preferred the latter.

By the autumn of 1908 Little was receiving offers of employment that would allow him to relocate in Boston – offers he could not afford to ignore, for technically he was still a volunteer. Fearful of losing such a valuable colleague, Grenfell offered him a permanent staff position at $1,000 a year (later raised to $2,000). But by doing so he compromised a basic principle of the Mission, namely the recruitment of medical staff who were evangelical Christians, doctors and nurses who viewed themselves as missionaries first. Little, a Unitarian, had told Grenfell he did not object to the Mission's religious motivations but knew he was 'unfitted by habit, custom of thought and former associations' to take an active part in the religious work.[17] His objective was professional advancement, and he preferred not to be bound by contract for the future. However, he assured Grenfell that he would devote himself to the work even though his attitude towards it contrasted sharply with Grenfell's broader priorities. That year he was enraged when Grenfell published a number of letters he had written home. In an unusual display of anger, he told his parents, who had shown Grenfell the letters,

> What I do up here is done simply and I don't intend to have people misunderstand it or have mawkish sentiment made out of it, and as for my professional work, I happen to take it seriously and do not intend to have printed matter about it that I do not edit. I quite understand Dr. Grenfell's attitude about advertising his work, and he is so constituted, and is so really simple that there is no harm about it, only good for other people and for the work. But I am not like Dr. Grenfell and cannot appear as a tin hero any more than I can lead prayers.[18]

While he revelled in the frontier existence and developed professionally from his surgical work, he could not bring himself to promote it the way Grenfell had. For the first time an important part of the Mission's work lay in the hands of a man who did not share Grenfell's religious ideas or his manly assumptions.

Grenfell himself spent the winter of 1908–9 fund-raising in the United States. He was received as a hero wherever he went, and newspapers, with romantic excess, referred to him variously as the 'angel' and 'patron saint' of Labrador.[19] Dr Harvey Kellogg, the health reformer at Battle Creek, Michigan, devoted a complete number of *Medical Missionary* to his work. 'G. has apparently suffered no damage at all from his experience on the ice,' Daly was relieved to see. 'He continues to win volunteers for the work right and left.'[20] In May he returned to Providence to stay with Jessie Luther's family before sailing to England to confer briefly with the council, then bring back his mother to see him receive honorary degrees at Harvard and Williams College. He had arranged for Jessie Luther to come and look after Mrs. Grenfell, and Jessie travelled up to Cambridge, where the Grenfells were staying with Dr Edward Moore. 'I fell in love with Mrs. Grenfell at once,' she wrote. 'A charming, gracious lady, and the doctor's affectionate devotion to her was beautiful to see.'[21]

By now, Jessie Luther had become an important part of the Mission's enterprise. During the winter she had lectured about the Mission and written an appeal for special funds to develop pottery and brick-making. She subsequently received another leave of absence from the Butler Hospital and in October would return for another year to St Anthony, where the plans for the proposed brickyard remained unsettled. Thus, she was quite unprepared in August, when Grenfell wrote to her with startling news. In the short interval since she saw him in the summer he had become engaged to a young American, Anna MacClanahan of Lake Forest, Illinois, whom he had met aboard the *Mauretania* on his way back from England. Now Anne, as she was called, was writing enthusiastically about her interest in the industrial work and her desire to help. In November, Grenfell announced, they would marry and in December arrive in St Anthony, where a house was to be constructed for them.

No one could have been more surprised at this intelligence than Jessie Luther, who was as close to Grenfell as anyone and aware of his tendency to rush into things. Indeed, she expressed misgivings about the new departure and wrote in her journal, 'Everyone rejoiced with the Doctor in his happiness, but it was difficult to think of him as a domestic man (although we knew he enjoyed and appreciated what comforts and amenities we were able to offer him at the Guest-House) for his absorption in his work, and its precedence in all his thoughts and actions was so great – irrespective of the hazards involved in implementing such work – that any thought of his connection with the possible restraints of married life had seemed remote.'[22] Miss Luther was probably correct. The pattern of conventional marriage did not seem suited to the kind of life Grenfell was leading. But she had not met the future Mrs Grenfell and could not know of her considerable abilities. Indeed, Grenfell himself was probably unaware of them as he wrote excitedly to break the news to Mackenzie King: 'God has been pleased to give me better than a degree – the love of a girl of college training, a true Christian – of sound body – and independent. She is American, and I shall hope to introduce you sooner than you perhaps guess. I have not told anyone yet, but it will soon be out and no one will rejoice more in my happiness than yourself (and [José] Machado).'[23]

The bride-to-be was barely twenty-three, with blue eyes and handsome features that a close friend described as 'almost beautiful.' At over five foot ten she stood a full inch taller than Grenfell, who was conscious of the difference. She had graduated from Bryn Mawr in 1906 with a degree in politics and economics and gloried in her privileged education. She would announce to her mother-in-law, 'The longer I live the more I am thankful for my university education. It has given me resources and pleasures that I could never have obtained in any other way – better than all the parlour tricks imaginable.'[24] When Grenfell encountered her, she was returning from a tour of Europe with her friend Dorothy Stirling and Miss Stirling's father, the Chicago banker William R. Stirling.

Anne MacClanahan came from southern stock. Her father, Edmund Burke McClanahan, was the son of a lawyer in Madison County, Tennessee. He had practised law in Jackson before enlisting in the Confederate Army as a private in 1861. The next year, as a captain in the 6th Tennessee Infantry Regiment, he was wounded slightly at the battle before Murfreesboro but served out the war on the staff of the judge advocate general with generals Bragg, Johnson, and Hood.[25] At the close of the Civil War, he resumed practice in Nashville, then moved to Chicago in 1873. There he married Rosamond Hill of Burlington, Vermont, who since the death of her parents had lived in the suburb of Lake Forest with her sister, Mrs Anna C. Durand, widow of the prosperous wholesale grocer Charles Durand.[26] McClanahan himself had died in 1883, after settling in Lake Forest. His widow taught English and deportment in the Chicago public school system, and she and her daughter occupied a house on the Durand estate. Nearby lived the Stirling family, and the two young ladies had been friends since school. When Anna Durand died the year before, she had provided for her niece generously, leaving her, besides her diamond jewellery, her homestead, one and a quarter acres of land and an additional property situated at 2141 Calumet Avenue, Chicago.[27] She was indeed, as Grenfell described her, 'independent.' Later, she converted these valuable real estate holdings to stocks and bonds.

Grenfell had met Stirling and what appeared to be his two daughters on the second day of the voyage. Despite the attention devoted to his activities in the press, Anne had heard of him only once before: when he had spoken at Bryn Mawr the previous year. On that occasion she had refused to go and hear him for fear of having a dull evening. But Grenfell, who was overwhelmed by her, had no time to waste. The *Mauretania* could cross the Atlantic in four and a half days, and the captain seemed intent on establishing a speed record. As long as his elderly mother kept to her cabin, he was left free to pay court, and by the time he reached New York he had proposed without actually knowing her real identity, assuming she was one of the Stirlings. 'Fortunately,' he recalled later, 'I remembered that it was not the matter at issue, and explained, without admitting the impeachment, that the only question that interested me in the least was what I hoped that it might become.'[28] Even so, the matter was not settled there. Anna Elizabeth Caldwell MacClanahan (as the name was respelled) was not ready to give her answer until Grenfell and his mother had visited Lake Forest. But on the strength of that visit, a wedding was planned for November, and Grenfell's life moved at a more dazzling pace than before.

He put in a full summer's work on the coast, then returned to Anne's Chicago home for the wedding on 18 November 1909. The bride wore a long satin gown, and the groom looked uncomfortable in tails, white tie, white gloves, and the miniature decoration of the Order of St Michael and St George. The couple then departed for Virginia to spend a few days at the Hot Springs before sailing for St John's. Meanwhile, Grenfell had chosen a piece of land situated on the bedrock behind the hospital, and during his first visit to Lake Forest the two agreed upon a design for a house. By the time he left St Anthony, he could report to his mother, 'It was being covered in when I left. It is most unique and I think very "Grenfellian".'[29]

Whatever he might have meant by 'Grenfellian,' the house stood out among the more conventional dwellings of the region as it took shape in January 1910. Built in the New England cottage tradition, it was a three-storey structure with a pitched roof, dormer windows, and a glassed-in verandah – a feature that had worked well at the Guest House – running around three sides. As it filled up with clutter, it did become distinctively Grenfellian, with its reindeer and caribou antlers, furs, prints of the British Isles, snowshoes, dog whips, hunting and fishing gear, Indian clubs, boxing gloves, and a brass tablet memorializing Moody, Watch, and Spy. Strongly built with double floors and fitted windows, it was comfortably equipped with a coal furnace, steam heat, plumbing fixtures, and electricity. The living-room, its walls covered with green burlap, featured a huge fireplace with irregular pieces of gleaming Labradorite set into the grey stone. By contrast, the dining-room walls provided a dark red background for the mahogany furniture. On the second floor were the bedrooms, and on the third a den fitted out with shelves and cupboards where Grenfell could work. 'The house itself is delightful,' observed the author Fullerton Waldo a few years later, 'and it is only too bad that the Doctor and his wife see so little of it.'[30]

While the work progressed, arrangements were made for Grenfell's triumphal arrival. The men of St Anthony had built a traditional arch of spruce boughs, hung with a large banner that proclaimed 'WELCOME TO OUR NOBLE DOCTOR AND HIS BONNIE BRIDE,' and a komatik had been decorated with cushions and red and white streamers, ready to convey the couple ashore. Every available flag flew, and the village lived in a state of expectation. Finally, on 12 January 1910, the *Prospero* arrived, and as soon as the navigation lights appeared around the point, the celebration began. Guns went off along the shore, and bonfires blazed. Fireworks rose and burst aloft, drawing shrieks from the children, who had not witnessed such a spectacle before. The ceremonial komatik, drawn by twenty men, started off across the ice towards the vessel, returning at length at the head of a long line of people that snaked its way across the harbour and up to the hospital. A strange silence prevailed. 'There was no demonstration,' wrote Jessie Luther; 'the people were very quiet, with only an occasional whoop.'[31] In front of the house, still unfinished and lacking a cook, the two struggled to their feet and went inside to meet the Mission staff, who strained to form their first impression of the bride.

She was above all dignified: handsome, well dressed, and very tall. Grenfell hovered nervously, still a little unsure. Not until two days later, when they gathered in the hospital for a staff dinner could the staff form opinions. This time the women came dressed in their unaccustomed finery, the men in high, stiff collars, to drink the health of the bride and groom. The following Sunday afternoon, young Mrs Grenfell received them for tea in her living-room, now spread with a huge polar bear skin, and Grenfell told them he wanted to have them meet there regularly for tea and talk. However, through the following weeks, Anne Grenfell was not well enough to receive visitors and rarely went out. Instead, Grenfell organized a Saturday afternoon snowshoe club to roam over the countryside. 'In planning these walks the Doctor has, I think, tried to revive the weekly wanderings so much enjoyed two years ago by our happy winter family,' wrote Jessie. 'It is what the active Doctor likes to do, and it must be a disappointment that Mrs. Grenfell is, at present, not strong enough to share this form of enjoyment with him.'[32] Clearly, Anne Grenfell did not prefer vigorous outdoor sports. As time would reveal, she was in some ways the very antithesis of her husband: systematic and orderly but also squeamish at sea, numb in cold weather, and impatient with robust activity or hardship.[33] After a year in St Anthony, she purchased a retreat cottage in Swampscott, Massachusetts.

Her interests seemed more aesthetic and intellectual than Grenfell's, but her talents were oddly suited to the task he had set for himself. It was not long before she had taken over as his secretary, a role previously filled by a succession of young men from Britain and the United States. The Reverend Henry Gordon of the Colonial and Continental Church Society, who saw her in action during the summer of 1917, observed, 'This was my first meeting with Mrs. Grenfell, and it didn't take long to come to the conclusion that she was the ideal mate for the dynamic doctor. The fact that he was not in his usual mad rush, and announced his intention to stay put for three days, was abundant evidence of her restraining influence. During their visit, I took up my quarters on board *Strathcona*, where such peace and order prevailed, that I hardly recognized her.'[34] But there was one other important difference. She not only typed letters; she often wrote them, and she worked over her husband's manuscripts thoroughly, knowing he lacked the patience to do so himself. During the first year she took credit for the success of 'Suzanne,' a pathetic tale of a girl's loss of virtue aboard a fishing schooner, after Houghton Mifflin had praised it as an effort worthy of Tolstoy. 'I did all the polishing and worked for days over it,' she revealed to her mother.[35]

Above all, Grenfell prized her judgment, a quality that operated quietly behind the constant buzz of publicity attending her husband's many projects. Within a few years he could look back and remark to W.R. Stirling, 'Suddenly out of a blue sky there came into my life, as ten thousand Providences have – so obvious that a fool can't mistake them – a woman, young, talented, beautiful, independent, but infinitely above these attributes gifted with the courage of an inspired judgement. (Even you do not know it.) She has made me feel often like the sculptor [Sir Charles Bennet] Lawes, who took all the credit for the wonderful sculptures his assistant [Richard Claude Belt] created.'[36] Anne Grenfell's other qualities manifested themselves as time went on. She was sensitive rather than sentimental, and a stubborn sense of humour persisted beneath her dignified exterior. A committed anglophile, she clearly enjoyed the role of Englishman's wife, sending out notepaper bearing the Grenfell arms and sprinkling her letters and talk with polite anglicisms. She thanked people 'ever so much' and noted that things were 'splendid,' 'really jolly,' 'cutting' and 'top hole.' She expressed to her mother-in-law the wish to employ an English servant, 'for they are more reliable.'[37] On the other hand, she did not share her husband's tolerance of Jews. Several years later, for example, when Grenfell reported to his mother that the debt on the Swampscott cottage had been reduced to $4,500, he added, 'It let late for $1,200. A Jew offered $2,000 & Anne, I thought foolishly, would not rent to a Hebrew, which cost us $800 & a month later out of our house.'[38] With the added presence of another strong personality, life for the staff in St Anthony had changed considerably since the ice-pan incident two years before.

On the larger scale, the Mission had continued to grow. In 1909 the Grenfell Association of America collected $71,000, and its paid-up membership exceeded 1,850. On the medical side, the in-patient returns more than doubled over those of the previous year, and the number of out-patients had risen by 30 per cent.[39] There were twenty-eight children resident in the orphanage, and the reindeer herd had increased to six hundred. The Mission abandoned the idea of renovating the existing sailors' home in St John's and purchased property on Water Street for the construction of a new building under the supervision of Charles Karnopp. With the aid of $10,000 from Boston, raised by Dr Little's sister, the size of the hospital had practically doubled, and the Yale Grenfell Association had arranged to build the forty-four-foot *Yale* for use in Hamilton Inlet. There never seemed to be a shortage of Ivy League students or medical staff eager to be associated with the work. But the sense of romance that had clung to the early efforts of the Mission was slipping.

Grenfell's movements were more circumscribed. No longer could he run off on impulse to deal with daily occurrences. His wife worried about his safety. Nothing illustrated the changes in his life better than the way in which his forty-fifth birthday was observed. That February morning in 1910, Anne surprised the staff by inviting them to a buffet supper and set the Lake Forest style firmly on the house. She received them in the living-room, looking thinner but gorgeously dressed in a red velvet Liberty gown with train, elbow sleeves, and collar and cuffs of Irish lace. Grenfell appeared in his customary homespun trousers but had put on a black coat and white collar and waxed his moustache. 'Mrs. Grenfell was a gracious hostess, and the table was so beautiful with delicate linen and quantities of gleaming silver that it was hard to realize we were in Newfoundland,' Jessie Luther observed. 'It was quite like a formal luncheon at home.' With the candlelight sparkling, Anne served creamed rabbit with a salad of tinned asparagus tips and the firm parts of tinned tomato, several kinds of fancy sandwiches, olives, and coffee. For sweets, she had laid out an assortment of cakes and wafers with chocolates, candied fruits, and ice cream. Later, the company joined the crowd at the Orangemen's Hall, where Grenfell gave an illustrated lecture for the benefit of the football club. Clearly, St Anthony was entering a new period of development. Looking back on the previous two years, when a staff of four worked with no modern conveniences, Jessie could not help noting that they had not been happier since. 'Do ease and self-indulgence, when emphasized as a goal, bring greater happiness than when they are balanced by self-denial?' she wondered. 'An uneasy question often asked.'[40]

PART THREE

Living Legend

— 11 —

Running a Railroad Accident
1910 – 1914

In the early days of our work on the coast the same range had to cook dinner for patients and staff, sterilize instruments, boil water for use in the operating theatre, and serve half-a-dozen useful purposes in addition. Too often the only nurse in the establishment was cook-general, too, and sometimes the surgeon, left to his own resources upstairs, could only regain the services of the nurse by hammering on the floor. We have advanced greatly since those stirring times, but the ever-growing character of the work demands increasing efficiency all round, and not least in the kitchen.

F.W. Willway, 'Medical Missionary Work
in Labrador,' 110

St Anthony was acquiring the look of a northern capital, with its own magistrate, archdeacon, and unelected deputy. During 1909–10 the Mission treated nearly six thousand patients at the various stations, more especially during summer, when the staff doubled or sometimes tripled with the influx of student volunteers. Apart from the primary medical or dental assistants, some of the volunteers performed a wide variety of non-professional tasks. They kept accounts and shingled roofs; they dug drains and kept the flotilla of Mission boats at sea, ploughed fields, and herded reindeer, taught school and unloaded schooners, conducted religious services and cooked. It was busy, satisfying work keeping up with the fertile mind of the presiding genius.

Twice a month the daily tasks would be suspended for the arrival of the northbound mail steamer *Prospero*, bringing the sick from around the coast.[1] Once the *Prospero* came alongside, a familiar ritual would be

159

enacted. A line of passengers composed of the limping, the sick, and the dying would leave the vessel and proceed along the path to the hospital. A few hours later another line would form, this time composed of those discharged, and make its way to the dock, some leaning on a nurse's arm, some conveyed in wheelchairs, some thankful to walk at all. Meanwhile, the first group required immediate attention so that they could be treated before the *Prospero* called again on the southbound run, and the medical staff often worked into the night in the small hospital.

With staff coming and going, the administration remained in a state of disorder, and there was no better example of that disorder than the dispensary. The dispensary was never created; it had emerged at the hands of a dozen different doctors from medical schools situated in Britain, Canada, and the United States, all using different drugs and all too busy to impose a system on what Dr Arthur Wakefield called its 'weird and fantastic' stock. Wakefield himself had tried to organize the dispensary but soon surrendered. He wrote,

> I have twice previously got things into some resemblance of order, and the shelves all nicely ticketed and labelled. But the gum is hardly dry on the labels, and my glow of satisfaction and well-earned pride has hardly spread half way from ear to ear ... when along comes a packing-case as big as a coffin, full of pills and bottles of all shapes and sizes, many unlabelled, the off-scourings of some antiquated G.P.'s spring cleaning or the unsaleable remnants of some clearance sale! Before I have got over the shock of this consternation, the Strathcona sends up a lot of stock she finds she hasn't room for, or can't use. And the next day the Prospero brings some volunteer specialist for a fortnight with his trunk packed full of all the latest patent mixtures and devices for the healing of his own art – *all* for the benefit of the Mission!! and so it goes on.[2]

But despite this sense of disorder, the process of reform continued. The medical work expanded, to be followed by new dental services. From 1910, a summer dental service began, staffed principally by graduates of the Harvard Dental School.[3] After two years the dentists moved out to the nursing stations, proceeding beyond simple operative dentistry to prosthetic restorations, then to a year-round service complete with the ministrations of dental hygienists. In addition to their clinical work, with the aid of volunteer workers the medical and dental staff maintained an intense program of instruction in hygiene, emphasizing the benefits of clean air in the growing campaign to curb the spread of tuberculosis. Beatrice Farnsworth, a graduate of the Johns Hopkins School of Nursing, reported by 1912 that 'The command "Do not spit" has been put up in all the hospitals – and these vital words are even woven by the natives into mats, which are frequently seen in their homes.'[4]

160

Grenfell himself did not slacken his own efforts. Instead, he pushed himself even harder, planning new projects and raising money. In 1910 he was especially interested in taking over the Moravian station at Makkovik, which appeared to be declining. For the past few years he had openly criticized the Moravians, especially for failing to contain the spread of syphilis among the Inuit population.[5] But generally speaking, the two missions coexisted satisfactorily, even if, from time to time, the Moravians complained about Grenfell's excursions into their proper sphere of influence. Such an event occurred in 1910, when Grenfell first offered to send a doctor, run the boarding school, and set up home industries.

Considering the changes imminent in his own organization, it is difficult to imagine why Grenfell would make such an offer, but his intentions were clear. 'I happen to have on hand a large voluntary staff,' he wrote, 'and should be able to place a doctor there without any expense to myself if he were to work in connection with our Mission. In summer he would run the hospital at Indian Harbour, with a beautiful launch at his service, and where he would be in touch with many of the settlers who need so badly both spiritual and medical aid. In the fall he would retire to Makkovik and be a splendid centre from Hopedale to Stag Bay for the sick and suffering.' The merits of such an offer could not be denied, despite Grenfell's criticisms, and the Moravians took it seriously as long as the resident doctor did not 'meddle' at Hopedale or anywhere else in the Moravian 'sphere.'[6] But they were still unclear about the nature of the co-operative venture. Were they dealing with the RNMDSF, with Grenfell as an individual, or with the American association? They couldn't be sure, and by the spring of 1911 they decided against joint occupation of the Makkovik station.

The constant pursuit of further projects tired Grenfell even further. That spring, Daly informed King, 'Grenfell is so near the breaking point physically that something ought to be done to help *him*, and endowment is the only solution I can see. He will die in his tracks if some of the financial burden is not taken off him! He stayed part of two weeks in our house and I saw how terribly tired he is now.'[7] Grenfell had also continued his seemingly endless output of journalism as well as producing manuscripts for a series of books, including his edition of essays, *Labrador, the Country and Its People* (1909), and two collections of yarns, *Down to the Sea* (1910) and *Down North on the Labrador* (1911). To these he added a series of preachments on life and religion for the *Congregationalist and Christian World* (later published in booklets by the Pilgrim Press) as well as the William Belden Noble Lectures for Harvard University.

More than ever he depended on the loyalty of men such as Daly and King, men well placed to assist him. King had succeeded in getting himself elected to Parliament in 1908, and the following year was invited into the cabinet of Sir Wilfrid Laurier. Grenfell viewed him as a possible successor to the leadership of the Liberal party of Canada.[8] But the governor general, Earl Grey, assisted him even more.

Grey continued to be impressed with Grenfell's reforms, especially with the reindeer experiment, for such a scheme fed his dream of expanding Canadian sovereignty into the Arctic and offsetting the perceived American encroachment that followed the sale of Alaska. He had visited the Mission in 1910 and communicated his enthusiasm about reindeer to both the king and the minister of agriculture. 'They grow as fat as butter on the mosses & the bush growth of the Tundra,' he reported enthusiastically to George V. 'They cost absolutely nothing to keep. They are most gentle and docile. Their Milk is rich, their meat excellent, and as Transport animals they excel the Dogs. I am pressing upon Your Majesty's Canadian Ministers the desirability of establishing a herd at every one of the N.W.M.P. Posts in the North of Canada. Under proper management, which the N.W.M. Police could supply, without any substantial increase of Cost, Reindeer might become the Dairy, the Larder, & the Transport of the North.'[9]

Grey already possessed a reputation in England as a strong reformist Liberal who organized co-operatives, developed plans for garden cities, promoted temperance, and advocated proportional representation in Parliament. Since his Ottawa appointment in 1904, he had strenuously maintained a proconsular influence in Canadian political affairs and liked to promote his sense of the British empire and Canada's place in it. Throughout his term of office he took it upon himself to encourage Newfoundland's entry into confederation so as to offset its growing trade relationship with the United States.[10] Grey not only admired Grenfell as a missionary but regarded him as a valuable pro-confederate who could assist him in bringing Newfoundland in. Grenfell, for his part, had publicly advocated confederation, notably in an address to the Canadian Club of Toronto in 1905. But he had also advocated reciprocity with the United States if it would improve the price of fish.[11]

In January 1909 Grey entered into an ill-advised conspiratorial scheme with Harry Crowe, a Canadian businessman and imperialist, to bring about confederation by taking advantage of Newfoundland's political instability.[12] According to Crowe's proposal, Sir Edward Morris and Sir Robert Bond, two Newfoundland political opponents who were both anti-confederates, would be made to unite in a common cause to support confederation if Canadian financial interests could influence the railway developer W.D. Reid. In exchange for an anticipated railway monopoly, Reid was expected to bring Morris to support Bond. Morris, in turn, could then choose between the provincial premiership that would be created or a Canadian cabinet appointment. Bond, who was thought to be tired of Newfoundland politics, would retire to the House of Lords. Such a scheme, however, was made impossible by the personal bitterness between Morris and Bond, and Grey made a delicate withdrawal for the time being, realizing he could not induce confederation during his tenure of office. He did not, however, abandon the confederation scheme, but encouraged it more subtly through exchange visits and the spread of propaganda.

In 1910 he suggested to the prime minister, Sir Wilfrid Laurier, that Grenfell's mission stations might be used as a 'medium of enlightenment' to convey the advantages. Such an idea originated not with him, however, but with his former son-in-law, Arthur Morton Grenfell, a cousin of Grenfell's, who had been touring the Harmsworth timber interests.[13] Later that year Grey advocated to Wilfred Grenfell a co-operative organization in British hands that would purchase the Labrador catch, transport it, and market it as a hedge against American capitalists who might enter the Newfoundland economy and make confederation more difficult. Meanwhile, he suggested that Grenfell might engage in a little 'political missionary work' among the migrant fishermen he treated in the north:

I know that you are as keen as I am to make Newfoundland into one of the Canadian Provinces. This ought not to be difficult. The railway interest, the banking interest, the iron industry on Bell Island, the pulp and paper interests, the educated Protestant vote, Archbishop Howley, are all Confederates, and I believe that in their hearts Bond and Morris are Confederates also. Strong as these forces are, they would appear to be powerless in face of the prejudices of an ignorant electorate. I am told that no one can publicly advocate Confederation without being denounced as a traitor who is prepared to sell his country. If this is the case do you not think some action should be taken to educate the Newfoundland elector?[14]

From here, the confederation campaign proceeded more subtly. Early in 1911, when Grenfell wrote Grey with an assessment of the political support in the colony, he expressed his willingness to carry out a propaganda campaign. Crowe, for his part, urged Newfoundlanders resident in Canada to put pressure on Morris.[15] On the next trip to Britain, Grenfell spent three-quarters of an hour at Marlborough House with George V, who commended him for his enterprise and showed a particular interest in the reindeer experiment. But Newfoundland was not yet ready for confederation, and Grenfell would be left to deal with the colonial government.

While Grenfell enjoyed new celebrity as a builder of empire, public recognition flowed from other sources. The Royal Geographical Society, to whom he had lectured in February on Labrador's promising future, awarded him the 1911 Murchison Bequest for his geographical work. In the United States one of his principal supporters, George B. Cluett, offered to build a three-masted, 135-foot schooner to be used for transporting cargo and staff to Labrador. The schooner, to be named after Cluett himself, was launched in July 1911. And in St John's, on 22 June, Coronation Day, the cornerstone was laid for Grenfell's projected fishermen's institute after the king began the complex electrical process by pushing a button in London.

As Grenfell involved himself more and more in public affairs, his private life also changed. In September 1910 Anne gave birth to their first son, Wilfred Thomason, Jr, and two years later a second son, Kinloch Pascoe was born. (The couple's only daughter, Rosamond Loveday, would be born in 1917.) Without breaking his pace, Grenfell slowly came to terms with the demands of domestic existence. He provided some sense of his attitude to these new responsibilities in the wry sketches he turned out for Anne's amusement, showing himself as a small fisherman of Pickwickian configuration dealing with a towering but fashionable-looking mistress (sometimes displayed as an enormous cat).[16] In these sketches, Grenfell portrayed himself variously as an over-sized idol, seen from the point of view of students; as 'General Hooker,' continually on call to fasten the back of the lady's dress; or as dwarfed by the Noble lectures, which he carried on his back. Anne herself was featured as a forceful figure shouting 'Who wrote the Harvard Lectures?' or as 'Nemesis,' meeting him at the door with 'You're late again, Hubby.' In a drawing labelled 'Deportment,' the huge cat instructed the fisherman in manners and dress, and in 'Fresh from the bargain counter' the fisherman challenged the cat, who appeared freshly outfitted. In 'Nurse Maids for Wilfred,' the fisherman was shown bringing six girls from a boat while Anne stood waiting, hands on hips. The fisherman explains, 'I had to go and see 'em safe. There's only six this time!!'

Meanwhile, as Grenfell's range of projects expanded, the council were not quite so sanguine about some of the new initiatives, especially his 'business' ventures and the expensive new seamen's institute in St John's. The response of the Rockefeller Foundation provides some indication of the way in which the concept of a seamen's institute grew. In 1907 Grenfell had approached the Rockefellers to assist with the construction of a building estimated at $25,000. Two years later the plan was presented again, this time estimated at $100,000. The Rockefeller Foundation declined each time. Now the estimated cost had grown to $150,000, and the Rockefeller Foundation suggested that this particular branch of the work was being promoted excessively. Grenfell had appealed for part of the cost on the grounds that the financial burden crippled his usefulness in other spheres. In a New York boardroom, however, this was not viewed as a dilemma but a diversion. 'The great success of his labors heretofore and the splendid service which he has been able to give to the people of the Labrador Coast has been because of his direct personal contact with them in their homes,' wrote a Rockefeller adviser. 'He has a unique personality and an almost unexampled consecration, and the sooner he drops the matter of brick and mortar and gets back to the personal contact the better for him and his work.'[17] Once again, the foundation declined.

The Mission council had previously voiced its misgivings about the haphazard manner in which these undertakings began and complained about the increasing costs. Now, more than ever, it pressed for a restructuring of the whole Labrador branch so as to shift the primary responsibility to the numerous American and Canadian committees, leaving it free to devote its energy to the work in Britain. The work in Labrador had by now grown virtually unchecked, and the council had merely thrown the occasional block or diversion in Grenfell's way. Grenfell proceeded as he had before, striking out in new directions, taking on volunteers not qualified for the tasks before them, and holding the organization together through the sheer force of his personal magnetism and energy. But such a policy would no longer suffice. The work required tighter control on where it was actually going on, and no one knew this better than Dr Little.

Little watched events unfold during his periods in charge of the St Anthony hospital. A rudimentary facility had been transformed under his leadership into a well-organized medical institution. 'It is practically the work of Dr. Little,' wrote Dr Arthur Wakefield, 'and it reflects the greatest possible credit on his genius.'[18] Dedicated more than ever to promoting a public health policy for the region, Little had also engaged in scientific research. He had studied the effects of diet and hygiene and linked the cases to the early stages of beri-beri. In an article he was preparing for the *Journal of the American Medical Association*, he would advocate radical changes in diet that would break down the prejudice against whole-wheat flour.[19] As Grenfell left Britain for the United States in the spring of 1911, however, Little privately expressed misgivings about the overall administration of the Mission. He wrote his mother in Boston, 'The poor man has a frightful muddle to straighten out. It is of his own making I am sorry to say. I do hope he is rested so that he will be a bit more like his old self, able to make decisions. He has got to knuckle under and allow organization along proper lines with a certain amount of restraint. I think he has so thoro'ly tied himself up that it is inevitable. I have seen it for a long time.'[20]

Little thought part of the difficulty arose from Grenfell's own personality, from the very qualities that led people to perceive him as heroic. He continued, 'It has been a hard thing to see so powerful, able, unusual a man, doing such a unique, useful, noble work, but showing such weakness as he has in certain ways lately. You know I love him and would not criticise him unkindly. I know that he has worked so hard that he got into a condition that in anyone less strong would have been a nervous breakdown. I know that at times he seemed to me actually irresponsible. It has been frightfully hard working with him at times.' Little was not just disappointed with Grenfell but with the sense of drift, the lack of leadership that existed while the Mission worked out how it would proceed. He added:

> Of course now, we are all in the air. Nobody has any authority. Old methods and systems are knocked on the head, new ones not yet instituted and the whole responsibility very vague. There has got to be machinery. I think the New York committee a very able body, thoro'ly interested, able and willing to provide the machinery. Smaller organizations have got to cooperate or amalgamate. You see, this thing can be run as though it were a railroad accident, but why run it with that amount of fuss, flurry, excitement, expenditure etc. How long would the giving public continue to support a charity run on such lines? I don't believe that today in spite of enthusiasm, faith etc. etc. any charity should be run that is not run along sensible lines. Modern business methods should be used. Now I think that any man who says he is working for Christ has got to do [it] this way or he is not doing the best work and had better quit, just as I believe that any surgeon who is working on a mission should be a top-notcher. If we are going to recommend Him by service it has got to be A. no. 1 or he is not recommended, all shouting, preaching, advertising, enthusiasm etc. notwithstanding.

Little may be forgiven for his vexed tone. At the time he was undertaking long journeys by dog team and carrying the burden of surgical work in St Anthony. More important, his cultural assumptions were different: he did not share Grenfell's Christian manliness. But he had gone to the heart of the matter, and his frustration was shared by the New York committee.

The year before, 1910, the Grenfell Association of America (GAA), had tactfully written the council in London to discuss what seemed to have become an unusually loose relationship between the two bodies in view of the growth of their joint activities. To that point, the GAA had been satisfied to operate as a fund-raising and advisory body, and it emphasized its long-standing policy of not interfering in the 'permanent and paramount relations' that had existed between Grenfell and the Mission.[21] But it also provided the greater proportion of funds and required some form of control commensurate with its support. In response, the council sent the secretary to New York to investigate. Now, in 1911, the GAA wrote to ask for the transfer of administrative authority, by which time the council was ready to agree in principle to what seemed a sensible solution, provided that the terms of the transfer would secure the continuance of the work on a 'Protestant Evangelical' basis and protect the Mission against financial liability.[22]

Grenfell himself was delighted with the arrangement. 'You know I can't carry on a work like ours with a comm[ee]. tied and bound like the English one – though they are good men,' he wrote privately to W.R. Stirling, the father of Anne's close friend. 'I don't want my liberty to be licence, & I don't want to pledge a comm[ee]. to what it might embarrass it to perform.' But there was more to it than that. Grenfell had felt constrained by the Mission's theological position and less comfortable with it as time went on. He was beginning to prefer the liberal theology of his New York committee and its chairman, Henry Van Dyke, to what he referred to as 'the old stereotyped message of future salvation.'[23] For their part, the Mission disliked Grenfell's theology of optimism and action. When his collection of lectures, *What Life Means to Me*, appeared in a British edition in 1913, *Toilers of the Deep* damned it with faint praise. 'We do not endorse some of the views he expresses, nor do we agree with all he says,' it stated.[24]

Thus, when Grenfell returned to England early in 1912, he found himself unexpectedly caught up in the negotiations between the two organizations. When Stirling arrived in February, he found Grenfell worried about a letter from the council's auditors, passed to him without comment by the London office. As Stirling interpreted it, the letter virtually charged him with mismanagement and hinted at the misapplication of funds.[25] As a trusted friend since the time of Grenfell's speedy courtship at sea, Stirling was by now an important adviser and confidant. A few years later Grenfell would write him with characteristic overstatement: 'It is you who I depend on most for advice. You are more to me and Labrador than any one single person on any of our councils. Anne & I go far more by you than anyone. We believe you love & therefore understand better.'[26] For the moment, lacking an official audit of the Labrador branch, the Mission was not able to reflect Grenfell's activities in its annual report. To spare Grenfell the worry, Stirling himself met the chairman of the council, W.F.A. Archibald, to straighten out what he called a 'tangled situation.'

Stirling thought Archibald a warm supporter of Grenfell. But he also noticed what he considered to be a 'narrow' and 'critical' attitude among members of the finance committee, through whom the auditor's letter had been sent, and he reminded them frankly that American support had been attracted not by the Mission but by Grenfell and his work. For its part, the Mission expressed its own misgivings. According to its charter, it was constituted to do medical missionary work, not to carry on commercial ventures, no matter how justifiable. Since Grenfell remained its official representative and superintendent, it feared he might undertake further financial liabilities for which they could not remain responsible. To satisfy both sides, Stirling suggested an independent audit of the New York books by Price, Waterhouse. As for the council's terms, Archibald assured Stirling they were not so inflexible as they appeared. The Mission merely wanted to engage evangelically minded doctors as far as possible, when no other course lay open. Also, it did not expect an indemnity bond from the GAA but the simple assurance that the Mission would not be expected to assume any future debts. To ensure that no debts occurred, it expected someone other than Grenfell to take charge of routine business matters, leaving him free for medical work and for what it called the 'constructive and progressive movements' designed for the welfare of fishermen. Accordingly, the Mission undertook to contribute in the future not less than $10,000 a year – more if Grenfell could campaign specifically for his purposes.

The GAA started to feel more comfortable already. Frightened perhaps by the ice pan episode, the committee hoped to avoid the collapse of the Labrador work that would surely follow if Grenfell injured himself or died. They perceived themselves as administrators, yet they still lacked administrative control, and they depended upon the personal magnetism of an adventurous and sometimes reckless individual who could be lost to them without warning. After receiving a report from Price, Waterhouse urging them to put their accounts in order, they proposed to the Mission a plan to reorganize on 'a more permanent and orderly basis.'[27] The generous American support, they argued, was attributable to Grenfell's 'forceful and winning personality'; otherwise, the Labrador work made 'no strong claim' on the American public. Thus, they suggested a pattern of management that would be 'representative of the contributing interests' and 'responsive to local sentiment.' What they had in mind was a new association incorporated under the Companies Act of the Newfoundland legislature with power to hold assets and transfer properties held in Grenfell's or the Mission's name, and a board of directors representing each of the contributing interests. Each country would maintain an auxiliary committee with a secretary or business manager. But another year would pass before the council agreed to the details, and in the interim two unrelated events, at Pilley's Island and St John's, reinforced their decision to retreat from Labrador after twenty years.

Grenfell could not resist the opportunity to involve himself in the growing cottage hospital movement in Newfoundland. In the autumn of 1910 he had received a petition from Green Bay, asking him to locate a cottage hospital supported by public subscription. The need was manifest: no hospital existed along the coast between St John's and St Anthony, and no doctor between Twillingate and Tilt Cove. Nearly three hundred people sought treatment in St Anthony that year, many of them unfit to travel, and complaints about overcrowding had been heard from passengers on the mail steamers. This kind of practical social problem appealed to Grenfell, who responded by recommending a hospital to be situated at Pilley's Island, a central location visited regularly by two mail steamers yet remote enough to avoid interfering with the livelihood of any Newfoundland practitioners. Once established, he thought, the hospital could be financed by local subscription, supplemented by an annual grant from the Newfoundland government to account for those unable to pay.

In the intervening year he succeeded in acquiring two recent graduates of the Harvard Medical School, Hugh Greeley and Harrison Webster, and three nurses. Together, they would set up a small hospital in an abandoned hotel at Pilley's Island and live in the community for eighteen months. In a letter to the *Evening Telegram* in November 1911, he clearly laid out the Mission's expectations. The government, he pointed out, had made the formation of a cottage hospital system part of their election platform: 'At present the Government has promised $1,000 a year, but if this grant cannot be increased, it seems to be probable the scheme will fall through unless the people are prepared to pay three times as much as was ever required of any people in support of their hospital. This means without outside help, such a scheme in our estimation in no way is possible. Indeed, the staff laboured to make the project work and provide some of the social and educational life accepted as part of the Mission's programme.[28] But the Pilley's Island cottage hospital, for a variety of reasons, was doomed from the start.

Even before the two physicians departed for Newfoundland, Grenfell had changed his mind, realizing that sufficient local funds would not appear. Instead, he thought the experiment would have a better chance in the more prosperous Bay of Islands, situated on the west coast. Here, with the support of the community, he would have the privilege of nominating medical officers but not invite the charge of 'pauperizing' the people by giving them free medical care. 'I am so strongly in favour of Bay of Islands that though our finances are very strained this year, owing to the Institute, I think I can guarantee that the committee will endorse what I have said,' he wrote; 'and if not I think I could give you the money myself within a very short time.'[29] He left it to Greeley to rearrange matters with the government when the young doctor arrived in St John's, expecting that neither the council nor any of the committees was likely to provide funds while the Mission went through its transition.[30] He wrote the manager of the Bank of Montreal in the Bay of Islands to test his proposal:

169

Local doctors would send cases of two classes – those that cannot pay for treatment and those that can pay but need treatment that cannot be obtained outside. We seek cases sent to Boston and Montreal from the prosperous Newfoundlanders. Our hope is to bring within the reach of all the people that which cannot be excelled in the way of medicine and surgery in any city, and that I am certain we have at St. Anthony. Paying patients in the hospital can be attended by any doctor they care to choose.[31]

At the same time, the hospital committee at Pilley's Island reminded Greeley that they had not asked for a hospital in their district, only a doctor. When Grenfell had suggested opening a hospital, they had agreed, expecting it would add to the income of any doctor they might conceivably attract.[32] On the strength of this, Greeley decided to begin work anyway, realizing that the hospital might not continue long.

After a year he presented his findings to the prime minister of Newfoundland. Pilley's Island could be reached by mail steamer, he pointed out, but not during the winter. He expected the hospital would close at the end of the summer of 1912. Grenfell regretted the threatened closure but felt relieved of the possibility of having to maintain another hospital for patients who could not pay for themselves. He could also point to the experience in answer to those Newfoundlanders who insisted the colony did not require the assistance of the Mission. Ordinarily, he would have looked to his committees to keep the hospital going. 'But we are disorganized – at great expense in reconstruction – & unable to do what I never intended to do, guarantee a hospital I couldn't control, as you see I can't P.I.,' he told Greeley.[33] Thus, he wrote the prime minister to announce that the hospital would close unless the government grant were increased. But preoccupied with other matters, he did not press further in St John's. Greeley and Webster decided to go elsewhere, and Grenfell accepted defeat.

Grenfell now turned his attention to a second problem at the King George V Institute. When the institute opened in 1911, he had appointed as superintendent Charles F. Karnopp, an American highly recommended by the international committee of the YMCA, with a view to making an important contribution to seamen ashore in St John's: not only fishermen but naval reservists from the outports and men from Royal Navy ships on station. An ambitious building of brick and reinforced concrete, 115 by 144 feet and four storeys high, the structure had been designed free of charge, at an estimated construction cost of over $150,000, by the New York architectural firm of Delano and Aldrich, incorporating up-to-date features suggested by Sir Frederick Treves. Unlike the seamen's institutes run by the RNMDSF in Britain, it modelled itself on the Rowton Houses, working men's lodging houses run successfully in England at affordable rates, not as charitable institutions.[34] The basement contained a cobbler's shop where men could repair their shoes, a laundry where they could wash their clothes, a forty-five foot swimming pool, and a bowling alley. The main floor featured a large hall that could seat 350, a dining-room, a reading room and a temperance bar. The third and fourth floors consisted of bedrooms, the upper floor reserved exclusively for the use of women in the fishing industry. The superintendent also lived here with his family. With these facilities constructed, the institute proceeded to insert itself into the life of the seafaring community.

But the institute encountered difficulties during its first years of operation. Some St John's citizens complained it was too grandly conceived for ordinary fishermen, others that they could not use it themselves. In August 1912, during his survey of the Mission's assets, Cecil S. Ashdown, the public accountant sent out by Price, Waterhouse, discovered that the superintendent had embezzled over $1,000 in Mission funds during the first year. Karnopp, perhaps because of his wife's illness and her need to return to the United States, had over a period of months deposited donations and proceeds from the sale of equipment into three separate bank accounts without reporting the transactions. Moreover, with the arrival of the accountants, he had burned the official receipt book, thus destroying any trace of the amounts that might have appeared on the stubs.[35]

Under less pressing circumstances, Karnopp might have been permitted to make restitution and the matter might have passed unnoticed. But Grenfell did not want to risk the Mission's reputation. When he returned from Labrador to take a personal hand, he consulted the Mission's counsel, Sir Edward Morris, and decided to press charges.[36] At the trial Karnopp pleaded guilty and threw himself on the mercy of the court, claiming he could have made good the funds if called upon to do so. He had come to St John's, he said, with the impression his board and lodgings would be paid but instead found he was being charged $100 a month.[37] Nevertheless, he was convicted and given a prison sentence of six months.

The institute also lost the services of its female worker, Miss Strangman, sent out by the Mission to work with girls in the fishing industry. Miss Strangman also claimed she found things different from what she had expected. To begin with, there were no facilities provided for her and no girls with whom to work until October, at the end of the fishing season. More important, she insisted the institute was being run as a social club, not as a charity like the ones at home, and that the secretary, Abram Sheard, had cut the daily prayers from the rules she had drawn up for her department. Alarmed by these reports, the chairman of the council wrote

Grenfell, 'We hope you will never allow that noble building to miss its Spiritual use and to be turned into a mere Club, Coffee house and Recreation rooms.'[38]

More positively, though, in 1912 Grenfell enjoyed one significant success when he obtained the services of Dr Harry Paddon, a reserved, highly articulate Englishman who, unlike Little, *did* share his cultural assumptions and who would soon prove to be his most outstanding and longest-serving labourer in Labrador. Paddon seemed destined for missionary work among seafaring men from the start. Born at Thornton Heath, Surrey, the son of Colonel Harry L. Paddon and Mary Van Sommer Paddon, he declared as a boy of eight, during a summer holiday near the fishing fleet of Sheringham, that some day he wanted to go as a missionary. He learned of Labrador from Grenfell himself when he visited his school at Repton on one of his lecture tours. After taking a degree in classics at Oxford, Paddon enrolled as a medical student at St Thomas's Hospital. Following Grenfell's example, he too spent his summers in the North Sea as a physician with the Royal National Mission to Deep Sea Fishermen, and after qualifying for the conjoint medical degree, he entered himself for fifteen months of practical medical and surgical work at the Guest Hospital, Dudley, before launching himself into the missionary field as the medical officer at Indian Harbour.[39]

Upon first arriving in Labrador, Paddon was impressed by Grenfell's energy and broad vision. He remembered in particular the frenzy of Grenfell's first visit to Indian Harbour:

Firing questions and suggestions like shrapnel, helping with an operation, holding an impromptu service for the patients, manhandling rocks from the reservoir bed, anon extemporizing a picnic, inditing a few letters or writing a chapter of some book, sharing the griefs or joys of any fresh comer always with complete detachment from all other interests, trying out new fungi on reluctant 'volunteers,' preaching the gospel of brown flour to a septuagenarian widow while his own dinner cooled and the local Martha worried thereat, ubiquitous yet elusive, always happy and enthusiastic, Dr. Grenfell ever made his visit the event of the summer. When he could think of nothing more to do or say, he breezed off forty miles up the inlet for a goose hunt. This was his annual holiday. A marsh with a hundred or so square miles of area, a river and legions of waterfowl, was his Mecca.[40]

Paddon took more than a transient interest in Labrador as the years went on. He shared Grenfell's view that medicine was but one means to an end. Like Grenfell, he also believed in Labrador's economic potential and consistently dismissed the notion that the resident population should be shifted to a more agreeable location. During his first year he met the nurse Mina Gilchrist and married her a year later, at which point Grenfell could barely contain his glee. 'Paddon is a gem,' he wrote. 'He is *full* of enthusiasm and sanity mixed & courage & hope thrown in. His wife will I think make him a good second.'[41]

Soon Paddon was speculating about Labrador's economic future and delivering opinions such as the following on the benefits of a sound public health program: 'Preventive medicine is, to us, quite as sacred a duty as curative. Hundreds and hundreds of people are killing themselves and one another with consumption by careless spitting and bad ventilation, to say nothing of causes which cannot be helped in many cases (defective diet and clothing).'[42] He began early to preach a gospel of self-help and independence that he wove into his religious services, and as a believer in common-sense living habits he developed his own practical methods for the treatment of minor disorders. During his long residence he would do much to dispel the unfortunate myth of Labrador as a wasteland conferred upon Cain.

Meanwhile, Grenfell had not heard the last of Ashdown's audit. Even before Ashdown arrived back in New York, someone had approached the *New York Herald* with the details of his report and suggested the possibility of mismanagement. On 2 September 1912 a front-page story gave the false impression that the investigation had followed from the defalcation of funds at the institute: 'Bad management of the thousands of dollars donated to them annually, misappropriation of funds, the diverting of property of a charitable institution to private uses, the evasion of customs duties and the renting of their hospital ships and launches for pleasure cruises or for commercial purposes are charges made against some of the men promoting the Labrador missions of Dr. Wilfred T. Grenfell which will be made public today.' While it did not attack Grenfell personally, these distorted and sensational details raised again the continuing question of his role. In addition to the Karnopp affair, it cited the shutting down of co-operative stores and food stations. It reported that Mission vessels had been leased for private or commercial purposes during the season of open water, contrary to the terms for which they had been donated. While the renting of these vessels would benefit the Mission, it argued, it would not materially relieve the fishermen on the coast. The motor launch *Yale* had been chartered by the government to carry mail and the *George B. Cluett* by W.R. Stirling to take his daughters on a cruise to Hudson Strait. Then there was the matter of the Mission's duty-free status. Provisions, clothing, and hospital supplies regularly arrived duty free, and the Mission benefited greatly from the privilege. Someone watching these events was carefully repeating the rumour that articles brought in by the *Cluett* were sold at what had been the St Anthony co-operative store, recently taken over by Grenfell himself. There was also the matter of the reindeer project, 'bungled' through a serious error in selection when dairy deer had been brought in instead of draught deer.

The following day Willis E. Lougee, secretary of the GAA, issued a reassuring statement defending the Mission and pointing out that the planned reorganization would prevent further embezzlement.[43] Ashdown himself gave an interview to the *New York Times*, declaring that Grenfell favoured the reorganization and the application of more up-to-date business methods. But the reports did the most damage, perhaps, when they were carried by the St John's newspapers, presenting further ammunition to those who had struggled to discredit Grenfell, and Abram Sheard suspected the source came from within rather than at arm's length. He told Grenfell, 'I intuitively form the conclusion that it is a "nigger in the fence", someone who has been at close quarters, in confidence, and either has had smouldering dissatisfaction, loss of business, revenge, or a weakness to see an effusion of his, or hers, accepted, and in print. However that may be it is, I read it so, a very serious matter, and I fear will require you, and you only, to use the full force of the love and influence you have engendered in the hearts of many to undo the harm of the criticisms circulated broadcast throughout the world, especially in the United States and Canada.'[44] The perpetrator was never identified. As Sheard, a relative newcomer sent by the New York office, realized, serious damage had been done to the Mission's name because the charges contained an element of truth. If Grenfell did not move quickly to dispel the perception of incompetence, the Mission would lose its principal source of income.

Sheard was one of those who thought Grenfell's highly centralized organization brought difficulties inevitably upon itself. As Dr Wakefield observed, 'There are so many branches of the Mission, with sub-branches and side-branches, and innumerable twigs on each of them, and there is no tap-root, but such vast numbers of roots and rootlets drawing sustenance from pretty nearly all quarters of the globe that efficient organization is not only very especially necessary but also very especially difficult.'[45] Grenfell had directed the Mission virtually single-handed, only occasionally putting his trust in a variety of individuals to carry out his wishes. Over the past four years, however, the Labrador budget had doubled. Labrador services now cost from $50,000 to $60,000 a year, and the Mission stood on the edge of a new phase of its development. Clearly, the Mission could not easily maintain its reputation and continue its commercial interests. Grenfell took the advice seriously, but he also resisted the restraints that stricter organization would place upon his ability to respond personally.

There remained as well the difficulties of the King George V Seamen's Institute, struggling to find its proper role in St John's. Still disturbed by undisputed rumours and the poor image Grenfell had given the colony abroad, the city had not yet reconciled itself to the presence of the Mission, for the council in London wanted to create at the institute a Christian environment, not a public gathering place. It had thus refused the use of the building to organizations as disparate as the St Andrew's Society and the Fishermen's Protective Union. 'You can run the place successfully as a City Institute or a Seamen's and Fishermen's Institute, but not as both,' Secretary Wood wrote Sheard from London, 'and I could point out to you over here several instances where the attempt has been made to run similar undertakings on the dual footing, which have failed so far as the seamen's side of the work was concerned.' The London council was also surprised to find that the local committee had passed a resolution banning religious meetings, clearly at variance with the terms for which the Mission had appealed for funds. 'No doubt there are Christian congregations of different kinds in St. John's,' wrote Wood; 'but we understood one of the main objects of the Building was to provide spiritual help in the way of meetings for men who could not or would not attend an ordinary place of worship.'[46]

Sheard, once referred to by Harry Paddon as 'a genial human ledger,' recommended to W.R. Stirling that the GAA carry out its reorganization cautiously in view of what he perceived to be the prejudices and antagonisms in the colony. He counselled, 'Do you know that I am constrained to conclude that generally speaking the Mission does not command here that respect and that popularity or admiration which it should. The Catholic authorities are deadly opposed to it, the Church of England unfriendly, the Leader of the Fishermen's Union [William F. Coaker] not an upholder: all this combined with indifference on the part of the public, at any rate here in the city, causes me to advise care, if not hesitation, in connection with the whole project.' In view of this, Sheard also opposed the plan to make St John's the headquarters of the new organization, even though he thought the administration and board of governors could be located there. Mostly, he feared that the attendant loss of royal patronage, an honour accorded the British organization, would eliminate a valuable source of prestige. 'If the Royal Patronage is maintained the organization would have to be British,' he told the New England Grenfell Association. 'Far better than a Newfoundland philanthropic Company.'[47]

Instead, the new international structure that fell into place, to be known as the International Grenfell Association (IGA), took on a distinctly American style. The council in London rejected the plan of reorganization in April 1913 but finally approved it in October.[48] The first meeting convened at the Harvard Club early in 1914 with the following founding members present: W.R. Stirling and Cecil Ashdown (Grenfell Association of America); Dr. Clarence J. Blake, Boston, and Professor Reginald A. Daly, Harvard (New England Grenfell Association); José Machado, vice-president of the Canadian Bank Note Company, and Herbert B. Ames, MP (Labrador Medical Mission, Ottawa); the Honourable Robert Watson, manager, Newfoundland Savings Bank (Newfoundland Grenfell Association); and Abram Sheard, secretary. The group represented a wide range of business and financial interests, and they were used to upholding sound financial principles. Two directors from London could not attend.[49]

Tired by the strain of the year's events, Grenfell followed Anne's advice and took a month's holiday in Europe and Asia Minor. After an early Christmas in England, the two spent the following weeks away from the worries of the Mission in Rome, Athens, Smyrna, Constantinople, Budapest, and Vienna. Never satisfied to remain a mere tourist, Grenfell grew impatient with the round of churches and religious art and the obvious wealth devoted to maintaining them. 'It is possibly a defect in my development, like my inability to appreciate classical music,' he wrote.[50] But the change of scene and the historical features of the trip obviously invigorated him. As he returned to England, he wrote W.R. Stirling, 'We had lovely experiences and learnt a thousand things we could never have learnt otherwise, & indeed never even expected. The patriotism of the Greeks, espy Americans, the courage of Greeks & Armenians in Asia, the incapacity of the Turk, the superiority of the races "as you get north," the endless evil done by superstition aping real religion, the efficiency of the American missionary work at the colleges – the marvellous scope & value of their lives – & a thousand other things, make me long to be able to describe them for others' comfort & encouragement. I am a more confirmed optimist than ever.'[51]

Once he returned home, however, Grenfell was not entirely satisfied with the way things were changing. He feared that with its devotion to order and regularity, the International Grenfell Association would lose sight of his religious goals. He confided to Stirling, 'I have written at length to Sheard today. He cannot see that organization doesn't & never can, alone accomplish our ends. We want to bring men to God – to make better children of men – and there must be the human element of personal human contact in that process.' Clearly, he did not fully agree with Sheard, another Price, Waterhouse accountant who he feared would crush the Mission's religious spirit by giving undue attention to organization. He continued, 'Affection & shrewd "organization" sense don't seem to harmonize in me any more than in Sheard. I think I'm softer inside & harder outside than he. Less homogeneous.'[52] As he approached his fiftieth birthday, he could perhaps feel the pioneering phase of his work coming to a close. That summer, he confided in his brother about his state of mind: 'The responsibilities of life are terribly taxing, & unless one has a huge faith in the value of what one little life can do, one is often left wondering if it is "worth the candle." I sometimes do pine for somewhere to get out of the limelight, somewhere where one needn't fight other people's battles, as one has to do here. Whether, when I retire & only come north in summer, I shall find such with headquarters at "Swampscott," I can't say. Anyhow our little house will be readily saleable & a good investment I believe.'[53]

In August a businesslike general meeting was held at the King George v Institute to receive audited reports, elect directors for the coming year, and deal with the budget. The orderly accounting mind had prevailed, and what now came to be known as the 'Grenfell Mission' was established on a sound financial footing, well fixed to meet operating expenses of nearly $67,000 (excluding the institute).[54] By now the war had intervened, making it difficult to conduct business with the United Kingdom. The International Grenfell Association, Incorporated, had put its house in order just in time.

─12─

Coping with War
1914 – 1918

He was one of the people who don't seem to need more than three
or four hours sleep and worked both himself and his associates at full
pressure. It was the same when he took time off for recreation, which
he did for part of one of the days he was here. This took the form of a
fishing picnic up Muddy Bay Brook. By the time we had rowed a heavy
ship's boat the five miles there and back, with some tough scrambling
up the side of the brook, we were pretty tired – but not Grenfell.

Reverend Henry Gordon, *The Labrador Parson*, 76–7

With the outbreak of war in August 1914, Newfoundland, though remote from the centre of hostilities, immediately felt the consequences. The colonial government immediately committed itself to raise a force of one thousand naval reservists and within months sent overseas the first draft of the Newfoundland Regiment. Men volunteered from all over the island and from as far north as Labrador. But more important for Grenfell were the economic consequences. In London the Mission staff scattered into the armed services, and donations dried up. The generous Americans, though not officially at war, experienced a decline in prosperity as a result of market conditions in Europe. The war pinched the fishermen from both sides. No trade took place with the Mediterranean, and war risk insurance discouraged merchants from sending their vessels out. Meanwhile, the price of fish dropped from $7.50 per quintal before the war to $4.00, and the fur market disappeared; the price of sugar rose, and there was a scarcity of flour and meat. Dr Wakefield's wife wrote from Battle Harbour, 'The effect of the war on the people here is disastrous. There is very little fish, and what there is can only be disposed of at lowest prices, as the merchants

178

are never sure whether they will be able to collect the cost of their fish from the firms to which they consign it. In addition to this, the price of everything has gone away up, so that even those who have ready cash get less for their money than formerly.'[1] By the spring of 1915, Grenfell reported, 'The people are having hard times; many families have been without butter or sugar for weeks – there is not a pound to be purchased or borrowed.'[2] Once again, these conditions were felt acutely in the remote, cash-poor communities.

Tuberculosis continued to be the most serious medical problem in the colony, even though the numbers afflicted dropped slightly in 1914. The Mission carried out a strenuous propaganda campaign to curb spitting and encourage fresh air in private dwellings. It also wrestled with beri-beri, a form of neuritis widespread in the northern areas.[3] Normally associated with the tropics, beri-beri had already been traced to a diet based on polished rice, the discarded husks containing the necessary substance to prevent degeneration. In the north, where rice was not normally eaten, a heavy diet of bleached flour produced the same deficiency, and it was necessary to overcome the prejudice against whole-wheat flour as being somehow 'soiled.' The whole notion that nutritious food must contain certain organic trace nutrients in addition to adequate fats, carbohydrates, proteins, and minerals was still emerging in 1912, for the most common deficiency diseases were still associated with infection. Once the principle had been established, however, the Mission took care to promote a balanced diet while attacking the habit of spitting and advocating open windows and proper drainage. Nutrition provided one more dimension for Grenfell's reforms.

The actual experimental work on white flour pressed forward under the direction of Dr Little, who clearly understood the theory of vitamin deficiency. As early as 1912, he had seized upon white flour as the source of the problem, though he carefully added it might not be the only source. Lacking adequate facilities in St Anthony, he conducted experiments with chickens at the Harvard Medical School through one of his assistants, Richard Ohler, who was able to show through the strict diet of nine groups of fowls that the group fed exclusively on white bread, with or without yeast, developed definite polyneuritis. Thus Little concluded that in a wheat diet restricted to milled flour, the necessary vitamins were also absent and that the disease developed with the same certainty.[4]

While Little continued his research, Grenfell turned his attention to social problems. He struggled to create work by employing loggers to cut wood, and Anne sought out new types of home industry. During the winter of 1913–14 she worked at the factory of the Mayfair Flowers Workers in London so that she could bring back the craft of artificial flowers. 'Quite aside from the pecuniary advantage which should accrue to the girls who are making these plants and flowers, we value the effect which the production of beautiful things must have in opening up the minds of the workers,' Grenfell thought.[5] Anne also developed a modest mat industry and found a market for her products in the United States. Frustrated at having to follow a delicate course between Miss Demarest (the Boston secretary), Sheard, and 'certain directors' in New York, by 1916 she was complaining, 'It takes me three and a half hours every day to get ready the necessary mats; and with them and Wilf's correspondence I can refute the statements of certain ones who declare that I do nothing all day long! I am really not nearly so vindictive as I sound, but I have worked now for years very hard on this mat industry, and I am interested to see it go ahead.'[6] Undoubtedly her single-mindedness clashed with the intentions of Jessie Luther, who had run the industrial program for nearly ten years. In the spring of 1915 Miss Luther had expressed satisfaction with the progress made so far in the production of high-quality craft work.[7] But at the end of the summer she submitted her resignation and after a year doing occupational therapy with the US army returned to her place at the Butler Hospital.

The difference of opinion that precipitated her departure undoubtedly arose over the way the mat industry should be run. Jessie Luther had altered the indigenous designs she had encountered and carefully trained her artisans to a high standard, in keeping with the precepts of Mrs Albee, to meet the demands of the market. 'In a country where exactness has not been part of the general native training,' she later wrote, 'this rule has sometimes been difficult to enforce, but it is by no means beyond the powers of anyone who tries, and the effort itself does no harm to the individual, to say the least.'[8] Grenfell, on the other hand, was looking for ways to spread the modest income from the industry among as many people as possible, including those not so highly skilled or talented. In giving notice of her resignation, Jessie Luther hinted at what had happened. 'Your attitude in regard to the Industrial work and your frank statement that your written as well as verbal agreements are to be disregarded make it utterly impossible for me to longer work in connection with one whose views are so at variance with mine and on whose word I cannot rely,' she told him.[9] But Grenfell would not concede that a conflict existed. He suggested she had misinterpreted him and cited 'increasing differences' between her and the Mission staff, including Grieve, Wakefield, and Paddon. 'You cannot expect anyone living right alongside hungry people not to find work for them to earn bread at once because of any rules. I could not work with any colleague who would expect it,' he said. Typically, he refused to dwell upon the past. 'We must all resign sometime,' he added.[10]

Jessie Luther had been sensitive to the need for maintaining the trickle of cash. In a summary of the industrial program written at the end of 1913, she had emphasized the need for a high standard in order to develop a profitable market. 'This is the principle of the work,' she announced, 'but there have been, and are exceptions, when in cases of extreme poverty poor work is accepted because the immediate need of assistance is great and what the people bring in is all they have to offer in return for money or clothing.'[11] Indeed, she appears to have sent a copy of this article to her mentor, Jane Addams, who hoped she would visit Chicago again 'when your work among the deep-sea fisheries is impossible.'[12] But from Anne's point of view, Miss Luther stood as an impediment to the industry, for she seemed willing to sell only at a 'high profit' and employ only a few women who could do 'extra good work.' Moreover, Anne told the Boston office that Grenfell's designs were 'more interesting,' and her judgments were passed on to Jessie.[13] There was room in St Anthony for only one chatelaine, despite Miss Luther's devotion to Grenfell. After discussing the matter with Little and acknowledging what were referred to as Miss Luther's 'physical troubles' of recent years, Grenfell recommended that the board accept her resignation.

In the colony, where the Mission treated well over seven thousand cases in 1914, Grenfell now looked for ways to retrench. Everything the Mission imported had risen in price. Thus, the customary autumn trip north was curtailed and the *Strathcona* tied up for the winter. The *Cluett*, due to bring in expected winter supplies, was again chartered commercially to bring in needed cash, and the sudden change of policy inconvenienced practically everyone in St Anthony. Dr Little, who expected a large consignment, including his winter supply of coal, considered the decision insensitive. He complained, 'All these arrangements which were to have bettered conditions and saved money were upset by one minute's work of the Doctor's. He having the power and thinking to make some money made the charter off his own, not realising the money would be more than eaten up in repairs, freights and losses from changed plans. The change simply announced to Mr. Sheard as having taken place and Sheard being responsible for the running of supplies, etc. Did you ever hear such a ridiculous thing?'[14] Little reserved his severest scorn for Grenfell himself. To Little, the decision confirmed Grenfell's inability to handle finances, even though his power permitted him to do so. He wrote ominously:

The directors have a good deal to learn and they are in a hard position as he is the originator of the whole thing, is the money getter, and yet has been so spoiled and is so childish that he wants to stick his fingers into everything and gets pettish if he is checked in any way. He is so remarkable and likable in so many ways and such an inspirer of youth, and age for that matter, and seems to be able to present religion in such an acceptable shape, and is such a worker and with such a fresh outlook that it is a shame to see his faults hinder his work and crop out in his life. He has no business however to handle anybody's money but his own and should be absolutely forbidden by his trustees from having anything to do with the business affairs of the mission. They will learn so someday if they stick to him. His former way of managing his trustees has been to give them the slip and change them. I don't believe he will this bunch. He is now in the state of making a tremendous fuss about doing less work that counts than anybody I know and is wearing himself and everybody else out doing it.

From his position at St Anthony, Little could see subtle changes occurring. Grenfell was still the founder, but he no longer held power, and he still seemed unaware of the limits placed upon him. To some degree, his role in the north had become marginal. While he contemplated whether to offer his services at the front, he received another reproach, this time from the Dominion government.

As one of his retrenchment measures, he had brought the reindeer herd, diminished by poachers, closer to the hospital in St Anthony to save the salaries of herdsmen. Through Sir Herbert Ames he had also approached the Department of Agriculture to inquire about payment of the annual $1,000 maintenance grant. But by now the department was not so liberally disposed. Only fifty reindeer had been shipped to the Canadian mainland, and these had gone to Fort Smith, in the North-West Territories. Otherwise, the herd had not been delivered to Canadian territory as promised. One attempt had been made in 1910, when the government sent a vessel to the Strait of Belle Isle, but the captain's intentions were misinterpreted, and the herd waited a month at St Anthony, ready for transport, before the error was discovered. This time the minister of agriculture took a narrower view of the whole enterprise. He wrote Ames, 'Now while I have every sympathy with Dr. Grenfell in his noble work for the amelioration of the adverse conditions under which the people on the coast of the Canadian Labrador and elsewhere struggle for existence, I cannot but feel that in continuing to pay to him monies voted by Parliament which, although no doubt advantageously expended by him in the maintenance of the reindeer elsewhere, are not being used for the specific purpose for which they were voted, I am laying myself open to criticism.'[15] Despite his seat in Parliament, Ames did not carry the same authority as Mackenzie King, and King, who had been defeated in 1911 with the Laurier government, could no longer put in a good word to assist his friend. The reindeer continued to languish in St Anthony until 1918, when they were taken over by the Dominion and transported to the north shore of the Gulf of St Lawrence. In 1922, when Grenfell again sought the help of Mackenzie King, by then prime minister, to reintroduce the reindeer into Labrador, the government refused. The considerable cost of the 'experiment' had not shown sufficient results to warrant it.[16]

Most lamentable of all, Grenfell decided to close the hospital in St Anthony for the winter and treat patients in their homes. The hospital, built hurriedly nearly twenty years before out of the enthusiasm of Grenfell's first winter, had not been put on a secure foundation. After it had heaved up and down with each successive winter's frost, the doors would not close and the windows would not open. As soon as the wood dried out, it became difficult to heat, and coal was difficult to obtain. Faced with these conditions, Grenfell worried about the Mission's future. 'We are all right for this year but we shall see next year,' wrote Little.[17]

Other important changes occurred on the coast. In 1915 a new co-operative store was formed at Cape St Charles, but its presence stirred up opposition from the start. The Newfoundland merchants, led by Baine Grieve, complained bitterly about the Mission's interference in the market. In this instance, the IGA board agreed that a blunder had been made and instructed the doctor in Battle Harbour, John Grieve (no relation), to sever his connections with the co-operative as soon as possible. But Baine Grieve was not appeased, and he asserted that Dr Grieve was manipulating Grenfell. He resigned as a member of the Newfoundland Grenfell Association and threatened to do no more business with the Mission. 'When the Executive Officers of the International Grenfell Association settle down to the beneficent work which lies before them, and when fantastic day dreams, which appeal to sentiment or procure notoriety are laid aside,' he wrote ponderously, 'I shall be ready to resume connection with you if it be desired.'[18] Within a year, the merchants petitioned the Newfoundland government for a commission to investigate the Mission's business dealings.

More positively, in 1915 Dr Paddon opened a cottage hospital at North West River, making it possible for him to carry on working after Indian Harbour shut down for the winter, and the Physicians' and Surgeons' Club of Columbia University took over a summer clinic at Spotted Island.[19] But Sheard resigned from his position at the King George V Institute, obstensibly on the advice of his doctor, and sought a more salubrious climate. He was replaced by Dr John Grieve, who had, despite the notoriety at Cape St Charles, impressed Grenfell with his aptitude for figures and management. Dr Hare also resigned from the Harrington hospital. He had complained of heart trouble since 1913, and Grenfell was enraged because the collection of medical fees for that year was so low, amounting to only $27.50. Complaining of his wife's health and his own heart trouble, Hare struck out for Florida.[20] Amidst all of this, Dr Charles Curtis appeared on the coast as a summer volunteer.

Curtis was perhaps the complete antithesis of Grenfell: reserved and modest, with an occasional display of crustiness, but quietly competent. After graduating from the Harvard Medical School, he had encountered Grenfell when he was twenty-eight, when he went to hear him speak in New Haven, Connecticut, and decided to volunteer. He then followed him around the coast during the summer of 1915. Though like Dr Little he shared none of the assumptions of Christian manliness, he was overwhelmed by Grenfell's relentless impulse to serve and make himself useful. He wrote his sister:

> My admiration for Dr. G. grows daily. There are few men of his class walking this world today, *or else* it would be a different place. The talks *he gives* to these people are more eloquent than any of the *oratory* you hear in Boston pulpits. What a difference here on this bleak and rocky coast in some ramshackled building out of the paths of war with half-starved fishermen for an audience in comparison with the grandeur of the city churches. Many a minister could take a lesson from Dr Grenfell. He is certainly one of the leaders of this generation.[21]

Curtis also recognized the other side of Grenfell's personality: his childlike faith, his impracticality. In later years he liked to illustrate this with a story of an event that occurred the following summer. After a visit to Harrington Harbour in the *Strathcona*, Grenfell decided to visit his old friend George Whiteley at Bonne Esperance, though it was blowing hard with a dense fog. There were, of course, no lighthouses, and the coastline was strewn with reefs. While the crew stood about looking uncertain, Grenfell ordered the captain to stop both engines, and they drifted into the Gulf of St Lawrence while he sounded the ship's horn. Curtis recalled,

> We were all standing on deck and in those days we were always very free in our conversation. Someone said, 'We shouldn't be out here anyway; we should never have left Harrington. We're lost.'
> Suddenly out of the fog, evidently having heard the *Strathcona's* horn, came two men in a punt. Grenfell said, 'Ah, God has sent two men out to guide us into the harbor,' and he turned to us who had criticized and said, 'You unbelievers, go below.'
> Instead of going below we all rushed to the rail as the two men scrambled aboard. Dr. Grenfell asked, 'Will you guide us into the harbor?'
> 'No,' said the men, 'we can't. You aren't within twenty miles of "Boney." We have been out here all day and we don't know where we are.'

At that, all of us 'unbelievers' went below, seeing no celestial pilots had arrived.[22]

This story, of course, was told with the benefit of hindsight. At the time Curtis welcomed the chance to do so much good, and he remained in St Anthony that winter to take charge of the hospital during Dr Little's furlough. Grenfell, on his return, took pleasure from reports of his hard work, since the New York directors had discouraged him from placing the responsibility on anyone so junior. 'Wilf gives the same report of him on the boat,' wrote Anne, 'that he gets up at 5 and is never idle one second till he goes to bed. If it isn't medical work it is something else of a practical and useful nature.'[23] Curtis showed more than surgical skill. He genuinely enjoyed the philanthropic side of the Mission's work, even though he manifested no exceptional missionary leanings himself.

While the Mission made economies, Newfoundland began to enjoy relative prosperity during the conduct of the war.[24] After an initial period of confusion, the European markets opened again: Newfoundland surpassed its rivals in the dried fish industry, and prices soared. Prior to 1914 the colony had suffered successive losses in its balance of trade, but during the period 1914–19 it maintained steady gains. Wartime prosperity afforded a level of spending far above what the average Newfoundlander had experienced in peace time, and the Newfoundland government enjoyed a surplus each year, even though it borrowed heavily in New York and London to finance its war effort, thus increasing its national debt. With the ancient cycle of success and failure in the fishing industry swinging upward, the government met its fiscal obligations. For the time being, there was no need to consider what might happen if the market dropped again.

Grenfell wanted to get into the war and see it for himself, but he also wanted to lecture and raise money in case he would have to close more hospitals. When he went to Boston in 1915 to attend the National Congress of Surgeons and receive an honorary fellowship, his mind was made up for him. There he received an invitation to join the Harvard Surgical Unit, a group of thirty surgeons and thirty-six nurses led by Dr David Cheever, which was sailing from New York in support of the Royal Army Medical Corps.[25] The unit was recruited on the basis of six months' service (although not all could be spared to serve out the full time), and Grenfell decided to give his vacation time for three months, knowing he would have to do the mandatory lecturing and return to the coast by June. On 14 December he and Anne embarked for England, arriving in time for Christmas.

At the end of October 1914 Grenfell had written his brother Algie to inquire about the state of Mostyn House and as Britain entered the war announce his intention of volunteering. Algie reported that their mother was vigorous and active and that their brother Cecil was still 'filling a useful niche' in the Royal Marines. But Algie was curbing expenses too. There were ninety-seven boys in residence, ten of those 'guests' and ten more about to leave. No new entries were scheduled for January 1915. By then, 211 Old Mostonians were fighting or training, and despite the carnage in Europe Algie regarded the war in positive terms, as a 'discipline' and 'tonic' that would serve to wake up a country heading into ruin. He blustered about the loss of 'really good chaps' and feared that after the war Britain would fall into the hands of the 'socialists, boozers, skunks & general riff-raff' left over, 'breeding like rabbits, and turning out a disgusting offspring like unto themselves.' He deplored the Dreadnought policy as foolhardy and expensive and condemned the handling of the Royal Navy under Winston Churchill, whom he looked upon as a 'braggart, interfering, cocky little cad.'[26] He urged his brother to stay in Labrador, where he could make himself more useful. Grenfell disregarded his advice. While Anne remained in Parkgate, he took a temporary commission in the rank of major and busied himself getting kitted out for the front lines.

The Royal Army Medical Corps, a body numbering under twenty thousand at the start of the war, grew to about one hundred and fifty thousand by the time hostilities ended. Its strategy, in most instances, was to carry out emergency surgery with knife, bandage, and morphine at the casualty clearing stations, for the first year of combat had revealed that if dead or injured tissue was treated within thirty hours, considerable sepsis and gangrene could be avoided. Still, the RAMC worked without some of the advantages of modern medicine. There was no practical x-ray facility, and blood transfusion was still in its infancy. Without the antibiotics available during the Second World War, field wounds went septic within six hours, and if infection was present from the outset, surgery could only provide more radical treatment, such as amputation. Wounds often had to be kept unstitched, filled with gauze and drained regularly to allow slow healing from the bottom up. Much of the wounding produced by trench warfare, the complex effects of bullets and explosive devices, was new to surgeons.[27] Under these conditions, the RAMC performed efficiently. Of two and a quarter million men requiring treatment in England, one and a half million were patched up sufficiently to return to the front.

Arriving at the northern front in January 1916, Grenfell was immediately given all the work he could do, but as usual he spotted opportunities for reform. By now a stark medical truth had become clear: more damage was being done to the soldiers by exposure and the physical deterioration of trench life than by the enemy. Wallowing in mud and filth during the winter months, men would be brought to the medical stations in a deplorable state, sometimes never having seen the enemy or fired a shot in anger. The trench provided a hospitable breeding ground for the gas (anaerobic) bacillus, which promoted a kind of gangrene, and the tetanus bacillus, often driven into the body with shreds of uniform. The wet mud and exposure also produced trench-foot, a condition confused with frostbite but actually a kind of foot rot. And there were vermin: fleas, typhus-producing lice, and the microscopic mites that put thousands out of action from scabies. After a year's experience, the RAMC brought these conditions under control. As Grenfell showed in an article he sent to *The Times* in 1916, the complex system of casualty clearing stations, field ambulances, advanced dressing posts, and fixed hospitals could now provide reasonably quick care, and close behind the trenches huge vats served as baths for the troops while their uniforms received attention.

The design of appropriate uniforms in particular interested Grenfell. Impatient with convention and fashion at the best of times, he chafed under the army dress regulations, especially the gentlemanly affectations of what he called 'the everlasting little walking cane & kid gloves.' He wrote his mother, 'I feel a little odd – the uniform is most uncomfortable. Very good to *look at* – but for weather, for wind & water, for warmth & for fighting just about as silly as could be devised. What on earth do I want with heavy hard boots – hard beastly gaiters – great heavy leather belt and shoulder straps. They would all freeze you in Labrador & would catch in everything that came along, & the cloth would soak mud & let water through & be cold & beastly.'[28] An interest in reforming dress continued to preoccupy him during the early days at the base camp in Boulogne and then in the trenches at Ypres, Bethune, and Armentières, and he fastened on the idea that clothing itself promoted disease. A month after his arrival, he wrote W.R. Stirling:

> The heavy losses from the gangrene of gas bacillus has [sic] been fairly well met. We can handle it, though it means making terrible large wounds. Trench feet are no longer the problem they were, though not nearly all regiments are equally persistent & therefore successful in preventing a very costly source of leakage to their strength. I have been taking very naturally much interest in that, as we have greater cold in Labrador & *never* have the disease. For it is a disease eventually & not merely a frostbite of temporary importance only. It *permanently* unfits men. Then again the problem of light, warm, waterproof, suitable, economic clothing interests me.[29]

Within two weeks, his recommendations for practical clothing to resist wet and cold conditions, illustrated with his own drawings, appeared in the *British Medical Journal*. Meanwhile, he set Anne to work in England to start a model suit that he was having finished by a *couturière*.[30]

Then there was the vexed question of armour. The helmet, he noted, had already been adopted and had saved numerous lives. But the War Office was reluctant to supply the men, especially the wire cutters and bombers, with protection for the other vital areas. He wrote impatiently, 'I'm hoping something will be done. But everyone seems afraid to talk of "armour" as if it reflected on courage. It could be so light & only over vital places – thus practically *all* abdominal wounds die. There are a thousand other problems. But except in laboratories, where excellent work is being done, everyone is so busy & everyone hates any new departure, till it is proven or is conventionalized, & so no advance is made.'[31] He also wanted to do something about what he called 'soul suffering.' At the beginning of his tour he had ordered a set of slides and with these visited the wards three or four evenings a week, using pictures to gather groups of patients and medical staff. But he did not attract the attention to which he was accustomed. The war was changing men's attitudes to heroism and religion. The business of war was suddenly less chivalric than before, and the experience revealed something to him. The men, in their loneliness, did not feel inclined to talk of following Christ, and the experience made him uncomfortable. 'For much as I honour my colleagues, we are not of the same school exactly or generation either,' he concluded, 'for I am over 50 & they nearer 30.'

Having returned to England at the end of March, he turned his attention to defending the RAMC against charges of incompetence and promoting the war effort. Soon he was at work on an *apologia* to be submitted to *The Times* and a fuller account sent to the *Atlantic Monthly* in the United States.[32] 'How can people feel peace of mind if every day some ignoramus advertises himself by abusing the best friends of their loved & wounded & no one answers them?' he wrote Stirling.[33] The result was a brief survey of the medical and surgical innovations the war had generated, and for this gesture he received the thanks of the War Office and the surgeon general in France. In New York he gave an interview to the *Outlook* in which he described conditions in the field and stated that unless the United States entered the war it could not be won soon. Appealing to their democratic sense, he urged Americans to come in and prevent world domination by the Kaiser: 'It puzzles me ... why America worries over the details and does not admit that to escape what must result if Germany wins was exactly what necessitated America's birth,' he wrote.[34] The warm reception accorded his journalism encouraged him to do more, and he began to think that when the time for retiring from Labrador was right, he could take up the pen to supplement his income.[35]

On returning to St John's, Grenfell once more found himself under attack by the press for an address to the Canadian Club in Montreal, misquoted in the *Montreal Gazette* and the *Montreal Star*.[36] In general, the report was favourable, for he had said nothing this time to offend Newfoundland pride. But the reporter had confused the 'drinking hells' and 'diseases' he had experienced in the North Sea with his description of life on the Labrador coast before the arrival of the Mission, and after the report was carried in the St John's newspapers, he again defended his actions at a lecture at the Casino Theatre.

Grenfell's critics had not been concerned so much this time with the representation of Newfoundland life as with the way in which he had tended to dramatize conditions and portray himself as the saviour of Labrador. The *Daily News*, in an unusually sarcastic report, suggested that the young volunteers of military age working in Labrador would be better employed defending humanity in Europe and mocked the claim that the King George V Institute had been responsible for prohibition. In a letter to the editor, the Reverend Canon F.W. Colley also took strong exception to the report: 'It goes without saying that many of the statements in your paper of yesterday accredited to Dr. Grenfell, are simply false – abominable lies – he has once more been most unfortunate in his report and Newfoundland's reputation suffers.' Colley charged that Grenfell overlooked the sacrifices of earlier missionaries, men content to go about their work unnoticed. A Methodist minister, the Reverend John Reay of Whitbourne, agreed. Dr Grenfell and his workers had done a great deal of work, he acknowledged, 'But Newfoundland got on pretty well before any of them were heard of, and things were improving every year according as the country's means increased.'[37] After Grenfell's Montreal board member, Sir Herbert Ames, investigated the matter, the *Star* issued a public apology, claiming it had reproduced an erroneous report from the *Gazette*,[38] but the *Daily News* remained unrepentant.

Once Grenfell arrived in St Anthony, hoping to get back to work, a fresh set of problems assaulted him there. Since the reindeer herd had now shrunk to 230, he decided to cut his losses and sell the remainder to the Canadian government. In his absence, the replacement for the tight-fisted A.C. Blackburn, his secretary, had made 'a horrible mess' of things. He also needed someone to take over the sheet-iron business that would collapse in the spring when his Penn student married his head nurse and took her back to Pennsylvania. As usual, Grenfell felt the temptation to take it over himself, but this time he was overruled by Anne, who convinced him that such a venture would encourage his critics. 'There was a time when I said "Critics be hanged",' he wrote W.R. Stirling, 'but now I say "get on to your shelf, you're too old for words".'[39] Fortunately there were bright spots as well. He was bringing out another collection of stories, *Tales of the Labrador* (1916). He was enjoying the success of the Mission's non-denominational school, and giving his support to a new Anglican church. He had also managed to erect, on the strength of a gift of $5,000 from a lady in New Bedford, a 'rest house' for visitors to St Anthony awaiting medical treatment. But again, the achievement was not clear cut. He had built the house without passing the proposal through the committee in New York, and as a result his first conflict with the IGA emerged into the open.

Grenfell had rushed the rest house into construction in advance of the winter without confirming it with the New York office. As he acknowledged, the new business procedures had been arranged to prevent just such an occurrence, but he did not regret what had happened. 'My business attributes a long and somewhat sorry connection have made plain to you,' he confessed to W.R. Stirling; 'and you have, with Ashdown and Sheard, possibly saved the otherwise inevitable catastrophe when force of circumstances forces large business concerns and responsibilities on an unbusinesslike man.'[40] The new procedures protected him from the perception of fraud; now, however, he needed something to safeguard him from the dissatisfaction of his own directors, since he had forgotten a minute from the New York office requiring him to send back the plans and estimates to them. Frustrated by this after all his efforts to systematize the Mission's spending, William Adams Delano threatened to quit the IGA board. But Grenfell felt justified. Preoccupied by surgery, the war, and critics in St John's, he had gone ahead as usual.

The episode brought home to Grenfell the limits of his powers. Though fit and enthusiastic, he was no longer a young man, and what he used to ignore now bothered him. 'These attacks from my best friends leave me not enough ability to be the up to date surgeon that I once was and ought now to be,' he confided to Stirling, 'and moreover, I know daily that the courage and idealism I once had is being sapped.' Instead, he charged the directors with misplacing their sympathies. In the summer of 1916 Baine Grieve had shown that business was not prepared to encourage co-operatives. In Grenfell's view, the directors cared more about whether Grieve had withdrawn his support because his earnings had dropped or whether Robert Watson had resigned from the IGA because Paddon had attacked the ineptitude of the colonial secretary's office. Since he could not carry on without his directors, he felt justified in offering his resignation and taking one of the unspecified 'softer' jobs he said he had been offered.

If he felt disillusioned, he never lost interest in the work of other reformers, especially those who could apply the message of Christianity to contemporary social problems. He respected Elwood Worcester of the

Emmanuel Movement and his application of psychotherapy to nervous disorders. He also approved of Arthur Ponsonby of the League of Democratic Control, with his analysis of social convention in *The Camel and the Needle's Eye* (1910) and his attack on class divisions in *The Decline of Aristocracy* (1912). He had also rediscovered his interest in 'natural' medicine. In an article published in *Modern Hospital*, he spelled out the dangers of over-indulgence and noted the benefits of reformers like Dr Richard Cabot, who had demonstrated the importance of social work as a diagnostic and therapeutic aid, and William Graham Sumner, the social Darwinist and advocate of eugenics.[41]

More significantly, he was attracted to the work of Dr John Harvey Kellogg, perhaps the foremost health reformer of the Progressive era. Kellogg's theories about 'rational' diet and abstinence suited Grenfell, whose own unconventionality had begun with H.H. Almond, headmaster of Loretto, many years before. With Kellogg, however, he encountered a surgeon thirteen years his senior who had reduced an alternative style of living to rational principles in the tradition of such reformers as Sylvester Graham and Horace Fletcher.[42] Kellogg, a Seventh Day Adventist, was director of the Battle Creek Sanatarium. Here he advocated total abstinence not only from alcohol but from tea, coffee, chocolate, tobacco, and condiments and recommended the use of meat, milk, cheese, eggs, and refined sugar sparingly. Instead, he promoted foods more 'natural' to humans: whole-grain breakfast cereals, fruits, legumes, peanut butter, and nut-based meat substitutes. He also refrained from administering drugs, maintaining that the best medicine lay in a sensible diet, sensible clothing, correct posture, regular exercise and rest, and exposure to fresh air and sunshine. Grenfell admired him unreservedly as a specimen of what such care could achieve. In the years ahead, he turned to Battle Creek for treatment on numerous occasions.

There were also subtle changes in the way Grenfell thought about religion and its practical applications. A few months after his return from Europe, he had revealed these changes in a letter to his mother:

> The older I get, I'm not nearly as young as I once was, the more I realize there is no lasting joy, & no excuse for life, outside service to man, & so to God. We have to take a larger view of what Christ asks of us, as we get older – & it seems to me, He asks, 'Good faithful work – & doing what we can *well*.' I read more & more of God the *righteous* judge into Christ's teaching 'only believe.' I think I see that, why you always preferred the Church [of England] to the Methodist meeting, & I am more & more of your mind.[43]

He admired Methodist enthusiasm, but he would not embrace it entirely.

He secured money to build an Anglican church in St Anthony and continued to contribute to it, even though his instincts ran counter to the
Anglican sensibility. Having consented to participate in the service of
consecration, he expressed his discomfort with the ceremonial, for as he
explained it to Stirling,

> The keen young parson, v. high church, wore a large red carpet covered with
> Xmas filigree. He looked for all the world like an ambulatory Xmas tree
> without the evergreens, but he has been so keen, so unselfish, & so enthusias-
> tic I followed him round in a black petticoat & short white 'nighty,' to the
> 'awful' astonishment of many of my ultra-Methodist friends who came to
> give us a 'send off.' It seemed a poor send off for so auspicious an occasion
> but the parson was *so* grateful, I felt I would gladly have waded round on my
> hands.[44]

Thus, he was encouraged by the resignation of the bishop of Newfoundland, Llewellyn Jones, whom he considered 'a veritable stone wall.' To
replace him, he supported Dr Edgar Jones, rector of St Thomas's Church
in St John's, whom he considered 'a splendid man.' Dr Jones was an avid
prohibitionist. 'He could make the Episcopal Ch. a real live wire for the
Kingdom of God & not be a befrocked figurehead,' Grenfell said.[45] By the
time the war drew to a close, he again wrote his mother,

> Anne & I have a lessening value for the emotional doctrines of Methodism
> & c. than we had. I never quite understood your own love for the old Church
> prayers & service. But I'm getting it now – this easy, cheap, emotional religion
> does *not* produce trustworthy men. Algy is quite right. They have cheated &
> deceived me so often, & you never can be sure of their *loyalty*. Kindly,
> generous, inoffensive on the whole, pious, churchgoing & as far as possible law
> abiding, but not to be *counted* on, not fighters & sticklers for righteousness,
> squashy & timid, & inefficient in public service except so far as it relates to
> making converts to Methodism. So we rejoice in our dear little Church of
> England here, where we do subscribe to & help both – we are coming to your
> views, which are much those of Kingsley.[46]

At this time, influenced perhaps by Anne's episcopalianism, he regained
his denominational origins. In other subtle ways, he was falling into line
with trends in Protestant thinking, trends associated not with what he
called the 'emotionalist religionist' but with what was becoming recognized
in the United States as the Social Gospel.

The Social Gospel constituted a reforming element in late nineteenth
and early twentieth century religious thinking that brought scientific

knowledge and historical criticism to bear on theological ideas. Its aim was to bring Christian energy to bear upon the social problems of the time, especially those associated with urban living and the conditions of labour. The leaders were largely evangelicals or Christocentric liberals whose approach to social issues was shaped politically within the Progressive movement. And though the more radical espoused some form of socialism, in general they were progressive and reformist rather than revolutionary, aiming their churches in the direction of what Grenfell called 'public service.' As one religious historian has observed, 'The social gospel from its first appearance was critical of the individualism of the earlier evangelicalism, and insisted that the older *personal* ethic was not sufficient for the day of big industry and sprawling cities, for a *social* ethic was also required.'[47] Thus, the transcendant elements expressed by nineteenth-century evangelicals did not continue to receive the same attention. And to some extent, their vision encompassed a Christianized America into which other religious groups did not conveniently fit – particularly the growing Jewish population, a group they regarded apprehensively.

At the same time there was a countervailing fundamentalism centred upon the traditional orthodoxies such as biblical inerrancy, the virgin birth, and the Second Coming. Pre-eminent among those liberal Protestants who would engage the fundamentalists was the Reverend Harry Emerson Fosdick, a Baptist minister whose writings Grenfell admired.[48] Grenfell had once preached at Fosdick's church in Montclair, New Jersey, and since that time Fosdick treated him as a heroic figure whose practical missionary work served as an example of how much difference an individual Christian could make to the world.[49] Grenfell had continually advocated the entry of the United States into the war, and when he read Fosdick's book *The Challenge of the Present Crisis*, written in 1917 to justify American intervention, he became an admirer of Fosdick's ideas.

One other indication of Grenfell's thinking at this time was his interest in the novels of Winston Churchill, a social melodramatist whose representations of social and moral regeneration through service to others made him one of the novelists most widely read by the American middle class. Grenfell admired Churchill's novels and recommended them to others, undoubtedly because of the intellectual assumptions on which they were formed – an ethical optimism whereby characters free to make ethical choices saw justice inevitably done. Churchill was a romantic seeking to accommodate himself to the scientific changes brought about at the turn of the century. Grenfell himself was a man of nineteenth-century sensibility who from this point onward searched for a way of accommodating a nineteenth-century Christian belief to twentieth-century social change. Both Churchill the novelist and Grenfell the reformer faced the irreconcilable differences between two assumptions: that the human spirit is free of material considerations to make moral and ethical choices and that we are confined in our dealings by the material universe. More and more, Grenfell was seeking a way of reconciling the two.

While he reconsidered his religious stance, important changes were occurring in the running of the medical services in St Anthony. Dr Little, after a decade of work, was tiring of the adventure. To begin with, his eyes had begun to fail, making surgery more difficult. His three children required an education, and his father had called for him to come home. With the United States about to enter the war, he felt less secure about remaining so far away from Boston. Perhaps more important, he was tired of Grenfell's lack of management and could no longer tolerate it. Many years later, Curtis recalled,

> One of the main reasons that Dr Little left the Mission was that he found there was little co-operation between himself and Dr Grenfell. The hospital was packed with patients; its equipment was primitive and it had very few facilities, and at that time when the medical situation was very arduous and complicated, Dr Grenfell built an orphanage, which Dr. Little didn't approve of at that time because he thought the hospital was much more important. There was often disagreement between them.[50]

In 1916 Little spent a furlough in Boston. Then, after his father offered to back him if he entered the competitive Boston medical world, he made up his mind. His wife Ruth, though she shared his misgivings, agreed that the time had come for him to prove himself in a larger context.[51] In June 1917 Little wrote an affectionate letter to Grenfell in which he offered his resignation:

> My father is getting old and wants me. My wife's mother is growing old, is not well, and needs us. My children are growing up and in this life I cannot make a permanent home for them, assure their future education or my wife's comfort in case of casualty. I have not been well for two years and the rough side of the life does not seem to help me. The hospital part of the work which has been mine more especially is constructed on its present scale and further development seems unlikely. My part of the work will run along well. The war has been a great unsettler and men are needed at home. It is perhaps unnecessary to go farther.[52]

The news discouraged Grenfell, but he thought Little was justified. In October he took him and his family aboard the *Strathcona* and brought them to where they connected with the train. It was a sad parting. The two had been through a great deal together, including the ice pan episode. And as Grenfell acknowledged, it was Little who had systematized the hospital and maintained its professional rating. But he was not one to sentimentalize for long. Luckily there was a substitute close at hand. 'We have however a fine fellow in Dr. Curtis,' he wrote triumphantly, 'a man much more quickly beloved by the individual than Little. He is a good surgeon, an agressive [sic] Christian & a tireless physical worker. Gloria sit Deo.'[53]

Charles Curtis also sprang from New England roots. Good natured and easy-going with ruddy cheeks, a hearty guffaw, and an ever-present pipe he relit constantly, he nevertheless appeared reserved, if not shy. During his winter in charge of the St Anthony hospital, he had demonstrated a strong ability for administration and decision. In addition, he loved the winter, as Little had, and his first exciting year killed what remained of an ambition to settle into a more predictable Beacon Street practice in Boston.

Having found a replacement for Little, Grenfell faced in the autumn of 1917 the most serious challenge to his legitimacy so far, the investigations of the Squarey Commission. That year, the merchants and traders who felt threatened by the prospect of competition finally made a formal complaint to the Newfoundland government in two separate petitions that, among other things, charged the Mission with competing in the market, benefiting unfairly from customs concessions, misrepresenting Newfoundland abroad as a society of paupers, and operating with the capital of American philanthropists. It recommended that the privilege accorded the International Grenfell Association by the government be abolished. At last the long-standing conflicts with local merchants and government placemen had come into the open. 'For over twenty years this sort of vapouring has gone on, Sir,' Paddon wrote Sir Richard Squires. 'God knows we have nothing to fear from investigation; whereas others have a good deal to fear, if the investigation be thorough & unbiased.'[54]

The commissioner was Magistrate R.T. Squarey, then seventy-one years old. 'He has a reputation like his name, which is Squarey,' observed Grenfell condescendingly. 'Educatus Newfoundlandian & limited but a good, honest hearted man he seems.' Squarey made his rounds accompanied by the opposing lawyers and a court stenographer. After hearing evidence in St John's, he interviewed merchants at Harbour Grace and Carbonear, then boarded the *Strathcona* with his entourage en route to St Anthony. 'Well, I picked them up at Norris Arm,' wrote Grenfell, barely checking his glee, '& before we were round Cape John all were very ill, except the old sailor magistrate, & an atmosphere of sympathy began to distill.'[55] Long before they reached Battle Harbour, all idea of a 'yachting cruise' had dissipated, and when Grenfell entered a harbour for the night the commissioner inadvertently witnessed one of his over-the-side clinics. Patients came aboard at once, some with teeth to be pulled, and the screaming through the bulkheads alerted the investigators to what Grenfell called the 'weirdness' of his practice. At St Anthony, Squarey met Dr Fallon, the Roman Catholic who happened to be in charge, thus scotching the charge of 'narrow proseletyzing' by the Mission. In the hospital itself, he witnessed the removal of a pin from a baby after it had been detected by x-ray and watched Grenfell remove an upper jaw for cancer. Prevented from leaving by a strong head wind, the whole commission ended up Sunday night singing hymns with the staff. By this time Squarey felt kindly disposed, for he had not yet found anything to support the petitioners' claim. While Grenfell regretted having to take the time, he acknowledged that the report would ultimately do him good. 'It certainly is the best thing, so far as I can see, that ever happened [to] this mission,' he assured Stirling.

After hearing evidence at Battle Harbour, Cape St Charles, Forteau, and the 'experimental' hospital at Pilley's Island, Squarey concluded that considerable misunderstanding about the work of the IGA existed. He had by then examined sixty witnesses without finding a single connection between the Mission and the co-operative stores, and he had received no complaints about religious interference.[56] Consequently, he offered a single recommendation to ensure harmony. In 1916 the value of imported clothing amounted to nearly $3,000. In future, he recommended, all imported clothing should be liable for a duty that the government would rebate annually, thus avoiding any doubt. While the sum was not extensive in commercial terms, Squarey considered it a 'burning sore' that would have to be removed before friendly relations could exist between the IGA and the businessmen of Newfoundland and Labrador.

As the war ended, the leadership of the Mission changed hands. Jessie Luther had left over a disagreement. Sheard had resigned from the institute after only four years. Dr Wakefield had gone to the front, and Dr Little had felt the prods of frustration and time. With the death of W.R. Stirling in 1918 Grenfell lost his confidant and father confessor. The Mission seemed to take a new direction, and more and more, he turned to Anne for support and advice. He had spent twenty-five years straining to keep together the precarious network of hospitals, nursing stations, and vessels, and his age would not permit him to keep up the same pace for ever. Having lost money by investing in his ventures, he needed a form of income other than the modest salary paid him by the IGA. It was time to take advantage of his reputation through writing and lecturing while he could still promote the interests of the Mission.

— 13 —

Promoting the Mission
1918 – 1920

*Sitting down to write one's own life story has always loomed up before
my imagination as an admission that one was passing the post which
marks the last lap; and though it was a justly celebrated physician
who told us that we might profitably crawl upon the shelf at half a
century, that added no attraction for me to the effort, when I passed
that goal.*

Wilfred Grenfell, *A Labrador Doctor*

The autobiographer, unlike the biographer or the historian, faces special
problems of composition. Unable to distance himself completely from
the events under review, he must nevertheless convey to the reader an
impression of a life while it still goes on and force himself into imaginative
choices about how to reveal himself satisfactorily. He must literally invent
himself in retrospect as he shuffles, selects, and discards the accumula-
tions of a lifetime. In this way the autobiography resembles the novel. Just
as the novelist dissolves theoretical statements into personal relationships,
the autobiographer imposes upon his own life a theoretical or intellectual
pattern with which he has come to identify himself or aims at the imagined
coherence of his own character and attitudes.[1]

Critics have drawn attention to further similarities between autobiography and the novel, especially the shared use of repeated narrative struc-
tures. We find, for example, that some autobiographers, particularly those
of the last century, have chosen a metaphor of the self and developed it in
a narrative sequence so as to create a kind of personal myth. Others,
especially politicians, have viewed their lives in heroic terms, granting
themselves special qualities for overcoming obstacles in the service of

some great cause. Still others, usually religious writers, have cast their lives as journeys of the soul. Such strategies require the restructuring of events, not merely the reporting of them. Moreover, the writer is often tendentious. He may be an individual of stature or reputation taking advantage of an unwonted period of leisure, retirement, or reflection to celebrate his service to society at large; or he may be an apologist for his cause, his profession, or his very life itself. Having followed Grenfell from the sands of Dee to the coast of Labrador, we must now stop to consider what construction he placed on the events that led him there. The authorial strategy, composition, and subsequent use of his autobiography reveal as much about the author as the autobiography itself.

While Grenfell's autobiography, *A Labrador Doctor* (1919), will not be read today as a faithful record of his life, it shows how the problems of autobiographical composition must be faced by a man of great reputation. To begin with, it holds no surprises, nothing to arrest the curious or awaken the bored – none of the startling episodes we are accustomed to finding among the confessions of professional athletes, movie stars, explorers, or politicians. This is an autobiography of a different order: the life of a physician conscious of the world's attention and accustomed to viewing his actions in spiritual terms. The title suggests a record of Grenfell's medical achievements, and we might reasonably expect something comparable to the autobiographies of other eminent British physicians and surgeons of the same period. But it is not like any of these.

It is not even like Dr Albert Schweitzer's *Out of My Life and Thought* (1931), an autobiography that invites comparison because the lives of the two medical missionaries have been compared so often. Schweitzer's autobiography is the work of an intellectual Christian. Schweitzer appears before the reader not in the persona of a pastor or even of a doctor of medicine but of a professor who is equally at ease with linguistic matters, Christian thought, or music. As he casts his life in retrospect, he never seems to tire of lecturing, whether he is talking about the difference between French and German, the history of the early church, or the mechanics of organ building. He seems equally comfortable with the humanities and the sciences. Barred from working in his own hospital while he was interned during the First World War, for example, he tells us he filled up his time writing a book about the philosophy of civilization so as to illustrate what he perceived to be its decline. Elsewhere, he informs us that his ethical catch-phrase 'reverence for life' flashed involuntarily upon his mind one day while he was steaming off to aid another missionary's wife. But Grenfell, the manly Christian, wrote within a different autobiographical tradition, the tradition of spiritual autobiography.

He had first begun to think about autobiography in 1911, after the ice pan adventure had turned him into an international folk hero. After observing the success of *Adrift on an Ice-Pan* (1909), his publisher, Houghton Mifflin, urged him to get his whole life story into print and offered to publish it.[2] But Grenfell was not yet ready for the task. He had married by then, and he was having to deal with the reorganization of the Mission. Not until 1916, after being encouraged by the success of his war journalism, did he take up the idea again seriously. That summer, fresh from defending himself in St John's and inclining towards retirement and a writing career, he informed his mother of a new book of stories he was preparing for the press. He also announced, with his usual enthusiasm for new ideas, 'some day I'm going to do my "autobiography". I wonder how it will be writing "all about oneself." I must read some autobiographies first. Do you know any good *auto*biographies? Tell me one or two you like best & better still buy for me two of the best you know. Mind *not* biographies but *auto*biographies, written by the man himself or woman herself.'[3]

He approached the task this time with greater confidence, for he could count on the encouragement and editorial support of Anne. Still, he did not intend a revealing book about his inner self. While he would employ an engaging and confidential tone, his life would be deliberately contrived to preserve the family's privacy and dignity while he accentuated certain traits of Christian manliness. We have some sense of the way he wanted to construe his upbringing from a letter written to his mother early in 1918:

It won't be a very formal affair. But I want some facts about Father for it. What scholarship did he win at Oxford? What poems or articles or anything else did he ever write? Did he ever publish anything? Did his father publish anything? If you can give me the words of anything nice he ever wrote I should be glad to have it. Also if you have any nice ones of Algie's. That one of the 12th of May or any nice one from the old Griffin or any nice hymn. Also any incident of my boy or babyhood that you remember as amusing or quaint or interesting. Do you remember Charles Kingsley visiting Parkgate and anything he said to me or anyone of any interest or anything interesting about him, also anything about your Father that was interesting or any incident in your own life that might be interesting, esp^y your reason why we boys were allowed to roam abroad alone so much & why you weren't anxious about us? It might amuse you, & it certainly would help me to have some of [the] things in the lives of our family away back, or present, that would interest others. Of course anything that you thought specially was of a formative influence, like special bible teaching also would be interesting.[4]

With this kind of information, he aimed to engage the reader and present a favourable impression of the Mission rather than, say, look within himself or invoke the spirit of the times.

If the choice of safe subject matter was important, so was the maintenance of a single point of view, for there were actually two 'authors' involved with its production. Anne Grenfell contributed to it substantially. Together, the two contrived an 'autobiography' that reinforced the popular conception of the missionary doctor without revealing much about him, and Anne assumed the management of it just as she managed so much of his other writing. The drafts preserved at Yale show that after Grenfell had framed them out by hand, she would transform them into a typed copy, eliminating excessive anecdote, softening judgments, and curbing Grenfell's tendency to dilate upon religious matters. As one of his summer secretaries reminded him, 'I know from the work I did in 1918 on "The Labrador Doctor" just how much of your literary efforts were produced through her love and wise editing and collecting.'[5] By now Anne had become an essential part of the writing process. While the book took shape, Grenfell revealed to Dorothy Stirling that Anne was, in fact, the author of another forthcoming book. 'The autobiography, shameless product of egotism, bursts on a suffering world next Xmas,' he said, 'and a little book of stories really written by Anne, but called mine, comes out at Easter.'[6] While it did not appear that soon, *Labrador Days: Tales of the Sea Toilers*, a collection of moral narratives 'collected and re-written' from a doctor's point of view, took shape in Anne's hands.[7] It was published by Houghton Mifflin the same year. Thereafter, the practice of joint authorship continued.

These and later productions did not simply provide an outlet for Anne's personal urge to write: they formed part of the publicity and fund-raising strategy, the titles widely advertised in the Mission's pamphlets and brochures and on the back pages of *Among the Deep Sea Fishers*. Thus, *A Labrador Doctor* was written with an audience in mind. It was the kind of 'wholesome' and 'instructive' missionary literature marketed by missionary societies throughout the world: the Bible commentaries, devotional tracts, and biographies of great and noble personages that might serve as an inspiration to believer and non-believer alike. Indeed, in his preface Grenfell offered his autobiography as a work of practical benefit, as unadulterated Christian experience that could be helpful to others.

While Grenfell was interested in writing an autobiography, he was also keen to obtain the best financial arrangement commensurate with his reputation and his experience as an author. In the summer of 1917, a month after Little's resignation, he instigated the bargaining process himself when he wrote Houghton Mifflin in Boston to report a 'very favorable' offer from an English firm but asking whether they would care to bid.

Within a month he received a reply from Ferris Greenslet, the literary editor, expressing interest but also insisting that in view of the urgency with which the firm had pressed the idea on Grenfell in the first place and their 'successful publishing relations' since, Houghton Mifflin possessed a 'priority of claim.' With that in mind, Greenslet thought the company should not have to make a competitive bid for an unwritten book. Instead, he offered a generous royalty of 20 per cent of the list price with an advance based on advance orders – 25 per cent if the book were marketed in England.[8] He assured Grenfell that, in any case, a 'generous' contract would undoubtedly emerge and urged him to tell the unnamed English publisher that he had promised the book elsewhere. Greenslet, a scholar with an instinct for making money, already sensed the book's potential and encouraged Grenfell to submit the manuscript by the end of 1918, pointing out that it would undoubtedly stimulate the sales of his other books as well.

In November Grenfell informed Greenslet that Anne had already sent for 'the necessary papers' and that he would have time to get the book under way that winter at the cottage in Swampscott, during his lecture tour.[9] After he visited the Boston offices in December, however, Greenslet was prepared to offer even more generous terms, a 'half-profit' sharing instead of regular royalties. This way, all the manufacturing and advertising expenses would be charged to a joint account, and the excess of the proceeds over expenses would be divided equally between author and publisher. We must note here that no charge was to be made for any of the publisher's expense for doing business, and the choice between profit-sharing and regular royalties was left open until the manuscript was complete. During this process, Greenslet took pains to make himself as hospitable as possible, bearing in mind the potential importance of the book. 'I cannot think of any other autobiography that we should welcome more heartily, publish with greater satisfaction, and for which we should expect a larger measure of success,' he wrote. 'And I make no bones of repeating what I told you yesterday, that I think this house can sell more copies of a biography or autobiography than any other house in America.'[10] Grenfell soon replied with his acceptance of the half-profit scheme at an irreducible minimum, and the company put the autobiography on its list of forthcoming books for the autumn.

By the end of the summer of 1918 Anne was doing most of the editing and working out the details with Greenslet, coaxing one chapter out of Grenfell at a time. She reported: 'By dint of hard labour on *my* part the Doctor has written some nine chapters of his autobiography. As the people of this Coast would say, he does the work "in punishment," it not being to his liking to be telling of himself.'[11] By October, with seventeen chapters roughed out, Greenslet was surprised by the quality and began to think in terms of two volumes, with perhaps fifty illustrations to bring out the 'picturesque backgrounds' of Grenfell's career. He thought the book would accomplish one of its purposes – attracting interest in Grenfell's work – and he judged that 'Dr. Grenfell has, I think, hit a happy vein from the very beginning. The story runs vividly and humorously, with the human quality, that is always the making of a good autobiography. It ought, when finished, [to] give a very keen pleasure to the wide circle of his personal admirers, and extend the radius of that circle still further.' Meanwhile, although he constantly refrained from revealing too much, Grenfell finished the final chapters early in the new year.[12] They had managed to complete the task in less than twelve months while Grenfell continued to go about his business and Anne worked with Katie Spalding, superintendent of the orphanage, on a book of pseudo-letters (*Le Petit Nord*) about life in St Anthony.[13]

A Labrador Doctor proved to be a commercial success both in the United States and in Britain. The question must therefore be asked, What construction or personal myth did Grenfell apply to his life to date to give it such widespread appeal? The answer is not far to seek. *A Labrador Doctor* is written, consciously or not, in the tradition of 'spiritual autobiography,' a conventional literary form long established by numerous Puritan autobiographies of the seventeenth century. The spiritual autobiography of old would begin with a recital of early providential mercies and opportunities for demonstrating virtue and then continue by describing a period of sin and resistance to the Gospel or, at most, a mere adherence to the externals of religion. The pivotal episode was an unforeseen act of conversion, often induced by an 'awakening' sermon. There followed a call to preach and a summary of the writer's 'ministry,' accompanied by anecdotes illustrating the nature of his pastoral work. Significant events in the convert's life, assumed to be direct consequences of his conversion, then constituted the main body. The book would end on a note of spiritual self-satisfaction as the writer oriented himself towards the future.

A Labrador Doctor, which followed this pattern, struck a chord with many readers. Like its forerunner, *Adrift on an Icepan*, it became a classic of its kind, and it is still remembered vividly by readers of a certain generation. *Adrift on an Icepan* remains today an outstanding example of the survival or personal history narrative, one that has maintained a life of its own long after Grenfell's death. *A Labrador Doctor*, on the other hand, became a kind of Protestant manual, a case history of cultural intervention in a remote society far removed from the reader. It was this practical feature of the book, its catalogue of benevolent accomplishment, that readers responded to as well as the familar motifs of spiritual regeneration. 'I believe you will find these reviews uncommonly pleasant reading,' wrote Ferris Greenslet soon after publication; 'certainly it is unusual for a book to meet with such unanimity of praise.'[14]

The *New York Times* review provides a good example of how this was done.[15] The reviewer makes the mistake of suggesting that the author was the centre of the story. He was not. The *Mission* was the centre. Only later on does the reviewer consider the book's real importance when he says, 'No one who is in the least interested in human endeavours to better the world can afford to miss it.' He then mentions that an endowment of one million dollars would be required to carry on the basic work of the Mission and suggests that the book itself would be enough to inspire the collection of many times that amount. Similarly, the *Outlook* praised the 'magnitude' of Grenfell's work and strongly suggested that many of those who read the book would want to assist with the million-dollar endowment already proposed by the IGA.[16] Thus, as Grenfell turned his attention more exclusively to lecturing throughout the 1920s, the book would become one of his principal instruments. In the year 1920 alone, royalties from the sale of all his books under the Houghton Mifflin imprint brought him $8,660.87 after taxes, a respectable earning for any writer. By 1921 Greenslet was observing with some satisfaction, 'You will notice that all of the books are enjoying quite a pleasant activity, and that *The Labrador Doctor* in particular has made a substantial contribution to our joint profit.'[17] Grenfell very quickly got into the habit of having copies on hand for his lectures and autographing them.

During the 1920s the insights provided by the autobiography encouraged a whole new generation of authors to write about Grenfell's life as heroic biography.[18] By flooding the market, they inadvertently reduced the sale of his own books. Dillon Wallace, an American author who had survived a disastrous trek through the Labrador wilderness and constructed a career from a string of children's books set in the region, was perhaps the worst perpetrator. His boys' book *The Story of Grenfell of Labrador* (1922) was intended as a tribute, but it drew so heavily on the autobiography that Grenfell considered taking court action for copyright infringement. 'Wallace is a well meaning man (I think),' he wrote Greenslet, 'but very silly to let Briggs of Revell's induce him to do this.'[19] In a previous unpleasant instance, Briggs had capitalized on the Mission's good will and prompted Norman Duncan to write *Dr Grenfell's Parish* (1905). The royalties from this book were to go to the Mission, but none had. Grenfell now feared that the cheaper book would show up where he lectured and cut into his own sales.

Journeying through Montreal, Ottawa, Toronto, Buffalo, and Philadelphia that year, he noticed that sales usually rose whenever he lectured, and he urged Greenslet to send review copies to the local papers. The sales were further encouraged by serial publication in journals such as *Onward*, a Canadian weekly, and the *Congregationalist*. As Grenfell's lecturing schedule intensified, he urged Houghton Mifflin to communicate with the organizers along the way so that they could press local booksellers to keep copies in stock, and like any other author, he did not hesitate to let the publisher know when copies ran short. In 1924, for example, he wrote from Tampa, Florida, 'I visited the book shops here – no Labrador Doctors – & I heard one lady ask for one! I am sure the sale will go up with the lectures if *only* the shops are apprised ahead. This ground is all new & I feel both books should be here. It would be a great help to our publicity if the schools took the Ice Pan book. That would sell the others. Can anything be done? They knew very little of us down here.'[20]

Generally speaking, however, he was satisfied with the sales. The autobiography was still selling well after ten years, especially if Grenfell autographed copies and drew one of his sketches on the flyleaf. By 1932, as a result of the half-profit contract, both Grenfell and Houghton Mifflin had earned just under $20,000 from the venture. This, together with Grenfell's other royalties, his journalism and his lecturing, augmented his income considerably. But despite the apparent success, the publisher actually lost money. Houghton Mifflin's share had failed to cover the book's proportion of the firm's general overhead by almost $4,000. Thus, while it had contributed substantially to the expense of carrying on the business, it had contributed nothing to the dividends due stockholders.[21] No matter how many books Grenfell sold, Houghton Mifflin could never come out on top. In the future, they would not issue such a contract.

Grenfell now prepared for another exacting winter of lecturing, knowing that each year of touring around the urban centres took more out of him than the one before. 'How quickly time passes,' he had written his mother after bringing the *Strathcona* back to St Anthony at the end of the 1917 season. 'Summer has flown, & we are going shortly to Swampscott. Such a migration: 3 girls, 3 kids & two old fogies!!'[22] This factual statement was offered partially in jest, but it betrayed something more. He had reached a stage in life where he was more conscious of the passage of time, and if he did not readily exhibit the effects of his age, he had at least learned to live with the accumulating ailments attendant upon advancing years. His energy remained high, but it was not the energy of youth. It was the energy of a man obsessed with a grand objective and conscious of the short time left to achieve it. That autumn, with a schedule planned by a lecturing agency, he toured the eastern United States with his lecture 'On Two Fronts,' not the usual promotion of the Mission but a personal account of the war and the duty of the Christian soldier. After only a week at the

Promoting the Mission

Swampscott cottage at Christmas, he took on a more ambitious tour of the Midwest and Canada in 1918. Only then did he realize how much he had lost the physical power he had always taken for granted.

Having left the three children in the custody of Anne's mother, Mrs MacClanahan, the two set off for three months. 'So far the lectures have been very successful,' Anne reported from Pennsylvania, 'but Wilf certainly does have to pay the price for this by hard labour. Now we are just starting out on another three months separation from our kiddies & we certainly do not anticipate it.'[23] After reaching Cleveland, Grenfell felt obliged to go to Canada – not for the money but for what he termed the 'sentiment' – for he did not look forward to the cold weather, and he could have raised more money in the States. Early in January, he wrote his mother, 'I *have* to work 7 days a week now & every night till late – so I just must have a holiday before the summer work comes on me.' As usual, the American audiences were attentive and generous, and a week later he wrote from Winnetka, Illinois: 'I have been speaking so much night after night. I get $100.00 a night & expenses guaranteed & whatever over is left after paying expenses. This pays the Mission very well, and it helps me to be more satisfied to be talking so much, that so many come & thank me for the spiritual uplift they get.'[24]

But soon he paid the price for talking so much, and the events of the tour illustrate the strain placed both on him and on the family as a whole. Soon after the start of the Toronto schedule his voice gave out entirely; he was put to bed and forbidden by his doctors to move for two days. When a spark returned and he threatened to get up, Anne was obliged to hide his clothes. 'To begin with Wilf has had a schedule which was enough to break down the constitution of a machine, which is exactly the light in which those who run his lectures seem to regard him,' she said. 'In Toronto, to cap the climax, he was given six & seven lectures a day with the result that he came down with an attack of bronchitis & just missed pneumonia.'[25] Advised to leave off lecturing and go to California for a rest, he refused until he had finished some engagements already promised. In the midst of this, Anne received a telegram from her mother, who was holding things together at Swampscott. A young Newfoundlander living in the house and studying plumbing at the Wentworth Institute had acquired pneumonia and was not expected to live. She herself could not procure any coal and desired to know what she would do if she could not heat the house. With Grenfell still in bed, Anne took the next train to Boston to straighten things out.

Two days later Grenfell was on his own in Lindsay, Ontario, making his way to Uxbridge and then Ottawa, where he had received so much support and where he needed to make his presence felt. By the time he had reached Ottawa he was clearly not fit to continue, and the Ottawa committee pressed him to go to Florida while he still could. The loss of control over his own schedule forced him to reflect more seriously about how he apportioned his time and that of his family, and with his own health at risk he took a decision about his future activities. 'This will be our very last winter in the north I expect,' he wrote his mother. 'We shall probably only go on going north for the open water season. I've had 30 years of the fishermen's work & feel as if I would like to ease up a little. We shall come home the following winter to England if the war is over & all goes well. The children grow apace, but alas we see little of them.'[26]

These words were written on the eve of his fifty-third birthday. Time was passing, and the continuance of the Mission had not been provided for. Now more than ever, the IGA recognized the need for an endowment fund to place their activities on a sounder footing. They decided at the annual meeting of May 1920 to raise one and a half million dollars, hoping to realize an annual income of $50,000 that would give a measure of self-sufficiency and room for expansion. Though the campaign was intended to relieve Grenfell of campaigning, it was he who would travel throughout Canada, the United States, and Britain to promote it. With a campaign office in New York and the organization in the hands of an experienced financial campaigner, Perry Burgess, by October he was ready to begin with a large meeting in Boston.

As he prepared himself for this new endeavour, he felt unsure of it. He could not imagine how long it would take to reach the objective, especially since he was looking for money at the beginning of a serious economic recession. Moreover, he had never once come close to making so much money during his whistle-stop tours of schools and parishes before. Burgess had organized the campaign in such a way that most of it could be pledged at large meetings in the major cities, not in local parishes and schools or among groups of friends. In keeping with contemporary fund-raising strategy, he had arranged it so that the major part of each audience was made up of an invited group, for as Grenfell rationalized it he wanted to interest middle-class philanthropy, the 'best people,' not the 'ultra-religious' like the YMCA. 'People are interested in this class of work in these days,' he conjectured. 'They have little or no interest in the old theological exposition of the love of God.'[27]

Grenfell was to open each evening with a stereopticon lecture featuring dissolving views of the Labrador, and Burgess was to follow with a direct appeal. This way, he could make maximum use of his time. Yet despite the thorough preparations, Grenfell still worried as the first lecture at the Symphony Hall in Boston approached. Burgess recalled, 'Somewhat to my amusement, Grenfell, the fearless, was very concerned ... No one would be interested in what he was doing, he thought, no one would pay any attention to such an appeal. The whole thing was going to be a dismal mistake.'[28] Accordingly, Burgess had not told him he had also rented the Horticultural Hall, across the street, to accommodate the overflow. But long before the lecture began, the hall filled and the overflow was directed across the street, where Grenfell's longtime colleague Francis Sayre took charge until Grenfell arrived to repeat his lecture. Many were turned away. He raised a substantial sum that night, and the campaign had made an encouraging start.

— 14 —

The Lecture Circuit
1918 – 1923

He hates – in fact, he refuses, like Peter Pan – to grow up or to grow old.

Fullerton Waldo, *With Grenfell on the Labrador*

As the campaign gained momentum, Burgess observed why Grenfell held such a grip on his audiences. Despite his lack of oratorical skill, he turned these public events into celebrations rather than formal lectures, even though he tended to ramble when he struck a subject that interested him, like sled dogs. And he was genuinely surprised by the enthusiasm he encountered. At the Boston meeting, he raised $19,000; at Massey Hall, Toronto, $5,000; at Carnegie Hall, New York, $13,000; at the Academy of Music, Philadelphia, $11,000; at the Orchestra Hall, Chicago, $12,000.[1] During the months to follow, as he reiterated the deficiencies of life in Labrador, the subscriptions and the applications for volunteer work poured in, not just from the large public meetings in cities like Baltimore, Des Moines, Denver, Omaha, and as far west as Los Angeles but in parts of Canada and Newfoundland, and also in Britain. Even when he was honoured with the gold medal of the National Institute of Social Sciences and elected a fellow of the Royal College of Surgeons, he could not free himself to receive either award in person. By the following spring he was writing confidently to Algie, 'I have over $800,000 endowment in sight now & hope for the million by June, or at least by Xmas.'[2]

Encouraged by these achievements, he was not prepared for a serious conflict with the Newfoundland government, whose economic difficulties had risen sharply since the end of the war. Besides Prime Minister Sir Richard Squire's own band of followers, the shaky coalition consisted of

208

a group of Liberals and eleven members representing the Fishermen's Protective Union, led by William F. Coaker. With the reassertion of nationalism in the markets after the war, Newfoundland had begun to feel the effects of a sharp recession. After five years of rising revenue and balanced budgets, in 1920–1 the colony ran up a deficit of over $4 million, a devastating figure amounting to half its revenue. At the same time, revenue fell by over $2 million, and expenditure increased by the same amount. Instead of controlling the economic causes of this state of affairs, the Squires government ran up annual deficits and borrowed heavily on the international market to meet the demands for public relief. By 1921 it faced a national debt of over $60 million, an impossible burden for such an unstable economy. It also suffered from an entrenched state of graft and corruption in which the prime minister, members of the House of Assembly, and certain public officials were implicated.[3] Furthermore, while negotiating loans in Washington, Squires was continually called to account for the dismal image of Newfoundland still fresh in American minds in the aftermath of Grenfell's campaign.

Even before Squires left the island for the United States in 1921, Grenfell had drawn attention to the dismal conditions existing on the Labrador coast. At the end of his summer voyage he had written a series of jeremiads to the St John's papers, detailing the consequences of economic change and citing cases of starvation. In September he wrote,

> Heavy clouds hang over Newfoundland, the direct rebound of war. Our main customers in the Mediterranean cannot pay the prices for fish that we must have in order to live; for our supplies are still at war prices owing to the heavy duties levied to meet a public debt which the country cannot afford. Practically all our industries are closed or at such a low ebb that the fisheries have to carry practically all the load, and are not able to do it. This means semi-starvation to quite a number of our people. It is an ugly word, and we do not like to use it, but only the successors of the 'Priest and the Levite' in our day can pass by and fail to see it, and the direct challenge to us to avert it.[4]

Grenfell was once again stepping outside the role of the conventional missionary and adopting that of political spokesman. His insistence that such dire conditions existed attracted the attention of the wire services in the United States, and at the end of September a sensational story crossed the country under headlines like 'FACE FAMINE IN NEWFOUNDLAND,' reporting that Grenfell, the 'Angel of Labrador,' had joined with William Willard Howard, a New York philanthropist, in an independent scheme to find a market for codfish. Taking Grenfell's assessment a step further, it reported that the population stood on the verge of famine and that Howard and

Grenfell had joined forces to send a ship full of provisions to the Labrador coast, to return with fish that could be sold to assist refugees from the Colorado flood.

Howard, a self-styled 'man of affairs,' had once founded an organization to raise funds for the relief of Armenians in Eastern Turkey and had formulated a relief plan for Cuba. One of the vice-presidents of his organization was Lyman Abbott.[5] Howard had first become interested in the living conditions in Newfoundland when two of his vessels were carried ashore at Rose Blanche, on the southwest coast, in January 1921. On that occasion, he claimed, he was horrified by the poverty and destitution he encountered. 'Sickness due to undernourishment was in every house.' he later wrote in *Among the Deep Sea Fishers*; 'families had eaten nothing but fish heads for days; outlying communities had had nothing to eat except dry bread for two weeks; men, driven desperate by the hunger of wives and children, had looted a local merchant's warehouse in broad daylight without arrest or restraint.'[6] While the fishermen had plenty of salt codfish on hand, he noted, the Newfoundland government's restrictions on the sale of salt fish in Europe had prevented them from selling it, except at the price desired. Howard then purchased the catch and attempted to sell it in the United States at bargain prices. But he could not. The wholesale fish merchants, amply supplied with fish, were selling on consignment at wartime prices. Finally, he sold the fish himself after painting a bleak picture of conditions in Newfoundland in the evangelical magazine *Christian Work*. He then suspended his fish merchandising during the summer of 1921, but not before the St John's press had taken issue with what it considered excessive language contrived to encourage support in the United States.[7]

Howard resumed with fresh supplies of fish in November 1921, after he received 'appeals for help' from Newfoundland, and continued through until June. He also claimed that Grenfell had heard of his efforts and had come to see him at his office in New York. In an emotional appeal published in November, the *Outlook* reported, 'So great is the destitution already that when Mrs. Grenfell came south from Labrador recently and stopped in some of the harbors on the northwest coast of Newfoundland the fishermen's families flocked to the hospital ship and offered their most cherished possessions – mats, rugs, cushions, their poor little luxuries – in return for clothing, making this confession of poverty in spite of the fact that they are among the proudest, most sensitive, shyest people to be found anywhere.'[8] It also reported that Howard bought fish from needy fishermen with Grenfell's 'advice' and 'co-operation.' Howard's direct, practical solution to a social problem constituted the kind of unconventional action that appealed to Grenfell, and Howard now suggested that the IGA might wish to take over the enterprise and carry it on as a permanent relief measure.

On his return from the United States in September 1921, Prime Minister Squires was handed a clipping of the story from a newspaper in Indianapolis and immediately charged Grenfell with 'blackmailing' Newfoundland so that he could extract more money for his endowment campaign.[9] He also insisted that Newfoundland's financial standing abroad remained satisfactory but that the exaggerations of Grenfell and Howard had injured the colony's credit and reputation. A newspaper quoted him encouraging the people of Newfoundland to 'rise up' and drive the 'blackmailers of the Grenfell class' out of the country, and Grenfell now found himself the object of Squires's intemperate public wrath.[10] The prime minister, grasping any rhetorical advantage he could find, fell back upon the sure footing of local pride and, in the colony's best nationalist tradition, attempted to discredit Grenfell as an interfering outsider.

By so doing, he placed the governor, Sir Alexander Harris, in an awkward position. As chairman of the Grenfell Association of Newfoundland, Harris naturally sympathized with Grenfell's work. But as governor, he found it necessary to draft a communiqué claiming Grenfell's descriptions contained only an element of truth 'twisted into generalities' and that anyway Grenfell's knowledge applied to only a small portion of the island.[11] At the same time, he cautioned Squires for what appeared to be 'rather strong language.' Grenfell, realizing that Squires strained to discredit him, ostentatiously turned the other cheek, issuing a mild public statement acknowledging the attack and betraying only a hint of the animosity he actually felt. He wrote in a letter to the *Daily News*, 'Criticism is easy. Just criticism is not nearly so easy. When it comes to a question of distrusting the methods of another man, every politician will realize that it is possibly a mutual emotion. When Sir Richard Squires returns to private life, if he would honor me with a debate in any acceptable public place in St John's, and when my visit to the city makes it possible, I feel sure we should have at least an interested audience.'[12] But Squires, undeterred by Grenfell's attempt at an ethical manoeuvre, decided he required vigorous public censure and wrote the governor to request a meeting with the Grenfell Association of Newfoundland, enclosing a copy of the offending letter.[13]

Harris attempted to play the role of mediator. In preparation for the association's meeting, customarily held at Government House, he arranged a private dinner for Squires and Grenfell in order to 'smooth the way' for some kind of *rapprochement*, withholding the usual invitation for Grenfell to stay at Government House, where he had customarily lodged for each visit to St John's since 1892. Squires, maintaining an air of outraged decency, accepted, for as usual there was a kernel of truth in his claim. Grenfell had indeed overstated the case. Outmanoeuvred for the moment, Grenfell found it necessary to accede to the prime minister's demand for a public statement, and in a letter to the *Fishermen's Advocate* he acknowledged he had indeed informed Howard about unsold fish and contemplated raising an emergency fund through a joint committee.[14] When the prime minister insisted there was no need of outside help, he explained, the committee was dissolved. Grenfell now took pains to distance himself from Howard. 'I am in no way responsible for statements he makes; they are entirely his own observations,' he said.

Grenfell seemed oblivious to the new tensions he had created in St John's. He now chose to publish in the daily newspapers two critical articles entitled 'The Lure of the Labrador,' intending to show that those who chose to live in the north were misunderstood by those in St John's and that, generally speaking, Labrador itself was a desirable place to live. Indeed, he invoked Kipling's explorer, who anticipates,

> Ores you'll find there; wood and cattle; water-transit sure and steady
> (That should keep the railway-rates down), coal and iron at your doors.
> God took care to hide that country till He judged His people ready,
> Then He chose me for His Whisper, and I've found it, and it's yours![15]

For the most part he confined himself to promoting the desirability of living in Labrador and explaining where its potential lay. At the same time, however, he could not resist characterizing himself, by implication, as one of those misunderstood. His words were full of the assumptions of heroism and Christian manliness. He wrote, 'There must be a quota, however, in every British audience, who have that ineradicable British trait of character which makes them actually crazy to go and leave the flesh pots and dwell in the uttermost parts of the Empire. There will always be some who will never understand and believe this, and they will, [ac]cording to their temperament, class the "explorer" of Rudyard Kipling as a hero, a fool, or politely, an "exaggerator," as their own measure of generosity and stature permits.'[16] Harris, who had declared his own moratorium on public debate while the differences between Squires and Grenfell continued, considered Grenfell's timing insensitive. As chairman of the Grenfell Association of Newfoundland, he had so far maintained the position comfortably and remained above the fray. Now he could no longer do so, since he owed allegiance to both sides. He immediately announced his resignation as chairman, to take effect at the end of the year, and arranged for the association to meet Grenfell and the prime minister the following day.[17]

When the meeting opened, the turbulence of the past month was suppressed by the presence of the governor and sixty prominent St John's citizens.[18] Grenfell complained about the difficulty of controlling reporters who did not actually attend his lectures. Squires insisted that Grenfell should take more advantage of the unusual opportunities presented him to boost Newfoundland internationally instead of constantly presenting its raw side. When Squires withdrew, however, the association voted to let the matter die rather than draw further attention to it, particularly after Labrador planters such as Captain George Whiteley of Bonne Esperance spoke vigorously about Grenfell's thirty years of work. But the resolution failed to satisfy Squires when he heard about it. The next day he rang up the governor in a state of agitation, desiring to know whether Grenfell would include in his lectures a statement about Newfoundland's trade figures and contradict the article in the *Indianapolis Mail*. Accordingly, another meeting was arranged between Squires and Grenfell at Government House. This time Grenfell signed a statement declaring that he had given no interview about a state of famine in Newfoundland and denied the existence of a relief fund. This Squires released immediately to the American wire services and issued to the St John's papers.

If Squires thought he had contained Grenfell with this measure, he had underestimated him. A few days later the *Evening Advocate* published a letter Grenfell had submitted in October, trying to confront the Squires government with what he had observed himself: 'Chronic starvation exists now in some form in every simple hamlet I have visited this summer, and spells an inevitable aftermath of burdens for the Colony,' he wrote. 'Is the Government making any rational attempt to meet this?' Moreover, two days later the papers reported an address to the Empire Club in Toronto in which Grenfell was supposed to have repeated the details about the rising public debt in Newfoundland. He was also quoted as saying the colony should have entered confederation with Canada in order to improve its position and predicted that some day it would.[19] Again Squires found it necessary to issue a denial, arguing that most Newfoundlanders preferred independence, and he referred with satisfaction to the favourable terms given Newfoundland bonds. Once again Grenfell's alleged statements brought outrage from the boardrooms. Dominion Securities, who had negotiated a $6 million loan with New York and Boston brokers earlier that year, immediately urged the prime minister to challenge Grenfell's statements, fearing they would discourage investment in Newfoundland securities. But the Empire Club quickly defended him. It insisted that his remarks had once again been misrepresented by a reporter. On the contrary, it insisted, Grenfell had represented Newfoundland optimistically. His remarks about confederation had constituted only his personal opinion.[20]

Regardless of his intentions, Grenfell had failed once again to consider the consequences, prompting Harris, in a polite letter, to instruct him that the topic of confederation was 'more or less taboo' in Newfoundland. He also urged him to leave the whole question of the island and its economic prospects out of his public statements in the future. Weary of the whole matter by now, the governor confessed to Squires that it was difficult to keep Grenfell in line. As for Grenfell himself, the altercations with the prime minister had drained considerable energy he required for his endowment campaign. 'The nervous strain of the past months was as much as one man could bear,' he told Harris. 'If if didn't play [hand]ball & tennis every day possible, I should have broken down physically.'[21]

But the matter was still not finished. Grenfell would not abandon the issue of confederation, and during the spring of 1922 he wrote privately to Mackenzie King, by now the prime minister of Canada, 'One thing I do want to do is to secure confederation. That villain Squires (P.M. of Newfoundland) is so unreliable & so untruthful, I am glad I can be independent of him. I had to tell him that he was bidding for the Roman Catholic vote by telling gross untruths about our methods. He was again mad because I so openly & always favor confederation. It must be, and I would love to bring it about in your regime.'[22] That summer, while Squires visited England, Grenfell returned to haunt his deliberations, this time when portions of his 'log,' an occasional report of proceedings distributed to the newspapers, appeared in Canada and the United States with fresh accounts of nakedness and starvation.[23] In Harris's absence, Squires furiously cabled the administrator, 'Grenfell's publicity has long been a menace to Newfoundland, and he usually succeeds in timing the publication of his articles when he can do the most damage.'[24] For Grenfell's despatches from isolated communities had again created the impression that Newfoundland as a whole was destitute. This time the St John's press agreed with Squires, and Grenfell felt their disapproval. 'I am not the saint I ought to be,' he told Captain George Whiteley, 'but I have tried to do what I thought the Master would do in my place – and if I have failed it is not because I purposely tried to mislead as Sir R. Squires believes. I love the coast, I love the Fishermen. I am older than I was, and I know I might have been wiser – but I have tried and had great joy in it.'[25]

As the quarrel with Squires wore on, two events in Grenfell's personal life distracted him from his aim of publicizing the Mission. The first occurred in April 1921, when Jane Grenfell died at Mostyn House at the age of eighty-eight. With the death of his mother, Grenfell lost a central part of his religious life and a link to the school, still his only permanent home. He had corresponded with his mother faithfully from the start of his venture into the mission field, measuring his achievements year by year and affirming his Christian idealism. Still sentimentally attached to her, on three occasions he had rushed home when her death seemed imminent. This time, however, the demands of the lecture tour had kept him away, and Algie, whom she thanked in one of her last letters 'for all your kindness to me, in this long illness,'[26] had seen to the burial in Neston churchyard. Her death now raised further difficulties, for the brothers were once again brought face to face with the complexities of their father's controversial will, and their differences over the provisions brought unresolved hostilities to the surface for the next few years.

Under the terms of the will, A.G. Grenfell was to take possession of their father's real and personal property, provide an income for their mother, pay Wilf £4,000, and invest funds that would provide an annuity of £160 for Cecil. If Cecil were to predecease his mother, another £1,500 was to be paid out of the estate to Wilf. In 1895, however, all three brothers had 'agreed' to set aside the will so that A.G. (as he had come to be called) could take over sole ownership of the school and develop it the way he wished. Once this was done, A.G. proposed that Wilf take the rest of the estate and pay Cecil £160 a year from the proceeds. It is difficult to tell what part Cecil played in these proceedings; however, in 1912 he retired from the Royal Marines, still a private, and then married. At that time he agreed to a new arrangement of the family estate proposed by his mother. His mother was to advance him £60 a year until her death, after which time he was to receive £100 a year and pay A.G. back at the same rate of £60 a year. In other words, for every year he had received £60 before his mother's death, he agreed to receive only £100 after it, instead of the full £160 he was supposed to receive.[27] But Cecil died of heart failure in 1920, and the brothers generously decided to provide £80 a year to his widow to compensate her for Cecil's pension, which stopped immediately.[28]

Following his mother's death, Grenfell did not immediately concern himself with the implications for his patrimony but left the legal details unresolved until the autumn of 1922, when he arrived in England on a fund-raising tour. On the understanding that the amount due him would be difficult to raise, he accepted a promissory note for £5,500 from A.G., payable on demand, at 5 per cent interest. A.G. later instructed his eldest son, Daryl, to pay Grenfell from the proceeds of his life insurance policy if he died in the interim.[29] The arrangement seemed to suit both parties until a few months later, when A.G. complained that he was being pressed to pay up so that Wilf could invest the money in the United States at a higher rate of interest. This sudden change of attitude he blamed on Anne, who he suspected was encouraging her husband to insist on claiming what was now legally his. 'She is very keen on money,' A.G. wrote in his diary.

'The matter was only settled last November.'[30] But there was more to it than that. Grenfell was not a wealthy man, and the demands on his limited income were increasing, particularly with three growing children.

The second significant event in Grenfell's life occurred in October 1922: the *Strathcona*, which had carried him along the Labrador coast for over twenty years, sank off the coast of Newfoundland. After leaving St Anthony for Bay Roberts, where she was to remain that winter, the vessel had encountered rough weather and begun to leak. Having reached a safe haven until the weather moderated, she had again struck a heavy sea and stood on with her pumps checking the influx of seawater. When a blowout pipe parted, disabling the boiler and pumps, the crew could not contain the tide below decks and abandoned ship. Fortunately all hands were picked up, and for twenty-five minutes they watched as the *Strathcona* slipped below the surface in fifty fathoms.

The loss hit Grenfell hard. He knew the vessel could not have carried on indefinitely after twenty years of grinding along the coast; yet the *Strathcona* had symbolized everything he stood for. He had watched the Mission grow from his commanding position in the wheelhouse as he piloted himself in and out of the coves and bays. He had kept his books and his home-made charts in that same wheelhouse. There he had done his writing and planning at odd hours between stops. And there he had slept, wedged in to keep himself from rolling onto the deck. The loss signalled the end of his most vigorous years, and he knew it. In one of his most lyrical moments, he lamented, 'How many busy days we have shared together! How many ventures we have assayed! How many, many times her decks have been crowded with our brethren seeking healing of the body – relief from pain – counsel in anxiety! Babes have been born aboard her; helpless children saved and carried to the permanent care of loving hands. Some have been married, and others have died in her accommodating shelter.'[31] The sound of her distinctive signal, an adolescent falsetto followed by a groan, would no longer bring hopeful faces to the gunwhales. The 'Holy Roller' would tow no more shipwrecked crews to safety, save no more drowning sailors. No one would gather on the deck to sing hymns. A trifle maudlin, Grenfell read correctly the significance of the loss. 'As I look in the glass,' he wrote, 'there comes back to me no longer the vision of the young man just setting out in life that the old mirror in the chart-room returned to me when first the *Strathcona* and I started work together. Gray hairs and furrows warn me now that my turn, too, must soon come, and the torch from failing hands must then be flung to others.'[32] At the end of December he wrote the directors of the IGA to announce he would spend no more winters in the north.

If Grenfell sounded demoralized by this loss, there were other losses to come. In December Sir Frederick Treves, his chief counsel in the early days, died in a nursing home in Lausanne. In January 1923 a fire wiped out Dr Paddon's hospital at North West River. But despite these setbacks, he insisted on pointing to the accomplishments of the past year. A new brick orphanage had been built in St Anthony, the home of fifty-seven children, and already there were plans for a new brick hospital. That year 24,731 patients were treated, 1,186 of them as in-patients. The endowment fund was closing in on its goal, and the IGA, with its new executive officer, Colonel Arthur Cosby, had created a new system of departmental organization, each department to be run by a qualified staff member. The new organization reflected fresh thinking. As Dorothy Stirling remarked, 'I do think the Mission is everlastingly indebted to volunteer labour, but I am more and more impressed by the fact that the organization is too large and doing too important a work to be as dependent in the future as it has been in the past upon the uncertainties of volunteer labour.'[33] Anne's friend Harriot P. Houghteling was placed in charge of staff selection, and Dorothy Stirling the clothing department. Marion R. Mosely was to direct child welfare, and Catherine Eloise Cleveland, an instructor at Cornell, became head of the industrial department. With the conduct of the Mission passing into younger hands, during the winter of 1923 Grenfell undertook another strenuous three months of lecturing under the management of the Coit-Alber Platform Service, leaving the family in the three-storey brick townhouse acquired at 53 Monmouth Street, Brookline.[34]

As Grenfell approached his fifty-eighth birthday, he set off across the United States by train, taking with him a single assistant to make the arrangements, operate his slide projector, and look after him. Without Anne to supervise and keep him on track, he learned a great deal about the intricacies of the lecture circuit. The lectures themselves followed the established pattern. First, he would devote himself to what he called 'propaganda,' getting his audiences interested in Labrador through its physical beauties and its potential. Then he would make a special plea by showing that it had lost its markets during the war and now needed as much help as the dispossessed in Turkey, Russia, or Armenia. Couldn't Labrador have a little favoured treatment by revising the tariff on fish? He wrote the new governor of Newfoundland, Sir William Allardyce, to see whether such a solution would be acceptable to the politicians. But Allardyce was supporting Squires, and Grenfell soon realized that he could no longer take Government House for granted. 'The Governor is a meticulous ass in many ways,' he would tell Anne later that summer. 'He declares now that the colony is solvent, more so than ever, Squires a hero; the real enemy of King George is the Bank of Montreal, who won't go on paying perfectly good debts. He would like the poor people to take their money out of the Savings Banks and lend it Squires or King George!!!'[35]

Grenfell also learned that the choice of a compatible assistant was crucial, for as usual he was so preoccupied with lecturing that he often forgot the time and place of meetings and lost track of his belongings. Left to his own devices, he simply could not organize himself. Perry Burgess once recalled that during the endowment campaign, Grenfell failed to show up for a speaking engagement in Montreal, and he ran into the street to find him: 'At length he rushed into view, hair streaming in the wind, eager face wearing a worried expression as he scanned the buildings, hoping to find some sign that would indicate in which of them he was supposed to be. He was in full evening dress but, as an unexpected touch, he was wearing bright red socks.'[36] Grenfell found hats particularly hard to manage. His son Pascoe remembered that, on one winter tour, he left his hat at the first stop and had it replaced by a generous host. As he continued, leaving a hat behind at each successive stop, it was replaced again, until at the end of the tour 'father returned home to Boston to find several packages waiting for him. In each of them was a hat.'[37] As he started out in 1923, he quickly lost control of his wardrobe. He wrote home, 'Have my trousers turned up? Have the other oranges? I lost my gloves today. But I have wired for them & *may* get them.'[38]

As he made his way west, often travelling overnight between distant stations, the Labrador doctor observed the transformation of post-war America. Passing through Pennsylvania, he was distracted by large groups of flappers with 'frizzy' hair, dashing in and out of the train. Many of his fellow travellers, those he referred to as 'Poles, Jews and general heretics,' spoke no English, and the train was packed tight with sober, good-natured coal miners, all carrying identical lunch buckets. Everywhere there were new kinds of American faces, mothers with screaming children and strangers who patted him on the back familiarly. The world was changing before his eyes. Why was he putting himself through this ordeal? During those early days of the tour, the train gave him an opportunity to reflect about the need to go through with it at this stage of his life. What went through his mind during these early weeks?

To begin with, he needed income other than his modest Mission salary. His most active years were already behind him, and so far he had depended too heavily, he thought, on Anne's private income. As he journeyed through Pennsylvania, he took time to reflect upon his career and consider without remorse the sacrifices he had made. He wrote Anne, 'In 1889, when I refused $4,000 and expenses and took $1,500 without, it was because I hated to be doing altruistic, much less Christian work, for Charity money, and I've fought off a bigger salary ever since. I see plainly now without *your* income & my side issues (books), we couldn't have lived even decently. When I see other workers so young & half educated & terrible murderers even of our English language earning thousands to our hundreds, it seems wrong.' He also regretted the sacrifice she had made. Looking around him, he observed professional women in public and commercial positions and speculated about what she could have accomplished. Each night he commanded a fee of $300 but took home only $100, and before long he regretted his arrangement with the lecture agency. He was making numerous connections throughout the country and drawing in volunteers for Labrador work, but the return for his efforts continued to rankle. While the discussion of money clearly made him uncomfortable, he admitted privately to Anne that the modest salary he drew from the Mission was simply not adequate:

> As I look at $300 a month I see it is an *absurd* return for two people, highly educated, well connected, I think I may say of more than ordinary ability – and our very same society [the IGA] paying [Perry Burgess] a little Methodist minister $12,000 & [Colonel Arthur Cosby] a divorced army officer $10,000. This new $10,000 sticks very hard in my throat. I will talk it over with you before I do anything. But I am not going to settle down to $300 a month again & leave you using all your private income to keep our house afloat. With our entertaining, which we must do to be efficient & which we love doing – all that should be taken care of by my salary, and I am going to ask for $500 a month & get it easily. (Now I can demonstrate that I can make $3,000 a month.) Then no one, not even my conscience, can say 'You are overpaid.' Then I can give you your $300 a month & clear your private income entirely to do what you want.[39]

Quite simply, for all his efforts, Grenfell had provided no financial cushion, except what he made himself. He did not require more luxury. He wanted more freedom – the freedom to add to what he termed his 'efficiency' and 'longevity.' The Mission was changing, and he required more time to devote to its added complexities.

By March, as the tour continued, he was convinced he was being held back by the lecture agency. He drew large crowds, composed substantially of the loyal church-going constituency who regarded him as a hero, but he sometimes lost opportunities to speak. There were awkward gaps between engagements and embarrassing complaints that he was not always available through the agency. With this experience, he felt confident enough to manage his own tour in 1924 without the direction and expense of Coit-Alber, who he discovered were offering him as part of a package with other lecturers. Already he had decided to lecture with the agency only one more year before setting out on his own. 'I like Coit – as far as I saw him – but I'm just *not* going to be a stalking horse for Will Rogers & Daisy Darling & Tootsie Flapper,' he fumed. Nevertheless, at the end of the three months, he felt more satisfied with his earnings and reckoned he would clear about $9,000, far more than he could make from his salary alone.[40] By then he had come to better terms with Coit-Alber for 1924. The improved conditions left him a greater margin of independence and allowed him to enjoy the lecturing more – so much that he confidently recommended the bureau to Sir Frederick Banting.[41]

Grenfell did not simply seek a higher income; he craved the independence of working for the Mission without drawing his full income from it, thus maintaining technically the status of a 'volunteer.' The conflict between working for a charity and earning money from it bothered him, and he resisted the trend towards hiring more specialized staff. Up to this point the Mission had moved along mainly through volunteer labour and low salaries. Its increasing complexity, however, made this policy less practical. Rationalizing his added income, he wrote, 'But above all it makes me able to be a "volunteer," & if I am a volunteer then I can talk differently to the jealous & the evil minded in Nfd. The Mission can pay Cosby & Burgess at $10 & 12,000 – but I can't accept it – & in 14 or 15 weeks at 700-800 a *week* which their offer means we get enough to be on easy street.'[42] Anne had reached the limit of her patience with the terms of the contract and Grenfell's complaints, and she was about to write to Coit-Alber herself. Grenfell, however, urged her to wait. For the time being, he was happy with the new arrangements. In a rare expression of puritan self-analysis, he revealed how his financial state had chastened him. He added, 'Don't you see how it hurt my pride? You *know* I hated taking a cent & *never* took more than bread and butter. I never had money to give away. I never could finance anything after I lost my money in co-ops & Mills. The Good Lord has opened *this* way: I never could see *any* way, & He disciplined me the other way first. I have so often said Xt must have found it hard to accept Charity.'

Regarded now as one of the highest-paid lecturers in the United States, Grenfell had learned that the man he chose as his assistant made the difference between a pleasurable journey and a monotonous grind. His current assistant simply did not suit him. He complained that the man smoked too much and was 'effeminate.' The next time, he decided, he would choose his own assistant, pay him a better wage, and cover his travelling expenses. He needed someone to operate the array of stereopticon and film projectors put at his disposal and adapt them to the various electrical currents. He also needed someone bright enough to get him more easily from place to place. But above all, he needed someone more socially compatible, someone who fitted in better with the college presidents, schoolmasters, and clergymen he encountered. As he wrote his brother during the 1923 tour, 'Of course my present man is only a mechanic & never comes with me to friends' houses. The man next year is to be a gentleman, & he will visit with me universities, schools, clubs, homes, public institutions of every kind.'[43]

Grenfell had also learned something about the price to be paid for celebrity. He was no longer the young missionary doctor seeking help for his growing enterprise. The Mission ran along in capable hands, and as he approached his sixtieth birthday he was aware that he was no longer viewed simply as a frontier doctor. He was a man with a mythology surrounding him – a public figure required to endure the loneliness imparted by fame and the pressure to live up to it. That year, he wrote Anne, 'I never had a trip like this. The Canadian part nearly finished me off – 3 times a day – day after day – no escape and such endless repetitions of useless questions & impertinent questions really. These two days in *hotels* have been almost in heaven. I refused to see anyone or accept any callers.'[44] When his throat gave out again, he realized he had been wise to refuse any further speaking engagements. 'I can't do it, Pussie, & keep sane,' he wrote. 'Too much notoriety makes it impossible. One lecture per day in future, & only one.'

For the second winter with the Coit-Alber agency Grenfell acquired the services of a more compatible assistant, Geoffrey Milling, an old boy of Mostyn House who still maintained a close connection with A.G. An Oxford undergraduate and a keen oarsman, Milling was prepared to take a few months off before returning to row at Henley in June. He possessed not only the intelligence but the social graces Grenfell required. Moreover, Grenfell could beat him at squash and handball. 'He is on the job *all* the time,' he soon disclosed, '& refused to stay & row for the varsity this year to come. He would be rowing now. He doesn't smoke or drink – we work together, & he always kneels for evening prayer. There is *some* good result for Mostyn House School.'[45]

The two achieved a mutual understanding. Milling liked Grenfell's casual approach to his lectures and marvelled at how he never seemed sure about what he would say next. Sometimes he would spend so much time talking about a slide it would crack. The promotional films broke continually and in the end hardly seemed worth showing. 'But despite this he was a great success as a lecturer and there was something charismatic about him which appealed to the largely midwestern audiences he lectured to,' Milling recalled.[46] To Grenfell, Milling embodied the qualities of manly Christianity. He introduced Milling to Endicott Peabody of Groton, headmaster of his sons' school. When Peabody attended the Henley regatta the next summer as Milling's guest, he offered Milling a mastership. Grenfell was on hand also as Milling rowed for the English Rowing Club challenge boat and helped win the challenge cup. 'I do love to see a man who is not afraid to admit he loves God and his fellow men enough to work openly for them, and to show at the same time he can beat at their own games the men who live only for the *things* of life,' he observed.[47]

During this second winter on the road Grenfell maintained a stream of letters home as he struggled again with his loneliness. He kept up a barrage of personal jokes, puns, racist slurs, and sexual innuendo in these letters, aimed playfully at keeping Anne amused while she managed the home base. Sometimes he praised her; at other times he upbraided her for not seeing to her administrative duties. When the lectures went well, he conveyed his joy and excitement. When they did not, he complained about the lack of pamphlets on hand or told her the clothes she had sent did not match. He chided her for her idleness, cautioned her about giving him unnecessary 'nervous' worries, or teased her about running off with another man. Above all, there were tender letters addressed simply to 'Pussy' and signed 'Lamb.' After seven weeks he had decided he would never tour without her again. 'Life has so little – so little worthwhile – all we can do is to fill it to the full,' he wrote tenderly on the eve of another birthday. 'Oh darling Pussie – it is running away and we are far apart.'[48]

— 15 —

Public Figure
1923 - 1927

Indeed, all my leanings, hereditary or otherwise, were towards a life of action. My forebears have almost all been physical fighters, and I presume I could hardly have escaped the heritage of a hatred for peace and platitudes.

Wilfred Grenfell, *The Adventure of Life*

As Grenfell travelled about promoting Labrador and the Mission during the 1920s, he himself emerged into prominence as a phenomenon distinct from the Mission itself. He had always been treated by authors and journalists as a romantic figure. Now he acquired the quality of a folk hero, a venturing Christian with an acute sense of duty – the ordinary person's idea of what he or she could ideally become without the clogs and responsibilities of everyday life. Saul Bellow, in whose novel *Henderson the Rain King* (1959) Grenfell stands out as a model of humanitarianism, has recently written, 'In boyhood, two books by Sir Wilfred Grenfell deeply influenced me – one was *A Labrador Doctor* and the other stirring narrative called *Adrift on an Icepan*.'[1] Bellow acknowledges Grenfell's attraction during those materialistic years following the war when he, with other popular heroes, embodied the spirit of idealism.

Something similar occurred in Britain. A fresh series of biographies, drawing on the recent expansion of the Mission's work, returned to the preoccupation with romantic genealogy. 'It is worthy of observation,' wrote Cuthbert McEvoy in 1922, 'that one whose life was to be lived in unceasing conflict with apparently insuperable difficulties came of a great fighting stock.' W.C. Piggott attributed Grenfell's qualities to 'the spirit of an ancestry of fighters by land and sea.' Other authors of the 1920s, clearly aiming at a juvenile readership, seized upon the achievements in Labrador as a wholesome example for school children. 'In him the Viking and the Elizabethan adventurer are alive again – though his sea-raids have a kindlier but not a less courageous quality than those of Eric the Red and Sir Richard Grenville of the *Revenge*,' judged Basil Mathews.[2] In the popular imagination, Grenfell wore the mantle of the venturing Christian, the man of action and accomplishment.

In 1924 the IGA suggested that if he were to continue to work at the same level much longer, he would need a holiday. (Curtis later claimed they wanted to get him abroad while they built the new hospital uninterrupted.)[3] They proposed that he should give up all lecturing and medical work and take time off to travel through the East on a kind of sabbatical. He agreed reluctantly, and when he left New York in June 1924 he spent a few months lecturing in England before setting out for Egypt, Palestine, Lebanon, Iraq, India, Malaya, China, Korea, and Japan. In England he looked for a replacement for the *Strathcona*, and with the help of a Sussex firm he found what he needed: the ninety-five-ton steam yacht *Runa*, smaller than the *Strathcona* but more manoeuvrable and more comfortable to sail. This vessel, renamed *Strathcona II*, would impose new conditions on the Mission's marine work.

For a start, the IGA insisted that the Mission employ *Strathcona II* exclusively for its own missionary activities and never for transporting cargo. Secondly, the new vessel, which had been fitted out expensively as a yacht and sold at a sacrifice, was much more comfortable than the first *Strathcona*, which had become so leaky that the crew had often slept and taken their meals on deck or in the wheelhouse. In the new vessel there were comfortable bunks in separate cabins, so that heads of departments and nurses could be carried on board from time to time. While Grenfell continued on his tour, the RNMDSF set about reconditioning and equipping *Strathcona II* in Gorleston. The British Mission also engaged a crew to sail it to Newfoundland and held a dismissal service on board before it departed in May 1925.

Meanwhile, Grenfell and Anne had begun their tour of the Near and Far East, their professed objective to examine other ways of dealing with social problems. After sightseeing in Cairo, they spent a fortnight in Jerusalem and made a thorough tour of Palestine. As they progressed eastward, visiting a succession of British officials, American missionaries, doctors, educators, and archaeologists, they received a privileged view of these countries of the empire and its protectorates. They crossed from Beirut to Damascus by car, then over the Syrian desert before taking the train through Mesopotamia. At length, they steamed down the Persian Gulf to tour Iraq and India. Grenfell took note of the movement for Indian self-rule that followed the attempts at parliamentary reform engineered by Edwin Montagu, secretary of state for India. His attitude to colonial self-government, with its implications for Newfoundland, emerged in a letter to A.G. from Kashmir. ' "Self-Determination" is [the] most dangerous cant ever started,' he reckoned, ' "natural" I mean. It just means handing over ignorant, miserable, defenceless millions to a few scheming, rapacious lawyer sharks. It is the same in India, & nowhere more plain than in Cashmir. I am with you entirely, a benevolent autocratic govt. is the *only* one. But it must govern. That rotten fool Montague did endless harm & cruelty by his ignorant self-conceit & folly in my opinion.'[4] After proceeding through Malaya, China, and Korea, the two completed their journeys in Japan. Grenfell wrote optimistically about the changes in China since the revolution and discovered what he called a 'beautiful unity' amongst Christian workers there.[5]

Accustomed to seeing himself as a social critic, two years later he published his collection of notes, *Labrador Looks at the Orient*, a traveller's guide to the East produced with the usual editorial assistance of Anne. *Labrador Looks at the Orient* was full of observations, anecdotes, local knowledge, and political thoughts based upon the reworked contents of reference books and the received opinions of the authorities met along the way. Thus it lacked a sustained point of view and a particular audience and took the reader on a ramble through disconnected opinions, expressing an unrelenting surprise and amusement at intractable political problems, strange local customs, and indecipherable artistic concepts. Lacking a specialized knowledge of Eastern cultures, Grenfell sometimes fell back upon inept truisms and religious sententiae while maintaining an embarrassingly consistent condescension. His brother A.G., who worked dutifully through it the following year, found the book interesting, but he was surprised by the weird American spellings, the ungrammatical sentences, the 'flippancy,' the 'finest mixture of metaphors,' and the 'naive slaps at democracy.'[6] The book reveals more about Grenfell's influence as a public figure than the judgment of Hodder and Stoughton. Certainly, it did not add to his stature as a writer.

During his absence the Mission had moved ahead with new initiatives, demonstrating, under its new organization, that it could operate on its own with a strong board of directors, the heads of the 'departments,' and confident leadership from Dr Curtis in St Anthony. Yale students had started raising money for a new public school in North West River. The YMCA had taken over the management of the King George V Institute, left comparatively under-used by changing patterns in the fishing industry. The Industrial Department had opened an office in Boston. The Canadian government had made a grant for the hospital at Harrington. But above all, work had begun on a new hospital in St Anthony, constructed chiefly by local tradesmen the Mission had sent abroad to be trained. This new steel and concrete hospital, more up-to-date than any other facility in the colony, would move the Mission's medical work squarely into the twentieth century. Together with *Strathcona II*, it would mark the Mission's break with its frontier beginnings and accentuate Grenfell's continuing distancing from the work in the field.

Grenfell himself was conscious of losing touch. From time to time he wrote private notes to himself in his copy of the New Testament, acknowledging the existence of ideas as good as his own and the need to hand over the work to others. Nothing accentuated these changes more than the premature death of Dr Little in the spring of 1926 at the age of fifty-one. Since leaving the north, Little had carved out a place for himself in Boston, but despite his ambitions he seemed never to regain the same sense of authority and accomplishment. He had been a surgeon in the out-patient department of the Massachusetts General Hospital for a decade, and also assistant visiting surgeon at the Long Island Hospital, and instructor in surgical technique at the Harvard Medical School. He had become assistant medical director of the New England Mutual Life Assurance Company and chief surgeon of the Boston and Albany Railroad. At the same time he had served the Mission in other capacities, first as a director, then as president of the New England Grenfell Association, then as a director of the IGA. 'It had often puzzled me why the good Lord made it, as we saw it, inevitable, that so great a help in our lonely field should have to leave for Boston, where already were so many wonderful men able to give the best aid to sufferers that the world could afford,' Grenfell memorialized.[7] But even had he not disputed Grenfell's tactics, Little could not have continued to meet the physical demands in St Anthony. He had developed a tumour near the heart that finally brought about his death. Only then were his wishes fully satisfied. His ashes were returned to St Anthony and sealed in the rock on Fox Farm Hill, the first of Grenfell's inner circle to rest at the scene of their most fulfilling work. Little's premature death reminded Grenfell again that he had 'no time to waste.' The day of the funeral in Brookline, he wrote to his brother, urging him to pay him his patrimony.[8]

Grenfell's demands renewed the acrimonious exchange between the two begun a year before, at a time when A.G. assumed Wilf was being prompted by Anne. In his diary, A.G. acknowledged a variety of solutions, including selling off his considerable rubber shares, raising the annual payment, and paying Grenfell's income tax until the capital was paid off. 'I am trying to satisfy Anne's peddling avarice about interest,' he noted to himself after receiving this most recent demand, '& to give a very sure guarantee of my anxiety to pay off the patrimony as soon as possible.'[9] But he did not move fast enough to satisfy Grenfell, and in April 1926 Grenfell wrote to review the way the will had been interpreted. He reminded his brother:

> You wanted to reduce the fifty-five hundred pounds left to me. One reason you gave was that Mostyn House was only worth a thousand pounds when father bought it. When I showed you a letter of his asking for the 'last installment,' which was stated and not denied to be eleven hundred pounds, you simply annexed the letter, and I presume destroyed it. I reminded you in the lawyer's office, and he reminded you, that mother's estate should have been worth more than fifty-five hundred pounds if you had paid rent for the thirty years in which you had enjoyed the use of the property and during which I had received not one cent, on which you agreed at once.[10]

Because of the disruption caused by the general strike, A.G. did not receive this letter for a month and could not refute the assertion. Meanwhile he was enraged by the charge in a subsequent letter that he had somehow convinced his mother to alter her will so that she would leave all her property to him. He assumed that Grenfell was being pressed by Anne, and continued to resist paying the capital.

Two weeks later Grenfell wrote again to explain why he preferred to have the money invested in the United States. Again, he questioned his brother's financial judgment and charged, 'Your money affairs are to me nothing but a series of speculations: Marks, Francs, Rubbers, Houses, Cottages, Baths, etc., etc. I want now to put my money into stocks that will bring in a regular income. As for the future of Mostyn House – well, I heard Father prophesying it was going to the Dogs, & I suppose Old Price did the same. It all depends to my mind on the man, not on the school or the British finances, & I'm certain it is still worth a great many thousand dollars.'[11] By now Grenfell had placed himself in an intractable position. He had originally acquiesced in A.G.'s interpretation of both parents' wills; but having changed his mind, he insisted on what was rightfully his after all. When A.G. once again asked him to leave the money in his hands, Grenfell attempted to justify his previous actions and replied:

> When you told me after her [their mother's] death that she had left it all to you and that you intended to keep the whole of it, I said nothing for your sake. Had you paid off the Father's legacy, you would never have been reminded of that by me, & I stand by what I said then. In addition to that, had I not (by the merest chance) found the letter demanding Father's 'Final Payment' of £1100 for Mostyn, I should have believed what you told me and Gamon, the lawyer, that at the time Father bought it, it was only worth £1000. And I

should have worried about accepting £5500 in the face of your statement, &
nearly did agree to your proposal to reduce the amount.[12]

Grenfell also claimed his brother had discouraged him by claiming he and
the school would have been embarrassed if he had taken out such an
amount. Rather than quarrel then, he had accepted the sacrifice. Now, he
found, his money was being used to finance A.G.'s various investments.
At this point, Grenfell's letter of 8 April, with his notion of a 'last
instalment,' arrived, and A.G. wanted to set the record straight. In the
most conciliatory tone, he questioned the existence of any letter asking
for a last instalment of £1,100, reminding Grenfell that their father had
sold nothing but goodwill and furniture. He also questioned Grenfell's
ability to remember details. 'It is perfectly obvious that you never understood my attitude at that meeting in Dickson's office,' he wrote. 'I wasn't
fighting or arguing. I was asking you to do what I had asked for years, and
trying to show the reasonable equity of my proposal.' He was also eager to
show that he could not possibly have influenced their mother to change
her will in his favour. As he revealed, she had never actually written down
the terms of her will, contrary to what Grenfell believed, but dictated it.
Those terms had not been altered since 1898. He added:

> This is the subject I told you recently was very painful to me to dig up –
> because it looks like *bragging* about what I did for the old darling – but you
> have dug it up now, with a vengeance. God knows I was glad enough to do
> what I could, and wish I were still doing it. You *couldn't* do anything for her,
> of course – and there was no-one else. For Heaven's sake don't let us ever
> refer to this subject again, and let it be sacred from discussion with anyone
> else. My conscience is quite happy about what I did for her – and also about
> what she did for me.[13]

Quite simply, A.G. wanted to show that Grenfell did not understand the
whole matter and indirectly to warn Anne that she should not interfere.
'Sent reply to W.T.G. disproving Anne's infamous charges & insinuations,'
he wrote in his diary.[14]
Grenfell himself remained unmoved by these revelations but decided,
with so many imponderables, to forget the whole business for the time
being as long as his brother understood he wanted to be paid as soon as
possible. 'Life is short,' he wrote, 'and neither of us will go hungry.'[15] But
A.G. remained adamant. As far as he could see, he had done nothing wrong
and had not misrepresented the details of the wills. With no resolution in
sight, he preferred to believe that his brother simply failed to understand
the facts and contented himself with waiting until Grenfell's next visit to

set him straight. In October, when Grenfell arrived at Mostyn House in advance of his extended lecture tour, the hostility between the two brothers seemed to have abated. Grenfell spent a good deal of time treating his brother's osteomyelitis, which had advanced, and with cleaning out one of his sinuses.[16] Moreover, Anne was not present.

Grenfell came to Britain in 1926 intending to lecture until the middle of December, according to a full schedule of events organized by Gerald Christy. Beginning in mid-October, he and Anne spent six weeks touring the major English centres, as well as Glasgow and Edinburgh, in a car piled high with pamphlets, slides, and reels of film. The response was unpredictably warm. In Britain Grenfell was recognized not just as another fund-raiser but as a *bona fide* public figure. People wanted to shake his hand and obtain his autograph. On he went through Manchester, Liverpool, Cheltenham, Oxford, Cambridge, Reading, Newcastle, and Gravesend, at times addressing audiences of two to three thousand people. But the greatest response came in London. Here, during his final fortnight, he tried something new: instead of moving from one platform to another, he hired the Polytechnic Hall in Regent Street and lectured twice a day. As it happened, the Judicial Committee of the Privy Council were finishing their hearings on the Labrador boundary dispute, and Labrador was in the air. Grenfell and Labrador drew in large crowds, and the overflow had to be turned away.

Encouraged by the display of enthusiasm, Grenfell made another of those spur-of-the-moment decisions that left others to labour with the details afterwards: he took the campaign a step further and gathered supporters to form a new organization to collect funds in the United Kingdom. Customarily, he had collected money under the auspices of the RNMDSF, one of the societies represented on the board of the IGA. But the Mission would no longer guarantee an annual quota, and contributions had fallen off. At its latest annual meeting, the IGA had authorized Grenfell to open an office for this purpose in London without explicitly authorizing him to found a new agency, and the council of the RNMDSF expressed surprise when it discovered he now acted independently.

In objecting to the impending organizational changes, the RNMDSF also took the opportunity to inquire about Grenfell's altered theological position. The Mission itself remained an evangelical body, yet Grenfell seemed surprised when the council objected to a list of patrons that included the chief rabbi. The council also knew he had recently published a book entitled *Religion in Everyday Life*, in which he had taken an even broader position. Here, in keeping with his long-standing antipathy towards organized religion, he had provided a particularly liberal interpretation of Christ's intentions which was in keeping with changes in liberal thinking throughout the 1920s. He had written, ' "Well done" was what his religion aimed at, not "correctly thought." The one man whom he condemned to "the place prepared for the devil" was not the agnostic (today every modest man admits that impeachment) but the unprofitable man.'[17] He also claimed he had never made belief a criterion for employment in Labrador. 'We have made religion ridiculous by insisting that others should think as we do,' he added. Such notions did not sit comfortably with Grenfell's evangelical colleagues, for he seemed to suggest that religion no longer mattered in the Labrador mission. (In a new edition of *A Man's Faith*, also published that year, he embraced the testimony of the Hindu and the Moslem and expressed his admiration for Gandhi, whom he had met in India, as a 'Christlike' man.)[18] That summer, the Moody Bible Institute had also taken issue with these notions and in an editorial published in the *Moody Bible Institute Monthly* expressed shock. The editorial had been read at a meeting of the council in September and referred to the spiritual work committee, who had discussed Grenfell's religion. The RNMDSF was obviously disturbed about his unorthodox views, yet we cannot now know its attitude exactly. Inexplicably, the section of the minutes of the September council meeting dealing with the question has been obliterated.[19]

Grenfell now set about organizing a body of supporters being referred to as the 'Grenfell Foundation of Great Britain and Ireland.' He also opened an office at 92 Victoria Street, SW1, and placed in charge Miss Katie Spalding as honorary secretary with the promise of a loan of $2,000 from the IGA to get things moving. (Once the office was opened and the rent arranged, the promised $2,000 was never heard of again.)[20] Then, while he kept up his busy lecturing schedule, he formed a temporary advisory board and a treasurer and opened a bank account. Smaller committees were now organized by former workers in other parts of the United Kingdom, and all of this had been accomplished without the assistance of the Mission to Deep Sea Fishermen. In fact, no mention of the Mission had been made at any of Grenfell's lectures.

Grenfell had been directing the proceeds of his British lectures into his own special fund since 1922. 'I wanted to show them that without any special preparation I could raise in a month more than they did in twelve, which was no trouble to do,' he explained to the directors of the IGA at the time. 'There is a tremendous interest in England in our kind of mission work, but except with a very few, there is scarcely any interest in their methods of work. To me they seem to live in a long by-gone age.'[21] Challenged by the RNMDSF this time, he rationalized his actions again in a report to the council. He explained that a 'demarcation line' had been required to set the Labrador funds apart 'as some interested in our work in Labrador had sent subscriptions to the RNMDSF without earmarking them, under which circumstance, as I understand from their resolution forwarded to the IGA Board, those subscriptions would not be credited to the Labrador.'[22] His aim, therefore, was to form in Britain a separate body eligible to receive contributions exclusively for Labrador and would forward to the IGA only those donations specifically intended for the Labrador work. The council must also have known that throughout September and October he had run weekly instalments of his *apologia*, *What Christ Means to Me*, in the church paper *British Weekly*, pressing his own interpretation of practical Christianity and justifying the measures he had taken to improve life in the north. 'Christ called for faith in Himself,' he proclaimed. 'He never called for intellectual comprehension. He sent out to preach His gospel men who had not any creed or any intellectual faith, only a dumb sort of faith that Christ was more than man. I believe that he sent me out also to help make a better world.'[23]

On 9 December, a week before he was to return to the United States, Grenfell and Katie Spalding attended a climactic meeting with the council. The day before he had written Hopwood (now Lord Southborough) and explained the radical change thus: 'They have lost interest in our work because our method of carrying what we believe to be the Gospel of the Grace of God does not insist on their theology. We think the world has got to where it does not listen to what you say any longer. It is interested infinitely more in what you do, which, anyhow, brings infinitely greater satisfaction to the preacher.'[24] As he discovered, the council wanted to understand its relationship with the new committee and find out whether its formation had been authorized by the IGA. In *Toilers of the Deep*, the RNMDSF officially expressed its 'great pleasure' at meeting Grenfell for a 'special sitting' to discuss his 'latest efforts' in Britain, but in fact the meeting was not as cordial as it sounded. Grenfell had expected some kind of welcome from his former colleagues or at least an expression of congratulation, even though he had not involved them in his latest initiatives. On the contrary, the meeting became an intense and lengthy interrogation in which the council, including Walter Wood and Frederick Willway, reviewed the intricate relationship between the IGA and its contributing associations and challenged Grenfell's right to organize what looked like a new body.

The council began by expressing its dissatisfaction with Grenfell's free interpretation of the IGA's intentions. According to the IGA minutes, Grenfell had been directed to carry on a campaign in Great Britain and Ireland to increase interest in the IGA, to select a suitable office, and to pass all the money he raised through the hands of the RNMDSF. He had already raised £2,000, and for this reason the council were especially eager to know how this amount had been handled. Moreover, on the basis of their own experience, they did not fully trust Grenfell's ability as an administrator. As the chairman put it, referring to the Karnopp affair, 'What we have felt was, we know your enthusiasm and how you are apt to entangle people and infect them with your enthusiasm, but it does not always work well when you come to put men into the work, the right man does not always get into the right place.' One other matter bothered the council: the degree to which Grenfell had taken full credit for the accomplishments in Labrador and neglected to mention the role of the RNMDSF. 'What we feel a little bit,' said the chairman, 'is, if all goes well, you get all the kudos – we wish you to have it; we do not want anything, but if anything goes wrong, they come down on us.'[25] The Grenfell Foundation for Great Britain and Ireland did not yet exist as an incorporated body. The council wanted to know why the foundation received funds for which its individual members could be made liable as individuals and not the RNMDSF.

According to Grenfell, the new committee had apparently decided to hand over the collections at the end of the fiscal year and review their whole collecting procedure. Grenfell contended that the busy lecturing schedule had prevented him from informing the RNMDSF of these arrangements – but neither had he informed the IGA. Walter Wood, who had attended the last meeting of the IGA, recalled the discussions vividly and did not recollect any suggestion about forming a new board in Britain. Rather, he recollected something more tentative: an 'experiment' to find out the level of response. Grenfell did not recall the discussion, and when he was asked why he had not informed the two British members of the IGA about his plans, he replied dismissively that he had not done lots of things. Wood, who had himself engaged in long discussions with the IGA members in New York, insisted that nothing had been said about a new association.

Once this issue had been clarified, the council members reiterated their support for Grenfell's work but insisted on more information about developments in Britain if they were to continue to support him. They also insisted on receiving public acknowledgment and requested that Grenfell refer to the RNMDSF at his lectures at the 'Parent Society.' In the end, nothing had been resolved but a great deal had been said – enough for Grenfell to realize the extent of the council's hostility. After thirty years, he recognized, he no longer shared the same theological ground with the mission. From now on the long relationship would be honoured publicly, but the two organizations would go their separate ways. In the new year Grenfell urged the IGA to incorporate the foundation. He told José Machado, his Ottawa representative, 'By their own conversation, England has rejected the RNMDSF and its interpretation of the gospel. You can understand when I say that the youth of England needs exactly the message we are giving it – to have an outlet for its religious emotions. You can see how it jumped at and responded to the message, and to allow that obsolete, narrow-gauge lot of fundamentalists to choke the issue is too bad to believe possible.'[26]

The London committee subsequently incorporated itself as the Grenfell Association of Great Britain and Ireland, and the contributions of the RNMDSF diminished further. An important link with the origins of the Labrador mission had now disappeared. The Royal National Mission, more oriented towards its British objectives and more theologically conservative, had done what it had perhaps always wanted to do – relieve itself of its responsibilities outside Britain. In 1929 the council agreed to transfer all its overseas properties to the IGA by cancelling its lease of 1918. In 1934, when the transfer formally took place, it ended its official connection with the work in Labrador.

If this important change was not immediately apparent, the growth of the IGA became more apparent in St Anthony, where the new hospital was being constructed under the eye of Dr Curtis. Here, after ten years of work, Curtis effectively controlled the day-to-day medical work and, while Grenfell dealt with matters overseas, prepared to bring it gracefully into the modern era. The old wood-frame hospital, hewn out of the surrounding forest by Grenfell twenty-five years before, was about to be replaced by the most up-to-date hospital in the colony, and the new concrete building, pushed ahead with local labour and expertise since May 1925, now neared completion. Early in the new year the last wiring had been done, the steam was up, and the beds were made. Then, on 27 January 1927, a procession of patients made its way between the two buildings, stretcher by stretcher. An hour later, liberated from the creaking floorboards and narrow hallways of the old structure, they were dazzled by fresh stucco and waxed linoleum.

It would be difficult to exaggerate the difficulties presented by the old building, with its cramped spaces, narrow staircase, and creaking floors. The very atmosphere reeked of combustible fuels. Kerosene stoves heated the water, and these, together with the old burner heating the sterilizing room and the adjoining operating room, combined with the ether to produce an uncomfortable atmosphere that clogged the head and eyes. The building itself was laid out in such a way as to provide maximum discomfort. Wooden floors separated the wards from the staff bedrooms above and the staff quarters below. When the staff was not disturbing the patients, the patients disturbed the staff. In summer the arrival of the coastal boat would bring extraordinary problems of management. The staff could cope with forty or fifty patients, but if thirty arrived without notice they had to be accommodated somehow. 'After every one supposedly had been settled,' wrote one observer, 'some sleeping on chairs, benches, tables, and even on the floor of the reception room, on the examining table, in the dentist chair in the dispensary, or in outside tents, the staff would heave a sigh of relief and prepare for their long delayed supper, only to discover several who had been overlooked and for whom accommodation would have to be provided in nearby houses.' Once, at least eighty-three patients slept in the hospital.[27] But the new building, with its new equipment and its wide corridors, incorporated what Curtis fondly regarded as the best of medical planning and technology.[28] The staff, lodged in a three-storey building connected with the hospital, could live their lives separately.

A distinguished assemblage turned up in St Anthony for the official opening ceremonies on 25 July. First there was Governor Allardyce, whom Grenfell had described as a 'meticulous ass,' arriving ceremonially from HMS *Wistaria*. Judge F.J. Morris represented the prime minister, the Honourable Walter Monroe, and Admiral Sir James Startin represented the RNMDSF. Allardyce immediately took Grenfell by surprise, informing him that the king wished to make him a knight of the Order of St Michael and St George, and expected the public recognition would delight him. Yet Grenfell seemed unsure about accepting the honour. Anne, who would become Lady Grenfell and relinquish her American citizenship thereby, was completely sure. Nothing, perhaps, could have given her more pleasure. The discussion rested upon the message this new dignity might convey. Would Sir Wilfred Grenfell find it more difficult to communicate with simple folk? Would he be able to throw open doors to private endowment and government assistance previously denied him? In the end, he was convinced that the prestige would help the Mission. He explained to Lord Southborough, 'I never sought this kind of personal honor – but it will be useful, & may help me in England with the interest we need.'[29] No longer simply a missionary, as Sir Wilfred Grenfell he could command more attention than before.

The official opening of the hospital transformed the missionary into a public institution. No longer able to ignore the advances in the northern part of the colony, the St John's authorities joined their voices with those of the RNMDSF in praising him. Governor Allardyce lauded the thirty-five years of devotion and self-effacement that had 'won the esteem and admiration of all.'[30] Grenfell's work, he announced, had produced exemplary results: four hospitals, two orphanages, three public schools, and an industrial scheme. Grenfell had influenced people, largely through his own efforts, to give their money and time to the people of Newfoundland and Labrador. Finally, he read a congratulatory message from the king, and when the applause died he announced that the knighthood had been conferred.

At first, the assembled crowd, many of them Americans, seemed unsure about the significance of it. But when he added his personal congratulations to 'Sir Wilfred Grenfell,' there was warm applause and cheers. The Mission had acquired new legitimacy. As for Grenfell himself, he did his best to treat his new-found dignity ironically. In a letter to the three children, he refused to take it too seriously and sketched himself in a suit of armour, battling Labrador black flies. 'How do you like my tin suit – all nights were tin suits – some call them "Nighties",' he wrote. 'I am still in homespuns – and have not found any ostrich feathers yet growing out of my top knot. Perhaps it will come on in time, like the tomato plants I hope are doing.'[31] But privately he must have known that the hospital represented the climax of his work and that it had brought his best years to an end.

That summer he spent his time on the Labrador coast in *Strathcona II*, returning to sea again as soon as the excitement subsided. There seemed to be young Americans everywhere, putting in long days without pay and caring nothing about the hard work. Something had subtly changed. No longer was he taking the lead. Instead, people were concerned about his health, and they questioned everything he did. From Tickoralak he wrote Anne a melancholy note full of irritations. The new Mission vessel was no longer his to command, but he was not content to be a passenger:

I do my best to keep young – but the crew gets on my nerves. One is *never* alone, and the boys, especially this huge Varrick [Frissell], are so much at home that they use everything you have & sit in your seat & have dirty clothes anywhere & even now have natives in my cabin to show them movie pictures 'downstairs.' You see you *must* keep them satisfied, or it would be worse. Then every ... meal is Eberbach – Self – Herbert (that's all should be there) – the Varrick – Gibbs – & always someone else, such as Paddon – a nurse – a wop – & forward was Ted [Badger] – & now is Charlie. All are exceptionally fine & good *at soul*, or I would have to expire. But late for every meal, eternally wet & dirty, and a sense of waste, tho of course they pay ten times for it – gets on human nerves. I had to sail into Nurse Anderson yesterday. She had taken *three* brand new towels, with the labels still on, soaked them in water, wrapped up lettuces & cabbages in them, & left them out on deck. They were black & filthy – she apologized – but what good is that? She has mended my socks – my rugs – made a fine lining and edging for a mat. She is as good as gold & has fine spiritual vision. I suppose I am getting old.[32]

Something had gone wrong. Details he would normally take in stride were suddenly too much for him. He had become fussy and difficult. Before the trip finished, he collapsed as he climbed a hill. For the first time he was brought back aboard *Strathcona II* a patient in his own hospital ship.

WTG as major in Harvard Surgical Unit, 1915

WTG aboard the *Bowdoin* at sea, July 1925

A Boston newspaper records the departure of volunteers for the coast of
Labrador 'to relieve suffering among the people of this bleak region.' *Left to
right*: Dr Joseph Andrews, ophthalmologist; unidentified man; Elizabeth Fuller,
Ruth Taylor, and Marion Mosely of Boston; WTG; Anne Grenfell; Harriot
Houghteling of Chicago.

International Grenfell Association hospital, St Anthony, opened July 1927

Crew of the *Maraval*, Belfast, Maine, June 1929. *Third row*: Hoyt Pease, Al Gould, Jr, Nelson Rockefeller, Wilfred Grenfell, Jr. *Second row*: George Williams, Smitty, Doc Faunce, Bill James, Dudley Merrill, Lawrence Rockefeller. *First row*: Skipper Al Gould, Sr, Gibbs Sherrill

WTG and his brother, A.G. Grenfell, at Mostyn House School, *c.* 1932

WTG and Lady Grenfell, 1930

Mrs Milton Seely and WTG outside Copley Plaza, Boston, publicizing the
Grenfell Bazaar, 1932

The last family picture, Kinloch House, Vermont, 1937: Willie, Rosamond, Pascoe, Lady Grenfell, WTG

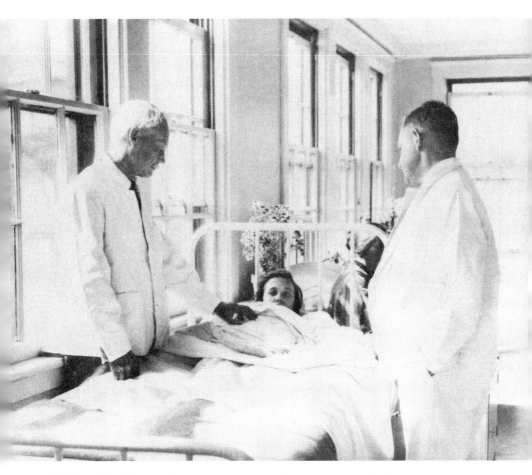

WTG and Dr Charles Curtis in the sun porch of the IGA hospital, St Anthony, July 1939

WTG and Dr Harry Paddon aboard the *Maraval,* summer 1939

PART FOUR

Spent Runner

—16—

The New Mission
1928 – 1931

*I wish those old simple days could come back again, sometimes when
I had an hour to sit down and smoke a pipe on Cartwright platform.*

Wilfred Grenfell to Ralph Parsons,
15 April 1930

The opening of the new St Anthony hospital brought the years of Grenfell's
direct influence virtually to an end. Hand-hewn lumber had given way to
reinforced concrete, the mails to radio, the two-stroke gasoline engine to
the diesel. Equipped with modern facilities and a professional staff, the
Mission could no longer be considered a struggling enterprise required to
demonstrate its value to the people of Newfoundland and the world at
large. But even as the hospital opened, the technological limits of medicine
had already manifested themselves. Major diseases had, in fact, been
curbed, but in the colonial world one could see that disease was also
associated with poverty and malnutrition. The Mission was now acting
upon the widely accepted knowledge that the lack of nutrition as well as
disease inhibited social development.

In St John's, where the Water Street merchants had given up part of
their domination of the economy with the arrival of paper and mining
interests, what was now familiarly known as 'the Grenfell Mission' had
achieved unquestioned status. When the annual report for 1927 was
released, the *Daily News* saluted the new hospital as an admirable institution, and the *Evening Telegram* could hardly contain its approbation. 'It
stands as a monument to the foresight, energy and humanity of Sir Wilfred
Grenfell who gave the best years of his life in ministering to the needs
of the people scattered along the northern shores of Newfoundland and

Labrador,' caroled its editorialist. 'St Anthony is more than fulfilling the visions of its founder, and in its ministrations to the sick and afflicted it has proved itself an indispensible factor in promoting the general welfare of the community.'[1] By 1930 the *New York Times*, which regarded the Mission as an American institution, characterized the work as one of the great adventures of the twentieth century.[2] Such rhetorical bursts not only acknowledged Grenfell's unimpeachable achievements; they revealed a new, unquestioned acceptance of his international stature.

The opening of the hospital occurred at a time when the colony enjoyed a fleeting illusion of promise. At the Imperial Conference of 1926 Newfoundland had been granted the same dominion status as Canada and thus an improved constitutional position that added a measure of independence. In 1927 a second paper mill was opened at Corner Brook, and the Privy Council ruled on the boundary dispute between Newfoundland and Quebec, awarding Newfoundland an area of 112,826 square miles and opening up what were imagined as untold possibilities for timber production, mineral exploration, and hydro-electric power. In 1928 American capital financed a new lead and zinc mine at Buchans. Fish prices began to rise, and Brazil returned as an important market. As a significant force in the medical and social life of the northern districts, the Mission experienced a spasm of optimism soon to be calmed by two unforeseen changes.

First, Sir Richard Squires, whom Grenfell still regarded as a political brigand, returned to power in 1928 with a strong majority, promising further industrialization and relief from Newfoundland's dependence on the fishery. Instinctively, Grenfell despised the prime minister, especially for his neglect of public welfare in what was now a greatly expanded Labrador, and when the government refused to install a water supply in Cartwright he wrote pompously to the manager of the Hudson's Bay Company, 'Do try and make it so hard for the Government that they will see how badly they will stand before the whole world, if I were to publish the fact that they were unwilling to do even that small amount for the development of the vast area entrusted to them.'[3] But secondly, Squires arrived in office just when the world was about to experience the consequences of a world-wide depression, and by 1930 Newfoundland was already suffering the effects. Fish prices dropped to an unusually low level, bringing down revenue at a time when the government received greater demands for relief. While it would be easy to blame Squires for the economy's swift collapse, with the odour of previous scandal still hanging about him, more complex economic pressures prevailed. As S.J.R. Noel has shown, 'It would, of course, be wholly wrong to suggest that the government in power was responsible for this state of affairs. They were but the hapless victims of a trap constructed by preceding governments, one of which had been Squires's own, and devastatingly sprung by economic forces beyond their control.'[4] With this state of affairs, investors retreated, and when the government invited tenders for a major loan to offset its anticipated debts in 1930–1, not one was received. Newfoundland began to sense a slide into total financial collapse and a default on its debts. With the government at the mercy of bondholders and the depression choking the flow of charitable support from the United States, the Mission's task appeared even greater.

As a self-governing dominion, Newfoundland now enjoyed the same constitutional status as the other dominions of the empire. If it defaulted on its national debt, it would establish an embarrassing precedent. In May 1931 the four Canadian banks operating on the island briefly came to the government's rescue and jointly advanced a temporary loan of $2 million, postponing the default temporarily. Consequently, the government decreased its expenditures even further, and Squires asked the British government to appoint a commissioner who would investigate its financial structure and recommend necessary changes.

As the collapse of the Newfoundland economy loomed, Grenfell renewed his fund-raising efforts, setting forth on lecture tours of Britain and the United States despite the tiring process. 'It wrings my heart to think that such a man, at his age and not in the best of health, is forced to lecture all over the United States to produce the amount of money necessary to produce his splendid character-factories along the Labrador coast,' Charles H. Sherrill wrote John D. Rockefeller.[5] While he laboured to keep up contributions, honour and recognition continued to pour in. Princeton gave him an honorary LL.D., and so did Bowdoin College. The students of the University of St Andrews elected him lord rector by a majority of 157 over Lord Melchett, the Liberal reformer. But donations remained low. In March 1929 his brother wrote and warned him to ease up. 'For Heaven's sake do give yourself a bit of a chance – & "repoze",' he said. 'I am sure it can't be good for any man of our age to be such a human tornado. The mere *sight* of a crowd, indoors or out, always makes me feel miserable – always did: but to have to live all the time haranguing a crowd – help!'[6] The warning proved justified. Before the end of the month, Grenfell suffered a severe attack of angina and cancelled all speaking engagements. He and Anne returned for a period of rest at Dr Kellogg's sanitarium in Battle Creek, where Kellogg had been treating the rich and famous of America with short periods of stringency and rest. Still, he refused to ease up and was already planning his schedule for the year ahead. His unwillingness to accept what his body told him disturbed the family. 'You know best how much you can do,' A.G. advised him, 'but for goodness' sake be guided by your prudence rather than by an insatiable keenness to cram as much activity as possible into the Last Lap. The programme you sketch out for the rest of the year would reduce *me* to mutton.'[7]

While Grenfell continued as the Mission's only fund-raiser, the extremely high incidence of tuberculosis in the region required an effort to offset the low resistance of the population, and the Mission renewed its campaign against the disease with a program to reform living habits. Tuberculosis still ranked as the most common cause of death in Newfoundland. In the one-hundred-bed St Anthony hospital alone, during a fifteen-year study begun in 1923, there were approximately nine hundred admissions for tuberculosis, some requiring imaginative surgical intervention for which Curtis was the acknowledged master. On any given day Curtis performed a variety of operations, ranging from the restoration of a deformed ankle to the removal of a cataract to the treatment of a tuberculous hip joint.[8] He possessed the strength and dexterity required for these and other elaborate procedures – such as thoracoplasty, an orthodox operation for tuberculosis which required the surgeon to expose the chest wall by opening a huge flap, removing the ribs from one side, and allowing the lung within to collapse. Curtis was capable of performing two such laborious operations in a single morning, then turning his hand to putting bone grafts into another patient with tuberculosis of the spine and leaving enough time before lunch to take out most of a thyroid gland and a gall bladder.[9] With procedures such as these, the new hospital treated numerous cases of tuberculosis or consigned patients to a regimen of fresh air and exposure to sunlight in the tuberculosis sanatorium.

The Mission exhibited the same energy in its nutrition campaign. After fifteen years, the general adoption of whole-wheat flour had produced no ostensible effect. Since the flour checked only one deficiency, in any case, it was thought wiser to aim at encouraging a greater variety of food, and the attack on deficiency diseases proceeded by challenging taste and tradition. In 1929 Dr Helen Mitchell of the Battle Creek Sanitarium concluded from a nutritional survey that although the vitamin content of the usual food supply in the region was low by American standards, she was surprised by the lack of clinical evidence of disease. Yet she did draw a cultural conclusion from the data. 'There does exist, however, an ill-defined lack of "pep" and ambition, chronic under-nutrition, and a low resistance to various diseases such as tuberculosis, all of which may be due to the poor food eaten,' she wrote.[10] The understanding of the effects of vitamin A was by now assuming greater importance, especially its part in the resistance to generalized infection.[11] In 1930 a newspaper story emanating from Battle Creek announced that Margery Vaughn, a nutritionist with two years' experience with the Red Cross in Texas, had volunteered to go north and work among the 'hardy settlers from Devonshire' along the coast.[12] Though Miss Vaughn's work among what she called the 'quaint people' of the region was curtailed by weather and transportation, she proceeded with an ambitious program of baby shows, cooking demonstrations, health talks, good teeth campaigns, and other competitions and reported remarkable gains in the health of younger children.[13]

She was especially satisfied with the increase of interest in gardening and reported that in 1932 food shortages seemed reduced as a result. Since 1928 the Mission had benefited from the annual visits of Professor F.C. Sears, a horticulturalist and orchard pioneer at Massachusetts State College who had come north to begin a gardening program. Sears had met with some considerable success once he recognized the speed with which plants could grow during the extensive daylight hours. But he also recognized what in Grenfell code was politely called the 'conservatism' of the people and took steps to enrich the sandy soil and drain the gardens by fashioning narrow beds with deep ditches.[14] The Mission also employed teams of volunteer workers to teach people to plant gardens and lecture them on hygiene and nutrition. Thus, during the brief summer months remote communities suddenly came alive with young university students, the so-called wops – not only as labourers and ships' crews but as schoolteachers, nutritionists, district nurses, and instructors in home industries, mostly Americans of comfortable, sometimes wealthy families, attracted by the opportunity to perform public service in a location remote from their own lives. As Grenfell explained the origins of the term, years before a spoiled young man who felt superior to the work deemed it fit only for 'wops,' as the Italian labourers in the United States were known. Grenfell replied that in Labrador everybody was a wop and did his or her share of useful labour.[15] Henceforth, all volunteers were known by the term, even though Grenfell later tried to suggest that it was an acronym for 'without pay.'

The Mission treated the recruitment of these volunteers with the same seriousness as the selection of medical staff and carefully briefed them so as not to offend local sensibilities, especially those of the Methodists. 'Methodist people in these small settlements are very conservative,' wrote a Methodist clergyman, 'and would be shocked if any young lady indulging in the modern accomplishments of smoking or dancing should be sent among them.'[16] Candidates were first interviewed at the New York office by the recruitment secretary, who determined whether they were best suited to teaching or nutrition, office or industrial work, labouring or agriculture. They were then dispatched to a Mission hospital or station for seven weeks, during which time they paid their own expenses.

Fearful of any cultural conflicts that might occur when exuberant students were introduced into a colonial environment, the IGA handed out a set of instructions to prepare them for their encounter with the native population. In addition to advising workers on travel and equipment, these instructions consisted of directions for suitable behaviour. The workers were told that the population differed from themselves in custom and speech but that they were 'white' and 'of the same stock as we.'[17] At the same time, however, they were encouraged to see the experience as adventure. 'It is a tremendous adventure as well as very hard work,' an applicant was told, 'for you would be the only twentieth century person in a seventeenth [sic] century environment.' To maintain good relations, they were urged to observe the Sabbath strictly. Though women were asked not to smoke in public or in private and cautioned never to wear knickerbockers, the direction was not followed universally. In 1926 Anne Grenfell complained to the staff selection committee that Vassar girls had been banned from the coast because the captain of the boat bringing them north complained that they had smoked and behaved in an 'objectionable' way.[18]

With these warnings in mind, this ever-changing group of genteel, well-educated individuals set about the task of bringing their knowledge and up-to-date attitudes to the sequestered way stations of the coast, sometimes working without supervision, direct mail, or their accustomed diet for weeks on end. For the most part, they went about these duties seriously, living among a people set apart from themselves by culture and tradition. During the summer of 1924, for example, Mary Grace Coates, a junior at Wellesley, taught fifteen children at a one-room school in Eddy's Cove, Newfoundland. Besides her formal duties, she conducted church services, gave health talks, encouraged gardening, promoted rug-hooking and seal-skin work, and assisted the visiting doctor or dentist.[19] Throughout the winter of 1926 Carolyn Galbraith, a young teacher from Vermont, lived in Forteau, Labrador, then a village of twenty-five 'desolate' houses with ten or a dozen children resident in most of them, all clothed by the Mission store. 'We now have an evening school three nights a week,' she reported excitedly to a college friend. 'I am to teach cooking, sewing, weaving, knitting, wood carving etc. – to all women & girls who wish it, men at weaving & carving. I will also have evening classes for the young people who have left school – teaching the three R's – as needed.'[20] Miss Galbraith also gave six piano lessons a week but never complained about too much work. Each day, she insisted, she awoke ready to begin again. Other volunteers exhibited the same satisfactions as they went about the task of meeting the perceived needs of a population with which they had virtually nothing in common. Clearly they were far removed from the lives of local people. The first Newfoundland volunteer observed from Cartwright in 1930, 'They seem to be very fine chaps and very capable of doing heavy work. However, the main objection to their company is that they have unlimited wealth at their disposal, and this makes it rather difficult for a Memorial College student to hold up his end of the plank, as they say.'[21]

In later life these young Americans looked upon such a period of intense philanthropy, lived out during the gilded age conveyed in the novels of Fitzgerald and Hemingway, as a precious interlude. Nursing journals and alumni magazines reported personal experiences in the north,[22] and there were enthusiastic annual reunions in Boston, New York, and London. The alumni made considerable financial contributions and gradually took over the boards of the supporting associations, forgetting the moments of unrelieved loneliness, boredom, and frustration, the occupational hazards of the missionary. For at such moments they had turned to one another, and the coast had provided a convenient launching place for countless liaisons, some of which developed into lifelong friendships – some even into marriages. A crew of young American oceanographers who ventured into St Anthony during the summer of 1926 came away convinced that Grenfell volunteers were not the pale, sober-sided missionary types they had expected. A young woman in charge of the craft store succeeded in attaching herself to two scruffy crewmen and selling them her whole inventory of local crafts. 'Jordan on the other hand was captured by three nurses who only let him go when he promised to work there all next winter,' the skipper recorded. Not surprisingly, as one doctor observed, visitors, especially French sailors, were always welcome in all the Grenfell institutions, where the resident staff was composed almost entirely of women.[23]

If Grenfell inspired these young people to labour on the coast, he left it to others to carry the work through. In 1928 he engaged the thirty-seven-year-old Eric H. Thomsen, a practical Christian with a desire for social justice, to supervise the labourers. Thomsen soon recognized how the organization was falling into the hands of the New York managers whom he considered more preoccupied with the 'shell' of the enterprise while losing sight of the 'real thing.' In a passage he struck from a draft letter to Grenfell that summer he wrote:

> Out of loyalty to the vision which both of us can see – you so much more boldly and courageously than I – I feel compelled to say that much is being lost by your not being here in person, which it must have taken you years to build up, not in dollars and cents only ... but rather of those far more elusive qualities which make the essence of the Christian life, and I cannot help but think that some who help to share your glory and exploit your name, have never succeeded in catching a glimpse of the tremendous vision to which you have consecrated your life.[24]

Donald Johnson, an Englishman of the same education as Grenfell who had left what he called a 'dull rut' to relieve Dr Donald Hodd at Harrington Harbour during the winter of 1928–9, experienced something similar when he visited St Anthony the next summer. Johnson, a sharp-witted radical with a good deal more experience than the average university student, took in what appeared to be a new spirit, a departure from the zest that had previously informed the work. Instead, he encountered that year a less orderly group. 'Amongst the summer volunteer workers,' he said, 'young college men and women, mainly from the Eastern United States, who had been induced by Grenfell's eloquence to spend their summer in doing the humbler tasks about the hospital, the result was disillusionment and a tendency for natural high spirits to find their outlet in horseplay of various kinds, most of it of such a kind as to lead to friction and misunderstanding with the more sombre-minded permanent staff.'[25] While some allowance must be made for Johnson's grouchiness, without Grenfell's presence and personal inspiration, volunteer interest was declining. The same wops did not return as frequently, and ten years later their loyalty had fall off considerably.[26]

Johnson was impressed by the hospital in St Anthony, where he worked as a temporary house surgeon, but surprised by the awful manifestations of tuberculosis, particularly the acute pulmonary cases and the multiple joint afflictions that required repeated amputations. He was also disappointed by Grenfell himself, whom he had admired from a distance. Johnson would have read Grenfell's pronouncements about the development of the north, routinely printed in the pages of *Among the Deep Sea Fishers*. He would have known that his name carried sufficient authority to carry through a benefit performance of *Faust* at the Metropolitan Opera, bringing in as much as $7,500 for the Mission. He would have watched, occasionally, when Grenfell donned a white coat and walked the wards, performing the familiar rituals of the consultant. But clearly he was no longer in charge. Curtis, who had since married Harriot Houghteling, Anne's childhood friend, quietly commanded the medical facility, transforming it for the task at hand. Grenfell looked tired, and his hair had turned white. Johnson observed: .

> The Grenfell house on the hill at St Anthony was now occupied for only some few weeks in each year during the summer when 'Sir Wilf,' together with the dignified and charming Lady Grenfell, would appear as the figureheads of the establishment. But with Grenfell, as so often with others of brilliant early fame, advancing years had already taken their toll. Now, at the age of sixty-four, though socially and publicly lionized in Great Britain and the United States, he was a potterer divested of real authority in the organization which he had built up

during the hey-day of his powers. The whole latter part of his life had been devoted to platform appeals for funds in the big centres of population, while the work on the Coast of Labrador had fallen into other hands – it was institutionalized and organized from the head office in New York.[27]

Grenfell may have lost his zest, but he was not quite a 'potterer' yet. He could still charm or, if necessary, transfix a recalcitrant worker with a stern glance. Elliott Merrick, a volunteer in Indian Harbour during the summer of 1929, has maintained that Grenfell resisted the ceremonial but still preserved his air of authority, leaving no doubt about who had founded and built the Mission as soon as he stepped aboard *Strathcona II* and started issuing orders. Merrick, who had already taken his degree at Yale and worked in New York, was not so readily impressed by the easy assumption of command. 'Grenfell expected us to unload tons of freight from *Strathcona* in the rain into a dory and row everything ashore and carry it about a hundred yards up to the hospital by hand, not even a wheelbarrow,' he has said. 'That was all right. That was the code, and, after all, we'd never been adrift on an icepan.'[28] Others, like Johnson, were disappointed. Laurence and Nelson Rockefeller, who worked as deckhand and cook aboard the *Maraval*, regarded the experience as 'disillusioning.'[29] Grenfell sensed their dissatisfaction and took relief from a polite letter from Nelson the next winter, fearing he had 'strained sacrificial self-effacement to the limit!'[30] But it confirmed his belief in the efficacy of volunteer labour. 'To nine tenths of those who go down it is a real insult to offer them money,' he wrote his Ottawa director. 'They have never earned money in their lives, and the only way we can really pay them is by showing them the pleasure of a sacrificial service.'[31]

That same summer Grenfell refused Harry Paddon the use of *Maraval* for a medical cruise to northern Labrador in co-operation with the Moravians, commandeering it for a trip along the coast of Newfoundland. But in 1930 Paddon and an eye, ear, and throat specialist from Cincinnati accompanied a Moravian doctor to Nain. Paddon wanted to go as far north as Hebron the following year, even though Grenfell did not give him his wholehearted support. He told the Moravian superintendent:

I was notified that 'the experiment will be watched with interest,' by Sir W. Grenfell, who was rather sceptical about the amount of service Maraval would render, and was inclined to use her for all sorts of purposes outside of Labrador Medical Mission cruising. Of course he always is erratic. Our Directors sincerely wish the boat to be used in this way &, once clear of the freighting etc., associated with our extensive reorganization at this time, I am confident I can cruise the whole coast from Belle Isle Strait to Nain 2-3 times, with 1 trip to Hebron, annually. If I have your backing it will strengthen my case with Sir Wilf & the Directors, & will help the latter to counter any impulsive scheme of Sir W's, by pointing out that the boat already has imperative duties on the Labrador Coast.[32]

The Moravians, who had looked sceptically upon Grenfell's intrusions into their domain over the years, welcomed Paddon's offer. For even though the two missions co-existed satisfactorily, the Moravians sometimes felt like minor characters in the grand drama Grenfell had created in the public mind. In conveying Paddon's request to his headquarters, the Superintendent argued:

> You are aware of the reasons why visits of Dr Grenfell to our stations have not been welcomed in the past. In many cases they have not been mission trips at all, but advertisement, and collecting of material for advertisement. In his lectures and reports Dr. Grenfell has been in the habit of intentionally avoiding mentioning the existence of the Moravians on the coast. While we do not ask Dr. Paddon to proclaim for us the merits of our mission, we ask to be treated as cooperators if he wants our cooperation. Dr. Paddon's letter not only but his attitude during his recent visit make us hope that he is sincerely seeking to work with us in the same cause and for the honour of the same Master.[33]

He therefore asked the board to encourage such visits as Paddon proposed. Grenfell knew he was sometimes the author of such conflicts. 'I am so often cross & so often say what I don't the least mean to be anything but kind – it hurts – & I am hurt more than anyone else – esp. afterwards,' he wrote Anne. But as he acknowledged in a letter he wrote to the *New York Times* a few days later, Labrador was changing despite him, and so was the Mission.[34]

Paddon had taken time to reflect upon the Mission's changing circumstances during a six-month furlough. By now he could see that, despite the great achievements at St Anthony, the Mission seemed more centralized, leaving the outposts and nursing stations on the Labrador coast to proceed as best they could. He was by now the most experienced of the 'pioneer' doctors in Labrador, accustomed to covering long miles by dogsled in winter and aboard *Maraval* in summer. He knew the Moravians and the scattered population intimately and had accustomed himself to the unorthodox situations imposed by isolation with characteristic competence and understatement.[35] As the permanent medical officer in Labrador, he had by this time devoted himself to developing the medical, educational, industrial, and agricultural work aimed at improving daily life, and he took a personal interest in schools and gardens as a means of raising the standard of living. He had written the London secretary in 1928, 'I am fifteen years older than I was my first winter on this Coast, and cannot go on doing 1600 miles a winter forever.'[36] Florence Cozad, a nurse in St Anthony, thought Paddon less 'infectious' than Grenfell but more practical and businesslike with 'fewer flights of fancy and more continuity.' She added, 'I have seen & am seeing more and more too many results of the mission's unwise generosity and acts of brotherly love not founded on good sociological principles.'[37]

In two nostalgic articles entitled 'Ye Goode Olde Dayes,' published in 1929, Paddon paid due attention to the great progress made in St Anthony since his arrival in 1912. He noted the new hospital and orphanage, the school, the stock farm, the machine shop, the haul-up slip, and the greenhouse. All of these were indisputable features of the Mission's stature, he acknowledged. But by dwelling so heavily upon the past, he also made an implicit judgment about the present, a judgment of which he was fully aware, and he apologized for what might be interpreted as an expression of discontent. He wrote, 'Improvements are needed and right; in terms of community progress they are essential. Yet in 1912, though buildings were primitive, equipment defective and communications slow, there was intense *joie de vivre*.'[38] While rejoicing in the material progress, he looked back upon a different kind of Mission.

As for Grenfell himself, a sense of resignation had crept into his public utterances. He sounded increasingly like the runner trying to cram everything into the last lap. He arrived in the United Kingdom in the autumn of 1929 to follow a familiar pattern: six or eight weeks of lecturing followed by a winter holiday, usually somewhere in the southern United States. He gave an enthusiastic talk about Labrador's potential at the British Broadcasting Corporation.[39] At St Andrews he assumed for a year the largely ceremonial position of lord rector and received yet another LL.D. On his arrival for this event, he was mobbed at the railway station by the students and driven ceremonially through the streets in a horse-drawn carriage, conscious that he would sit in the place once occupied by John Knox and his own latter-day heroes, Kipling, Barrie, and Nansen.

During the post-war years the students of St Andrews had avoided politics in their choice of a rector and favoured candidates whom they considered men of character and personal appeal. Haig had come straight from his conquests in France. Barrie, Kipling, and Nansen had advocated the qualities of courage, independence, and adventure. For Grenfell, the familiar accolades poured out: Cornish stock ... fighting temper ... athletic record ... mariner's skill ... saga of endurance and escape on the ice ... forty years of work for deep-sea fishermen. A *Times* editorialist remarked the following day, 'At first it is a little difficult to think of him, as we must think of him since yesterday, as Rector of a University, since never was a man of intellect less academic. But St. Andrews University – true, as SIR WILFRED GRENFELL suggests, to the spirit of its patron saint – likes men of adventure for its Rectors.'[40] Grenfell, however, did not address the students as a modern-day hero, as he had done in countless schools and colleges. He presented himself as one whose day was past. 'Today,' he told them haltingly, 'I am but the spent runner, handing the torch to you, who are bursting with greater potential for the race than ever I had, and I am trying to say *Moriturus vos saluto*.'[41]

One other important matter he did not wish to ignore during his time in the United Kingdom was his patrimony. To date, he had still received no satisfaction from his brother, and as his years as a lecturer diminished and his two sons prepared to enter university he felt the need to claim his portion again. For the past two years, the brothers had continued to discuss a settlement through correspondence and long discussions at Parkgate. A.G. wrote in his diary in 1927, for example, 'Usual avaricious letter from Anne (signed by W.T.G.) about feared hardship of having to pay English Income Tax on the money earned in England.'[42] But the time could not have been less propitious: the advancing world depression had eaten into A.G.'s holdings, making it even more difficult for him to settle, and his health had deterioriated. The osteomyelitis that had troubled him through-out his life grew painful, and Grenfell sent his brother to Liverpool to see Sir Robert Jones, a surgeon he admired. Yet Jones, despite his acknowl-edged skill, could not work a miracle, and A.G. continued to suffer.

On Grenfell's return from St Andrews, the meeting between the two turned unusually emotional. A.G. noted, 'W.T.G. came v. early: I had had a rotten night – doped with Kalmine – I broke down rather badly: like a fool. He told me not to worry about his patrimony £5500: quite satisfied to leave it in the business. E.C. Grenfell has invested a sum to cover cost of his children's education. So he is not hard up.'[43] For the next year, A.G. did indeed examine alternatives, but with the depression well advanced he asked his brother to lessen the interest. Grenfell felt conciliatory, grateful for the hospitality afforded his family on numerous visits.[44] And so, once again, they laid their financial differences to rest.

When A.G. heard from him next, Grenfell was celebrating his sixty-fifth birthday in Texas, complaining about his heart, and feeling disappointed that the stock market crash and the restrictions placed upon his own movements had prevented him from filling the Mission's coffers. By March he was staying with Henry Ford in Florida and sounding encouraged. Ford was two years older than Grenfell and at that stage of his life a good deal fitter. Grenfell was impressed with his liberal employment policies, his flamboyant charitable activities, and his desire to raise wages despite the national policy of retrenchment. Soon after, he wrote, 'Mr. Henry Ford is preaching, I believe, the most wonderful industrial social gospel today when he raises the wages of the worker. Increase of population and low wages mean misery, Bolshevism, war. Piety is good; but the enabling of the worker to maintain a decent home is a better safeguard of civilization than laws and guns.'[45] But if Grenfell expected Ford to make a contribution to the Mission, he was disappointed. Ford, an even more accomplished publicist than Grenfell, donated some construction machinery instead. As the *George B. Cluett*, the Mission's new freighter, left Boston in the spring of 1930, he came aboard for less than an hour, having put the crew up at the Wayside Inn the weekend before, and had his photograph taken with Grenfell for the Boston papers.

Grenfell himself sailed with the *Cluett* for St Anthony, making his customary display of manliness for the young crew. In the course of the voyage he would take his turn at the wheel, scramble up the shrouds, perch on the crosstrees, and come down the other side. Every morning he would scoop up a bucket of seawater, douse himself and run up and down, swinging his arms with great exuberance. One morning in the Strait of Belle Isle, a young wop recorded in his diary, he stopped the *Cluett* in sight of an iceberg and ordered all hands overboard for a dip. But he did not take the rough weather easily. His food came up, his head ached, and privately he resorted to quinidine.[46]

That summer he heard rumours that Squires would sell off Labrador to Canada. After making what was now an unusual visit to St John's to discourage the plan, at a public lecture at the King George v Institute he declared that the Newfoundland government would be acting in a shortsighted manner if it disposed of the territory.[47] In those days, Grenfell liked to propagate the popular myth that Labrador was a land of promise, 'rich in natural wealth.' Thus, drawing a parallel with Alaska, he argued that northern territories were not beyond the reach of industrial development and that Newfoundland would be blind to its own interests if it parted with a rich territory to relieve a temporary shortage of cash. A decade before, such an intrusion into political debate would have brought scathing letters to the editor and public denunciations. This time Grenfell's place was secure. Even before the lecture took place, the *Daily News* had vigorously celebrated his efforts against privileged interests and suggested in an editorial that his tendency to 'overcolor' the deprivations of the north might have been justified. 'The cry of the poor and needy will not be listened to by the world unless it be a cry: a whisper for help will go unheeded,' it now insisted.[48]

During these early depression years Anne seemed to take on more of the burden of promotion than ever. She continued to accompany him on lecture tours, planning schedules, showing slides, and handing out pamphlets, worrying about his health. Consequently, she was rarely left sufficient time for family gatherings, except during the summer at the house purchased in Charlotte, Vermont. Instead, she attempted to keep the family together with frequent letters to the three children, Willie and Pascoe at Groton, and Rosamond at Havergal, Toronto. As she acknowledged in 1929 in a letter to Rosamond, then twelve, 'I was so pleased to hear [you loved your school], for it makes me so much more satisfied to think that you are not homesick, though I must say that you have always been a brick in never making a fuss, and in standing by in making sacrifices for the sake of letting me help Father in his work.' From a train crossing Newfoundland in 1930, she wrote Willie, 'I hate to think of you all by yourself & deserted by your family! But you are a jolly good sport & not given to the vice of self pity.'[49]

With the Mission's work changing its emphasis, she herself had taken a special interest in the education of young Newfoundlanders and Labradorians of promise and arranged for them to attend American training schools like Berea College so that they could return to work as nurses, teachers, plumbers, and machinists. She also took it upon herself to encourage home industries so as to bring ready cash into families suffering from the slump in the market. Though the Industrial Department had been established for a decade, it had never been able to generate much above $500 a year in sales. But with the rise in demand for its work, it had grown to $27,000 in 1926. In 1929, through the production of specially designed hooked mats, weaving, ivory carving, basketwork, and curios, the sales had risen to $63,000, and the products were highly regarded in the field of occupational therapy.[50] The Mission claimed that as many as a thousand people benefited from such sales to one degree or another. Suddenly, the IGA found it had created a growing enterprise with no adequate building in St Anthony, no capital, and no business organization, and it reluctantly put up the capital itself out of the general fund. Stores were needed, catalogues, and staff. Anne, with the help of an industrial committee, took the task on herself. She was an influential part of the process of cultural intervention to which the Mission was committed.

She spared no opportunity to advertise her product. Shoppers on Oxford Street would find a window in Selfridge's dedicated to Grenfell crafts for a fortnight; opera-goers at the annual benefit would find displays in the foyer of the Metropolitan at intermission. 'The problem today is not one of production,' she wrote enthusiastically in an article printed in the *New York Times*, 'but of sales. If we could get a sufficiently large market for our goods, there is practically no limit to the amount which could be produced on the Labrador and Newfoundland coasts and this quite without any loss in the quality of the articles.'[51] As for the products themselves, they had by now lost their traditional designs. The Mission furnished the materials to spare the women the financial outlay, and it also developed most of the designs and the colours through a combination of simplification, miniaturization, and novelty to accommodate the preconceptions of the market. In particular, the ethnicity of the Inuit was featured as cute and exotic, and Grenfell himself designed the rug patterns, usually incorporating familiar northern scenes and dog-team motifs. To ensure a steady sale, two shops opened in the United States, one on Madison Avenue and the other on Locust Street, Philadelphia. Later, the Dog-Team Tavern, a salesroom and tea-shop, opened in a New England farmhouse on the Champlain Highway near Ferrisburg, Vermont.[52] In 1934, a second Dog-Team tea-room and shop opened in Oxford, Connecticut.

At this stage of industrial development, Jessie Luther returned to St Anthony on holiday, arriving by way of a new summer cruise scheduled by the Clarke Steamship Company. After an absence of fifteen years, she measured the advances made since her departure. The old Guest House now served as a lumber shed. The Industrial Department itself occupied what was once the orphanage, incorporating a weaving room, a dye room with steam vats, and separate spaces for toy-making and ivory carving. The mat industry had since reached a high degree of refinement. Workers were busy tearing long strips of flannel for hooked mats, others cutting silk stockings for the finer grade. 'I know of no work of the kind found anywhere to compare with the excellence of workmanship of these mats, many of which resemble tapestry,' she judged. 'It is difficult to make purchasers believe they are hooked, the work is so fine and even.'[53] In the designing room a group cut stencils and marked the burlap to be used for hooking. Finished products waited to be shipped. In the intervening years, despite the lack of a large market, the products had achieved a high degree of artisanship and a wide reputation.

The Mission was still expanding its province beyond purely medical work, and there was a price to be paid for the time and energy the Grenfells had devoted to such progress. As they prepared for a lecture tour of Britain in the autumn of 1930, they were suddenly aware that Willie, their oldest child, had grown up in their absence and, after six years at Groton with Endicott Peabody, had left to take a degree at Oxford, where his parents wanted to expose him to gentlemanly British habits. His fees would be paid by Grenfell's cousin, Edward Grenfell, the London banker and Conservative MP (soon to be Baron St Just). So much time had gone by. Grenfell had grown no closer to his sons, and as the first term approached he wrote Willie with his best advice and a warning about upholding the family name and living a godly life. Stay away from 'harmful indulgences,' he warned, and cultivate simpicity. And the old athlete asked his son to keep his learning in perspective. 'It is the love of your heart, and the devotion of your life to His (Christ's) standard and standards, that alone can give you – Wilfred Grenfell Jr. – the vision of truth and reality, Oxford and Harvard even cannot,' he wrote.[54]

Anne, on the other hand, advised her son on the fine points of social pragmatism. She wanted to make sure he paid his bills and wrote thank-you notes. During the first days of term, as he adjusted himself to the new social conventions, she told him how to behave according to the qualities she admired herself. With a touch of wishful thinking, she counselled:

> Be pleasant & courteous *always*, but don't make intimates yet. English people are *slow* & sure. Your friends will come later, never fear. I expect it is jolly lonely at times – but stick to your work & your rowing & be always a quiet, (not noisy) pleasant, helpful, self-controlled *gentleman*, & they'll take your measure & seek you out for your merit. They hate pushing, noisy, grouchy people. Be a good & interested listener to everything the English boys have to tell you. You'll learn a lot & you will flatter them. Meantime don't be discouraged a bit.[55]

As she and Grenfell toured Scotland, she reminded him of the need to make good as a scholar so as to uphold the family honour. She also urged him to write his benefactor, Edward Grenfell. 'He will be pleased,' she assured him, 'especially as he does not know I am suggesting it, and will think you are writing out of friendship and appreciation to him.'[56]

By the second term Willie had acquired the freshman's intellectual self-confidence and a taste for controversy after imbibing the socialist economics of G.D.H. Cole and the views of Alfred Zimmern on international relations and felt up to challenging her conservative assumptions. He was finding England a trifle isolationist but enjoyed his weekends with A.G., who filled him full of ideas about the futility of prohibition and the dark future of the church. He was also concerned about his father's health after observing him for a summer aboard *Maraval* on the Labrador coast. But Anne felt the need to place these matters in perspective. She insisted, 'We may laugh at Father's childlikeness, and his absent-mindedness, but when it comes down to solid facts of life, he is the straightest man I know; and though I laugh at him and get furious because he keeps me waiting for trains and meals, and does not know what he has eaten, and loses his clothes, and gets up from a meal before he has eaten and says, "What are we waiting for?" – still, I would take his judgement on matters that really concern life before I would take anybody else's.'[57] Her letters did, however, admit one regret: the lack of a conventional family life. Willie's twenty-first birthday reminded her that her son had achieved his majority without having had his family around him during his formative years. Yet she refused to reject the path she had taken and explained, 'It has not been exactly as I would have wished it, for I have been so tired for so many years that it has been hard on you children, but you have been wonderfully good children and wonderfully understanding and cooperative, and I hope that the knowledge of having a father like yours has been some compensation for having only an apology for a home. I think often of what you have had to give up, but I seem to have done all I could about it, and I must leave the rest, hoping that you understand.'[58]

Manhood, as Grenfell remarked, had crept up on Willie with a vengeance. He had joined the Labour Party Club, and with his reading of political theory, his fashionable admiration for Soviet economic experiments, and his attachment to his Uncle Algie, he kept his mother busy with challenges to conventional wisdom. Most of the clergy were hypocrites; communism seemed to offer an answer to current problems. She carried the debate forward, and as he entered his second year, she laid out a religious and political philosophy that sounded very much like Grenfell's own:

> I am certain that in Christ we have the highest revelation of God which mankind is capable of, and I do not in the least confuse Christianity with the collections of crowds in city cathedrals, to hear time-worn formulas. That sounds to me very much like Uncle Algy. I do not think the collection of crowds to hear time-worn formulas has anything to do with Christianity, and what you say about De Tocqueville stating that no stable society could exist without a form of religion I do not think applies to Russia, because don't you think that the form of religion has a great deal to do with the stability of society? From as close observation as I could give to Russia, it seemed to me that it had not hit upon a form of society that was either stable or would endure, because its basic principle is rotten. It begins at the wrong end of the stick.[59]

And as she matched herself against her son's undergraduate certainties, she knew that one of the least stable political societies lay in Newfoundland itself. Could a society set so firmly on the road of responsible government give up all claims to democracy? As Newfoundland sank further into economic decline, the signs suggested that it could not.

— 17 —

The Death of Democracy
1931 – 1934

*The crowd grew very still, and a deep, low, happy sigh, as of people
who see the theatre curtain go up at last, breathed from innumerable
throats.*

George Orwell, 'Shooting an Elephant'

In all of Newfoundland and Labrador, no public monument honours the
first Baron Amulree (1860–1942), the British commissioner who fathered
the political and economic changes of the 1930s. For it was Amulree, a
Scots lawyer skilled in matters relating to local government, a superb wage
arbitrator, an experienced commissioner, and a former member of Ramsay
MacDonald's cabinet, who presided over the royal commission that prepared the way for the loss of responsible government and the political and
economic reforms to follow. The Amulree Commission was the child of
unprecedented public disorder. By the end of 1931, when the emergency
loan advanced by the syndicate of four Canadian banks had run out,
Newfoundland faced economic collapse once again. But the Canadian
banks came through with a second six-month loan to service the national
debt, this time attaching more stringent conditions. During this second
reprieve, no one, least of all Sir Richard Squires, expected the government
could eventually avoid default. As more public services were cut, the
government itself began to feel the threat of an increasingly distressed
population. For, with unemployment spreading, voters conditioned to
drawing directly on the government for a grant, a job, or a favour of some
kind expressed their frustration. Crowds of unemployed workers gathered
in St John's, and when the legislature opened in February 1932 their anger
was inflamed by the resignation of the minister of finance, Peter Cashin,

who charged the prime minister and other members of the cabinet with corruption.

It would be difficult to imagine a worse time to call the integrity of the government into question. On 11 February a mob invaded the prime minister's office at the Court House. The prime minister himself was jostled, and the crowd did not disperse until dole orders were issued.[1] As the Squires government manoeuvred to stay in power throughout the rest of the winter, it passed further stringency measures, including additional charges on basic foodstuffs. Public resentment continued to grow. By 5 April, the day the House was scheduled to adjourn, an orderly crowd gathered outside the legislature to demand an investigation into allegations against Squires's ministers. When a delegation failed to receive a hearing, even as the legislature continued debate inside, the crowd turned into a mob and stoned the building, breaking the windows. Then the demonstrators surged in, brushing aside the small force of policemen, and took possession of the basement, where they destroyed furniture and scattered public records over nearby Bannerman Park. Squires himself escaped through a side entrance but was roughed up before he found refuge an hour later in a private dwelling nearby and later escaped from the city.[2]

With Squires in hiding, the rioting subsided. And when he announced he would seek a dissolution and called an election on 11 June, the results surprised no one. Squires lost all but two seats, including his own, to a reform party under the leadership of F.C. Alderdice and a collection of businessmen. As part of his electoral manifesto, Alderdice had promised to inquire into the possibility of placing the Dominion under a commission of government, subject to the approval of the people. Throughout the sequence of events that led to commission of government, however, the electorate were never given another chance to make their preferences clear.

Alderdice's government, though it appeared more honest than that of Squires, could not avoid Squires's dilemma. The country could afford no further loans to service the debt, but it could afford no further stringencies either. There seemed no way open except default. At this point, the British government intervened and once again persuaded the Canadian prime minister, R.B. Bennett, to prevent such an outcome, one that would be undesirable for Canada. Thus, as S.J.R. Noel has shown, the Alderdice ministry began its preparations for rescheduling the debt 'without knowing that the first step to prevent it from doing so had already been taken.'[3] No part of the empire had ever before defaulted on an external loan, and the British government feared that such action would impair the prestige of the empire as a whole, perhaps impair the credit of Canada, Newfoundland's close trading partner. As a result of these negotiations, Britain and Canada agreed to a joint loan if Newfoundland accepted a royal commission to examine its economic prospects. Grenfell, at least, was encouraged by his relations with the new government, especially by its proposed initiatives for self-help.[4]

Meanwhile the commission, consisting of Amulree and two Canadians, Charles A. Magrath and Sir William Stavert, received their appointments on 17 February 1933 with wide terms of reference and began hearings *in camera* in St John's the next month so that, the commission decided, it could ascertain the 'true current' of public feeling. They then moved to the outports and the interior before conferring with bankers and politicians in Ottawa, Montreal, and Halifax. When they concluded in Newfoundland in July, they had held some one hundred formal sittings and heard 260 witnesses. Their report, which recommended a suspension of the legislature – what it delicately termed 'a rest from party politics for a period of years' – surprised no one.[5] Amulree was proposing a commission of government consisting of three members from Newfoundland and three from the United Kingdom, each presiding over a separate portfolio, and a governor empowered to enact legislation. And while this proposal was being considered, the British government took steps to secure Newfoundland financially. It caused Newfoundland bondholders to convert to a new issue at a lower rate of interest, thus lowering the cost of the debt. Instead of a default, it had engineered the kind of conversion Alderdice had wanted in the first place, except that now the bondholder was guaranteed both interest and principal by the British government.

Without a transcript of the evidence submitted to the Amulree Commission, it is impossible to judge the wisdom of these recommendations. However, bearing in mind the choice of commissioners and their backgrounds, it would not be difficult to imagine the assumptions on which they operated. To this day, doubts about the inevitability of their conclusions remain. Peter Neary has written,

> The public argument made for intervening in Newfoundland picked up a characteristic idea of the 1930s, a thought encouraged perhaps by hard times generally. This was that democracy and economic efficiency could sometimes conflict, that left to his own devices the party man would often seek to bribe the electorate and so invite economic disaster through over spending. What was needed to restore economic health was an end to partisanship and the introduction of impartial administration according to business precepts.[6]

But with local politics in such disarray, the assumptions were accepted in St John's without strong opposition or public protest and endorsed in London without difficulty. As J.L. Paton, the British president of Memorial College, interpreted events to the Royal Institute of International Affairs in January 1933 -- eight months before the report was submitted – it was not possible to suspend the politicians. Thus there was no alternative but to suspend politics, 'and so let the whole generation of vipers die out from atrophy.'[7] Both Grenfell and Lord Amulree attended this meeting and participated in the discussion. The next day, in a letter to *The Times*, Grenfell expressed his satisfaction with the way events were developing and drew attention to the 'gallant' attempt by Newfoundlanders under the present 'wise direction' to live up to their tradition of loyalty and integrity. It must be remembered that this meeting occurred a full year before the Alderdice government gave up power, for the Commission of Government did not assume office until 16 February 1934.

As the political drama played itself out in St John's, Grenfell kept up his personal efforts to maintain the level of services in the north. While he could not possibly keep in touch with all the developments of the Mission, he remained its nominal superintendent, lecturing, writing, travelling, going up and down the Labrador coast. As his vitality declined, Anne carried him through the schedule he set for himself, still attending public events, reminding him, keeping his clothes in order, consoling him, and managing the affairs of the three younger Grenfells from a distance. Early in 1931 it was already apparent that she herself was being drained by some unknown disorder as well as by Grenfell's unwillingness to slow down and hand over what remained of his tasks to younger hands.

Emily A. Fowler, an influential board member of the Grenfell Association of America and a close friend, wrote her to warn about her own limitations. She had found her 'overstrained' and 'nervous,' unable to relax. Still in the prime of life and able to look ahead to many productive years, she had shown signs of rapid aging. Miss Fowler put the matter plainly:

> I know that you are so conscious of the fact that Wilf is more and more dependent on you to carry on things that he has forgotten, or dislikes to face, and generally to keep things going straight for him, that you feel naturally that yours are the only shoulders onto which he can & will slip his burdens. This makes you dread to face the truth that unless you get yourself into better physical shape, and renew your nervous condition in some way, you will be very soon a weak and broken reed for him to depend on.[8]

Miss Fowler did not simply speak for herself. She spoke on behalf of those involved with running the Mission, directors and supporters who could not understand why the two could never rest, why they could not accept the fact that the organization could continue without them.

By now the IGA had grown into an efficient and businesslike organization. There were many hands to do the work. Yet Grenfell himself refused to spare himself, often disagreeing with decisions already made. Miss Fowler suggested that, by slowing down, he would in fact benefit the Mission more by giving it more years of attention: 'The directors are all unhappy and distressed because they cannot always see things in the same way that Wilf does, and because they have to disagree with him so often, and cannot conscientiously carry out his plans, because many of his suggestions conflict seriously with work already undertaken and which they can see no reason to cancel casually and throw into the scrap heap.' These observations seemed to make no difference at all. The two drove themselves as much as before. But Miss Fowler did reveal subtle changes in the management of the Mission's activities.

Grenfell, with his single-mindedness and his desire to help individuals in distress, did not always regard the larger picture. The Mission absorbed his every waking hour. He had never cultivated a conventional home life, never spent time with the neighbours, and his children had grown up independently. Working compulsively, he had grown accustomed to the relentless activity and the public acclaim. During the summer of 1931 he took the *Strathcona* to sea to assist Dr Alexander Forbes, the Harvard Medical School physiologist, with his aerial survey of the Labrador coast, but not as a passenger. He wanted to get involved in the whole operation since he had suggested it in the first place. As the voyage progressed, he wrote Anne from Quirpon, 'It is a *good* thing we should be parted for a while – we are both strong personalities, & it is a rest *to have one's own way "without words".'*[9] Dr Hilton Willcox, who was required to look after him, saw it differently. A month later, he noted in his journal:

> Sir Wilf is having rather frequent heart attacks these nights; but he looks very well, and seems to stand up to a long day's work as well as, if not better than, most of us. I was told, before we left St. Anthony, that one of my responsibilities on these two *Strathcona* voyages would be that of ensuring that Sir Wilf 'did not overdo it' – this by special request of Lady Grenfell. With all due respect to Lady Grenfell, such a request must be the joke of the summer! – as if I, or anyone else, would have the slightest chance of keeping this ball of fire under any sort of control![10]

But Grenfell's display of energy was misleading. From Flower's Cove that autumn he wrote to Anne, 'I am become a garrulous old man – it is very hard to conquer the desire to TALK. All this notoriety & flattery is very hard for anyone.'[11] Fortunately, as he approached his fortieth year of Labrador work, an opportunity to rest presented itself. Offered a villa in Alassio, Italy, he agreed to do some writing. He would rewrite the autobiography, bring up to date his book of natural history, *Labrador, the*

Country and the People (1909), and reissue some of his stories under a new title.

That winter, though he applied himself to the task at hand, the onset of years had made the act of writing less agreeable than before. Day after day he returned from the bottom of the garden, clutching not the promised revisions but new reflections on religion and science.[12] Once again, the burden fell upon Anne to meet Houghton Mifflin's deadline, for by the spring the publishers were considering how to market the book. Grenfell wanted to call it 'Forty Years in Labrador,' but the publishers preferred 'Forty Years *for* Labrador' in the interests of accuracy.[13] Returning to the United States, he soon left for the coast, leaving Anne to get the manuscript ready for printing after he had gone over it again and filled it with corrections and alterations. When she came to edit this time, she discovered such 'glaring discrepancies' and 'acrobatic leaps' that she needed to change the order of chapters to maintain coherence. Moreover, the emphasis had changed. Having thought this over carefully, she decided the book sounded more retrospective than its predecessor and needed the point of view of someone who had more or less 'rounded off' his career. For this, she took full credit. 'While he was about it was hopeless to do anything, as no matter how "fair" a copy I made, nor with what Scotch canniness I hid it, armed with a shears and an enormous pen and no blotting paper, he was certain to find it out,' she explained to I.R. Kent of Houghton Mifflin. 'As it is I have had to rush it under pressure, and it has been done when I was jaded.'[14]

When she joined Grenfell in St Anthony later that summer, he had already planned to take the Mission vessel *Jessie Goldthwait* to sea as supply vessel for the continuation of the ambitious survey carried out by Alexander Forbes. But he suffered several more attacks of angina, and again Anne nagged him into resting. Moreover, he insisted on sailing the *Goldthwait* at night and failed to get enough sleep. As Anne reported with exasperation, he did this not simply to complete the task but because the competitive schoolboy in him wanted to show Harry Paddon he could still do it. Paddon remained the Mission's presence in Labrador. He had never left it except for a furlough. Anne wrote to Dr Theodore Badger:

> He [Grenfell] has been showing a lot of bravado about running the boat, because, (I tell you this as his medical advisor), Dr. Paddon had run the *Strathcona* aground, and Sir Wilf wanted to show Paddon he could run his boat entirely with a volunteer crew. I tried to persuade him, if he had one good man like Abe Mercer, he would still have a volunteer crew, but he was determined that Dr. Paddon, who had been twitting him with the number of times that he, (Sir Wilf) had run the *Strathcona* aground, should see that he

could run this boat with nobody but himself. I have had a terribly uneasy summer as a result.[15]

Returning to Boston, she began preparations for an ambitious bazaar at the Copley Plaza that surprised everybody by bringing in $6,000. At this two-day event the IGA mounted displays of the Mission's achievements, and Boston debutantes presided over tables of goods. To publicize it a team of sled-dogs with a police escort ran the Boston streets between the State House and Copley Square. Grenfell himself was in attendance to sign copies of *Forty Years for Labrador*.[16]

Forty Years for Labrador caught the same class of reader and carried much the same information as its predecessor fifteen years before, bringing the process of social reform up to date. But the note of self-satisfaction struck the reader now as more of a general manager's annual report than an autobiography. Once again Grenfell characterized himself as a runner entering the 'last lap,' and the last quarter of the book included a recital of new projects with a list of acknowledgments to friends and colleagues. Nevertheless, the sheer weight of Grenfell's reputation ensured its success both in the United States and Britain. Over five thousand copies were sold in the first six months, a remarkable sales record for a time when bookstore sales had dropped from a half to two-thirds their normal volume.[17] Book reviewers gave it generous if not reverent attention. 'Not merely is this book a stirring record of hardships met and human suffering alleviated. It is an addition to literature that is other than biography [*sic*],' the *New York Times Book Review* declaimed. 'How Conrad would have liked – and would all but have envied – this!' The *Glasgow Herald* chimed, 'There is no more knightly figure in the world today than that of Sir Wilfred Grenfell.'[18] In 1934 he followed with *Deeds of Daring*, his collection of stories, and *The Romance of Labrador*, a collection of natural history essays by divers hands with Grenfell as nominal editor. But once again Anne had put it together. He acknowledged in a letter to Rosamond, 'The Royal British Empire Society has presented me with another gold medal – for service & for the "Romance of Labrador book" which mother wrote.'

With the book out of the way, Grenfell turned his attention to the Amulree Commission. Ten days after its appointment, Charles Curtis, who had been taking clinics in Vienna, pressed him to pursue an extensive hearing with the commissioners and to 'tell them a few facts.' From his considerable experience in Newfoundland, Curtis shared Grenfell's belief that it was government rather than economics that required reform and that Newfoundlanders in general would welcome a change of government, even in the hands of bureaucrats. He also wanted to make sure the commissioners got out of St John's and into the outports, where they could talk to fishermen. He insisted:

> It's not the world general depression that's the cause of Newfoundland's trouble. It's rotten government, and unless there is a change, the rotters will be in again because the Alderdice government will be unpopular with the masses and out they will go. A million Royal Commissions will never otherwise do any good ... a Royal Commission governing the country and the cheap politicians are out for good and all. If I were a Newfoundland government bond holder, I would never accept a single cent less in interest rate under the present form of government because the differences would be stolen and the people would not be any better off.[19]

In his representations to Amulree, Grenfell chose to dramatize Curtis's position and his dedication to the operation in St Anthony. To strengthen his argument, he told Amulree, 'He feels inclined to chuck the whole Colony and go back to the United States if the Squires regime buy their way back into power, as he feels that they are trying to do already.'[20] He also added his own contempt of the Squires government for good measure and urged Amulree to keep his views in strict confidence, fearing the further deterioration of his relationship with the authorities in St John's. And he added something more: he suggested that whatever good the Mission had been able to accomplish had been 'hampered seriously' by government 'jealousies,' citing as an example the government's unwillingness to protect his reindeer herd. He concluded, 'I long for the welfare of those splendid people whom I have seen robbed and skinned for so many years by bad government. Alderdice is all right, but I am afraid the very fact of his doing justly will make him unpopular and he may lose control.'

That spring he worried about the deteriorating political state of Newfoundland and felt sure that commission government was the right choice. He personally admired Alderdice, he told his old friend Lord Southborough, and thought him honest and capable, but considered the people incapable of sustaining government in the Westminster style. Without a skilled commission, he saw no hope for the future. Thus, when Amulree sought his opinion within a month of his appointment, Grenfell did not hesitate. There could be no development without an independent government, he said: 'Personally I do not believe it can be secured by the present form of government with our people. They need either a dictator or a small commission of experts. Confederation will be too slow an evolutionary method in the present crisis.'[21]

Grenfell's recommendations contained practical solutions to immediate problems. He advocated a permanent civil service based on ability and a 'stern' revision of the post office. He recommended the building of more roads, especially on the west coast, to assist rural development. He wanted to abandon the railway and the coastal steamers as the principal means of travel between the districts and suggested turning to motor-driven traffic to improve the transportation of goods, bring in tourists, and give access to peat bogs, berry marshes, and game. He called for a northern Newfoundland centre like St Anthony and one in Labrador, perhaps at Cartwright. He, of course, thought Newfoundland would greatly benefit from the development of co-operative stores. He would handle pauper relief through community clubs. He would start small industries, such as those begun by the Mission. And he suggested the schools teach more technical subjects like cooking and crafts rather than Latin and French. These and other recommendations were considered seriously, and some were included in the final report.

Grenfell's second encounter with the Amulree Commission occurred after the report had been submitted. While the House of Commons considered the bill that would bring its recommendations into effect, he was ensconced at St Ermin's Hotel, Westminster, where he received visitors, lectured, and prepared for a meeting of Grenfell alumni. The bill was introduced on 8 December, but Grenfell had already written Lord Amulree on 25 November to seek an interview, informing Amulree that there were 'many things which I shall value very much having the opportunity of talking over with you.'[22] Amulree welcomed the opportunity, for he admired Grenfell. Four months later, at a lecture Grenfell gave at the Royal Society of Arts, he described him as 'one of our Empire builders' whose name belonged on a list with those of Livingstone, Rhodes, and Stamford Raffles.[23] But at the present meeting, he probably went a step further and raised the possibility of having Grenfell preside over the inevitable Commission of Government as governor of Newfoundland.

On 8 December, as the bill received first reading, a press story released from Ottawa conjectured about the appointment. It quoted a 'report' (possibly from one of Amulree's two Canadian commissioners) speculating that Grenfell's appointment would be 'received with approval' in Newfoundland and 'welcomed' by the Canadian government. The next day, when the story received the authority of the *New York Times*, it was carried by Reuter to newspapers in the United States and Britain. Undoubtedly someone had made an offer, but few people knew that Grenfell's state of health prevented him from pursuing the day-to-day business of his own life, much less running a bankrupt colony. No one knew it better than Anne, who did not hesitate to scotch the idea. She wrote to Willie at Oxford:

Very privately, we were approached unofficially as to Father's being Governor. I turned it down definitely, as I knew it would certainly be the end of Father, and what is more, I doubt if in his present state of health, he would stand it. I have no illusions – the politicians are certain to try every sort of underhand game to get back into power, and Father's life would be one long misery, even if his heart would stand it.

On the other hand he can be of immense use to them all in an advisory capacity, and he has been having interviews with the Prime Minister, with Malcolm Macdonald, his son, and with various members of the Government. They have been coming in to dinner, and we have been running about like the proverbial chickens. After this Christmas recess of the House of Commons is over, there are more interviews and reports in store for Father, and you know I come in for a good amount of the detail working.[24]

Christmas passed, and the idea that he could still influence the problems of Newfoundland haunted him. The thought of making one last effort would not go away, even though so much else remained to be done and his condition had not improved. By the New Year, Anne reported to Willie, 'Father is very unsettled in his mind. People keep urging him to take the Governorship of Newfoundland and I know all the time that he is not up to it mentally or physically. Teddy Grenfell agrees with me, but no one else seems to do so. I am having some difficult days. The change of Government is all to the good, but it is entailing a lot of work on our part.'[25] There the matter ended. Grenfell finally realized his time for direct intervention had passed, and he forgot about what had seemed an attractive prospect. He returned to the business at hand, and after broadcasting to schoolchildren all over Britain and promising to answer their letters personally, he and Anne were buried in the avalanche of mail that descended upon the hotel.

The bill had speedily received royal assent. David Murray Anderson remained in place as governor, to be joined by three British commissioners: Sir John Hope Simpson, a former Indian civil servant; Thomas Lodge, an experienced administrator; and Everard Trentham of the Treasury. With these were paired three Newfoundland commissioners: F.C. Alderdice, the former prime minister, and two of his former ministers, William R. Howley and John C. Puddester. By early February 1934 they had received their briefings in London and prepared to sail, and the rooms at St Ermin's Hotel began to recover from their frequent visits.

The Grenfells saw the commissioners off on their task of rehabilitating a bankrupt society, even with the international economy in disarray and societies with much longer traditions of government adopting drastic measures, especially in Germany, where they liked to vacation and where they had sent Willie and Rosamond to learn the language. In January 1933 the Hitler cabinet had been installed, and a few weeks later the long agony of the Jews began. Grenfell realized that radical change would occur but, like so many foreign observers, he preferred Hitler's reforms to what was happening in the Soviet Union. As late as 1935 he was still trying to 'look behind' the mounting militarism and anti-semitism to see what he termed 'the real end.' In January of that year, he wrote Pascoe from Munich, 'We were dee-li-ted over the Saar settlement, not because we approve the Nazi Tactics entirely – there is too much greed & selfishness & silly conceit in some of the Prussion leaders. But as a man we think well of Hittler, and so far as peace goes we say "Heil Hittler" quite genuinely. The danger seems in the old Prussian bombast.'[26] Still, he seemed concerned about what was happening and wrote to the Bavarian Nazi staff in Munich to protest the treatment of the churches. He was told firmly that Hitler wanted 'deeds,' not 'loud confessions.'[27] Yet it was still possible to deny what was happening in Europe. 'I really believe those fellows don't want war on Christendom or Pagandom,' Grenfell wrote in the summer of 1935. 'Christian Italy I am not so sure of?'[28]

More changes awaited him in the United States. In March 1933 Roosevelt took the oath of office as president and launched the New Deal, prepared to use federal powers to the full extent to rescue the country from the devastation of the depression. In his inaugural address he expressed the desire to keep the money changers out of the 'Temple' of American civilization, restore more noble social values, and put the millions of unemployed to work.[29] Embedded in such economic nationalism, liberal thinkers smelled the potential for fascism in the United States itself. At the beginning of the New Deal, Roosevelt insisted that such changes could be brought about under the existing governmental arrangements, that changes in emphasis were possible without changing the constitution. But if the normal balance between the executive and legislative branches proved inadequate, he was prepared to ask Congress for broader executive power.

The times were out of joint. To the Grenfells, with their three children seeking a place in the world, these developments prompted serious considerations about how life should be lived. Through the years the two had shared a certain religious conservatism, although Anne seemed to prefer a more formal churchmanship than her husband. Culturally, Grenfell preferred the achievements of American science, American medicine, and American flexibility to the conventionality of his own country. Anne seemed to be a greater anglophile than ever, preferring Britain's apparent stability, tradition, and cultural unity to American variety and excitement. Roosevelt's economic experiments only fed her conservatism. Both she and Grenfell worried about the sharp rise in prices and the depreciation of the American dollar, and Anne claimed her own income had been reduced by 50 per cent. In the last quarter of 1933 she had gained practically nothing from her investments.[30]

They freely dispensed advice to their three young adults on matters of faith, personal morality, and vocation. As Pascoe neared the end of his engineering studies at Cambridge in 1934, he expressed the urge to return to the United States to look for a job. But his mother, though a true nativist, advised him against it, citing 'successful' men in Britain. She wrote Willie:

> They think that America is still unstable in business and in her mixed population, and in her banking system and in her sense of moral values in Business and that the chances for a happy life and future success are greater in England for a young man today than in America. Of course your moral values you make yourself, wherever you are, but certain surroundings can make you happy and others unhappy. Working in a scientific concern he [Pascoe] may find that he does not come up against business practices which he deplores – but I think he underestimates the foreign and hebraic influence in America today – though the true American is the most generous and delightful person possible.[31]

Nevertheless, Pascoe went to work for General Electric in Schenectady, New York, and remained there until he retired.

Grenfell also liked to lecture his sons on moral matters and warn them about the debilities of popular culture. In 1935, when Pascoe started his engineering career, he advised him, 'You can't do too much athletics to please me. They are the greatest help for a young fellow to let off steam in the right way – that and some form of class work for boys, or youths, less fortunate than yourself – one for the body, or both, & one or both for the soul. Nothing helps one to keep clean & keen like some work for others – definite time given to it.'[32] The same year, when Willie returned from China with the intention of becoming a teacher, his parents did not hesitate to reprimand him, even though he had reached the age of twenty-five, for what would be considered normal behaviour for a young American, if not for the son of Sir Wilfred Grenfell. Grenfell's letters, remarkable for their aloofness, their formality, their scoutmasterly tone, advised him in particular about wasting his time at the movies. After a life in pursuit of the ideal of moral manliness, he exhorted him:

> Do join an athletic Club of some kind – for *Squash* is good – or for rowing or golf for the open air. Knock off some of these beastly movies and late hours

at fuzzy dances. And get rid of that pale face – and the results of too much *indoors* – make your exercise – 'out of doors' – & if you can't afford it, let us know. *Red* blooded – common sense – hard living – taking ventures – and *doing* things, especially for others, are all character building, and happiness ensuring qualities – go for them. But also, though intellectually one cannot prove anything, venture that religion is real, works in the laboratory of life, and makes real men.[33]

Later that year, Anne herself lectured Willie on the pitfalls of popular culture. In a diatribe written in the firmest tradition of bourgeois puritanism, she wrote:

My feeling about your going so much to the films is this. You are a grown man, and a marked man by being Father's son, and one who is noticed. You are a highly intelligent man, and it is plain that you can and will be a leader whom boys will copy. It is no good to explain that you look at them from an artistic standpoint or a mechanical standpoint. They are at best fancy ticklers and time wasters and wasters of money which this wretched world needs for better uses than the pockets of Jew promoters and Tootsy Gishes, or worse. You lose caste, and influence and a great loss of dignity and make yourself a wee bit ridiculous at your age to be a film fan as you are. The world of the films is an unreal world, pictured through dirty or at best clouded spectacles. They do not depict life as it is. Some of them are good and worth seeing. If you do not want to read in the evening some good book, or do something like your Boy Scouts (an excellent idea) a good hobby like painting would make twice the man of you – and remember that now you are an example to young boys and are putting a stamp on their characters for life.[34]

For the same reason, she admired what she perceived to be Rosamond's sincerity and her scholastic achievements and preferred to think that she never smoked, drank, or used make-up. These concerns for the children arose partly as a response to the uncertain times. But it also came with the realization that they were no longer children and that her opportunity to influence them had passed. They, in turn, did not share her puritanism as she struggled to sustain the air of dignity required for her own place in life. As they went their respective ways, they took no direct hand in the running of the Mission.

While all these changes occurred in Grenfell's private life, the Commission of Government took up residence in St John's, where it remained, *mutatis mutandis*, until Newfoundland was finally brought into confederation with Canada in 1949. The Grenfells were pleased with only one British commissioner, Sir John Hope Simpson, whom they regarded as a strong, Christian man of principle. According to Grenfell's old chum, Sir Henry Richards, his colleague Trentham had been dismissed as a school inspector. That left Lodge, who had gone to Newfoundland with great reluctance and had not yet proved himself.[35] As for the Newfoundlanders, they feared the choices had been narrowed by the existing political circumstances. Anne wrote to Willie, who had just graduated from Oxford and taken a job with a commission of the League of Nations in China:

> The three Newfoundlanders are Alderdice (the former Premier) who proposes to take on Education as his branch in the Commission, and refuses to do away with the antidiluvian [sic] denominational school system of grants which is the curse of Newfoundland. Puddester is one of the better type of political healer. Howley is an ardent R.C. and an appointee of the Archbishop of Nfld. who refused to have [Lewis E.] Emerson (a far stronger man) appointed, as he was not sufficiently zealous as a Catholic. And so the story runs on, and human nature repeats itself, whether in Nfld. or China.[36]

During the summer of 1934 the commissioners turned up in St Anthony for the visitation of Prime Minister Ramsay MacDonald. By now, like so many of his contemporaries, Grenfell had adjusted to the idea of the new authoritarianism in government, including Hitler's, as an expedient for mobilizing the workforce and strengthening the economy.[37]

He had recently visited Italy under Mussolini. He admired Franklin D. Roosevelt – not so much for his economic nationalism as for his class – and liked the idea of having a 'gentleman' in the White House. In the pages of *Among the Deep Sea Fishers* he rationalized the experiment in Newfoundland this way: 'Even in the New World doubts are arising as to whether autocratic power may not have some advantages if tempered by a Christian spirit, if exercised under wise advisers, and if administered with courage. In the United States such power is apparently more respectfully regarded now than it was by the signers of the Declaration of Independence.'[38] But Grenfell had not changed his opinion of the individual commissioners. The bankruptcy of the colony and the subsequent withdrawal of grants to hospitals, coupled with reductions in donations and income, had reduced the overall receipts of the Mission by 26 per cent.[39] Only Hope Simpson continued to measure up to his expectations. He judged the rest 'too Fat' and 'too highly self-opinionated.' He was sorely disappointed with the highly intelligent but rude Thomas Lodge, who appeared to exhibit no vision, no 'real love for *people*, except one.'[40] For his part, Lodge suspected he was sacrificing several years of his life to what he termed a 'bizarre experiment' in dictatorship and for the next few years chafed under the petty jealousies and intrigues of St John's.

— 18 —

Resignation
1934 – 1937

Infirmity doth still neglect all office whereto our health is bound. We are not ourselves when nature, being oppressed, commands the mind to suffer with the body.

King Lear, II.iv.101–4

As Grenfell returned to Vermont in the autumn of 1934, he received the news of A.G.'s death. While the news did not surprise him, it distanced him further from Mostyn House. The headmastership now fell to a third generation of Grenfells, who took up with some uncertainty the relationship with their famous uncle and his continuing claim to a portion of the school. Two years before, in the autumn of 1932, A.G. had made a dramatic gesture when he wrote to pay interest on the 'loan' of £4,000 and 5 per cent on the £1,500, as usual. This time he surprised Grenfell by also paying off the £4,000 altogether, after taking out a loan from the bank. He also suggested that as a *beau geste* Grenfell himself might wipe out the £1,500, which he still claimed had never existed, even though he had paid the interest for a dozen years. He wrote in his diary, '*A ver loque dirá su mujer*! [Let's see what his wife will say].' But Grenfell refused, arguing that he regarded a legacy as a trust for his dependants and could not give it up without their consent.[1] A.G. noted again, '*La puta muy avara noquiso, loque temía yo* [The miserly bitch refused, just as I feared].' In preparing to give up the headmastership of Mostyn House, he had advanced a long way towards reconciling the remaining differences. He would not receive such an opportunity again.

In 1933, tired out and continually bothered by his painful leg, A.G. had handed over the school to his son Daryl. Early in the new year the leg had been amputated, and throughout the winter Grenfell wrote to give encouragement and recommend floor exercises and a low-fat diet so that A.G. could maintain his mobility and keep his weight down. But he still clung to his own interpretation of the will after looking it up at Somerset House and in fact chided A.G. for being too parochial in his business dealings: for not responding to hard times by mixing more and appealing to the 'county' set. 'A Duchess is not necessarily a snob or an idiot, and we have met a good many of these people in friends's [sic] homes of late, and I think Mostyn House could and should have gathered in boys from such,' he advised with an air of authority.[2] But A.G. refused to be impressed by titles and maintained boys who could no longer afford to pay their fees. At Easter, Grenfell visited his brother again. This time he thought he was making progress, despite his added weight, and encouraged him to fit himself with a bamboo limb. Meanwhile, he reassured Daryl, 'Don't you worry about the moiety or whatever it is – so long as A.G. is in any danger from reference to worries and troubles of (everyone's lot in) life, I'm happy. He must live on, & I think he wants to. Forget it, till I start the racket.'[3]

A.G. lasted until 29 September, when he died quite suddenly. In keeping with his independent and unceremonious style, his body was taken by his own men to the hill near his Welsh cottage in Nant-y-Garth for a simple funeral. At a memorial service that evening in chapel, Lord Leverhulme gave a short address and dedicated a new organ to his memory. Back in the United States, Grenfell reflected upon the loss of his brother and chief antagonist. Though the two had gone their separate ways, they had nevertheless maintained a mutual respect and a shared interest in the fortunes of the school, which they maintained through correspondence up to the last. Now that the relationship had ended, Grenfell wrote Daryl, 'As I reread your father's letter of yesterday I think over our long years of mutual relationships. Our minds were as different as chalk from cheese, with inevitable occasional frictions and misunderstandings. But we loved one another in a way that a human being, through the very nature of the machinery that kinship involves, is not prone to love a stranger. The loss or gap, when I get to England, will be *very* real to me.'[4]

But A.G. had died without making provision for the debt. In order to clear the account before the will could be probated, Daryl invited his uncle to make a formal claim for the remaining capital and interest so that it could be examined by the executors, warning him at the same time that the examination might result in a difference of opinion. With this measure, he clearly wished to avoid a family squabble and in fact would have preferred a private adjustment had he not been required by the law to proceed more formally. Grenfell therefore decided not to press his claim in order to give Daryl a chance to get the school on its feet. 'As I have said before,' he wrote, 'don't worry. Just make those lawyers understand that I settled this once and for all twelve years ago.'[5] By relenting at this difficult moment, he simplified the administration of the will without closing the matter entirely, and once again it was temporarily laid to rest. Having passed his seventieth birthday, he needed to pay closer attention to his own health.

On his last visit to London he had met Sir Michael Cassidy, the king's physician, who after a subsequent examination confirmed what Grenfell already knew: that his heart continued to fibrillate and probably always would. He recommended the conventional treatment of rest, light meals, and doses of nitroglycerine. By now the condition of his heart prevented Grenfell from undertaking normal activity. In fact, he suffered pain doing practically anything except walking slowly and standing erect. 'Any slouching or stooping seems to hasten it,' he complained. 'I can dig dandelions lying down in the grass not standing or stooping etc. I get pretty breathless sometimes in the night.'[6] Such adversity shortened his temper and clouded his judgment. The year before he had quarrelled with the directors over volunteers that he had appointed and sent to Flower's Cove. He was told he must consult E.A.B. Willmer (the executive secretary) and Curtis before making such appointments again. At that time he had agreed with the rule and allowed that his judgment might not have been reliable. But he lashed out at Curtis, who had been required to block his attempt to send money and food directly to people on the coast. 'This does not mean that I do not love him,' he wrote, 'and I am grateful to God for his affection and loyalty and good surgery; but somehow I do not think he has got the vision that will make or keep this Mission in the position it holds in the Christian world today, if you accept his judgment on policies.'[7] Curtis himself was upset by Grenfell's habit of sending out half-informed entrepreneurs to set up small industries without telling him first, thus embarrassing him and giving the Commission of Government the impression that it was dealing with an unstable and impractical organization. By the end of 1934 Curtis complained that he was sick of such tactics.[8]

Curtis was already recognized informally by the directors as a natural successor if Grenfell decided to step down, even though he had shown no hint of doing so. Thus early in 1935, when José Machado, chairman of the IGA board, retired from the Canadian Bank Note Company, he took the opportunity to ask Grenfell whether it might be time to hand over to Curtis, indicating that the directors would undoubtedly vote him a pension equal to his current salary. Released from his responsibilities, he could then devote himself to his interests as he saw fit. Behind this suggestion lay the directors' other concern, for they feared Grenfell, in his zeal, might subject them to further projects without complete financing. Already, the general financial picture in the 1930s gave them sufficient worry, and they did not want further burdens imposed upon them. Machado explained to Grenfell,

> I feel that this season we should make a very careful study of our situation, financial and otherwise, and not undertake any further building or other operations which would mean an increased budget, until we have made this study. I recommend this, because I feel we must realize that many years will pass before we can hope to get increased regular contributions. In fact, with the undoubted increase in taxes which is coming in the U.S., many people's contributions will have to be curtailed. Therefore, we must at this time look at the whole picture, and this would be a logical time for you to make a change if you have been considering it.[9]

Surprisingly, Grenfell liked the idea, and a week after his birthday he made up his mind to resign and devote himself to raising funds. He already expected an invitation from the Commission of Government, asking the board to send a 'deputation' that might discuss the IGA's continuing commitments, and to these he planned to send Sir Henry Richards to represent him because he shared his views. He was fully aware of how the angina attacks kept him 'out of the running' and had considered the matter for some time. 'Is it not hard to be sure if God's leading sometimes?' he wrote Machado. 'I've prayed & prayed for long months over what is best to do, & this is the outcome.'[10]

However, Anne was not so sure about the way of the divine will. Through her intervention he did not resign, and with Grenfell as superintendent the IGA board considered that winter how they should respond to the financial constraints imposed in Newfoundland and the emerging policies of the new government. For over forty years the Mission had grown through a set of *ad hoc* arrangements and maintained an ambiguous relationship with the elected authorities, principally because of Grenfell's forceful and independent style. Successive governments had left it to expand as it wished, for it had provided medical care in districts where the colony could not venture itself. By 1934, having grown unchecked, it stood in effect as a self-recruiting, self-disciplining, and self-financing principality with its own figurehead, prime minister, governing body, financial interests, folk-lore, and grateful public. In short, an establishment. But the Commission of Government endeavoured to exercise its authority throughout the whole of its domain. Having seen for themselves the deficiencies of Newfoundland and Labrador, they embarked on an ambitious program of reconstruction, led by the two dominant members, Hope Simpson and Lodge. The commissioners were a 'wee bit fed up' with the way Grenfell bombarded them with his own visionary schemes, so much so that the Newfoundland association found it necessary to go and explain how the IGA conducted its business.[11] The government thus invited the board to send for discussions their representatives, five of whom travelled to St John's during the summer of 1935 to establish more formal grounds for co-operation. But these were not the five Grenfell had recommended, and Sir Henry Richards was not among them. With its income falling, the board wished to secure its position and as a result of these discussions recognized fundamental changes in its own operation.[12] This recognition would alter the role of Wilfred Grenfell.

The extensive reconstruction Newfoundland required could have succeeded only with broad public support or with leadership from London. It received neither. The commissioners, unaccustomed to acting like politicians, did not mind if they displeased local interests. Moreover, the Dominions Office was prepared to go only so far in rehabilitating the economy. As Peter Neary writes, 'What the Dominions Office really wanted in Newfoundland was progress with economy and without adverse publicity. This was a typically bureaucratic goal and showed just how much the Commission of Government was at heart an administration of civil servants.'[13] Thus the week of discussions with the IGA proceeded like treaty negotiations. To begin with, the government formally recognized the Mission's responsibility for its chief business – medical care – and stipulated the accepted areas of operations: along the Labrador coast from Blanc Sablon to Indian Harbour and along the coast of northern Newfoundland, south to Port Saunders in the Strait of Belle Isle and south to Cape St John in White Bay. Considerable time was spent with officials of the Department of Health to clear up perceived 'misunderstandings,' and not until this was done did the two sides agree to bury the hatchet and proceed on the basis of 'hearty cooperation.' The government would permit patients to travel to and from the hospital free of charge. The IGA would maintain certain nursing stations and a hospital vessel to travel the coast during the summer. It would also build a tuberculosis sanitarium in St Anthony.

The government also recognized certain long-standing practices that had hardened into policy, notably the ever-present nervousness about customs privileges. No longer would the IGA import goods duty free (except for second-hand clothing) but pay the estimated equivalent value of $30,000 annually and receive it back, together with the annual operating grants already provided. With this arrangement, the government hoped to eliminate the perception that it accorded the Mission privileged status and demonstrate its willingness to co-operate. In turn, the IGA requested proportional grants for its non-sectarian schools, three of which were boarding schools. This the government also agreed to, provided the schools taught the curriculum newly applied by the Department of Education and employed teachers trained in the colony's system. Above all, regardless of these and other agreements worked out during the week of talks, the government expressed its 'complete sympathy' with the Mission's aims and its willingness to promote them. Both sides agreed in appropriately diplomatic language that the discussions had allowed them to 'consolidate' and 'clarify' their relationship.[14]

The expression of goodwill and the new air of efficient bureaucracy moved the IGA to examine its own structure. The Commission of Government, in effect, had left it to its own devices, realizing that no government could adequately serve the northern population itself. But it did request more accountability. The IGA's annual medical reports would be incorporated for the first time with those of the entire colony, and a chief medical officer would need to be appointed, someone resident on the coast who could co-ordinate the reports and consult with the Department of Health. The IGA, while it allowed each station to act as a separate unit, had already recognized the need for a 'supervisor' or 'superintendent' but had run into a terminological difficulty. Grenfell still held the nominal title of superintendent, even though he no longer visited the coast regularly. The directors therefore recommended that 'Logically, this Medical Supervisor or Superintendent on the Coast should be the Medical Officer in charge at St. Anthony conferring with our Superintendent. We believe that Dr. Curtis, after eighteen years of service on the Coast, is well qualified to fill this position.'[15] They also recommended that the IGA's executive officer spend several months a year there, making his headquarters in St Anthony so as to avoid the inefficiency of long-range operations. In this way, they faced the reality of Grenfell's advanced age and impairment. By dividing the business and medical duties and bringing them close to the scene, they hoped to improve their management of the changing problems and personnel on the coast.

The question of Grenfell's continuing role required delicate language. The authors reporting these proceedings, Cecil Ashdown and Theodore Greene, took care not to exclude Grenfell from any future plans. But they observed frankly that his inability to visit the coast required a structure in which he could be seen to 'generally direct' policies in consultation with the other two officers. They also viewed with some discomfort the growing commercial activities they faced, especially in the Industrial Department, where, Anne was now at work constructing a new Dog-Team Tavern in Vermont. They wrote, 'Without the closest cooperation between all three officials, friction will result. The Superintendent has the important duty of looking after the contributing associations and industrial sales in the various countries, and it is a question how far the Business Manager should be required to supervise these branches of the work or whether he should only have to do with the IGA.'[16] The report went further in identifying how Grenfell's continuing role presented an obstacle. After visiting St Anthony, they had heard of misunderstandings that had arisen when subordinates complained directly to Grenfell himself, by-passing the medical officer or the IGA's executive officer. Moreover, Curtis, exasperated by the degeneration of the St Anthony Co-operative Store, had suggested that he might not return to the coast the following year unless there was a radical change in policy and management.[17] The reorganization was aimed at eliminating such misunderstandings.

Accordingly, in January 1936 Grenfell wrote the directors to resign from the active management of the Mission's work but retained the title of superintendent on the advice of Anne. In his letter of resignation he explained that the previous year his announced intentions had brought letters of protest from supporters, and he had changed his mind. He gave two reasons for this: it would be more difficult to sustain support if his name were not connected with the IGA; and secondly, he wanted to maintain an influence on policy as long as he lived. As one who had given his life to the work, he was not prepared to surrender his influence entirely. He thus requested an annual salary of $6,000 for as long as he and Anne continued to work, noting that their income had fallen off sharply. As for giving up the superintendency, he maintained that it was unnecessary while he lived, and he wrote, 'My strong desire is that Dr Curtis be medical supervisor on the Coast, that Mr. Willmer be what his title defines, executive officer, *carrying out the policies laid down by the Directors*, (I feel he has had too much latitude in laying down policies of his own, spending special funds, having reports turned in to him which I have never seen, etc.) and that Mr. Ashdown be appointed Business Superintendent of the IGA.'[18] Finally, he also made his wishes known about lecturing. Any lecturing he or the doctors on furlough could not undertake he wanted delegated to Eleanor Cushman, secretary of the GAA. Miss Cushman, whose irrepressible energy and continual flow of chatter had earned her the nickname 'Sphinx,' had worked closely with the Grenfells for ten years and enjoyed the status of a family member. She knew the work of the branches and the work on the coast first hand, and Grenfell trusted her completely.

The change in Grenfell's attitude had been prompted by Anne, who was still tired from the effects of an unspecified illness during the past year but who remained more heavily involved in fund-raising and industrial activities than he. Without an official role, she would have no place in the Mission's future. Indeed, the day Grenfell relinquished the management, she reported to Willie, 'I have advised him against ever resigning till he dies. It would go too hard with the work if people thought he was out of it, so I shall never tell anyone, nor must you. But this step means that we lose at one bang 33% of our income and shall have to watch our step very carefully, the more especially as my income has gone to the proverbial "pot".'[19] Taking Grenfell's wishes into account, the board devised a new plan and passed it at an extraordinary meeting two weeks later.[20] As a consequence, Grenfell retained his title and his current salary. Cecil Ashdown became the executive director, Charles Curtis the medical supervisor on the coast, and Willmer the business manager in New York. To avoid the difficulty of challenging Grenfell's authority, Curtis and Willmer would report to Grenfell and the board through Ashdown.

Having finessed the reorganization painlessly, the directors now turned their attentions to the question of sustaining the Mission during a time of financial instability and political upheaval, since they could not count on Grenfell to act as its voice any longer. Throughout the winter of 1936, while he was living in the alumni house at Bryn Mawr, Grenfell's circulation deteriorated further. His ankles swelled, and he suffered losses of memory. Anne, who looked after him while she suffered her own mysterious pains and fatigue, struggled to maintain a facade of normalcy. That spring, she reported to Willie:

> It breaks my heart to see a great man like him so broken, though he is so patient and so darling and tries to be so humorous through it all that it makes it worse in a way. Keep this all to yourself absolutely. I want to protect Father. If rumours get out the next thing we shall hear is that he is losing his mind, which is absolutely not the case. This loss of memory is due to arterial changes in the brain solely and to lack of proper blood supply. So say nothing to anybody except to Rosamond.[21]

The directors were facing the elementary problem of any organization with a single charismatic leader: what to do if Wilfred Grenfell should die. Would the organization die with him? If not, how would they raise sufficient funds to keep things going? They operated six hospitals and seven nursing stations, the King George v Institute, four boarding schools, and assorted 'industrial' centres, greenhouses, clothing distribution stores, together with two hospital ships and assorted tenders, a supply schooner, and a haul-up slip in St Anthony. They maintained a permanent staff of fifty-seven and a pool of volunteers. As part of the Mission's widening commitment to social reform, they also included in their inventory experimental gardens, electric plants, animal husbandry, and assorted other enterprises. In short, they held almost total responsibility for the improvement of life in the region. To answer such questions, they engaged Tamblyn and Brown, Inc., a firm of managers and fund-raisers for charitable organizations, to help them see the way ahead.[22]

In 1936 the Grenfell organization maintained the same cumbersome structure with which it had begun. The IGA board continued to hire staff and allocate funds, but it still depended for financial support on five independent organizations with their own boards of directors and their own loyal donors. Each association maintained its own endowment fund and through conservative reinvestment husbanded it to meet expenses. The Newfoundland association still existed but remained weak. The British association had fallen off with the financial and political instability in Europe. It remained for the three principal agencies to carry the burden: the Grenfell Association of America (New York), the New England Grenfell Association (Boston) and the Grenfell Labrador Medical Mission (Ottawa). The survey conducted by Tamblyn and Brown demonstrated that in each case contributions had begun to decline and that the IGA needed to act quickly to raise more money or reduce services.

The Canadian group functioned quite independently. From a small downtown office in Ottawa, it raised money through lectures, collected clothing, sold Christmas cards, marketed industrial goods, and publicized the Mission. Unlike the American associations, it carried out its own budget allotment and distributed food and medical supplies in the Canadian sector of Labrador. Its twenty-nine Canadian branches raised $14,000 annually, and by 1937, through careful investment, its endowment fund stood at a market value of $374,515,[23] indicating a healthy growth. While donations remained constant from year to year, large contributions had fallen off.

The New England Grenfell Association, located in an office near Copley Square, Boston, functioned in a similar way. With a cumbersome board of thirty-four directors, it raised considerably more money through only six branches in four New England states. Its annual intake of about $15,000 came principally from small donations of three to five dollars, a far cry from the days when donors more frequently gave up to $500 annually, sometimes $1,000. But the association's assets had been greatly augmented in recent years by large capital gifts. At the end of 1935 the total stood at $571,391 and continued to grow.[24] The association also administered a special discretionary fund built up from money given to Grenfell to use as he wished. Because of Grenfell's readiness to give away money to those who appealed to him personally or to those who appeared distressed, the existence of this small fund of $11,160 sometimes interfered with the work on the coast and undermined the authority of Dr Curtis.

The Grenfell Association of America, by far the most productive of the three, was situated in headquarters on Fifth Avenue, New York. Its territory extended throughout the United States (excluding New England) and into foreign countries. This association, with its twenty-four board members, raised funds through seven branches, six along the eastern seaboard and one in Chicago, but without Grenfell's continuing presence in recent years the level of interest had diminished. The GAA raised funds in much the same way as the other associations and collaborated with the New England office to administer the Grenfell Juniors, a youth organization numbering 1,303. It also edited and produced the quarterly magazine *Among the Deep Sea Fishers*, with a circulation of 31,900, though it too had dropped from nearly 40,000 in 1930. As one of its principal sources of revenue, the GAA promoted the annual opera benefit, averaging $4,400 annually – $9,450 in the past year. The membership list, which stood at 3,508 in 1936, had dropped off sharply. Even though the association had improved its capital fund of over a million dollars through a steady flow of bequests and a shrewd program of reinvestment in securities, the return on investment and the number of bequests had dropped.[25] Income from subscriptions and lectures had also decreased, while at the same time demands had grown. In 1936–7, 140 containers of clothes, toys, books, and rug materials were shipped to the coast, the highest number since 1932.

The Mission had reached the limit of its growth under the present system. Where would it go from here? John D. Rockefeller had repeatedly denied the Mission large infusions of funds throughout the years (though he admired Grenfell personally), fearing it would not survive without Grenfell's presence. Now others were inquiring whether the work would continue, and with this perception in mind Tamblyn and Brown emphasized the need for strong leadership. It praised the appointment of Dr Curtis in St Anthony. It praised Ashdown's assumption of financial control. But it noted that none of the business managers controlled fund-raising throughout all the various associations. In fact, despite their representation on the IGA board, the supporting associations manifested a surprising lack of co-operation. In view of this, Tamblyn and Brown recommended that Grenfell accept the new title of founder and that Ashdown continue as executive director. It further recommended expansion of the position of business manager to give the incumbent the direction of fund-raising with the supervision of the supporting agencies and industrial merchandising.

Assuming such co-ordination would occur, it also recommended moving the Boston operation to New York and merging the two offices, each of which cost $9,000 a year to operate. Thus, a separate office would not be required to serve a regional population like New England and donors would then identify themselves with the work as a whole. Boston would remain a branch office with its board of directors administering its funds. In this way, the work would be substantially taken over by New York. Emphasizing the continuing need for personal communication with subscribers through lectures and meetings, it recommended a regular program of fieldwork and less reliance on correspondence. It also recommended a greater sharing of information and reports amongst the various offices and greater use of returned wops or 'alumni.'

One other matter, the relative importance of industrial activities, also reveals something of the changes taking place in the Mission's thinking. Some IGA directors believed the Mission had reversed its original emphasis: that the increasing development of industrial work had taken precedence over the medical and preventive activities and that the Mission had lost sight of its Christian appeal. Others, on the other hand, viewed the industrial side as a working model of social reform and a challenge for the Newfoundland government. Should carving and rug-hooking be regarded, like hospitals, as part of the Mission's duty (deserving of annual grants) or like a business, subject to the vagaries of the market? Regardless of this difference of opinion, Tamblyn and Brown viewed the Industrial Department as a failure in many respects. Limited by the quirks of its own organization, the department's work was further crippled by the lack of co-operation among the various offices and the independence allowed certain individuals. 'The entire set-up, involving a unit independent in its administration and supervision from other activities in the United States, seems entirely illogical from a business and organization standpoint,' it concluded.[26] In keeping with its preference for consolidation, it recommended the closure of the Philadelphia shop and the removal of the Grenfell Labrador Industries office to New York. It also recommended that the board abandon it as a business venture and instead make an annual grant of about $4,000, treating any losses as investments in social service work and advertising.

Finally, the report examined the financial position of the Mission. It discovered that in 1935 and 1936 it could not meet its normal expenses but dipped into capital funds to meet the operating deficits. It therefore recommended a reduction in expenditures that did not produce direct benefits for coastal people, a reorganization of the Mission's structure, and a concerted effort to increase donations and broaden the base of public support. By increasing its endowment by $600,000 as part of an aggressive public relations program, it proposed, the Mission would reassure the general public of its continuing vigour while Grenfell still lived and lent his name to the endeavour.

While the organization he had founded passed through this period of self-examination, Grenfell sank further into the mists of melancholia and forgetfulness as a result of what were referred to as arterial 'spasms,' and Anne was required to watch him more closely than ever. In January 1936 he began to experience further lapses of memory resulting from poor circulation to the brain. Yet he insisted on going off to New York alone to do a nationwide broadcast. Anne had to type two sets of directions that she pinned to his clothing, and she ordered Eleanor Cushman to meet him at the station.[27] In the weeks that followed, his ankles and legs swelled up, and his liver enlarged. Ordered to bed by his physician, he received no visitors that winter, wrote no letters, conducted no business. To make matters worse, Anne herself had just spent a month at the Massachusetts General Hospital, recuperating from emergency surgery to remove an ovarian tumour, for by now the source of her own difficulties had become obvious. Few people knew the tumour had been diagnosed as malignant, especially since she had helped plan the annual opera benefit and supervised Grenfell's daily routine, fearing he might have a relapse.

All that winter Grenfell suffered further spasms. Lapses of memory were broken by intervals of absolute clarity: he would grow excited; he would hear voices; he would fail to recognize colleagues and acquaintances; he would hallucinate at night; then he would appear normal again.[28] It was a distressing time. When Dr Theodore Badger, a director and friend, wrote in the spring to encourage him to get more active, Anne wrote back vehemently to say Grenfell could not risk the same ordeal again. 'Thank you for your advice,' she told him. 'I only wish I could take it. I know that it is good – but sometimes one just has to go on being bad and let consequences take care of themselves. That is what I am doing now.'[29]

With the inactivity imposed upon him, Grenfell seemed to improve and appeared not to remember his troubles. But the forgetfulness irked him. He instinctively worried about the day-to-day affairs of the Mission and the way it responded to conditions on the coast. Anne reassured him that Ashdown, Curtis, and the directors understood the people's needs and would act in their best interests. That winter she accompanied him to Beaufort, South Carolina, where the two could recuperate over the winter months. There Grenfell renewed his acquaintance with Dr John Harvey Kellogg, who operated a second sanatorium for the rich and famous in Miami Springs.

As soon as Kellogg received Grenfell's Christmas greetings, he wrote to invite him to Miami. Assuming Grenfell suffered from high blood pressure, he urged him to pack up and come there for a month as an 'honored guest,' assuring him he had treated many such ailments successfully. 'Nothing would afford me so much pleasure as to have an opportunity to render some service to those who have been of so great service to so many,' he said. But Grenfell had grown uncomfortable with crowds. He craved somewhere more private, preferably somewhere with a beach. Hampered by the inability to remember names or faces, he disliked going down to meals in public dining-rooms and found the attentions of admirers embarrassing. Anne assured Kellogg that there was nothing wrong with his blood pressure. 'In every other respect he is in first class physical condition,' she said, 'except that the nervous and physical strain and worry seems to be taking its toll. He comes of a highly intellectual and highly strung ancestry and it has always been hard for him to take anything placidly.'[30]

The two moved to a cottage at St Simon's Island, Georgia. There, on 28 February, his seventy-second birthday, an influx of letters, messages, and presents brought on another attack, accompanied by severe melancholia, which lasted until the end of March. Grenfell suffered one spasm after another but fortunately recollected nothing about these trying weeks. By the time they returned to their summer house in Vermont, Anne had given sixteen months of continuous care and could endure it no longer. Although Grenfell had always been a man of considerable intensity and independence, he possessed no means to defend himself. She explained to Theodore Badger, 'He was always a person of very touch-and-go temperament, but his control now is practically nil; and one of the hardest aspects of his illness is to see what a change it has made in his temperament. Whereas he used to be full of fun and gaiety he has lost it. Formerly he used to deplore complaints, and now the days are just one long complaint after another.'[31] She hired a male nurse to act as his companion and give him physiotherapy, and by the autumn he began to show signs of marked improvement. As for Anne herself, she suffered pain in the left hip and leg. As she prepared to return to St Simon's Island for another winter, her Boston surgeon, Joe Vincent Meigs, informed her that he was not satisfied with her most recent x-rays.

Meanwhile, the time had come to decide about the superintendency of the Mission, and already the question of a successor was being debated. Influential board members such as José Machado and Henry Holt pressed to abolish the fiction that Grenfell acted on his own behalf and favoured the appointment of the Reverend Theodore Ainsworth Greene. Others, including Anne, Curtis, and Sir Henry Richards, strongly objected. Cecil Ashdown favoured a British appointment but had no one particular in mind.[32] At the end of October 1937 Ashdown wrote to inform Grenfell that at their next meeting the board would formally assign to Dr Curtis full authority for the administration of affairs on the coast, making him medical superintendent and executive officer. 'Such action is, in my opinion, imperative if we are going to continue successfully,' he wrote.[33] He urged Grenfell to write Curtis a letter for delivery on 1 November, expressing confidence in his ability to continue the work and wishing him Godspeed before he went north aboard the *Cluett*. It was important, Ashdown believed, for Curtis to know that he went with the board's support and Grenfell's blessing.

Grenfell balked again. Curtis was not cut from the same manly cloth as he and his old friend Sir Henry Richards. Richards found Curtis a 'somewhat difficult person,' and he thought two of his tendencies needed watching – 'a lack of humour & tolerance and a not unnatural inclination to stress the medical work to the exclusion of social & religious work.'[34] Nevertheless, on the day Curtis left he received a telegram from Grenfell offering his good wishes. He had faced the inevitable and passed the torch, even though he found it difficult to approve of all that Curtis had done. 'I honestly love and trust him,' he wrote Ashdown fussily, 'but when I differ from him he seems to think I am blaming him for having a different opinion and I candidly confess he has just as much right to his as I have to mine. That is his personality. I shall do nothing except through you.'[35] Grenfell knew he was out of touch. He knew he was dogmatic. But he persisted in playing Lear. His pride, even in his advanced age, would not allow him to let go completely.

— 19 —

The Last Lap
1937 – 1940

I see Pres[iden]t Lowell of Harvard has 'permanently lost his licence to drive a car' (two accidents same day). He says he doesn't regret it. Must be 'Anno Dominitis' – an epidemic.

Wilfred Grenfell, letter to Anne Grenfell,
August 1937

As the Grenfell Mission shifted to accommodate the new leadership, its task was made more difficult by events in Europe. After inaugurating Germany's rearmament in 1935, Hitler had by this time begun a systematic occupation of the neighbouring countries. Mussolini had paid a spectacular state visit to Germany for the purpose of entering into a Rome-Berlin axis, then followed Hitler's lead by withdrawing Italy from the League of Nations. As a result, a League of Nations embargo closed off Italy as a market for Newfoundland fish. Hitler himself now developed a timetable of aggression to secure the necessary *Lebensraum*, or living space, for ethnic Germans in Europe. To remove any threat from the south, he planned to take over Austria and Czechoslovakia first.

In February 1938 Hitler took supreme command of the armed forces. A month later the first detachment of German troops crossed the Austrian frontier and Austria was proclaimed a territory of the German Reich. Having annexed Austria so easily, he decided to overwhelm Czechoslovakia the following autumn. Britain and France, who regarded these movements with alarm, believed peace could be maintained if the Sudeten German areas of Czechoslovakia were transferred to Germany. In a series of meetings with Hitler, Neville Chamberlain only succeeded in postponing the invasion temporarily. On 29 September a meeting with British,

French, and Italian leaders in Munich called for the evacuation of the Sudetenland. Since their countries shared no collective security agreement with Czechoslovakia, however, the Czechs were left with the choice of allowing their country to be partitioned or fighting Germany alone. Before leaving Germany the next day, Chamberlain signed with Hitler a declaration in which both parties agreed to consult with each other on matters of security. Three weeks later Hitler prepared for the invasion of Czechoslovakia, which was carried out in March 1939. Chamberlain then announced that Britain would resist any further German attempts at military domination. On 31 August 1939 Hitler ordered hostilities against Poland to begin, and on 3 September Britain and France declared war on Germany.

As these events unfolded at a distance, the IGA board consolidated their organizational changes. Ashdown now ran the headquarters in New York, and Curtis governed in St Anthony. Only the role of Harry Paddon still remained unclear. North West River seemed to be an expensive location for a small hospital, and Curtis, who had not visited Labrador since 1915, expected to go there for a look in the spring of 1938. Meanwhile, one of the board members, Theodore Greene, wrote Grenfell, 'I personally hate to think what this may mean to Paddon if he is not used somewhere in the new setup. Please be assured that we have no intention of not allowing him to continue with the Mission and to live on at Northwest River as he planned when he retires.'[1]

In St Anthony, Curtis viewed events with his newly acquired authority. Within his frame of reference, the fears of imminent war were aggravated locally by the loss of markets and another decline in the fishery. Within weeks of the annexation of Austria, he wrote Ashdown to respond to the Tamblyn and Brown report and at the same time gave his frank opinion about the conduct of the Mission. First, he thought there were too many wops at large, and the doctors at the stations were too busy to supervise their work. From his point of view, no one but Grenfell had the time or inclination to look after them. He wrote:

> You and the other Directors must realize that the years Sir Wilfred was on the Coast, at least for the last twenty years, he had no responsibility whatsoever at any station on this Mission. He could leave St Anthony the entire summer, and leave somebody he expected to carry on in his absence. One summer he left St Anthony in July, and went to a wreck on the Labrador, and was gone until the end of October, completely out of touch with the Mission's activities. Another summer he spent on the Labrador with the Forbes Grenfell survey. On these trips he had wops with him and naturally with close contact with Sir Wilfred, and the spectacular work way down on the Labrador[,] they had an excellent time and were very enthusiastic about it, but who else has ever

had that opportunity to be relieved entirely of responsibility of looking after patients and details of Mission work and be able to take a crowd of boys off as he did? Other doctors have had so much work to do at the Stations that they have had to keep their nose to the grindstone.[2]

Curtis therefore insisted that the number of wops be radically reduced. He also complained about the lack of staff for industrial work and the presence of infectious disease in the homes of the industrial workers. But most important, he complained about the lack of government support, and he discouraged another endowment campaign simply because the government would continue to neglect its own people in the northern districts. 'To launch an endowment campaign now would fortify the Government in their point of view that the United States money in unlimited amounts was behind the Mission. The news would have a bad effect on the people. Already they think the Mission can simply call on the United States for funds whenever they need them. It is not developing the right spirit,' he added.

Two weeks later he reported to Grenfell himself on his recent tour of the stations in the Strait of Belle Isle, where he had found conditions worse than ever. Fish had declined, the falling demand for newsprint had reduced wood-cutting, and co-operative stores had gone bankrupt. With money in short supply, more and more people were placed on the dole. Families lived in desperate circumstances, unable to feed themselves sufficiently and yet susceptible to the spread of tuberculosis. 'The Straits is full of tuberculosis as tuberculosis flourishes where there is undernourishment, poor living conditions and no clothing,' he said. To help alleviate these conditions, he recommended changes in the industrial policy. That year the Mission had paid out only $150 to a population of nearly two thousand. Yet there were only two trained industrial workers on the coast, one in St Anthony and one in Cartwright. More workers were needed, and the large overhead carried in the United States had to be reduced. 'It is perfectly ridiculous to be losing $4,000.00 in the States with the conditions here as they are. I do not wish to belittle the Industrial Department, but in order to justify its existence it must reach the community,' he insisted.[3]

Curtis's communications with Grenfell sounded less encouraging as the year progressed. As one of his pet projects, Grenfell had laboured to get cellulose-acetate windows installed in the tuberculosis sanatorium and build a solarium for convalescents. But, as Curtis pointed out, there existed a strong difference of opinion about the benefits derived from ultra-violet radiation for pulmonary tuberculosis. Some scientists considered it harmful in large doses; however, in bone and joint tuberculosis and tuberculous adenitis it seemed beneficial. He also reported that the Commission of

Government's program of economic reconstruction had not yet shown results and that government workers rarely visited the northern districts, perhaps assuming the Mission could look after itself. With the economy of the colony still in disarray, Curtis's reports conveyed a sense of gloom. The Commission of Government had indeed reformed the civil service, built roads, and standardized education, but Curtis preferred not to acknowledge these improvements. As an American, he remained sceptical about the government's chances for bringing about substantial change. 'I have not seen any great results from the Commission Government except that they have increased the salaries of civil servants about 100%,' he complained, 'but the fishermen are not better off. I have heard so much about the genius of the British for governing that I shall be very anxious to see what success they have in rescuing this colony from the doldrums.'[4]

In the spring of 1938 the board received the Tamblyn and Brown report at its April meeting. While the directors found the recommendations useful, they had passed the point where they could implement any of them. In fact, despite their own recommendations, Tamblyn and Brown openly discouraged a fund-raising drive in view of the continuing depression in the United States. The board also decided against appointing a managing director, leaving Ashdown to run their affairs in New York. Instead, they preferred to cultivate greater co-operation among the contributing associations, especially among the various secretaries. Thus the New England Grenfell Association continued as before, except that the Industrial Department was absorbed by the New York office. As for Grenfell's continuing role, Grenfell would be referred to thereafter as the 'Founder' and his suggestions welcomed as long as they were made through Ashdown.[5] He was enjoined not to correspond directly with the other officers of the IGA.

With the reorganization complete, the Mission's new structure accounted for all of its existing staff – except Harry Paddon. As the directors observed, the cottage hospital and orphanage in North West River served a small population. How could they justify the expense? To assist with its economies, the board considered leasing the property to Bowater Lloyd after the Commission of Government expressed an interest in starting a sulphite mill at Gander and an attendant community at North West River. Paddon, who had settled permanently there, received the proposal like a 'death sentence,' not knowing what medical facilities the company would provide for its town, but he rejoiced in the expected industrialization of Labrador. He had built his house in North West River and had governed there for over twenty-five hard years. He expected to retire soon, perhaps after the graduation from medical school of his son Anthony, who he hoped would succeed him.

Paddon insisted he bore no animosity towards Dr Curtis and his policy of centralization, and in a long testimonial to the London office he revealed his rationalization:

> Dr. Curtis is now Medical Superintendent and Executive Officer. That is quite as it should be. He is four years junior in service to me, and probably ten years younger; but he is our leading institutional physician and surgeon, and in closer touch with the Directors and Government. When I refused to take over Dr Little's work at St Anthony, I did it with my eyes open. Dr Curtis would never have stayed north of Belle Isle Straits for two years, let alone twenty. He has not my love for boats or long dog-team travel; and he is an institutional rather than a family doctor. So there is not the slightest jealousy or misunderstanding. If I had not stayed here to do what I have done, there would have been none to do it; and, despite many imperfections, I would not have missed it for anything. Sixty is the retiring age, as a general rule, for medical staff members, and sixty is not so very far away for me. Moreover, the annual budget comes so largely from the United States that it is hardly to be wondered if it is felt that more of the direction should come from there. It looks as if the work will be more and more centralised around St Anthony and Cartwright, apart from the Canadian-supported and operated little centre in and around Harrington, in Canadian Labrador. Times are certainly changing, and we must change with them.[6]

Still, he brooded over the possibilities. Though he realized the end of his small domain would be 'heart-breaking,' he also knew the employment and stimulation of increased logging operations could make his small hospital redundant – perhaps even spoil the area to which he was so deeply attached. But in any case, the advent of war shattered the idea of a third mill, and Paddon was left to wonder what the IGA would do with North West River next. 'I wish Dr. Curtis would come down himself,' he wrote that summer. 'Probably he will now. He has never been here since 1915, when the first little hospital was building.'[7]

If these events troubled Grenfell at St Simon's that winter, nothing troubled him as much as Anne's deterioration. Anne had appeared stronger after her surgery and carried on her usual pace of organizing and corresponding. She had also published two magazine articles and book of quotations to keep Grenfell's name in the forefront.[8] But she had grown increasingly tired and short-tempered, and as the year progressed she did not improve. She spent the whole of 1938 in varying degrees of discomfort, suffering at times from the effects of pleurisy and double pneumonia, which sent her to bed for five or six weeks, then phlebitis. After spending eight and a half weeks in St Luke's Hospital, she discharged herself and joined Grenfell in Georgia, where she developed phlebitis again and took to her bed for three weeks more.[9] At the end of April she returned to New York for a series of six-week radiation treatments and by September had limited her activities considerably. But she kept up a bold front and planned to spend the winter in Georgia. From now on, the radiation treatments would tire her out. She had lost sensation in her lower limbs and feet, and her body seemed inflated. She felt depressed. 'Discomfort does not describe my feelings – it is very severe pain,' she wrote in October. 'I can put up with discomfort with the best of them.'[10]

The radiation failed to arrest the spread of cancer, more apparently now the result of an intra-uterine radiation burn she had received after a miscarriage over a decade before. The cancer had now spread to the bones and the abdomen, reducing the chances of recovery.[11] Grenfell, seeking to try everything he could, placed her under the care of Dr Joel Goldthwait, an orthopaedic surgeon, and she entered the Brigham Hospital in Boston. But by November 1938 the reports showed there could be no hope. Faced with the inevitable, Grenfell still refused to accept the prognosis, even though his wife was deteriorating before his eyes. Charles Curtis arrived unexpectedly and spent many hours at her bedside. Grenfell wrote desperately to Dr Harvey Cushing, to whom he had turned for advice, 'Is nothing of any value but dope? and increasing dope? and the long drawn agony of perhaps a year of gradual living disintegration?'[12] Nothing was, and Anne had accepted long before the idea that she would not outlive him. On 9 December she slipped quietly away in her room at the Hampton Court Hotel, Brookline, her suffering ended.

Among the hundreds of letters Grenfell received, Queen Elizabeth sent her condolences, as did the prime minister of Canada, Mackenzie King. But these conventional expressions of grief failed to assist him in his desolation. He had lost his strongest ally and closest friend, and he took refuge more and more in the consolations of religion. Sensing the outcome several months before, when she had returned to Boston alone, he had written her touchingly, giving her full credit for easing the burden of his life. 'But one thing I know,' he wrote, 'the faith we hold does save from even the *desire* for more things – and God knows I had passions for glory and fame, and even sensual strong passions, and endless opportunities for indulgence in them – and strong temptations – that when this "faith" started me fighting (thank God very early in life) it showed me what a lot of "fear" *I* had also.'[13] With her ordeal over, he retreated again to St Simon's for the winter, and much of his time was spent handling the letters that had piled up. 'She flashed into my life out of the blue without my even knowing her name and she passed out of my life in a hotel ...,' he wrote her Bryn Mawr professor. 'Much younger than I, beautiful, brilliant, only living child of her widowed mother with younger suitors in the field and everything to keep her at home, she gave herself to me and to the north,' he wrote Harriott Curtis, 'though at the time, I was nearly twice her age, and she has recreated the work.'[14]

He received a letter from Mostyn House, commenting on the state of the school. Two weeks before Anne's death he had written to Daryl without telling her and in his agitated state of mind called in the remaining debt of £1,500, wishing to tie up loose ends in case they both should die. The request could not have come at a less propitious time. To begin with, Daryl had inherited a school in what he described as 'a very rocky state,' and since he had not inherited any of the cash, he was attempting to re-establish the school financially, much as his father had done decades before, by taking out a second mortgage from the bank and selling off property. He had since built up the school from seventy-eight pupils to its capacity of 117 without laying anything by for himself and his family. In short, Daryl could not pay the debt, and once again he called its legitimacy into question. He wrote, 'Whatever the strictly legal side of the matter (and I am no more prepared or qualified than Dad to decide this) he always maintained that morally a real, genuine & great mistake had been made ... not only by A.S.G. but later both by himself & you: for the whole matter was not thoroughly & sufficiently gone into at the time – not, in fact, until he paid you £4,000 of the complete sum alleged.' Both brothers had made an honest mistake, he insisted diplomatically, and their distinctive personalities had prevented them from agreeing on this sensitive issue. But Daryl need not have worried. In the meantime, Grenfell had asked Anne what she wished him to do about it, and she had without hesitation told him to forget it. He now conveyed the answer in the most sympathetic terms. 'Yes A.G.G. was absolutely honest – so was A.S.G.,' he wrote. 'God knows, I often wish I might have been able to do more for them.' On his seventy-fourth birthday he cancelled the promissory note and returned it to Mostyn House.[15]

In the summer of 1939 he returned to St Anthony with Anne's ashes. He had passed a comfortable winter at St Simon's, including a spell at Dr Kellogg's sanatorium in Miami, and he felt reinvigorated by the vegetarian diet and regular massages. He arrived aboard the *North Star* on 21 July, bringing Rosamond and the man she later married, his new secretary and companion, Wyman Shaw. Accompanying them was Mrs Vara Majette, a St Simon's lawyer. Grenfell's appearance generated the same excitement it had thirty years before, when he had brought his bride ashore to be greeted by a curious crowd and an arch of spruce bows. This time another spruce arch greeted him, and the flags and the muzzle-loaders were brought out for the occasion, but this time it was a welcome for a visitor. The next Sunday a group of mourners gathered at the rock face on the hill behind

the hospital. Early in the afternoon, the children of the orphanage surrounded it with a wreath and laid a carpet of wild flowers, and here Grenfell
conducted a short service, including the hymns sung at Anne's funeral in
the Church of Our Saviour, Brookline. The ashes were placed in a small
space next to the one provided for John Mason Little, and Curtis unveiled
the brass tablet. Then the group retreated down the hill again in silence.

Despite the solemnity, Grenfell seemed to enjoy the fortnight of
reunions that followed. He presided at the summer sports. He took an
excursion to Cartwright aboard the *Kyle* and met Harry Paddon. In mid-
August he ran down to Goose Cove aboard a trading schooner and crossed
Hare Bay, the scene of his survival on the ice pan. He journeyed across
the straits to Red Bay, the site of his first co-operative, and back to St
Anthony in a stomach-churning chop. But he had trouble making sense
of the changes presented to him. The Founder had over-extended himself,
and by the end of August his presence was clearly interfering with the
program of work. Curtis and Paddon had planned to visit all the Labrador
stations together aboard the *Maraval* that summer but realized Grenfell
would have wanted to go with them, making it impossible to investigate
any of the problems. Curtis complained later to Ashdown, 'In the future
Sir Wilfred must realize definitely that if he comes on the coast, that he
must not interfere with the running of the organization. Then again, last
summer he was accompanied, as you know, by his secretary, Lady Lawyer
from Georgia, Freddie Sears and Rosamund [*sic*]. Everywhere Sir Wilfred
went they went along also. I hope that you can impress upon the directors
how difficult this whole situation has been for me.'[16]

Grenfell himself was not insensible to his change of status. He knew he
was now a visitor. He wrote his old colleague Francis B. Sayre at the State
Department in Washington, 'In front of me as I write is the house Anne
and I built, and where our children were born. It is now the home of
"others." I am writing you from Dr. Curtis's house, where I am only a
guest. The beautiful new hospital is also in the picture as I look up, with
the flags of our two great countries flying side by side. The work is now in
the hands of "others," and the patients are so numerous that I hardly have
time to sit down and talk to my successor.'[17] Eleanor Cushman was asked
to take him home, and at the end of August he boarded the *New Northland*
for the return trip. A curious but tearful crowd assembled on the wharf on
29 August, perhaps sensing they were witnessing Grenfell's final appearance among them. They sang 'Auld Lang Syne' and 'For He's a Jolly Good
Fellow.'[18] Grenfell threw confetti from the guard rails. He stayed on the
upper deck until the ship had rounded the headland, then retreated to his
cabin, where he stayed alone for the next twenty-four hours in the full
knowledge that a door had closed for ever. He had left Anne behind, but

he took some consolation from the knowledge that a group of her friends had undertaken to raise $15,000 for a new industrial building in her memory, much of the money already in hand.

Within three days he grew absorbed by the hostilities in Europe, which were making it impossible for the Grenfell office in London to operate. With the British people preoccupied by air raid precautions and recruiting, the British branches held no meetings, and appeals seemed fruitless. All the British association could do was keep up their subscription list. Katie Spalding, the unpaid secretary, had written Anne before her death, 'What protection can there be from air raids when thousands can be killed at a time – and no medical service could be adequate to deal with the wounded in such numbers? One could only pray to be killed outright and not left in a mutilated condition.'[19] When the building at 66 Victoria Street was eventually bombed, Miss Spalding operated out of a single room with the windows blown out until the rest could be repaired.[20]

When the events in Europe threatened the work on the coast, the American volunteers withdrew for their safety to the United States. The industrial work now came virtually to a halt, and to make matters worse, the Newfoundland government held back its grants. Grenfell could not resist the desire to keep his hand in the business of the Mission even from a distance. He requisitioned cheques from his discretionary fund to send out to the distressed, creating the impression he could be approached directly. He urged Mackenzie King to take over Labrador. 'It seems to me that it would be the crowning act of your long premiership if you could complete this,' he assured him. 'I still have quite a number of friends in Canada who would be influenced by what I sponsor.'[21] At last José Machado, chairman of the IGA board, wrote unofficially to ask him to refuse contributions to the discretionary fund for the duration of the war and to turn over the balance to the treasurer of the New England Grenfell Association.[22] But nothing could have prepared him for what happened next, the death of a second irreplaceable ally, Harry Paddon.

Paddon, after twenty-eight years, had emerged as the Mission's chief Labrador presence. There was hardly a cove he hadn't poked into or a patient he hadn't treated.[23] He still believed in Labrador's great potential for hydro development, mineral extraction, and timber but despaired of the poverty and distress that still existed, especially among the native populations. While he hesitated to blame the politicians directly for allowing this to happen, he regarded the unchecked poverty in his beloved realm as nothing less than a 'tragic absurdity.'[24] With no one to replace Grenfell on the lecture circuit, he had come to the United States that autumn for a furlough, during which time he intended to spend Christmas with his sons, who were being educated there. He was heartened by the decision to keep open his boarding school for another year but still remained uncertain about the future. The day before he died he had taken the train to Philadelphia with his son Tony and come down with a violent chill, followed by severe headache and pain. By the next morning, Christmas Eve, he had collapsed, and he died later that day from a diffuse peritonitis, otherwise fit at the age of fifty-eight and still anticipating years of useful work.

When the family recovered from the shock, Mina Paddon decided to return to her post at North West River, and Tony, with two years of medical training left, returned to St Luke's Hospital, New York, fully expecting to succeed his father. In reporting his father's death to Grenfell, he made reference to the differences that had separated him from Curtis, fundamental differences that would not now be resolved. 'Dr. Curtis is a very splendid person,' he wrote, 'and though his particular talents and interests are not the same as yours, his love of the Mission is. He wrote me that my father's plans must not be allowed to lapse or fail, and that there would be a place for me when the time came.'[25] Paddon's ashes were buried on a hillside overlooking Hamilton Inlet.

That summer the war came to Newfoundland's doorstep when a pulp carrier bound for Europe took a torpedo and sank offshore. With the Commission of Government planning the defence of the island, Curtis prepared for more economies to follow. Large amounts of money were now being raised in the United States but diverted to assist oppressed nationals in Europe. Even if the Mission increased its income, it still would not offset the increased cost of supplies. Curtis put *Strathcona II* up for sale and called for a 10 per cent cut in salaries all round. From now on, the *Cluett* would be devoted exclusively to bringing in supplies, taking at least six trips the following spring to carry north the necessary freight. By closing the two Labrador boarding schools, he planned to save a further amount, and he intended to reduce North West River to the status of a nursing station, placing Dr Hogarth Forsyth aboard the *Maraval* the following summer to service the Labrador coast. As for the future of North West River itself, he advised Ashdown, 'I think it would be a great shame to abandon North West River entirely. Dr. Paddon of course, as you know, was not as much interested in the medical side as in the social service end of it and it will be impossible to find at once anybody who would go there and take his place. On the other hand, for years we have realised that North West was a very expensive station to operate. Some large requisition for supplies has been made here for next year.'[26]

In taking these measures, Curtis acted according to his best judgment, and the changes irked Mission officers such as Sir Henry Richards, who considered him unsympathetic to the social and religious dimensions of the Mission. Ashdown, however, credited him with greater understanding than anyone else and believed the Mission needed his firm hand. He reminded Richards that Grenfell's contribution lay in his vision and courage but that he would not stick to a plan and expected others to unscramble the 'hopeless tangles' he got himself into. 'I say this in no way to underestimate Grenfell's great genius ...,' he added defensively, 'but he could not have lasted long except for the extraordinary support of his Directors who have been long suffering and patient in the extreme and for the loyal and sustained interest of such men as Curtis.'[27]

Regardless of the Mission's policy, the Paddons had no intention of abandoning their new house, where Tony fully expected to return as soon as he had finished his two years of internship. Meanwhile, although Curtis himself considered the medical burden of North West River too great for a single nurse, he did not want to see the boarding school and agricultural work given up. Since the IGA appeared likely to grant Mrs Paddon a pension anyway, he suggested she take on the temporary management of the station together with whatever other operations the directors wanted continued. She could do this with the assistance of the Mission's technical man, Jack Watts.[28] Later that winter she returned to take charge.

Grenfell continued to divide his time between Georgia and his summer house in Vermont, preoccupied with his spirituality and the debate over American entry into the war. He read books such as Arthur Mees's *Broken Dream of Wilbur Wright*, Harry Emerson Fosdick's *Guide to the Understanding of the Bible*, and Fosdick's book of daily readings, *The Manhood of the Master*. Fosdick wrote him at this time, 'You are one of my heroes, and I find myself constantly mentioning you as an illustration of the things I should like to stand for.'[29] He took heart from the ideas of Arthur Stanley Eddington, who seemed to be able to harmonize his religious convictions with the new nuclear physics and to demonstrate that life was but one phase of a greater physical reality. He wrote Pascoe in February, 'Personally I am much better now – much clearer minded again – & much better able to express my own attitude in public when necessary. My 75th year is nearly closed. I wish we might have been together & WE are, for *this* carcase [sic] isn't me. God forbid, but it is mine & all I have left of the energy that now composes its electrons, atoms & molecules.'[30] He felt Anne's presence acutely and during his daily Bible readings recorded his communications with her in the margins. He received few visitors but kept up a stream of correspondence and answered individual appeals by attempting to issue cheques from his discretionary fund. When such cheques were blocked by his own office, he complained that he had no other means of accomplishing anything. Accustomed to working his will, he now attempted to play the directors off one against the other and criticized Curtis for his lack of faith. 'Very briefly,' he wrote that spring, 'the whole difference between this and the ordinary medical mission is that I don't personally regard the hospital work as the first work of the mission, and never did. I am far more interested in making a new man than a new body.'[31] Completely out of touch with the direction of the organization by this time, he made life difficult for those coping with restraint. But at other times he could be more generous. After reading Curtis's annual report in the fall, he congratulated him. 'We may not always see eye to eye,' he said, 'but I guess it won't be very long before I shan't be seeing anything.'[32]

He grew sentimental about England, having put aside his plans to visit Mostyn House. 'England is still *my country*,' he wrote Daryl. 'We are all *v* pro-British – a German doesn't show his nose hardly.'[33] By now the Germans were making incursions into Scandinavia, and it looked as if France would fall. During the spring and summer of 1940 the German army penetrated the Netherlands, and Winston Churchill became prime minister of Great Britain. Hitler entered Belgium, then France. As the British Expeditionary Force was extricating itself from Dunkirk, Grenfell wrote optimistically to Daryl. 'This butchery can't go on I presume and the ultimate dénouement I would think must be not far out of sight.'[34] He worried about the family at Mostyn House, expecting a bombing raid against nearby Liverpool, and in June, the day the Italians attacked southern France, he wrote offering to look after Daryl's children for the balance of the war. Daryl refused. The Battle of Britain had begun, and he had decided to run the school and keep his children about him. His reply was full of resolve, Churchillian resonance, and his father's sense of class responsibility:

> So long as I can run this school here and there is a demand for what we can and are doing, I'm sticking to it and the kids can help by helping and cheering others: I am sure that not only now – but later when they are older and can think more clearly – they would blame me if I were to have been responsible for depriving them of their chance and their right to serve even in this little way. I hope one day they may be leaders – and leaders must always show a good example, steadfastness, courage, faith and a desire to stand to one's post ... and be the last to leave the ship whatever danger she may be in: and I do not think this fine ship 'England' is in any danger (however great it may be temporarily, or appear to be) that she cannot and will not weather successfully to emerge victorious.[35]

The Blitz began in September. The Germans shifted their attacks from airfields and concentrated their efforts on bombing installations in London and provincial cities like Coventry and Liverpool. Grenfell wrote to Daryl,

'I think of you & pray for you all often.'[36] On 9 October he played a game of croquet with Wyman Shaw and Professor F.C. Sears and went upstairs to rest before dinner. When Shaw went to call him he did not respond. He had failed to survive one last heart attack, and a nitroglycerine tablet lay undissolved beneath his tongue.

Few men have been more thoroughly laid to rest than Grenfell. In all, there were three separate memorial services besides the official funeral held at Trinity Episcopal Church, Boston. The first memorial service was held at St James Episcopal Church, Madison Avenue, on his birthday in February 1941. Representatives of a range of Protestant tradition paid tribute: the Reverend Jesse Halsey (Presbyterian), the Reverend Theodore Ainsworth Greene (Congregationalist), the Reverend Harry Emerson Fosdick (Baptist), and the Right Reverend Henry Knox Sherrill (Episcopalian). The following summer the ashes were taken to St John's, where a second memorial service was held at the Church of England cathedral, long since restored to its neo-Gothic glory since the time Grenfell set foot in its ruins that first day in 1892. And on the afternoon of 25 July 1941 another procession wound its way up the hill behind the hospital in St Anthony, where another place had been prepared in the rock. Here the ashes finally rested. As the mourners gathered round, the parable of the Good Samaritan was read and St Matthew's parable of the Last Judgment. There were readings from St Paul, including the manly declaration to Timothy, 'I have fought a good fight, I have finished my course; I have kept the faith.' The last lap had finished, and Curtis had the privilege of placing the urn in the rock. To the accompaniment of a portable organ that had been wrestled to the site, the gathering broke the silence of the Newfoundland forest with the hymn 'For all the saints who from their labours rest,' and the silence returned. Then the procession retreated back down towards the hospital and the town of St Anthony. The sky was clear that day and the sea a dark blue. Over the hill a formation of huge icebergs drifted south in the Labrador Current.

Epilogue

Grenfell was publicly acknowledged as a hero of the modern day even though his contradictions were also acknowledged. He could sometimes act with great vision; yet he could also diminish the consequences of that vision with his impatience at detail and regulation. He possessed a genius for appropriating new ideas for social change; yet he left the implementation of those ideas to others. As a public speaker, he could ramble on about some unexpected subject; yet he could illuminate that subject by his simplicity and ingenuousness. He lacked the system of a philosopher or a theologian; yet he could arouse the learned, the wealthy, and the distinguished with a sense of urgency.

With all these qualities, one other is never mentioned – his desire for autonomy and authority. If one pattern emerges from his life, it is the struggle to control. He loved humanity idealistically; yet he attached himself to few individuals. He gave his life to Newfoundland; yet he disparaged its leaders and promoted the loss of its government. Despite his vast number of acquaintances, he had few close friends or colleagues, and he conducted his family affairs at arm's length. He loved his brother, but he would not tolerate the loss of his patrimony until his brother had died. He was, however, devoted to his wife, his chief adviser, who became an extension of himself and identified herself totally with him. When the time came for him to acknowledge that his days of leadership were over, it was she who insisted that he retain it, using the rationalization that the 'work' would suffer. As long as she maintained the illusion of his continuing presence, his authority was secure.

The mythology of chivalry gave Grenfell a language for expressing his altruism and maintaining his personal autonomy. For Grenfell was a soloist. From the beginning, as the agent of a missionary society, he worked

297

uncomfortably within the limitations imposed by organization, and his London colleagues found it difficult to exert their authority. By the end of the First World War, however, the chivalric view of life could not be sustained, and in any case it had become increasingly difficult for an unelected individual to impose measures upon a population arbitrarily. The board of the International Grenfell Association recognized this. As astute managers accustomed to sound business methods, they also recognized the need for a more systematic approach to benevolence, and as they imposed their own methods upon the Mission's activities in the north they moved Grenfell to the margin as fund-raiser and social commentator.

Grenfell seemed to accept the new role and maintained his autonomy by redefining himself as writer and lecturer. But by the last decade of his life a new generation had taken over the hospitals and boardrooms of the Grenfell Mission, younger men and women who did not share his cultural assumptions. Grenfell had become something of an anachronism, a crusader against vested interests living out his last days while the Mission reshaped itself in other hands. Under the leadership of Charles Curtis it concentrated on providing a high standard of medical and surgical care while slowly divesting itself of its other schemes for social improvement. Grenfell himself represented a dated paternalism – even in his relationship with his own organization, especially with Charles Curtis. Once bereft of real authority, he was governed by pride.

By the end of 1940 the Commission of Government had imposed a program of economic reconstruction, and throughout the Second World War further innovations were imposed by the needs of Canadian, British, and American armed services. The war transformed Newfoundland and Labrador in a way Grenfell could never have done, turning a destitute colony into a strategic base thrust forward into the Atlantic. Suddenly the island became a convenient transatlantic landing place and a launching platform for coastal patrols. By the time Grenfell died, Gander was already designated as a departure point for American military aircraft en route to the United Kingdom. Britain had granted the United States permission to build bases in Newfoundland, Bermuda, and elsewhere, bringing an unprecedented construction boom and relief for unemployed workers not directly engaged in hostilities. St John's itself turned into a staging area for transatlantic convoys. The United States built a base on the shores of nearby Quidi Vidi Lake, and the Royal Canadian Air Force opened up an airfield at Torbay. The Americans built a naval base and an army facility at Argentia as well as a landing field at Stephenville, on the west coast. At Goose Bay, twenty miles from North West River, the excavator's drone interrupted the stillness of Hamilton Inlet. Here the RCAF constructed an airport to serve as an alternative to Gander and built attendant radar stations along the coast. Before the war ended five years later, Newfound-landers and Labradorians had tasted North American culture and goods and joined the larger consumer society. While Mackenzie King was still prime minister of Canada, Newfoundland already contemplated the end of Commission of Government, but in 1949, when it entered confedera-tion, he was gone from office, narrowly missing the fulfilment of one of Grenfell's cherished desires.

With the coming of confederation, the perception of need also changed. Newfoundland and Labrador were now considered part of a greater Cana-dian constituency and beneficiaries of broader social and economic schemes. The politics of culture had suddenly altered. Curtis remained in St Anthony until he became chairman of the board a decade later. It was his task to lead the Mission into this next important phase, working closely with the levels of government while nourishing the myth of Wilfred Grenfell as a heroic, venturing Christian whose idiosyncrasies began to blur with the proliferation of memorials, tablets, stamps, and stained-glass windows dedicated to his memory. In response to Lennox Kerr's biography of Grenfell (1959), a book that relied upon the extensive testimony of Curtis himself, Curtis affirmed Grenfell's greatness but placed that great-ness in a different perspective. In a review printed in *Among the Deep Sea Fishers*, he portrayed him as a great originator with a fertile brain, but also as a restless individual who was often difficult for those who worked with him. Instead, he recognized Lady Grenfell as the great stabilizing influence, the strong force behind his success.

The Mission now occupied a different place in the world. Labrador no longer lay in the British Empire's isolated backyard; it was readily accessi-ble to the twentieth century. At the end of the war Curtis presided over a program of construction that produced a new hospital and doctor's resi-dence at Harrington Harbour; nursing stations at Forteau and Flower's Cover; a reservoir, dam, power plant, and tuberculosis sanatorium at St Anthony; and a new hospital at North West River, as well as other improvements to follow. Much of this new work was financed by generous endowments from Miss Louie Hall of Rochester, New York. But more and more, the facilities owed their existence not to philanthropy but to grants from the provincial and federal governments. They had become part of the 'health care industry.' In the King's Birthday Honours List for 1948, Curtis was honoured as a commander of the Most Excellent Order of the British Empire (CBE).

As the war subsided, the Mission continued to lose its links with the past. Month after month, *Among the Deep Sea Fishers* recorded the deaths of Grenfell's comrades in arms. Sir Henry Richards retired and Lord Southborough died in 1947. Selma Carlson retired in 1948, after twenty-five years as matron of the St Anthony hospital, and Cecil Ashdown died. Jessie Luther died in 1952 and a year later José Machado, both at the age of 91. Katie Spalding, who had kept the London office open during the Blitz, died in 1954 and a year later Henry Holt, the longtime treasurer of the IGA. William Adams Delano, the architect of the Mission's early buildings, died in 1960. As for the wops, they were running the world as bank presidents, politicians, headmasters, head nurses, professors, physicians and surgeons, and tending to the business of raising funds and recruiting staff.

During these years, the more conspicuous use of surgical intervention in the treatment of tuberculosis raised hopes. In 1946 Dr Gordon Thomas, a Montreal surgeon, came to St Anthony, and Curtis realized he had found a worthy surgical successor, one who was able to apply new surgical techniques, including the hospital's first lobectomy. With this trend in mind, the IGA authorized the building of a fifty-bed tuberculosis sanatorium, and Thomas took charge of the St Anthony hospital in 1954. That year he reported in the *New England Journal of Medicine* that since confederation the status of tuberculosis remained 'grave' but that substantial progress had been made. Pulmonary surgery, together with the advent of streptomycin and PAS, had reduced the death rate considerably. Meanwhile, the Mission continued to update itself in other ways. In 1955, it took possession of its first aircraft; it gradually replaced its aging vessels with the schooner *Lady Grenfell* and the steel-hulled hospital ship *Strathcona III*. Dr Thomas succeeded Dr Curtis as superintendent in 1959, his assistant superintendent the multi-talented Horace W. McNeill, born in St Anthony and educated by the Mission at Berea College, Kentucky. Harriot Curtis predeceased her husband in 1951. When her ashes were deposited in the rock on Fox Farm Hill, it was Dr Thomas who gave the eulogy. The leadership of the Mission had passed into new hands. When Curtis died in 1963 at the age of seventy-three, the ritual was repeated.

Meanwhile, Mina Paddon kept the North West River nursing station open until the end of the war. In 1949 she was made an officer of the Most Excellent Order of the British Empire (OBE), and she died in North West River in 1967 at the age of eighty-six. When her son Tony was discharged from the Royal Canadian Navy at the end of the war, he laboured as medical officer in Labrador until his retirement in 1977 and subsequently as lieutenant-governor of the province from 1981 to 1986. Dr Donald Hodd retired from Harrington in 1968, after nearly forty years of service. The same year, the IGA opened a large departmental hospital in St Anthony and dedicated it to the memory of Dr Curtis. While maintaining its Grade A accreditation, it gradually shifted its emphasis from the acute care of disease to public health, preventative medicine and community medicine. The same year, Selma Carlson died and her ashes were placed in the rock. Now the collection of brass plaques was complete.

The face of the Mission had been transformed. Dr Thomas retired in 1978, after thirty-two years on the coast, and the business offices moved from Ottawa to St Anthony. Dr Thomas's successor, Dr Peter Roberts, became the first Newfoundlander to take charge of the Mission's medical affairs. By now, the IGA administered not a mission at all but a distinctively regional health service, a complex organization with directors from the local population. In the face of increased governmental influence, greater change lay ahead. In 1981 *Among the Deep Sea Fishers* ceased publication. The International Grenfell Association itself withdrew and signed over its properties to Grenfell Regional Health Services, a provincial corporation designed to operate within its former domain.

In Britain that year the Royal National Mission to Deep Sea Fishermen completed a hundred years of continuous service to fishermen and their families, its work carried out in eighteen centres around the British Isles by thirty-five superintendents and assistant superintendents and a domestic staff of 150. These centres maintained an evangelical presence, providing accommodation, recreation, and canteen facilities as well as welfare services for families. A full-time uniformed staff offered counsel in the event of spiritual, moral and material needs. Fishermen's wives and children were cared for during the men's absence and in the event of disaster. Ship, home, and hospital visits continued, and the Mission staff helped the disabled and the distressed. The RNMDSF remained an interdenominational charity, receiving no government help and relying entirely for its annual sustenance on £700,000 derived from gifts, donations, and covenants. In its outlook and its services, it has remained virtually unchanged since the day Wilfred Grenfell became its first superintendent.

Notes

1 Mostyn House School

1 G.W. Place, 'Parkgate as a Port,' *Journal of the Chester Archaeological Society* 66 (1983): 47–55

2 This myth has been effectively examined in Michael McCrum, *Thomas Arnold, Headmaster: A Reassessment* (London 1989).

3 See Geoffrey Place, *This Is Parkgate: Its Buildings and Their Story* (Parkgate 1979); G.W. Place, 'John Brindley (1811–1873), Cheshire Schoolmaster, the Opponent of Atheism,' *Transactions of the Historical Society of Lancashire and Cheshire* 133 (1984): 113–32; Herbert J. Price, obituary in *Griffin* 6 (1899): 475 ff.

4 See reminiscences of A.G. Grenfell in *Griffin* 6 (1899): 475–80, and school photograph archive.

5 See William Collings Lukis de Guérin, *Our Kin: Genealogical Sketches, Pedigrees, and Arms of Sundry Families* (Guernsey 1890), 176–81, and Walter H. Tregellas, 'The Grenvilles of Stow,' in *Cornish Worthies: Sketches of Some Eminent Cornish Men and Families* (London 1884), 3–85.

6 See J. Horace Round, 'The Granvilles and the Monks,' in *Family Origins and Other Studies* (London 1930), 130–69; Arthur C. Fox-Davies, *Armorial Families: A Directory of Gentlemen of Coat-armour* (Rutland, Vt., 1970), I: 818.

7 Mostyn House Papers, J.G. Grenfell, 'The Story of My Life (1920).' This document, dictated to AGG in 1920, bears the unmistakable marks of his phraseology. See also 'Notes by A.G.G., 'apparently notes on a diary kept by Admiral John Grenfell, and Joseph Foster, comp., *Alumni Oxonienses* 1 (Oxford 1887–92), 562.

8 *The Rugby Register, from the Year 1675 [to 1853]* (Rugby 1853), 353

9 Foster, *Alumni Oxonienses*, 562

10 Mostyn House Papers, JGG's book of daily devotions contain annotations listing significant family dates.

11 Mostyn House Papers, J.G. Grenfell, 23

12 For these figures, I am grateful to Geoffrey Place.

13 Wilfred Grenfell Papers, WTG to AGG, undated

14 *Labrador Doctor*, 2–6, 9. See also A.G. Grenfell, 'Dr. Grenfell's Ancestry and Early History,' in James Johnson, *Grenfell of Labrador* (London [1908]), 15–23.

15 Mostyn House Papers, 'Notes by A.G.G.,' 2–3; *Labrador Doctor*, 29–30

16 *Labrador Doctor*, 8

17 *Toilers* 15 (1900): 266

18 *Labrador Doctor*, 24–6; *Malborough College Register from 1843 to 1904 Inclusive* (Oxford 1905), 349

19 L.E. Upcott, 'The Middle Years,' in *Marlborough College, 1843–1943*, ed. H.C. Brentnall and E.G.K. Kempson (Cambridge 1943), 20–7
20 J.A. Mangan, 'Athleticism: A Case Study of the Evolution of an Educational Ideology,' in *The Victorian Public School: Studies in the Development of an Educational Institution*, ed. Brian Simon and Ian Bradley (Dublin 1975), 157
21 J.A. Mangan, *Athleticism in the Victorian and Edwardian Public School* (Cambridge 1981), 135
22 Norman Vance, *The Sinews of the Spirit: The Ideal of Christian Manliness in Victorian Literature and Religious Thought* (Cambridge 1985), 26. See also Mark Girouard, *The Return to Camelot: Chivalry and the English Gentleman* (New Haven 1981).
23 See Mangan, *Athleticism in the Victorian and Edwardian Public School*, and J.A. Mangan and James Walvin, eds., *Manliness and Morality: Middle-class Masculinity in Britain and America* (New York 1987).
24 H.H. Almond, 'Football as a Moral Agent,' *Nineteenth Century* 34 (1893): 903. See also Robert Jameson Mackenzie, *Almond of Loretto* (London 1905), and J.A. Mangan, 'Almond of Loretto: Scottish Educational Visionary and Reformer,' *Scottish Educational Review* 11 (1979): 97–106.
25 *Labrador Doctor*, 17–21
26 Wilfred Grenfell Papers, WTG to AGG, c. 1881
27 *Labrador Doctor*, 39
28 Mostyn House Papers, 'Notes by A.G.G.,' 6
29 *Labrador Doctor*, 425–6
30 *Chester Chronicle*, 3 June 1882
31 Tower Hamlets Health Authority Archives, London Hospital House Committee Minutes, 1884–86: 180
32 AGG Diary, 2 November 1886
33 Undated letter in the possession of Dr Bevyl Cowan

2 The London Hospital Medical College

1 Charles Newman, *The Evolution of Medical Education in the Nineteenth Century* (London 1957), 200
2 See William B. Walker, 'Medical Education in 19th Century Great Britain,' *Journal of Medical Education* 31 (1956): 765–76, and W.J. Reader, *Professional Men: The Rise of the Professional Classes in Nineteenth-Century England* (London 1966).
3 See Sir Douglas Hubble, 'William Osler and Medical Education,' *Journal of the Royal College of Physicians, London* 9 (1975): 269–78.
4 *Labrador Doctor*, 41

5 Tower Hamlets Health Authority Archives, London Hospital Medical College, Register C: 257

6 *Labrador Doctor*, 44

7 See Stephen Trombley, *Sir Frederick Treves: The Extra-Ordinary Edwardian* (London 1989).

8 D.G. Halsted, *Doctor in the Nineties* (London 1959), 28

9 Wilfred T. Grenfell, 'Sir Frederick Treves: A Surgeon Who Happens to Be a Man of Genius,' *Putnam's* 5 (1909): 591

10 Treves's worldliness is emphasized in a portrait by his publisher, Newman Flower, *Just as It Happened* (London 1950), 109–26.

11 *Labrador Doctor*, 87. See also Michael Howell and Peter Ford, *The True History of the Elephant Man*, rev. and ill. ed. (London 1983).

12 See A.J. Youngson, *The Scientific Revolution in Victorian Medicine* (New York 1979).

13 *Labrador Doctor*, 71

14 Wilfred Grenfell Papers, WTG to AG, undated

15 *London Hospital Gazette* 12 (1896): 24

16 Halsted, *Doctor in the Nineties* 22

17 Ibid., 31

18 RNMDSF Miscellaneous Papers, typescript of interview with Duncan Carse, 2

19 [Cecil E. Tyndale-Biscoe], *Tyndale-Biscoe of Kashmir: An Autobiography* (London 1951), 42

20 *Labrador Doctor*, 57

21 Halsted, *Doctor in the Nineties*, 34

22 Wilfred Grenfell, 'How to Prepare for a Holiday Camp,' *Review of Reviews* 2 (1890): 575

23 RNMDSF Miscellaneous Papers, interview with Duncan Carse, 6–7

24 *Labrador Doctor*, 45. See also Ronald Rompkey, 'Elements of Spiritual Autobiography in Sir Wilfred Grenfell's *A Labrador Doctor*,' *Newfoundland Studies* 1 (1985): 17–28.

25 Wilfred Thomason Grenfell, *The Adventure of Life, Being the William Belden Noble Lectures for 1911* (Boston 1912), 8

26 RNMDSF Miscellaneous Papers, interview with Duncan Carse, 5–6

27 AGG Diary, 12 February 1988; RNMDSF Hospital Committee Minutes, 17 February 1888; Alexander Gordon, *What Cheer O! Or, the Story of the Mission to Deep Sea Fishermen* (London 1890), 139. Grenfell's personal account of this trip is recorded in 'A Winter Voyage with the M.D.S.F.,' *Toilers* 3 (1888): 238–43.

28 Wilfred Grenfell Papers, WTG to JGG, [March 1888]

29 Ibid., 20 [March 1888]

30 *Leeds Mercury*, 6 April 1888

31 Wilfred Grenfell Papers, WTG to JGG, 12 April [1888]
32 AGG Diary, 16 May 1888
33 Wilfred T. Grenfell, Jr., Papers, WTG to GR, undated [1888]
34 AGG Diary, 22 December 1888
35 *Times* (London), 6 February 1911
36 Harvey Cushing Papers, WTG to Cushing, 26 December [192?]
37 AGG Diary, 18 July 1888
38 General Register Office, will of the Rev. A.S. Grenfell, probated 25 October 1887
39 Mostyn House Papers, AMDG to WTG, 13 December 1938
40 AGG Diary, 18 February 1932
41 Mostyn House Papers, AGG to WTG, 11 May 1926
42 Wilfred Grenfell Papers, AGG to WTG, 28 February 1895
43 Mostyn House Papers, WTG to AGG, [May 1895]
44 Ibid., 8 April 1926; AGG to WTG, 11 May 1926
45 Wilfred T. Grenfell, 'What Christ Means to Me,' *British Weekly* 80 (1926): 447

3 The Mission to Deep Sea Fishermen

1 Jeremy Tunstall, *The Fishermen* (London 1962), 21–8
2 See Walter Wood, *North Sea Fishers and Fighters* (London 1911), ch. 15.
3 See C. Peter Williams, 'Healing and Evangelism: The Place of Medicine in Later Victorian Protestant Missionary Thinking,' in W.J. Sheils, ed., *The Church and Healing* (Oxford 1982), 271–85.
4 See E.J. Mather, *'Nor'ard of the Dogger,' Or Deep Sea Trials and Gospel Triumphs* (London 1887); Alexander Gordon, *What Cheer O! Or, the Story of the Mission to Deep Sea Fishermen* (London 1890); RNMDSF Miscellaneous Papers, A. Hague, 'Historical Summary of the Development of the Royal National Mission to Deep Sea Fishermen,' [1956].
5 Wood, *North Sea Fishers*, 201 ff
6 Mather, 'Nor'ard of the Dogger,' 304
7 Gordon, *What Cheer O!* 90–1
8 RNMDSF Council Minutes, 6 December 1889
9 Gordon, *What Cheer O!* 193
10 See R.M. Ballantyne, *The Young Trawler: A Story of Life and Death and Rescue on the North Sea* (London 1884), and *The Lively Poll: A Tale of the North Sea* (London 1886); Emma Marshall, *Daphne's Decision; or, Which Shall It Be?;* (London 1887); and James Runciman, *A Dream of the North Sea* (London [1889]).
11 *Yarmouth Independent*, 1 March 1890
12 *Yarmouth Mercury*, 19 October 1940

13 Ibid.

14 *Toilers* 6 (1891): 114

15 Ibid., 145

16 Ibid., 173

17 RNMDSF Council Minutes, 23 February 1891

18 *Toilers* 7 (1892): 66

19 RNMDSF Council Minutes, 6 December 1886

20 *Journal of the House of Assembly of Newfoundland* (St John's 1880), 126

21 RNMDSF Finance Committee Minutes, 10 July 1891; Southborough Papers, Lord Knutsford to Sir J.T. O'Brien, 1 August 1891

22 Southborough Papers, notebook entitled 'Notes on Newfoundland'; RNMDSF Council Minutes, 4 December 1891

23 James Alexander, 'On the Climate of Newfoundland and Some of the Diseases Chiefly Met with There,' *Dublin Journal of Medical Science* 65 (1878): 326–31

24 See R. Howley, 'The Fisheries and Fishermen of Newfoundland,' *Month* 61 (1887): 489–98; David Alexander, 'Newfoundland's Traditional Economy and Development to 1934,' *Acadiensis* 5 (1976): 56–78.

25 See *Report of Judge Bennett, Together with Evidence Respecting Bait Protection Service, 1891* (St John's 1891).

26 *Journal of the House of Assembly of Newfoundland*, 126

27 Southborough Papers, 'Notes on Newfoundland,' [p. 18]

28 William Chimmo, *Journal of a Voyage to the N.E. Coast of Labrador During the Year 1867 in H.M. Ship 'Gannet'*, ed. William J. Kirwin (St John's 1989), 74–5

29 *Toilers* 7 (1892): 41

30 *Canadian Gazette* 19 (1892): 8, 81, 298, 417

31 Ibid., 109

32 *Daily Chronicle*, 18 January 1892

33 *Canadian Gazette* 19 (1892): 81

34 Wilfred Grenfell Papers, Treves to WTG, 4 February 1892; RNMDSF Finance Committee Minutes, 21 April 1892

35 *Evening Herald*, 1 November 1892

36 Eliot Curwen, 'Trip to Labrador [1893],' 11. See also *Labrador Doctor*, 114.

37 *Yarmouth and Gorleston Times*, 18 June 1892. See also log of the *Albert* 15 June to 21 November 1892. At the Centre for Newfoundland Studies, Memorial University, an album of photos by Grenfell presented to the Rev. Moses Harvey provides a good visual record of the voyage.

38 Wilfred Grenfell Papers, WTG to JGG, 17 June [1892]

39 Ibid., [July 1892]

40 Curwen, 'Trip to Labrador,' 13

41 *Toilers* 7 (1892): 321
42 Wilfred Grenfell Papers, WTG to JGG, [July 1892]
43 *Toilers* 7 (1892): 322

4 The Voyages of the Albert

1 *Evening Herald* (St John's) 1 November 1892
2 See E.W. Hawkes, *The Labrador Eskimo*, No. 14, Anthropological Series (Ottawa 1916).
3 *Toilers* 7 (1892): 362
4 Ibid., 363
5 Ibid., 8 (1893): 72
6 See R.J. Freebairn, 'Presidential Address,' in *Bulletin of the Newfoundland Medical Association, Annual Convention* (1931): 11–19.
7 For a discussion of early deficiency disease in the region, see James J. Putnam, 'A Form of Poly-neuritis, Probably Analagous to or Identical with Beri-beri, Occurring in Sea-faring Men in Northern Latitudes,' *Journal of Nervous and Mental Diseases* 15 (1890): 495–505.
8 *Methodist Monthly Greeting* 4 (1892): 180–1
9 *Toilers* (1892): 364, 420
10 [Armine Gosling], *William Gilbert Gosling: A Tribute by A.N.G.* (New York [1935]), 30
11 S.J.R. Noel, *Politics in Newfoundland* (Toronto 1971), 17 ff
12 Philip Tocque, *Newfoundland: As It Was, and as It Is in 1871* (Toronto 1878), 86–7
13 *Report of the Newfoundland Royal Commission, 1933* (London 1934), 87
14 Wilfred Grenfell Papers, WTG to JGG, 22 October 1892
15 *William Gilbert Gosling*, 35
16 *Toilers* 8 (1893): 38
17 See David Arnold, 'Introduction: Disease, Medicine and Empire,' in David Arnold, ed., *Imperial Medicine and Indigenous Societies* (Manchester 1988), 15.
18 *Evening Herald*, 1 November 1892
19 *Toilers* 8 (1893): 35–6
20 Wilfred Grenfell Papers, WTG to JGG, 3 November [1892]
21 Ibid.
22 RNMDSF Council Minutes, 6 January 1893; *Toilers* 8 (1893): 128
23 RNMDSF Council Minutes, 3 March 1893
24 *Toilers* 8 (1893): 188 ff
25 Ibid., 219, 280
26 *The Griffin, Being the Chronicle of Mostyn House School* 1 (1893): 56
27 Wilfred Grenfell Papers, WTG to JGG, 26 June 1893

28 Eliot Curwen, 'Trip to Labrador [1893],' 17
29 Ibid., 29

5 The Voyage of the Princess May

1 *Toilers* 8 (1893): 280
2 Eliot Curwen, 'Trip to Labrador [1893],' 36–9
3 See A.P. Low, *Report on the Explorations in the Labrador Peninsula Along the East Main, Koksoak, Hamilton, Manicuagan and Portions of Other Rivers in 1892–93–94–95* (Ottawa 1896).
4 See Alexander Forbes, *Northernmost Labrador Mapped from the Air* (New York 1938).
5 Curwen, 'Trip to Labrador,' 81; Low, *Explorations*, 27
6 *Toilers* 8 (1893): 282–6; 346–52; 375–80
7 Curwen, 'Trip to Labrador,' 73
8 RNMDSF Spiritual Work Committee Minutes, WTG to Spiritual Work Committee, 8 August 1893
9 *Toilers* 8 (1893): 347
10 *Periodical Accounts Relating to the Foreign Missions of the Church of the United Brethren* 2 (1895): 437
11 *Toilers* 8 (1893): 349
12 Curwen, 'Trip to Labrador,' 92
13 *Toilers* 8 (1893): 351
14 Curwen, 'Trip to Labrador,' 101
15 Wilfred Grenfell Papers, Trezise to F.H. Wood, 26 October 1893
16 Curwen, 'Trip to Labrador,' 114
17 Ibid., 115
18 Ibid., 122
19 Ibid., 125
20 *Harbour Grace Standard*, 10 March 1893
21 Curwen, 'Trip to Labrador,' 113
22 *Toilers* 8 (1893): 379
23 Curwen, 'Trip to Labrador,' 129
24 Ibid., 131
25 *Toilers* 9 (1894): 12
26 Ibid., 12–13
27 Wilfred Grenfell Papers, WTG to JGG, 7 November [1893]
28 *Evening Telegram (St John's)*, 24 November 1893
29 RNMDSF Finance Committee Minutes, 20 April 1894
30 Wilfred Grenfell Papers, WTG to JGG, 30 November [1893]
31 See Rev. C.C. Carpenter, 'Toil and Triumph in Labrador,' *Christian*

Endeavor World, 18 April 1902: 545–6; [S.R.] Butler, *The Labrador Mission* (Montreal 1878); *Missionary Monthly* 1 (1926): 515–16.

32 Wilfred Grenfell Papers, WTG to JGG, 15 December 1893
33 *Montreal Weekly Witness*, 27 December 1893
34 *Toilers* 9 (1894): 41
35 Wilfred Grenfell Papers, WTG to JGG, 30 December 1893
36 Wilfred Grenfell Papers, Wakeham to Deputy Minister of Marine and Fisheries, 8 January 1894
37 Hudson's Bay Company Archives, Smith to Commissioner C.C. Chipman, 29 December 1893
38 Wilfred Grenfell Papers, Treves to WTG, 20 January 1894
39 RNMDSF Finance Committee Minutes, 20 April 1894
40 Ibid., 4 May 1894

6 Hard Times in Newfoundland

1 See C. Francis Rowe, James A. Haxby, and Robert J. Graham, *The Currency and Medals of Newfoundland* (Toronto 1983), 30–7.
2 *Toilers* 9 (1894): 208
3 *Montreal Gazette*, 19 July 1894.
4 *Toilers* 9 (1894): 281
5 Ibid., 282
6 RNMDSF Finance Committee Minutes, 21 December 1894
7 *Toilers* 35 (1920): 39
8 Ibid. 9 (1894): 340
9 Ibid., 344
10 Ibid. 10 (1895): 255–6, 245–7.
11 *Evening Herald*, 12 November 1894
12 *Illustrated London News* 105 (1894): 819
13 Wilfred Grenfell Papers, Jones to WTG, 24 January 1895
14 For a full discussion of these events, see J.K. Hiller, 'A History of Newfoundland, 1874–1901' (PHD dissertation, Cambridge University 1971), 286 ff.
15 Wilfred Grenfell Papers, Hopwood to WTG, 8 January 1895
16 Ibid., 18 March 1895
17 RNMDSF Finance Committee Minutes, 25 January 1895
18 Frederick Treves, in Wilfred T. Grenfell, *Vikings of To-day, Or Life and Medical Work among the Fishermen of Labrador* (London 1895), ix
19 RNMDSF Finance Committee Minutes, 22 March 1895
20 Ibid., 17 May 1895
21 *Evening Herald*, 15 June 1895
22 *Toilers* 10 (1895): 276

23 Ibid., 11 (1896): 71
24 Ibid. 10 (1895): 249
25 *Periodical Accounts Relating to the Foreign Missions of the Church of the United Brethren* 3 (1896): 37
26 RNMDSF Council Minutes, 13 September 1895
27 Wilfred Grenfell Papers, Hopwood to WTG, 8 December 1895
28 RNMDSF Council Minutes, 11, 24 January 1896
29 Wilfred Grenfell Papers, Treves to WTG, 1 February 1896
30 *Toilers* 11 (1896): 214
31 Ibid., 267
32 Ibid. 12 (1897): 54
33 Ibid. 11 (1896): 269
34 A.A. Chesterfield Papers, 'The Viking Doctor of Labrador,' 9
35 *Toilers* 11 (1896): 270
36 Ibid. 12 (1897): 309
37 RNMDSF Council Minutes, 29 December 1896
38 RNMDSF Finance Committee Minutes, 22 January 1897
39 Ibid., 20 February 1897
40 Ibid., 23 April 1897

7 Exile in England

1 *Toilers* 12 (1897): 244
2 Ibid., 15 (1900): 22
3 Ibid. 12 (1897): 329
4 W.H. Fitchett, *Deeds that Won the Empire* (London 1898), vi
5 *Toilers* 13 (1898): 100–1
6 Ibid., 14 (1899): 206
7 Ibid. 13 (1898): 160. See also Greta Jones, *Social Hygiene in Twentieth Century Britain* (London 1986), 18.
8 *Toilers* 12 (1897): 104, 232, 233, 235
9 Ibid. (1897): 279
10 *Daily News*, 27 May 1897
11 *Toilers* 13 (1898): 30
12 RNMDSF Council Minutes, 1 February 1898
13 *Toilers* 13 (1898): 161
14 Ibid. (1898): 301
15 RNMDSF Finance Committee Minutes, 17 February 1899. See also Wilfred T. Grenfell, *The Harvest of the Sea: A Tale of Both Sides of the Atlantic* (New York 1905).
16 RNMDSF Council Minutes, 24 February 1899

17 Wilfred Grenfell Papers, Willway to WTG, 6 February 1899
18 Hudson's Bay Company Archives, James A. Wilson to James Fraser, 26 October 1896; Fraser to Stuart Cotter, 16 December 1901
19 *Toilers* 14 (1899): 212, 295
20 RNMDSF Hospital Committee Minutes, 24 February 1899
21 RNMDSF Council Minutes, 10 March 1899
22 RNMDSF Finance Committee Minutes, 25 July 1899
23 See James K. Hiller, 'A History of Newfoundland, 1874–1901' (PHD dissertation, Cambridge University 1971), 337 ff.
24 *Ottawa Free Press*, 16 May 1899
25 *Montreal Gazette*, 17 June 1899
26 *Evening Herald*, 20 June 1899
27 *Daily News*, 26 June 1899; *Evening Telegram*, 29 June 1899
28 *Evening Herald*, 28 July 1899
29 *Daily News*, 28 March 1899
30 RNMDSF Council Minutes, 10 November 1899
31 Wilfred Grenfell Papers, Jones to WTG, 4 October 1899
32 *Toilers* 15 (1900): 108
33 Ibid., 109. See also Wilfred Grenfell Papers, WTG to AGG, 3 December 1899.
34 Lloyd's of London, Register of Agents, 284. Grenfell was sole agent for Labrador from 1903 to 1935.
35 *Toilers* 15 (1900): 219–20
36 Wilfred Grenfell Papers, WTG to AGG, 20 July 1900
37 *Toilers* 16 (1901): 72

8 The Hero Ascendant

1 For a full discussion of this phenomenon, see Robert T. Handy, *A Christian America: Protestant Hopes and Historical Realities* (New York 1971), and E. Digby Baltzell, *The Protestant Establishment: Aristocracy and Caste in America* (New York 1964).
2 See Helen R. Albee, 'A Profitable Philanthropy,' *Review of Reviews* 22 (1900): 57–60.
3 See Allen F. Davis, *Spearheads for Reform: The Social Settlements and the Progressive Movement, 1890–1914* (New York 1967).
4 For a full discussion of these social concepts, see Rivka Shpak Lissak, *Pluralism and Progressives: Hull House and the New Immigrants, 1890–1919* (Chicago 1989).
5 Caroline Williamson Montgomery, 'Settlements (Social, University, College, and Church)' in William D.P. Bliss and Rudolph M. Binder, eds., *The New Encyclopedia of Social Reform*, 3rd ed. (New York 1910), 1106–7

6 Lyman Abbott, *Reminiscences* (Boston 1915), ix

7 Frank Luther Mott, *A History of American Magazines* (Cambridge 1938), 3: 422–35

8 See Ira V. Brown, *Lyman Abbott, Christian Evolutionist: A Study in Religious Liberalism* (Cambridge 1953), 128 ff.

9 Lyman Abbott, *The Rights of Man: A Study in Twentieth Century Problems* (Boston 1901), 272

10 Lyman Abbott Memorial Collection, WTG to Abbott, 17 November 1909

11 W.L. Mackenzie King Correspondence, King to WTG, 11 April 1903

12 'Co-operative Stores Among Atlantic Fishermen,' *Labour Gazette* 3 (1903): 680–1

13 See Reginald A. Daly, 'The Geology of the Northeast Coast of Labrador,' *Bulletin of the Museum of Comparative Zoology* 38 (1902): 205–70.

14 Wilfred Grenfell Papers, Edwin D. Mead to Robert E. Ely, 15 April 1903

15 *Toilers* 18 (1903): 151

16 *New York Times*, 26 April 1903

17 See, for example, Wilfred Grenfell, 'The Lure of the Labrador,' *National Review* 97 (1931): 623.

18 'A Viking of To-day,' *Outlook* 74 (1903): 692

19 Wilfred T. Grenfell, 'Among the Deep-Sea Fishermen,' ibid., 695–701

20 RNMDSF Finance Committee Minutes, 24 February 1902, 29 May 1903

21 RNMDSF Council Minutes, 22 May 1903; *Toilers* 18 (1903): 155

22 *Toilers* 19 (1904): 121

23 Southborough Papers, WTG to Hopwood, 20 June [1904]

24 Wilfred Grenfell Papers, Hopwood to WTG, 10 October 1904

25 Southborough Papers, MacGregor to Hopwood, 27 October 1904

26 Ibid., 10 December 1904

27 RNMDSF Council Minutes, 29 September 1905

28 George Francis Durgin, *Letters from Labrador* (Concord, NH 1908), 47–8. Cf. Norman Duncan, 'The Codfishers of Newfoundland,' *World's Work* 6 (1903): 3617–38

29 Wilfred Grenfell Papers, Briggs to WTG, 7 July 1904. See also S. Edgar Briggs, 'Doctor Grenfell – Premier of the Labrador,' *Record of Christian Work* 23 (1904): 673–9.

30 Norman Duncan, 'Grenfell of the Medical Mission,' *Harper's* 110 (1904): 35

31 *Fishers*, July 1905: 24. See also Houghton Mifflin Papers, WTG to Ferris Greenslet, 20 November 1922.

32 Norman Duncan, *Dr. Grenfell's Parish: The Deep Sea Fishermen* (New York 1905), 7–8. See also Mary Bourchier Sanford, *The Wandering Twins: A Story of Labrador* (Chicago 1904).

33 *New York Times*, 15 April 1905

34 See Edwin W. Morse, *The Life and Letters of Hamilton W. Mabie* (New York 1920).

35 *New York Times*, 13 April 1906

36 Ibid., 17 April 1905

37 W.R. Moody, 'With Dr. Grenfell on the Labrador,' *Record of Christian Work* 24 (1905): 988

38 Rev. Edward C. Moore Papers, 'Journal of Trip to Labrador, July-Aug '05,' 17–18. See also Professor Edward C. Moore, DD, 'With Dr. Grenfell in Labrador – Three Weeks on the Hospital Ship of the Deep Sea Mission,' *Toilers* 21 (1906): 174–6.

39 Moore, 'Journal,' 33

40 See Bishop B. La Trobe, 'Visit of the Governor of Newfoundland to Nain, Labrador,' *Periodical Accounts Relating to the Foreign Missions of the Church of the United Brethren* 6 (1905): 235–51.

41 Moore, 'Journal,' 34

42 Jessie Luther Papers, 'Mission to Labrador,' 3–4

43 Moore, 'Journal,' 66

44 Durgin, *Letters from Labrador*, 51

45 *Trade Review*, 25 November 1905

46 *Evening Telegram*, 27 November 1905

47 *Trade Review*, 1 December 1905

48 *Evening Herald*, 12 December 1905

49 *Daily News*, 5 December 1905

50 *Daily News*, 13 December 1905

51 W.L. Mackenzie King Correspondence, WTG to King, 1 November 1905

52 RNMDSF Hospital Committee Minutes, 9 February 1906

53 See Ian Macdonald, 'W.F. Coaker and the Balance of Power Strategy: The Fishermen's Protective Union in Newfoundland Politics' in James Hiller and Peter Neary, eds., *Newfoundland in the Nineteenth and Twentieth Centuries* (Toronto 1980), 148–80.

9 Grand Almoner

1 RNMDSF Finance Committee Minutes, 28 December 1906, 14 January 1907

2 Ibid., 8 February 1907

3 *Fishers* 39 (1942): 110

4 Henry James Morgan, ed., *The Canadian Men and Women of the Time*, 2nd ed. (Toronto 1912), 500

5 *Toilers* 21 (1906): 43

6 Dr H. Mather Hare Papers, diary entry, 31 October 1905

7 Ibid., WTG to Hare, 2 May 1906

8 W.L. Mackenzie King Correspondence, Wakeham to Minister of Marine and Fisheries, 18 May 1905

9 Ibid., King to WTG, 26 May 1905

10 Ibid., 16 January 1906

11 Jessie Luther, 'Hooked Mats: How a Native Handicraft of the Women of Newfoundland and Labrador Was Placed on a Paying Basis,' *House Beautiful* 40 (1916): 106. See also Helen R. Albee, *Abnákee Rugs: A Manual Describing the Abnákee Industry, the Methods Used, with Instructions for Dyeing* (Cambridge 1903).

12 Jessie Luther Papers, 'Mission to Labrador,' 35

13 Luther, 'Mission to Labrador,' 39.

14 Frank D. Ashburn, *Peabody of Groton: A Portrait* (New York 1944), 38

15 Ibid., 117. See also D.P. Crook, *Benjamin Kidd: Portrait of a Social Darwinist* (Cambridge 1984).

16 Endicott Peabody Papers, WTG to Peabody, 17 April 1907

17 W.L. Mackenzie King Correspondence, King to WTG, 24 January 1907. See also Sir Wilfrid Laurier Papers, Grey to Laurier, 2 November 1906.

18 *Toilers* 22 (1907): 110

19 Rockefeller Family Archives, Starr J. Murphy to John D. Rockefeller, 16 October 1907

20 W.L. Mackenzie King Correspondence, Greenshields to King, 13 March 1907

21 See Gilbert H. Grosvenor, 'Reindeer in Alaska,' *National Geographic* 14 (1903): 127–48.

22 'Report of an Official Visit to the Coast of Labrador by the Governor of Newfoundland, During the Month of August, 1905,' *Journal of the House of Assembly of Newfoundland* (St John's 1907), 360

23 4th Earl Grey of Howick Papers, WTG to Grey, 8 February 1907

24 Department of Agriculture, Fisher to Grey, 25 March 1907

25 Department of Agriculture, Memorandum of Agreement, 22 March 1907

26 *Toilers* 22 (1907): 135, 136–8

27 Francis H. Wood, 'Reindeer, Dr. Grenfell, and Labrador,' *Toilers* 22 (1907): 176–8

28 W.L. Mackenzie King Correspondence, Daly to King, 15 December 1907

29 Russell Sage Foundation Papers, Charles F. Karnopp to Mrs Sage, 30 December 1910

30 See Luther, 'Mission to Labrador,' 79 ff.

31 Arthur and Marjorie Wakefield Papers, 'Labrador Diaries,' 24

32 For genealogical information about the Littles and the Keeses, I am grateful to Mrs Ruth (Little) Smith of Ashburnham, Mass., Dr Little's daughter, and Thomas M. Smith of Cambridge, Mass., his grandson. See also Theo-

dore L. Badger, 'Grenfell Vignette: Mrs. John Mason Little,' *Fishers* 74 (1977): 5–7.

33 Wilfred Grenfell Papers, WTG to RNMDSF, 1 November 1907
34 John Mason Little Papers, JML to Mrs John Mason Little, Sr, 17 July [1909]
35 See Cuthbert Lee, *With Dr. Grenfell in Labrador* (New York 1914).
36 Luther, 'Mission to Labrador,' 97
37 Ibid., 104
38 See Grenfell's account in the *New York Evening Post*, 7 March 1908.
39 For a description of the arrival, see Jessie Luther's account in the *Boston Evening Transcript*, 25 January 1908.
40 Jessie Luther Papers, 'Mission to Labrador,' 126
41 Ibid., 134, 135
42 *Labrador Doctor*, 293
43 Luther, 'Mission to Labrador,' 126
44 Wilfred Grenfell Papers, WTG to JGG, 6 September 1902
45 Luther, 'Mission to Labrador,' 127
46 Ibid., 139
47 4th Earl Grey of Howick Papers, WTG to Grey, 30 March 1908; WTG to Hon. Sidney Fisher, 3 April 1908

10 The Hero Confirmed

1 Jessie Luther Papers, 'Mission to Labrador,' 182
2 Wilfred Thomason Grenfell, *Adrift on an Ice-pan* (Boston 1909), 7
3 Ibid., 23
4 Ibid., 30
5 Testimonial of George Andrews in Stephen Taylor and Harold Horwood, *Beyond the Road: Portraits & Visions of Newfoundlanders* (Toronto 1976), 47
6 I am grateful to Mr Andrews's son, Edward, for relating his father's account.
7 Luther, 'Mission to Labrador,' 189, 192
8 John Mason Little Papers, JML to Mrs J.M. Little, Sr, 14 May 1908
9 Wilfred Grenfell Papers, WTG to William R. Moody, 30 April 198
10 *Toilers* 23 (1908): 253. See also *New York (Daily) Tribune*, 2 August 1908, and Wilfred T. Grenfell, 'A Voyage on an Ice-Floe,' *Wide World* 22 (1909): 403–10
11 Wilfred Grenfell Papers, WTG to AGG, 15 December 1909
12 Houghton Mifflin Papers, [William B. Pratt] to WTG, 21 May 1923; Ferris Greenslet to WTG, 3 April 1924
13 John Mason Little Papers, JML to Mrs John M. Little, Sr, 14 June 1908
14 See, for example, William Anderson, 'Surgical Cases Occurring in the Island of Newfoundland,' *Canadian Medical Journal and Monthly Record of*

Medical and Surgical Science 6 (1870): 160–4; and 'Surgical and Other Cases Occurring in Newfoundland,' *Canadian Medical Surgical Journal* 1 (1872): 289–96.

15 See John M. Little, 'Medical Conditions on the Labrador Coast and North Newfoundland,' *Journal of the American Medical Association* 50 (1908): 1037–9; and 'A Winter's Work in a Subarctic Climate,' ibid. 58 (1908): 996–7.

16 John Mason Little Papers, JML to Mrs John M. Little, Sr, 25 October 1908

17 Ibid., JML to John M. Little, Sr, 3 January 1909

18 Ibid., JML to Mrs John M. Little, Sr, 15 June 1909

19 A full collection of newspaper clippings for the years 1907 and 1908 is in the miscellaneous Grenfell papers at the Provincial Archives of Newfoundland and Labrador.

20 W.L. Mackenzie King Correspondence, Daly to King, 3 December 1908

21 Luther, 'Mission to labrador,' 253. See also Frances Bowes Sayre, *Glad Adventure* (New York 1957), 13–14.

22 Luther, 'Mission to Labrador,' 255

23 W.L. Mackenzie King Correspondence, WTG to King, 1 July [1909]

24 Wilfred Grenfell Papers, AECG to JGG, 11 August [1917]

25 National Archives, Records of the 6th Tennessee Infantry Regiment. See also *Tennesseans in the Civil War: A Military History of Confederate and Union Units with Available Rosters of Personnel* (Nashville 1965), 270; *The Bench and Bar of Chicago: Biographical Sketches* (Chicago [1883?]), 516.

26 Edward Arpee, *Lake Forest, Illinois: History and Reminiscences, 1861–1961* (Lake Forest 1964), 173; Frances Harriett (Bailey) Hewitt, comp., *Genealogy of the Durand, Whalley, Barnes and Yale Families* (Chicago 1912), 19; *Chicago Tribune*, 11 April 1894

27 State of Illinois, Lake County: Estate of Anna C. Durand, probated 5 October 1908. Although Mrs Durand's two adopted children contested the will in probate court, the will was sustained. See also *Chicago Tribune*, 13 October 1908.

28 *Labrador Doctor*, 335

29 Wilfred Grenfell Papers, WTG to JGG, 1 November 1909

30 Fullerton L. Waldo, *With Grenfell on the Labrador* (New York 1920), 44

31 Luther, 'Mission to Labrador,' 277

32 Ibid., 287

33 For personal knowledge of Lady Grenfell, I am grateful to Mrs Eleanor (Cushman) Wescott.

34 [Henry Gordon], *The Labrador Parson: Journal of the Reverend Henry Gordon, 1915–1925* (St John's, [1972]), 104

35 Wilfred Grenfell Papers, AECG to Mrs Rosamond MacClanahan, undated

letter, 1911. See also Wilfred T. Grenfell, 'Suzanne,' *Atlantic Monthly* 108 (1911): 347–52.

36 W.R. Stirling Papers, WTG to WRS, 8 October 1916

37 Wilfred Grenfell Papers, AECG to Mrs Rosamond MacClanahan, 9 March [1911]; AECG to JGG, 28 August 1911

38 Mostyn House Papers, WTG to JGG, 4 September 1917

39 *Toilers* 25 (1910): 56, 170 ff.

40 Luther, 'Mission to Labrador,' 288, 301

11 Running a Railroad Accident

1 For a full description of this procedure, see Dr. Emma E. Musson, 'Labrador: Interesting Account of the Country, Its Interests, Hospitals, etc.,' *Woman's Medical Journal* 20 (1910): 197–201; and Mary Keating, RN, 'Dr. Grenfell's Work in Newfoundland and Labrador,' *American Journal of Nursing* 11 (1911): 1020–6.

2 Arthur and Marjorie Wakefield Papers, 'Labrador Diaries,' 27

3 Richard Locke Hapgood, *History of the Harvard Dental School* (Boston 1930), 262–6

4 Beatrice Farnsworth Powers Papers, 'The Charm of the Labrador,' 4

5 Moravian Mission Records, WTG to Br Martin, 31 August 1907

6 Moravian Mission Records, WTG to Moravian Mission Council, 15 September 1910; ibid., Bishop B. LaTrobe to Br H. Osborne Essex, 25 October 1910

7 W.L. Mackenzie King Correspondence, Daly to King, 4 March 1911

8 Ibid., WTG to King, 16 June 1910

9 George V, Correspondence, Grey to George V, 6 September 1910. See also Department of Agriculture, Grey to Sidney Fisher, 6 September 1910.

10 See Mary Elizabeth Hallett, 'The 4th Earl Grey as Governor General of Canada' (PHD dissertation, University of London 1970), 179–214.

11 *Montreal Weekly Witness*, 26 April 1905

12 4th Earl Grey of Howick Papers, Grey to Sir William MacGregor, 25 January 1909; Grey to James Bryce (British ambassador, Washington), 26 January 1909

13 Arthur Morton Grenfell was first married to Lady Victoria Grey, who died in 1906.

14 4th Earl Grey of Howick Papers, Grey to WTG, 5 November 1910

15 Ibid., Grey to Laurier, 5 September 1910; WTG to Grey, 18 January 1911; Crowe to Grey, 5 February 1911

16 Wilfred Grenfell Papers, sketchbook inscribed 'Mrs. Wilfred T. Grenfell. St. Anthony, Newfoundland'

17 Rockefeller Family Archives, Starr J. Murphy to John D. Rockefeller, Jr, 11 April 1911

18 Wakefield, 'Labrador Diaries,' 21

19 John M. Little, 'Beriberi Caused by Fine White Flour,' *Journal of the American Medical Association* 58 (1912): 2029–30

20 John Mason Little Papers, JML to Mrs John Mason Little, Sr, 5 March 1911

21 Letter of GAA, 2 March 1910, cited in RNMDSF Council Minutes, 8 April 1910

22 RNMDSF Council Minutes, 13 January 1911

23 W.R. Stirling Papers, WTG to WRS, 1 December [1911]

24 *Toilers* 28 (1913): 71. See also Wilfred T. Grenfell, *What Life Means to Me* (London 1913).

25 Wilfred Grenfell Papers, WRS to Eugene Delano, [February 1912]

26 W.R. Stirling Papers, WTG to WRS, 7 February 1916.

27 RNMDSF Council Minutes, 15 March 1912

28 See Hugh Payne Greeley and Floretta Elmore Greeley, *Work and Play in the Grenfell Mission* (New York 1920).

29 Hugh Payne Greeley Papers, WTG to Dr Hugh Greeley, 23 March 1911

30 RNMDSF Finance Committee Minutes, 30 June 1911. At this meeting the committee refused to accept responsibility.

31 Hugh Payne Greeley Papers, WTG to L.S. Ruel, 17 April 1911

32 Ibid., E.C. Stuckless to Dr Hugh Greeley, 29 March 1911. See also undated petition to WTG, 1910.

33 Hugh Payne Greeley Papers, WTG to Greeley, 16 August 1912

34 Wilfred Grenfell Papers, WTG to Judge D.W. Prowse, 18 June 1910. See also photos in *Toilers* 28 (1913): 78–81.

35 *Evening Chronicle*, 8 August 1912

36 Wilfred Grenfell Papers, WTG to J.L. Karnopp, 12 August 1912

37 Ibid., Professor Wilson S. Naylor (Lawrence College) to WTG, 30 November 1912

38 Wilfred Grenfell Papers, Sir William Archibald to WTG, 12 August 1913

39 See Harry L. Paddon, 'Ye Goode Olde Dayes,' *Fishers* 27 (1929): 51–7, 155–63. See also W.A. Paddon, *Labrador Doctor: My Life with the Grenfell Mission* (Toronto 1989), 4 ff.

40 Paddon, 'Ye Goode Olde Dayes,' 56

41 W.R. Stirling Papers, WTG to WRS, 13 September [1912]

42 *Toilers* 28 (1913): 171

43 *New York Herald*, 3 September 1912

44 Wilfred Grenfell Papers, Sheard to WTG, 9 September 1912

45 Wakefield, 'Labrador Diaries,' 174.

46 Wilfred Grenfell Papers, Francis H. Wood to Sheard, 11 September 1912; Wood to Sheard, 19 November 1912

47 Ibid., Sheard to WRS, 27 January 1913; Sheard to Emma E. White, 1 February 1913

48 RNMDSF Council Minutes, 11 April 1913 and 10 October 1913
49 *Fishers* 12 (1914): 8. A complete set of IGA minutes is preserved at the Provincial Archives of Newfoundland and Labrador.
50 *Labrador Doctor*, 377
51 W.R. Stirling Papers, WTG to WRS, 25 January [1914]
52 Ibid., WTG to WRS, 19 February 1914
53 Wilfred Grenfell Papers, WTG to AGG, 10 July [1914]
54 See annual report in *Fishers* 13 (1915): 29 ff.

12 Coping with War

1 Marjorie and Arthur Wakefield, 'Labrador Diaries,' 266
2 *Toilers* 30 (1915): 144
3 George W. Corner, 'Hospital Work of the Labrador Mission,' *Modern Hospital* 3 (1914): 72–8
4 See J.M. Little, 'Beriberi,' *Journal of the American Medical Association* 63 (1914): 1287–90; W. Richard Ohler, 'Experimental Polyneuritis: Effects of Exclusive Diet of Wheat Flour, in the Form of Ordinary Bread, on Fowls,' *Journal of Medical Research* 31 (1914): 239–46; V.B. Appleton, 'Observations on Deficiency Diseases in Labrador,' *American Journal of Public Health* 11 (1921): 617–21.
5 *Fishers* 12 (1914): 87
6 W.R. Stirling Papers, AECG to WRS, 1 September [1916]
7 See Jessie Luther, 'The Industrial Work,' *Fishers* 13 (1915): 3–11.
8 Jessie Luther, 'Hooked Mats: How a Native Handicraft of the Women of Newfoundland and Labrador Was Placed on a Paying Basis,' *House Beautiful* 40 (1916): 106
9 Jessie Luther Papers, Luther to WTG, 17 September 1915. See also Jessie Luther, 'In Retrospect,' *Fishers* 28 (1930): 112–24.
10 Jessie Luther Papers, WTG to Luther, 20 October 1915
11 Jessie Luther, 'Industrial Work,' *Fishers* 16 (1914): 25
12 Jessie Luther Papers, Jane Addams to Luther, 6 April 1914
13 W.R. Stirling Papers, AECG to WRS, 6 August [1916]
14 John Mason Little Papers, JML to John Mason Little, Sr, 29 August 1914
15 Department of Agriculture, Martin Burrell to Ames, 5 May 1915
16 W.L. Mackenzie King Correspondence, minister of the interior to King, 15 February 1923
17 John Mason Little Papers, JML to Mrs John Mason Little, Sr, 14 October 1914
18 IGA Business Office Papers, W.B. Grieve to A. Sheard, 12 June 1916
19 See [F.P. Carleton], *P. & S. on the Labrador: An Account of the Work of the Columbia Unit of the Grenfell Missions at Spotted Islands, Labrador, Summer of 1922* (New York [1923]).

20 Dr H. Mather Hare Papers, WTG to Hare, 26 July 1914; ibid., diary entry, 22 January 1915

21 Theodore L. Badger Papers, Curtis to Helen Curtis, [October 1915?]

22 Charles S. Curtis, 'Summer on the *Strathcona,*' *Fishers* 60 (1962): 68

23 W.R. Stirling Papers, AECG to WRS, 1 September [1916]. See also Charles S. Curtis, 'First Winter,' *Fishers* 59 (1961): 35–40; 'Before Penicillin,' *Fishers* 59 (1962): 109–11, 114–15; 'Summer on the *Strathcona,*' *Fishers* 60 (1962): 44–6, 68–72.

24 See S.J.R. Noel, *Politics in Newfoundland* (Toronto 1971), 129 ff.

25 *Toilers* 31 (1916): 3

26 Wilfred Grenfell Papers, AGG to WTG, 28 November 1914

27 See John Keegan, *The Face of Battle* (New York 1976), 263 ff.

28 Wilfred Grenfell Papers, WTG to JGG, 2 January [1916]

29 W.R. Stirling Papers, WTG to WRS, 7 February 1916

30 A light canvass suit and a heavier one for winter were duly sent to the headquarters at St Omer for trial, but the contracts had already been let. Not until 1923 did he find a suitable light cloth that could be worn in the north, developed to his specifications by Walter Haythornthwaite, a Lanca-shire cotton manufacturer who later marketed it commercially as 'Grenfell cloth' with Grenfell's agreement. But Grenfell himself never profited from the product that bore his name. In the beginning, Haythornthwaite gave the British Grenfell Association a percentage of the profit at threepence a yard, later reduced to a penny. When Grenfell challenged the reduction in 1933, however, he was told that the firm had made voluntary contributions to the Mission, not a payment. Further, it did not view the practice as binding. Since this was constructed as an allowance to help the Labrador work, Grenfell was urged to accept it as the firm's position. Finally, in 1938 the British association formally agreed to the rate of a penny a yard on the sale of Grenfell cloth, except that sold for the use of the International Grenfell Association. GAGBI Papers, Haythornthwaite to WTG, 26 October 1925, 27 December 1933; Haythornthwaite Archives, deed made between T. Haythornthwaite & Sons, Ltd., and GAGBI, dated 3 February 1938

31 W.R. Stirling Papers, WTG to WRS, 7 February 1916

32 Wilfred T. Grenfell, 'Red Cross and R.A.M.C.,' *Atlantic Monthly* 118 (1916): 106–14

33 W.R. Stirling Papers, WTG to WRS, 1 April 1916

34 Wilfred T. Grenfell, 'Experiences in France,' *Outlook* 113 (1916): 215

35 Wilfred Grenfell Papers, WTG to JGG, 8 June 1916

36 See *Montreal Gazette*, 23 May 1916.

37 *Daily News*, 29 and 31 May, 6 June 1916

38 IGA Business Office Papers, C.F. Crandell, ed., to WTG, 19 June 1916. See also *Daily News*, 26 June 1916.

39 W.R. Stirling Papers, WTG to WRS, 28 December [1916]

40 Wilfred Grenfell Papers, WTG to WRS, 8 October 1916

41 Wilfred Grenfell, 'The Soul of Battle Creek,' *Modern Hospital*, 13 (1916): 277–80

42 See Richard W.Schwarz, *John Harvey Kellogg, M.D.* (Nashville 1970), and James C. Whorton, *Crusaders for Fitness: The History of American Health Reformers* (Princeton 1982), 201–38.

43 Wilfred Grenfell Papers, WTG to JGG, 17 October 1916

44 Ibid., WTG to WRS, 28 December [1916]

45 *Daily News*, 7 June 1916; Wilfred Grenfell Papers, WTG to JGG, 14 September 1917

46 Wilfred Grenfell Papers, WTG to JGG, [1918?]

47 Robert T. Handy, *A Christian America: Protestant Hopes and Historical Realities* (New York 1971), 159

48 See Robert Moats Miller, *Harry Emerson Fosdick: Preacher, Pastor, Prophet* (New York 1985).

49 Wilfred Grenfell Papers, Fosdick to WTG, 13 August 1918

50 GAGBI Papers, Curtis to Lennox Kerr, 7 January 1958

51 John Mason Little Papers, Mrs Ruth Little to Mrs Esther Keese, 3 June [1917]

52 Ibid., JML to WTG, 6 June 1917

53 W.R. Stirling Papers, WTG to WRS, 1 October 1917

54 Colonial Secretary's Correspondence, Paddon to Squires, 23 August 1917

55 W.R. Stirling Papers, WTG to WRS, 1 October 1917

56 A complete transcript of the evidence and a copy of the final report is contained in the Colonial Secretary's Correspondence.

13 Promoting the Mission

1 The point is discussed fully in Ronald Rompkey, 'Elements of Spiritual Autobiography in Sir Wilfred Grenfell's *A Labrador Doctor*,' *Newfoundland Studies* 1 (1985): 17–27.

2 Wilfred Grenfell Papers, Houghton Mifflin to WTG, 22 March 1911

3 Ibid., WTG to JGG, 8 June 1916

4 Mostyn House Papers, WTG to JGG, 12 February [1918]

5 Wilfred Grenfell Papers, Theodore Ainsworth Greene to WTG, 22 December 1938

6 Dorothy Stirling Papers, WTG to Stirling, 19 January 1918

7 Houghton Mifflin Papers, AECG to Greenslet, 23 August 1919

8 Houghton Mifflin Papers, WTG to Houghton Mifflin, 10 July 1917; Greenslet to WTG, 6 August 1917

9 Ibid., WTG to Greenslet, 5 November 1917; WTG to Greenslet, 24 January 1918 [1917?]

10 Ibid., Greenslet to WTG, 22 December 1917

11 Ibid., AECG to Greenslet, 23 August 1918
12 Ibid., Greenslet to AECG, 29 October 1918; AECG to Greenslet, 6 January 1919
13 Anne Grenfell and Katie Spalding, *Le Petit Nord, or Annals of a Labrador Harbor* (Boston and London 1920)
14 Houghton Mifflin Papers, Greenslet to WTG, 29 December 1919
15 *New York Times Book Review*, 9 November 1919
16 See 'A Saint in Trousers,' *Outlook* 124 (1920): 28.
17 Houghton Mifflin Papers, Greenslet to AECG, 25 October 1921; E.C. Robinson to Midland Bank, 12 September 1924
18 See Ronald Rompkey, 'Heroic Biography and the Life of Sir Wilfred Grenfell,' *Prose Studies* 12 (1989): 159–73.
19 Houghton Mifflin Papers, WTG to Greenslet, 20 November 1922
20 Ibid., WTG to Greenslet, 5 November [1919]; WTG to W.B. Pratt, [January 1923?]
21 Ibid., WTG to Greenslet, 15 December 1931; Greenslet to WTG, 21 May 1932
22 Mostyn House Papers, WTG to JGG, 4 September 1917
23 Ibid., AECG to JGG, 1 January [1918]
24 Ibid., WTG to JGG, 4 and 10 January [1918]
25 Ibid., AECG to JGG, 10 February [1918]
26 Ibid., WTG to JGG, 27 February [1918]
27 IGA Business Office Papers, WTG to José Machado, 12 March 1928
28 Perry Burgess, *Born of Those Years* (New York 1951), 18

14 The Lecture Circuit

1 *Fishers* 19 (1921): 43
2 Mostyn House Papers, WTG to AGG, 8 March [1921]
3 See R.M. Elliott, 'Newfoundland Politics in the 1920s: The Genesis and Significance of the Hollis Walker Enquiry' in James Hiller and Peter Neary, eds., *Newfoundland in the Nineteenth and Twentieth Centuries: Essays in Interpretation* (Toronto 1980), 181–204.
4 *Daily News*, 9 September 1921
5 William Willard Howard, *Horrors of Armenia: The Story of an Eye-witness* (New York 1896), 60; William Willard Howard, 'Cuban Relief: A Practical Plan,' *Outlook* 61 (1899): 963–6
6 William Willard Howard, 'Neighbors Who Need Help,' *Fishers* 20 (1922): 89
7 *Daily News*, 18 July 1921
8 Frank H. Potter, 'A Charity that Works Both Ways,' *Outlook* 129 (1921): 442

9 *Indianapolis Mail*, 30 September 1921

10 *Evening Telegram*, 4 October 1921; *Daily News*, 7 October 1921

11 Governors' Papers, draft of communiqué dated 7 October 1921

12 *Daily News*, 19 October 1921

13 Sir Richard Squires Papers, Squires to Harris, 19 October 1921.

14 Ibid., draft of letter to the editor, *Mail & Advocate*, 5 November 1921

15 Rudyard Kipling, 'The Explorer,' in *A Kipling Pageant* (Garden City 1936), 856–7

16 *Daily News*, 8 November 1921

17 Governors' Papers, Harris to Secretary-Treasurer, Grenfell Association of Newfoundland, 8 November 1921

18 *Daily News*, 10 November 1921

19 *Evening Advocate*, 16 November 1921; *Evening Telegram*, 18 November 1921

20 Governors' Papers, C.A.C. Bruce to Squires, 7 December 1921; Sir Richard Squires Papers, Empire Club to Squires, 8 December 1921

21 Governors' Papers, Harris to WTG, 9 December 1921; WTG to Harris, 28 April [1922]

22 W.L. Mackenzie King Correspondence, WTG to King, 8 March 1922

23 See, for example, *Edmonton Journal*, 'Newfoundland's Northern Fisher Folk Starving,' 11 August 1922; *Toronto Daily Star*, 'Is Pitiable Poverty Among Fisher Folk,' 4 August 1922.

24 Governors' Papers, Squires to Sir W.H. Horwood, 21 August 1922. Grenfell himself also became the victim of yellow journalism. That summer, when Marguerite Lindsay, a volunteer teacher in Labrador, went missing, the International Feature Service in Britain released a story claiming she had been kidnapped by 'savage Eskimos.' Five months later, when her body was found, it appeared that she had shot herself with her own revolver.

25 Captain George Whiteley Papers, WTG to Whiteley, 15 December 1922

26 Mostyn House Papers, JGG to AGG, [21] August 1920

27 Ibid., agreement dated 7 July 1912

28 Ibid., Katie Grenfell to AGG, 28 July 1920

29 See ibid., patrimony account of Dr Wilfred T. Grenfell; AGG Diary, 24 November 1924.

30 AGG Diary, 30 May 1923

31 *Toilers* 37 (1922): 102

32 Ibid., 103

33 Elizabeth (Page) Harris Papers, Dorothy Stirling to Page, 28 December 1922

34 See Pauline Chase Harrell and Margaret Supplee Smith, eds., *Victorian Boston Today: Ten Walking Tours* (Boston 1975), 64.

35 Wilfred Grenfell Papers, WTG to AECG, undated, and 22 June [1923]

36 Perry Burgess, *Born of Those Years* (New York 1951), 19–20
37 Pascoe Grenfell Papers, 'Life with Father,' typescript of talk delivered by KPG to the Fortnightly Club, Schenectady, NY, February 1952
38 Wilfred Grenfell Papers, WTG to AECG, 17 January 1923
39 Ibid., WTG to AECG, [January 1923]
40 Ibid., WTG to AECG, 11 March [1923], 1 April 1923
41 Frederick W. Banting Papers, WTG to Banting, 26 November 1923
42 Wilfred Grenfell Papers, WTG to AECG, undated [1923]
43 Mostyn House Papers, WTG to AGG, 28 February [1923]
44 Wilfred Grenfell Papers, WTG to AECG, 28 November [1923]
45 Ibid., [January 1924]
46 Wilfred T. Grenfell, Jr, Papers, Milling to Willie, 5 June 1978
47 *Fishers* 22 (1924): 93
48 Wilfred Grenfell Papers, WTG to AECG, 27 February 1924

15 Public Figure

1 Letter from Saul Bellow to the author, 10 December 1988
2 Cuthbert McEvoy, *Grenfell of Labrador* (London 1922), 3; W. Charter Piggott, *Wilfred Grenfell: The Doctor of Labrador* (London 1922), 8; Basil Mathews, *Wilfred Grenfell the Master Mariner: A Life of Adventure on Sea and Ice* (London 1924), 7
3 GAGBI Papers, Curtis to Lennox Kerr, 3 April 1958. Curtis refused to allow Kerr to use this detail for his biography.
4 Wilfred Grenfell Papers, WTG to AGG, 8 February 1925
5 See Wilfred T. Grenfell, 'Is China Making Progress?' *Contemporary Review* 128 (1925): 334–40.
6 AGG Diary, 5–20 November 1929
7 *Toilers* 41 (1926): 128
8 Mostyn House Papers, WTG to AGG, 25 March 1926
9 AG Diary, 7 April 1926
10 Mostyn House Papers, WTG to AGG, 8 April 1926
11 Ibid., WTG to AGG, 21 April [1926]
12 Ibid., 23 April 1926
13 Ibid., AGG to WTG, 11 May 1928
14 AGG Diary, 14 May 1926
15 Mostyn House Papers, WTG to AGG, 31 May 1926
16 AGG Diary, 5 October 1926
17 Wilfred T. Grenfell, *Religion in Everyday Life* (Chicago 1926), 10–11, 13
18 Wilfred T. Grenfell, *A Man's Faith* (Boston 1926), 25
19 RNMDF Council Minutes, 10 September 1926; Spiritual Work Committee Minutes, 6 October 1926

20 Katie Spalding, 'The Grenfell Association of Great Britain and Ireland, a Brief History,' *Fishers* 56 (1959): 116
21 IGA Business Office Papers, WTG to the directors of the IGA, 29 December 1922
22 RNMDSF Miscellaneous Papers, Dr Grenfell's Report, 15 December 1926
23 *British Weekly* 80 (1926): 542
24 Southborough Papers, WTG to Southborough, 9 December 1926 [*sic*].
25 RNMDSF Council Minutes, 9 December 1926
26 IGA Business Office Papers, WTG to José Machado, 28 January 1927
27 See Herbert Threlkeld-Edwards, 'The New Medical Era in St. Anthony,' *Fishers* 25 (1927): 51–7.
28 See Charles Curtis, 'This Northern Outpost of Modern Science Serves Large Area,' *Modern Hospital* 30 (1928): 79–83.
29 Southborough Papers, WTG to Southborough, 27 September 1927
30 *Evening Telegram*, 28 July 1927
31 Pascoe Grenfell Papers, WTG to Willie, KPG and RLG, 28 July 1927
32 Wilfred Grenfell Papers, WTG to AECG, 14 August [1927]

16 The New Mission

1 *Daily News*, 17 February 1928; *Evening Telegram*, 18 February 1928
2 *New York Times*, 7 November 1930
3 William Ralph Parsons Papers, WTG to Parsons, 15 November 1929
4 S.J.R. Noel, *Politics in Newfoundland* (Toronto 1971), 189
5 Rockefeller Family Archives, Sherrill to Rockefeller, 19 January 1928
6 Wilfred Grenfell Papers, AGG to WTG, 8 March 1929
7 Ibid., 3 July 1919
8 Hilton L. Willcox, *Beneath a Wandering Star* (Edinburgh 1986), 193. See also Charles H. Curtis and Evarts G. Loomis, 'Bone Tuberculosis in Northern Newfoundland,' *Journal of Bone and Joint Surgery* 23 (1941): 811–18.
9 W.A. Paddon, *Labrador Doctor: My Life with the Grenfell Mission* (Toronto 1989), 73–4
10 Helen S. Mitchell, 'Nutrition Survey in Labrador and Northern Newfoundland,' *Journal of the American Dietetic Association* 6 (1930): 33
11 See E. Ross Jenney, 'Some Newer Phases in Nutritional Therapy,' *Fishers* 29 (1931): 35–9; and David Steven and George Wald, 'Vitamin A Deficiency: A Field Study in Newfoundland and Labrador,' *Journal of Nutrition* 21 (1941): 468.
12 *Springfield Sunday Union and Republican*, 1 June 1930
13 Margery Vaughn, and Helen S. Mitchell, 'A Continuation of the Nutrition Project in Northern Newfoundland,' *Journal of the American Dietetic Association* 8 (1933): 526–31

14 See F.C. Sears, 'Farming in Labrador,' *Better Crops with Plant Food* 16 (1931): 43–4, 47–8; and Fred C. Sears, 'The Labrador Garden Campaign,' *Fishers* 30 (1933): 167–71.
15 Eric H. Thomsen Papers, 'An American Odyssey' (unpublished autobiography), 30–1.
16 Elizabeth (Page) Harris Papers, Dr Levi Curtis, Methodist Superintendent of Education, to Ethel Muir, 26 April 1923. A full picture of the appointment of summer staff is provided by the papers of Elizabeth (Page) Harris, executive secretary of the Staff Selection Committee and industrial secretary throughout the 1920s.
17 Pamphlet entitled 'Information and Instructions for Workers,' (International Grenfell Association, [n.d.])
18 Elizabeth (Page) Harris Papers, Harris to Elena Williams, 2 February 1924; ibid., AEMG to Page, 26 November 1926
19 Personal diary in the possession of Mrs Mary Miller-Blood
20 Carolyn H. Galbraith Papers, letter dated 15 September [1926]
21 J.L. Paton Papers, Herbert Cramm to Paton, 29 June 1930
22 Edith Tallant's *The Girl Who Was Marge* (Philadelphia 1939) presents a lengthy fictional idealization. See also William Adams Delano, 'Of Men and Fish,' *Fishers* 52 (1954): 18–19.
23 Columbus Iselin, *The Log of the Schooner Chance ...* (New York 1927), 22; Willcox, *Beneath a Wandering Star*, 200
24 Eric H. Thomsen Papers, Thomsen to WTG, 23 July 1928
25 Donald McI. Johnson, *A Doctor Regrets: Being the First Part of 'A Publisher Presents Himself'* (London 1949), 173
26 IGA Business Office Papers, 'Report to the Board of Directors of the International Grenfell Association by Tamblyn and Brown Inc.,' 1937–8; 44
27 Johnson, *A Doctor Regrets*, 173
28 Personal letter from Elliott Merrick to the author, 16 February 1986
29 Personal letter from Hugh Morrow, Nelson Rockefeller's press secretary, to Terence McCartney-Filgate, 28 January 1976. I am grateful to Mr McCartney-Filgate for permission to quote.
30 Harvey Williams Cushing Papers, WTG to Cushing, 14 January 1930. See also J.L. Paton, 'Newfoundland: Present and Future,' *International Affairs* 13 (1934): 408; and Charles Hitchcock Sherrill, *My Story Book* (privately printed 1937), 280.
31 IGA Business Office Papers, WTG to José Machado, 15 January 1930
32 Moravian Mission Records, Paddon to Rev. Paul Hettasch, 7 September 1930
33 Ibid., Rev. Paul Hettasch to Mission Board, October 1930
34 Wilfred Grenfell Papers, WTG to AECG, 18 July 1929; letter dated 26 July 1929 in the *New York Times*, 5 September 1929

35 See H.L. Paddon, 'Labrador To-day: A Lecture to the Medical and Physical Society,' *St. Thomas's Hospital Gazette* 35 (1936): 283–7. An account of growing up in North West River is provided in Harold G. Paddon, *Green Woods and Blue Waters, Memories of Labrador* (St John's 1989), 9–69.

36 GAGBI Papers, Paddon to Katie Spalding, 10 January 1928

37 Eric H. Thomsen Papers, Cozad to Thomsen, 7 December 1928

38 Harry L. Paddon, ' "Ye Goode Olde Dayes",' *Fishers* 27 (1929): 57

39 Wilfred Grenfell, 'Labrador in the Making,' *Listener* 2 (1929): 709–10

40 *Times*, 7 November 1929

41 Wilfred Grenfell, *The Fishermen's Saint: Rectorial Address Delivered at St. Andrews University, November 1929* (London 1930), 8–9

42 AGG Diary, 31 October 1927

43 Ibid., 29 November 1929

44 Mostyn House Papers, WTG to AGG, 14 October [1931]

45 *Fishers* 28 (1930): 9

46 See Alfred T. Hill, 'Rip Van Winkle Returns to St. Anthony,' *Fishers* 75 (1978): 7; Wilfred Grenfell Papers, WTG to AECG, 12 June [1930].

47 *Evening Telegram*, 30 August 1930

48 *Daily News*, 26 August 1930

49 Wilfred Grenfell Papers, AECG to RLG, 23 February [1929]; ibid., AECG to Willie, 22 August 1930

50 *Fishers* 28 (1930): 105. See also Gerald L. Pocius, 'Hooked Rugs in Newfoundland: The Representation of Social Structure in Design,' *Journal of American Folklore* 92 (1979): 273–84; Colleen Lynch, *Helping Ourselves: Crafts of the Grenfell Mission* (St John's, 1985); and Ethel C. Dana, 'Occupational Therapy in Labrador,' *U.S. Veterans' Bureau Medical Bulletin* (Washington 1929), 392–3.

51 *New York Times*, 5 October 1930

52 See *IGA* Industrial Department Records, Dog-Team Tavern.

53 *Fishers* 28 (1930): 123

54 Wilfred Grenfell Papers, WTG to Willie, 4 October 1930

55 Ibid., AECG to Willie, 2 November [1930]

56 Ibid., 16 November [1930]

57 Ibid., 17 January 1931

58 Ibid., 25 September [1931]

59 Ibid., 26 October 1931

17 The Death of Democracy

1 *Evening Telegram*, 12 February 1932

2 Ibid., 6 April 1932

3 S.J.R. Noel, *Politics in Newfoundland* (Toronto 1971), 207

4 Pascoe Grenfell Papers, WTG to KPG, 19 February 1933

5 *Report of the Newfoundland Royal Commission, 1933* (London 1934), 197–202, 223

6 See Peter Neary, *Newfoundland in the North Atlantic World, 1929–1949* (Kingston and Montreal 1988), 41.

7 J.L. Paton, 'Newfoundland: Present and Future,' *International Affairs* 13 (1934): 402

8 Wilfred Grenfell Papers, Emily A. Fowler to AECG, 4 February 1931

9 Pascoe Grenfell Papers, WTG to AECG, 5 July 1931

10 Hilton L. Willcox, *Beneath a Wandering Star* (Edinburgh 1986), 310. See also Alexander Forbes, *Northernmost Labrador Mapped from the Air* (New York 1938), 30–126.

11 Wilfred Grenfell Papers, WTG to AECG, 25 September [1931]

12 For information on WTG's writing habits I am grateful to Eleanor (Cushman) Wescott.

13 Houghton Mifflin Papers, I.R. Kent to Ferris Greenslet, 3 May 1932

14 Ibid., AECG to Kent, 2 July 1932

15 Wilfred Grenfell Papers, AECG to Badger, 23 August 1932

16 *Fishers* 31 (1933): 37; *Boston Herald*, 15 November 1932

17 Houghton Mifflin Papers, Greenslet to WTG, 29 April 1933

18 *New York Times Book Review*, 4 December 1932; *Glasgow Herald*, 23 March 1933

19 Amulree Papers, Curtis to WTG, 27 February [1933]

20 Ibid., WTG to Amulree, 4 March 1933

21 Ibid., 18 April 1933

22 Ibid., 30 November 1933

23 *Journal of the Royal Society of Arts* 82 (1934): 663

24 Wilfred Grenfell Papers, AECG to Willie, 26 December [1933]

25 Ibid., 1 January 1934

26 Pascoe Grenfell Papers, WTG to KPG, 18 January 1935

27 Wilfred Grenfell Papers, Herr Hoffman to WTG, 30 April 1935; WTG to Willie, 22 July 1935

28 Mostyn House Papers, WTG to AMDG, 29 June 1935

29 B.D. Zevin, ed., *Nothing to Fear: The Selected Addresses of Franklin Delano Roosevelt, 1932–1945* (Cambridge 1946), 14

30 Wilfred Grenfell Papers, AECG to Willie, 2 February [1934]; 12 May 1934

31 Ibid., 1 January 1934.

32 Pascoe Grenfell Papers, WTG to KPG, 18 February 1935

33 Wilfred Grenfell Papers, WTG to Willie, 24 May [1935]

34 Ibid., AECG to Willie, 24 October 1935

35 See T. Lodge, *Dictatorship in Newfoundland* (London 1939).

36 Wilfred Grenfell Papers, AECG to WILLIE, 2 February [1934]

37 *Fishers* 32 (1934): 4

38 Wilfred Grenfell, 'Dictatorship by Consent: The New Government of Newfoundland and Labrador,' ibid., 68

39 Ibid., 46.

40 Wilfred Grenfell papers, WTG to Willie, 18 August 1934

18 Resignation

1 AGG Diary, 20 October and 14 November 1932

2 Mostyn House Papers, WTG to AGG, 24 February 1934

3 Ibid., WTG to AMDG, 21 April 1934

4 Ibid., 30 September 1934

5 Mostyn House Papers, AMDG to WTG, 1 November 1934, ibid., WTG to AMDG, 6 November 1934

6 Wilfred Grenfell Papers, WTG to Dr Theodore Badger, 21 May 1935

7 Ibid., WTG to Rev. Theodore Greene, 2 May 1934

8 IGA Business Office Papers, H.R. Brookes to E.A.B. Willmer, [March 1935]; ibid., Curtis to E.A.B. Willmer, 17 December 1934

9 Ibid., Machado to WTG, 11 February 1935

10 Ibid., WTG to Machado, 7 March 1935

11 Ibid., H.R. Brookes to E.A.B. Willmer, [March 1935]

12 Ibid., 'Report of the Commission Appointed by the Directors of the International Grenfell Association, April 13th, 1935, to Confer with the Commission of Government for Newfoundland and Survey Conditions on the Coast of Newfoundland & Labrador' (hereafter IGA Commission Report)

13 Peter Neary, *Newfoundland in the North Atlantic World, 1929–1949* (Kingston and Montreal 1988), 105

14 IGA Commission Report, 13, 18

15 Ibid., 39

16 Ibid., 40

17 IGA Business Office Papers, Curtis to Cecil Ashdown, 4 November 1935

18 Ibid., WTG to the directors of the IGA, 8 January 1936

19 Wilfred Grenfell Papers, AEMG to Willie, 8 January 1936

20 IGA Business Office Papers, 'Suggested Resolution for Submission to the Extraordinary Meeting ... Jan. 21st, 1936'

21 Wilfred Grenfell Papers, AEMG to Willie, 4 April 1936

22 IGA Business Office Papers, 'Report to the Board of Directors of the International Grenfell Association by Tamblyn and Brown, Inc., 4 February 1938' (hereafter Tamblyn and Brown Report). Figures are quoted directly from the report.

23 Tambly and Brown Report, 15

24 Ibid., 20

25 Ibid., 25
26 Ibid., 78
27 Wilfred Grenfell Papers, AECG to Willie, 8 January 1936
28 John Harvey Kellogg Papers, AECG to Kellogg, 21 June 1937
29 Wilfred Grenfell Papers, AECG to Badger, 1 June 1936
30 John Harvey Kellogg Papers, Kellogg to WTG, 1 January 1937; ibid., AECG to Kellogg, 4 January 1937
31 Wilfred Grenfell Papers, AECG to Badger, 19 July 1937
32 GAGBI Papers, Ashdown to Richards, 25 August 1937
33 Wilfred Grenfell Papers, Ashdown to WTG, 28 October 1937
34 Ibid., Richards to WTG, 9 August 1938
35 Ibid., WTG to Ashdown, 8 February 1938

19 The Last Lap

1 Wilfred Grenfell Papers, Greene to WTG, 17 January 1938
2 GAGBI Papers, Curtis to Ashdown, 15 March 1938
3 Wilfred Grenfell Papers, Curtis to WTG, 31 March 1938
4 Ibid., 1 July 1938
5 Ibid., Ashdown to AECG, 20 April 1990
6 GAGBI Papers, Paddon to GAGBI, 26 April 1938
7 Wilfred Grenfell Papers, Paddon to AECG, 16 June 1938
8 See Sir Wilfred Grenfell, 'Labrador Days,' *Atlantic Monthly* 162 (1938): 824–8; 'Labrador, Lesson in Humanity,' *Rotarian* 53 (1938): 22–5; and *A Labrador Log Book* (Boston 1938).
9 Wilfred Grenfell Papers, AECG to Mrs Charles Curtis, 26 May 1938
10 Ibid., AECG to Dr Beeckman J. Delatour, 4 October 1938
11 Ibid., Dr Joe Vincent Meigs to Dr Harvey Cushing, 9 November 1938; John Harvey Kellogg Papers, WTG to Kellogg, 15 December 1938
12 Wilfred Grenfell Papers, WTG to Cushing, 8 November 1938
13 Ibid., WTG to AECG, 20 February [1938]
14 Ibid., WTG to Dr George Barton, 15 March 1939; WTG to Mrs Charles Curtis, 16 March 1939
15 Mostyn House Papers, AMDG to WTG, 13 December 1938; WTG to AMDG, 24 January [1939]; cancelled promissory note, dated 28 February 1939
16 IGA Business Office Papers, Curtis to Ashdown, 3 December 1939
17 Francis Bowes Sayre Correspondence, WTG to Sayre, 19 August 1939
18 *Fishers* 37 (1939): 90–1
19 Wilfred Grenfell Papers, Spalding to AECG, 29 October [1938]
20 *Fishers* 56 (1959): 117
21 Wilfred Grenfell Papers, WTG to King, 23 September 1939
22 Cecil S. Ashdown Papers, Machado to WTG, 22 March 1940

23 See W. Anthony Paddon's tribute to his father in 'Grenfell Mission Hospital Ships,' *Fishers* 63 (1965): 33–9.
24 Harry L. Paddon, 'A Viewpoint Twenty-six Years Long,' *Daily News* (Labrador Souvenir Supplement), 19 October 1938
25 Wilfred Grenfell Papers, Anthony Paddon to WTG, 22 January [1940]
26 IGA Business Office Papers, Curtis to Ashdown, 27 December 1939
27 GAGBI Papers, Ashdown to Richards, 26 January 1940
28 IGA Business Office Papers, Curtis to Kathleen Young (IGA bookkeeper), 6 January 1940. See also W.A. Paddon, 'Jack Watts of North West River,' *Fishers* 73 (1976): 9–12.
29 Wilfred Grenfell Papers, Fosdick to WTG, 22 July 1940
30 Pascoe Grenfell Papers, WTG to KPG, 25 February [1940]
31 Wilfred Grenfell Papers, WTG to Ashdown, 16 April 1940
32 Ibid., WTG to Curtis, 27 September 1940
33 Mostyn House Papers, WTG to AMDG, 22 April 1940
34 Ibid., 22 May 1940
35 Ibid., AMDG to WTG, 12 July 1940
36 Ibid., WTG to AMDG, 22 September [1940]

Bibliography

Works by Wilfred Grenfell

BOOKS

Vikings of Today, or, Life and Medical Work among the Fishermen of Labrador. London: Marshall Bros.; New York: Fleming H. Revell 1895

The Harvest of the Sea: A Tale of Both Sides of the Atlantic. New York: Fleming H. Revell 1905

Northern Neighbours: Stories of the Labrador People. London: Hodder & Stoughton 1906; Boston and New York: Houghton Mifflin 1923

Off the Rocks: Stories of the Deep-Sea Fisherfolk of Labrador. Philadelphia: Sunday School Times; Toronto: William Briggs 1906; London: Marshall Bros. 1907

A Man's Faith. Boston, New York, and Chicago: Pilgrim Press 1908

Labrador, the Country and the People. New York: Macmillan 1909

Down to the Sea: Yarns from the Labrador. New York: Fleming H. Revell; London: Andrew Melrose 1910

A Man's Helpers. Boston, New York, and Chicago: Pilgrim Press; Toronto: Musson Book Co. 1910

Adrift on an Icepan. Boston and New York: Houghton Mifflin 1909; London: Jarrolds 1909; London: Constable 1910

What Life Means to Me. Boston, New York, and Chicago: Pilgrim Press 1910; London: James Nisbet 1913

What Will You Do with Jesus Christ? Boston, New York, and Chicago: Pilgrim Press 1910

Down North on the Labrador. New York: Fleming H. Revell 1911; London: James Nisbet 1912

Bibliography

What the Church Means to Me: A Frank Confession and a Friendly Estimate by an Insider. Boston, New York, and Chicago: Pilgrim Press 1911

The Adventure of Life. The William Belden Noble Lectures at Harvard University for 1911. Boston and New York: Houghton Mifflin; London: James Nisbet; Toronto: William Briggs 1912

On Immortality. Boston, New York, and Chicago: Pilgrim Press; Toronto: McClelland & Goodchild 1912. Also published as *Shall a Man Live Again? A Vital Assurance of Faith in Immortality* (Boston, New York, and Chicago: Pilgrim Press 1912) and *Immortality* (London: James Nisbet 1913)

What Can Jesus Christ Do with Me? Boston, New York, and Chicago: Pilgrim Press 1912.

The Attractive Way. Boston, New York, and Chicago: Pilgrim Press 1913

The Price of Life. Boston, New York, and Chicago: Pilgrim Press 1914

Tales of Labrador. Boston and New York: Houghton Mifflin; London: James Nisbet 1916

Labrador Days: Tales of the Sea Toilers. Boston and New York: Houghton Mifflin; London: Hodder & Stoughton 1919

A Labrador Doctor: The Autobiography of Wilfred Thomason Grenfell, M.D. (Oxon.), C.M.G. Boston and New York: Houghton Mifflin 1919; London: Hodder & Stoughton 1920

The Story of a Labrador Doctor. Abridged edition. Boston and New York: Hodder & Stoughton 1920

That Christmas at Peace Haven and *Three Eyes.* Boston and New York: Houghton Mifflin 1923

Yourself and Your Body. New York: Scribner's; London: Hodder & Stoughton 1924

What Christ Means to Me. Boston and New York: Houghton Mifflin 1926

Religion in Everday Life. Chicago: American Library Association 1926

Labrador Looks at the Orient: Notes of Travel in the Near and Far East. London: Jarrolds; Boston and New York: Houghton Mifflin 1928

Labrador's Fight for Economic Freedom. Self and Society Booklet No. 19. London: Ernest Benn 1929

The Fishermen's Saint. Rectorial address, St Andrews University 1919. London: Hodder & Stoughton; New York: Scribner's 1930

Forty Years for Labrador. Boston and New York: Houghton Mifflin 1932; London: Hodder & Stoughton 1933

The Romance of Labrador. New York: Macmillan; London: Hodder & Stoughton 1934

Deeds of Daring. London: Hodder & Stoughton 1934

A Labrador Logbook. Boston: Little, Brown 1938; London: Hodder & Stoughton 1939

Bibliography

SELECTED JOURNALISM

'How to Prepare for a Holiday Camp.' *Review of Reviews* 2 (1890): 575

'Letter from Wilfred T. Grenfell. Esq., M.R.C.S.' *Journal of the Marine Biological Association* 3 (1893–5): 143–7

'Vikings of Today.' *Scottish Geographical Magazine* 11 (1895): 543

'Life in Labrador.' *Blackwood's* 170 (1901): 688–98. Reprinted in *Littell's Living Age* 232 (1902): 31–40

'Nursing Among the Deep-Sea Fishermen.' *American Journal of Nursing* 3 (1902): 161–6

'Curious Customs of the Labrador Esquimaux.' *Leslie's Weekly* (8 January 1903): 29, 32

'Among the Vikings of Labrador.' *Missionary Review of the World* 26 (1903): 481–9

'Among the Deep-Sea Fishermen.' *Outlook* 74 (1903): 695–701

'Leaves from the Log of the Lend-a-hand.' *McClure's* 24 (1905): 624–32

'How Santa Claus Came to Cape St. Anthony.' *Putnam's* 1 (1906): 331–6

'Two Leaders in Surgery.' *Outlook* 86 (1907): 404–9

'Christmas in Labrador.' *Churchman* 15 (1908): 895–8

[With W.J. Carroll] 'Reindeer in Labrador.' *Forest & Stream* 70 (1908): 611

'A Story of Labrador.' *Outlook* 89 (1908): 384–5

'A Man's Faith.' *Congregationalist and Christian World* 93 (1908): 726–8; 771–3; 820–2

'Experiences on the Labrador.' *Century* 78 (1909): 233–40

'Sir Frederick Treves: A Surgeon Who Happens to be a Man of Genius.' *Putnam's* 5 (1909): 581–91

' "T is Dogged as Does It": The Last Voyage of the Schooner "Rippling Wave".' *Putnam's* 6 (1909): 538–47

'Poisoning by Bad Air.' *Outlook* 92 (1909): 570–1

'Dr. Grenfell on Live Missionary Methods.' *Outlook* 93 (1909): 833–6

'The Optimist: A Case Where the Christmas Spirit Lasts the Year Through.' *Congregationalist and Christian World* 94 (1909): 870–2

'Missionaries as Writers and Speakers.' *Missionary Review of the World* 33 (1910): 135–8

'Land of Eternal Warring.' *National Geographic* 21 (1910): 665–90

'What Life Means to Me.' *Congregationalist and Christian World* 95 (1910): 320–2; 352–3

'What Prayer Means to Me.' *Congregationalist and Christian World* 95 (1910): 336–8

'What the Bible Means to Me.' *Congregationalist and Christian World* 95 (1910): 240–2

Bibliography

'What Christian Fellowship Means to Me.' *Congregationalist and Christian World* 95 (1910): 504–6

'What Will You Do with Jesus Christ?' *Congregationalist and Christian World* 95 (1910): 1008–9

'Labrador.' *Geographical Journal* 37 (1911): 407–19

'Partial Conversion.' *Independent* 70 (1911): 1052–5

'Brin.' *St. Nicholas* 39 (1911): 99–105

'Suzanne.' *Atlantic Monthly* 108 (1911): 347–52

'Sacrifice.' *Missionary Review of the World* 35 (1912): 128–9

'Shall Men Live Again?' *Outlook* 100 (1912): 502–7

'The Future of Labrador.' *Outlook* 101 (1912): 956–65

'A Labrador Adventure.' *Independent* 73 (1912): 553–6

'Christmas in Labrador.' *Quiver* 48 (1912): 201–4

'That Christmas at Peace Haven.' *Ladies' Home Journal* 29 (1912): 11–12

'Winter in Forteau: A Story of Hardship and Suffering.' *Quiver* 48 (1913): 1164–6

'Twenty Years in Labrador.' *Wide World* 32 (1913): 243–50; 330–8

'Real Sea Fight.' *Quiver* 48 (1913): 576–84

'Labrador,' in A.J. Herbertson and O.J.R. Howarth, eds, *The Oxford Survey of the British Empire* (Oxford: Clarendon Press 1914), vol. 4; 295–319

'By-products of Mission Work.' *Missionary Review of the World* 38 (1915): 318–23

'Misunderstood Eskimo.' *Travel* 25 (1915): 24–5

'The Year's Work in Labrador.' *Journal of the National Institute of Social Sciences* 1 (1915): 106–13

'Experiences in France.' *Outlook* 113 (1916): 210–15

'Queer Things.' *Canadian Magazine* 47 (1916): 173–5

'Notes on Clothing against Cold.' *British Medical Journal* 15 January 1916: 86–7

'Life-saving under Fire. The R.A.M.C. at Work. Wonders of the Clearing Stations.' *The Times* (London), 24 March 1916

'The R.A.M.C. at Work in Northern France.' *British Medical Journal* 1 April 1916: 500–1

'Red Cross and R.A.M.C.' *Atlantic Monthly* 118 (1916): 106–14

'Jim Wilson's Chum.' *St. Nicholas* 44 (1916): 109–12

'In Icy Labrador.' *Current History Magazine, N.Y. Times* 18 (1923): 823–9

'Is China Making Progress?' *Contemporary Review* 128 (1925): 334–40

'Some Impressions on a World Tour.' *Missionary Review of the World* 48 (1925): 688–91; 795–7

'Dr. Grenfell Endorses Feng: A Letter.' *Outlook* 142 (1926): 635

'What Christ Means to Me.' *British Weekly* 80 (1926): 447, 452, 473, 479, 487, 516, 523, 542: 82 (1926): 8, 16, 40

Bibliography

'Labrador,' in *Encyclopaedia Britannica*, 14th ed. (London 1929), vol. 13: 555–9

'Labrador in the Making.' *Listener* 2 (1929): 709–10

'Billy.' *English Review* 49 (1929): 336–73

'Optimism.' *Spectator* 146 (1931): 263, 301–2

'Education in Labrador.' *School Life* 17 (1931): 71–2

'The Lure of the Labrador.' *National Review* 97 (1931): 623–8

'Sir Wilfred Grenfell and His Dogs.' *Our Fourfooted Friends* 29 (1932): 1–2, 6

'Labrador Tragedy.' *Travel* 59 (1932): 36–40

'The Problems of Labrador.' *Canadian Geographical Journal* 7 (1933): 201–12

'Labrador Today: A Great Achievement.' *National Humane Review* 21 (1933): 3–5, 23

'Newfoundland and Labrador.' *Journal of the Royal Society of the Arts* 82 (1934): 652–63

'The Claims of Labrador.' *Spectator* 153 (1934): 830–1

'Warm Hearts in Labrador.' *Rotarian* 47 (1935): 6–10

'The Practice of Medicine in Labrador.' *Radiology* 26 (1936): 243–6

'Labrador Days.' *Atlantic Monthly* 162 (1938): 824–8

'To the North Lies Labrador.' *Rotarian* 53 (1938): 15–17

'Labrador, Lesson in Humanity.' *Rotarian* 53 (1938): 22–5

Manuscripts

CANADA

Kingston
A.A. Chesterfield Papers. Queen's University Archives

Montreal
Arthur and Marjorie Wakefield Papers. R.W. Wakefield.

North West River
Dr Harry L. Paddon Papers. Hon. Dr W.A. Paddon

Ottawa
Department of Agriculture Records. National Archives of Canada

Deputy Minister of Agriculture Letterbooks. National Archives of Canada

Sir Robert Borden Papers. National Archives of Canada

4th Earl Grey of Howick (Albert Henry George Grey) Papers. National Archives of Canada

Dr H. Mather Hare Papers. National Archives of Canada

W.L. Mackenzie King. Correspondence. National Archives of Canada

– Memoranda. National Archives of Canada

Bibliography

Sir Wilfrid Laurier Papers. National Archives of Canada
Mission to Deep Sea Fishermen Papers. National Archives of Canada
Dorothy Stirling Papers. National Archives of Canada

St John's

Hugh Cole Diary. Memorial University of Newfoundland Folklore Archive
Colonial Secretary's Correspondence. Provincial Archives of Newfoundland and
    Labrador
Governors' Papers. Provincial Archives of Newfoundland and Labrador
Grenfell Association of Great Britain and Ireland Papers. Provincial Archives of
    Newfoundland and Labrador
Grenfell Manuscript Collection. Provincial Reference and Resource Library
Moses Harvey Papers. Centre for Newfoundland Studies, Memorial University
International Grenfell Association Business Office Papers. Provincial Archives
    of Newfoundland and Labrador
Labrador Medical Mission (Ottawa) Papers. Provincial Archives of
    Newfoundland and Labrador
P.T. McGrath Collection. Provincial Archives of Newfoundland and Labrador
J.L. Paton Papers. Office of the President, Memorial University
Sir Richard Squires Papers. Provincial Archives of Newfoundland and
    Labrador
Dr Gordon Thomas Papers. Provincial Archives of Newfoundland and Labrador
Captain George Whiteley Papers. Miss Mary Whiteley

Toronto

Frederick W. Banting Papers. Thomas Fisher Rare Book Library, University of
    Toronto

Winnipeg

Hudson's Bay Company Archives. Provincial Archives of Manitoba
William Ralph Parsons Papers. Provincial Archives of Manitoba

UNITED KINGDOM

Berkshire

George V. Diary. Royal Archives, Windsor Castle
– Correspondence. Royal Archives, Windsor Castle

Cheshire

Eliot, Curwen. 'Trip to Labrador.' Mrs Ruth Gimlette, Lower Whitley
A.G. Grenfell, Correspondence. Dr Bevyl (Grenfell) Cowan, Burton
Diaries. Dr Bevyl (Grenfell) Cowan, Burton

Bibliography

Mostyn House Papers. Mostyn House School, Parkgate
Mostyn House School Records. Mostyn House School, Parkgate

Lancashire
Haythornthwaite Archives. Haythornthwaite & Sons, Ltd., Burnley

London
Examination Registers. University of London Library
Probated Wills. General Register Office.
Lloyd's of London. Register of Agents
Licentiates Register. Royal College of Physicians
London Hospital House Committee Minutes. Tower Hamlets Health Authority
  Archives
London Hospital Medical College Student Register. Tower Hamlets Health
  Authority Archives
Matriculation Register. University of London Library
Royal National Mission to Deep Sea Fishermen:
  Council Minutes
  Finance Committee Minutes
  Hospital Committee Minutes
  Spiritual Work Committee Minutes
  Miscellaneous Papers

Norfolk
Albert, Log. Norfolk Record Office, Norwich
Albert, Construction papers. Norfolk Record Office, Norwich

Oxford
1st Baron Amulree (William Warrender Mackenzie) Papers. Bodleian Library
1st Baron Southborough (Francis John Stephens Hopwood) Papers. Bodleian
  Library

Wiltshire
Marlborough College Register. Marlborough

UNITED STATES

Connecticut
Cecil S. Ashdown Papers. Mrs Ian Sidey, New Canaan
Theodore L. Badger Papers. Sterling Library, Yale University
Harvey Williams Cushing Papers. Sterling Library, Yale University
William Adams Delano Papers. Sterling Library, Yale University

Bibliography

Hugh Payne Greeley Papers. Sterling Library, Yale University
Wilfred Thomason Grenfell Papers. Sterling Library, Yale University
Elizabeth (Page) Harris Papers. Sterling Library, Yale University
New England Grenfell Association Records. Sterling Library, Yale University
W.R. Stirling Papers. Sterling Library, Yale University

District of Columbia
Varick Frissell Papers. Library of Congress, Washington
Francis Bowes Sayre Correspondence. Library of Congress, Washington
6th Tennessee Infantry Regiment Records. National Archives, Washington

Maine
Lyman Abbott Memorial Collection. Bowdoin College Library, Brunswick

Massachusetts
Carolyn H. Galbraith Papers. Smith College Women's History Archive,
    Northampton
Houghton Mifflin Papers. Houghton Library, Harvard University, Cambridge
John Mason Little Papers. Thomas M. Smith, Cambridge
Jessie Luther Papers. Mrs Marty Gendron, Swansea
Reverend Edward C. Moore Papers. Andover-Harvard Theological Library,
    Harvard University, Cambridge
Endicott Peabody Correspondence. Groton School, Groton
– Papers. Houghton Library, Harvard University, Cambridge

Michigan
Henry and Clara Ford Papers. Henry Ford Museum, Dearborn
John Harvey Kellogg Papers. Bentley Historical Library, University of Michigan,
    Ann Arbor

New Hampshire
Stefansson Papers. Dartmouth College Library, Hanover

New York
Commonwealth Fund Archives. Rockefeller Archive Center, Pocantico Hills
William Adams Delano Reminiscences. Oral History Project, Columbia
    University
Department of Nursing Education Archives. Teachers College Library,
    Columbia University
Rockefeller Family Archives. Rockefeller Archive Center, Pocantico Hills
Russell Sage Foundation Papers. Rockefeller Archive Center, Pocantico Hills

Bibliography

Pennsylvania

Moravian Mission Reports. Moravian Mission Archives, Bethlehem
Mrs Rosamond (Grenfell) Shaw Papers. Wayne

Texas

Eric S. Thomsen Papers. Mr and Mrs Erik Thomsen, Houston

Vermont

International Grenfell Association, Industrial Department Records. Dog Team
  Tavern, North Ferrisburg

Virginia

Pascoe Grenfell Papers. Richmond
Wilfred T. Grenfell, Jr, Papers. Charlottesville

Index

Index